STRANGER
in the NEST

Do Parents Really Shape
Their Child's Personality,
Intelligence, or Character?

DAVID B. COHEN

New York • Chichester • Weinheim • Brisbane • Singapore • Toronto

Published by John Wiley & Sons, Inc.
Published simultaneously in Canada.

No part of this publication may be reproduced, stored in a retrieval system or transmitted in any form or by any means, electronic, mechanical, photocopying, recording, scanning or otherwise, except as permitted under Sections 107 or 108 of the 1976 United States Copyright Act, without either the prior written permission of the Publisher, or authorization through payment of the appropriate per-copy fee to the Copyright Clearance Center, 222 Rosewood Drive, Danvers, MA 01923, (978) 750-8400, fax (978) 750-4744. Requests to the Publisher for permission should be addressed to the Permissions Department, John Wiley & Sons, Inc., 605 Third Avenue, New York, NY 10158-0012, (212) 850-6011, fax (212) 850-6008, E-Mail: PERMREQ@WILEY.COM.

This publication is designed to provide accurate and authoritative information in regard to the subject matter covered. It is sold with the understanding that the publisher is not engaged in rendering professional services. If legal, accounting, medical, psychological or any other expert assistance is required, the services of a competent professional person should be sought.

Library of Congress Cataloging-in-Publication Data
Cohen, David B., 1941–
    Stranger in the nest : do parents really shape their child's personality, intelligence, or character? / David B. Cohen.
        p.   cm.
    Includes bibliographical references and index.
    ISBN 0-471-31922-8 (hardcover : alk. paper)
    1. Nature and nurture.   2. Nativism (Psychology)   I. Title.
BF341.C55   1999
155.2'34—dc21   98-31371
                                                                                    CIP

Printed in the United States of America.

10 9 8 7 6 5 4 3 2 1

For her cherished love, enduring friendship, and wise counsel, I dedicate this book to my dear wife Leslie, and in deepest affection and gratitude offer her a timeless valentine that evokes something of the spirit of our relationship and the message of my work.

If Fate is just a roll of nature's dice
And happenstance is Fortune's main device,
Then love is blind, and mere caprice explains
Why romance comes with all its joys and pains.

But surely there is more to love than this:
When cupid's wound and Eros' artifice
Ignite two hearts with passions set in time
And merge two souls whose dreams are set to rhyme.

Since genes turn out to play a vital role
In how we sort in ways of heart and soul,
It means that instinct shapes our destiny
Though how this works is still a mystery.

And yet the sociobiologists
And biological psychologists
Admit that mental life is just as real,
That how we act will come from how we feel.

As feelings pushed by nature's inner dance
Compete with feelings pulled by circumstance,
The push and pull will merge like hand in glove
When past and future blend in deepest love.

I have made a dream poem of humanity. . . . I have taken stock. I will remember. . . . Deep into the snow mountains my search has led me. Now I have it fast. My dream has given it to me, in utter clearness, that I may know it forever.

—*Thomas Mann*

Acknowledgments

The ideal book," said the Roman poet Horace, "is that which at the same time instructs and entertains. . . . Avoid words that are new, obsolete, or sesquipedalian—foot-and-a-half words. Be as brief as clarity allows. Go straight to the heart of the matter . . . erase almost as much as you write. . . ." Horace also advised, "submit your work to a competent critic, and beware of your friends." I have tried to follow all this advice except, I must admit, the last injunction. For not only did I consult many competent critics, both laymen and professional, I failed to cultivate wariness of friends—a wise decision, for my friends, like so many others, have been an inspiration.

For helping me in countless ways to turn good ideas into better text, I am grateful to many. Let me begin with two people whose intelligence and common sense kept me on track more often than I care to admit: my wife Leslie, who has the love and patience of Penelope, and my son Jason, who has the logic and impatience of Spock. Also, I thank colleagues Joe Horn, for his intellect, wisdom, courage, and good sense, the common as well as the uncommon kind, and Judy Langlois, for her ideas, enthusiasm, and encouragement. And I thank my good friend John Street for his wise and supportive badgering—"Okay, then, what do we know?"—that forced me to think more deeply about the facts and their implications.

I want to acknowledge the special contributions of others: University of Texas colleagues Jan Bruell and Lee Willerman, whose passing is a great loss, and Arnold Buss, David Buss, Michael Granof, John Loehlin, Eldon Sutton, and Del Thiessen; students Victoria Beckner, Suejeudi Beuhler, Ben Scharf, Teresa Sokal, Lisa Stanton, and Marlene Tellez; and Linda Greenberg, Edward Miller, Allan and Vicki Rakoff, Alana Rosshirt, Stanton Samenow, Seymour Walzer, and John Bell.

Finally, to my indefatigable agent Jim Hornfischer of The Literary Group International, who knows what novelist Victor Hugo knew—that nothing is as powerful as an idea whose time has come—and to my enthusiastic editors Kelly Franklin and Dorothy Lin of John Wiley, whose wise counsel and high standards have made all the difference.

My heartfelt thanks to all these and others whose generous and, alas, insufficiently heralded contributions are nevertheless reflected in what is best in this work. And one other thing: in the spirit of Francis Bacon's philosophy, I would hope that *Stranger in the Nest* will be read not to contradict, nor to believe, but to weigh and consider.

Contents

Introduction

Great ideas often seem simple and self-evident, but only after somebody has explained them to us. Then, how interesting they become!

—*Theodosius Dobzhansky*

I was barely a toddler when my father began taking me for walks on Ocean Parkway. A few blocks from our apartment house the street gently rose over a pair of tracks, allowing free passage underneath for the lumbering freight trains of the Long Island railroad as they snaked through Brooklyn. My father would hold me firmly, patiently, just above an iron barrier from whose vantage I could see undulating cars that would disappear or emerge below us.

I loved the weekend ritual, taking walks and watching from our side of the street to see what he called the "Saturday train," and on the next day crossing to the other side of the parkway to see the "Sunday train." It didn't matter that they were the same trains, coming and going, viewed from either side of the street because each was a distinct experience separated in time and space by crossing over the wide and busy roadway, a journey not to be taken lightly by a 2-year-old.

Ocean Parkway was an eight-lane boulevard lined with rows of magnificent maples and sycamores that in some places met in the center to form a leafy canopy. Our apartment building was separated from buildings on the far side, not only by the great distance and natural obstructions, but by man-made divisions. These began on our side with a single-lane service road, after which came a bridle path and six traffic-filled lanes of main thoroughfare. Beyond were a bicycle path and sidewalk with benches, followed by a service lane at the far side. During my childhood, I rarely ventured beyond the bike path to the Sunday side.

The Saturday side was the boundary that marked my territory, where I lived and played and, for the briefest time, watched the trains. Now there is only silence with a trashy clutter of weeds and litter that marks the rusting tracks, giving the scene a melancholy quality. Thus mocked, old memories of sunny days and noisy trains nevertheless coalesce around an idea about the two sides of that street overlooking the tracks, not as they were but as a metaphor for two ways of looking at human behavior: one familiar, the other less so yet more intriguing. And another thought: We can stick to familiar territory or we can venture out and explore new ground.

Saturday Side: The Siren Song of Nurture's Sway

The *Saturday perspective*, the most familiar and popular, favors social explanations. To understand personality, think of it as shaped mostly from the outside by family life. To understand mental illness, think about dysfunctional parenting and stressful social situations. The *Sunday perspective*—less familiar territory—favors biological explanations. To understand personality, think of it as developing mostly from inborn influences. To understand mental illness, think of aberrant genes and harmful prenatal conditions.

Both views are true enough, for each focuses on inescapable facts of life. Clearly, Saturday people must accept evidence of inborn influences, just as Sunday people accept evidence of social influences. Yet most of us seem to live on the Saturday side, preferring environmental assumptions that people can be changed for the better, that inconvenient or embarrassing differences between them can be eliminated through encouragement or training, and that, through supportive social environments, one can create a happier world. But the downside to this environmentalist perspective is that if humane influences can bring relief, totalitarian influences can bring harm. If individuals are pliable clay to be shaped by external forces, parental as well as political, how does this serve their best interest, and how can they claim to have free will?

Academics, sociologists in particular, often push the environmentalist view while actively denying all but the most obvious genetic influence. Genetic influence in Alzheimer's, Down's syndrome, and maybe even in some mental illnesses is generally accepted, but not in personality and intelligence, and not in attitudes and achievement. College students, too, assume the overriding power of nurture, as evident when they are asked to rate the following 10 statements as mostly true or mostly false:

1. Most mental illness is caused by dysfunctional parenting or by stressful social conditions.
2. Abused children most likely will become abusive parents.
3. Genetically determined behaviors are mostly unchangeable.
4. The longer spouses live together, the more they resemble one another psychologically.
5. Children praised for extraordinary performance usually perform even better the next time.
6. Children of low-intelligence mothers generally wind up with comparably low intelligence.
7. Adults who were reared in adoptive homes are, in their personality and intelligence, more similar to their adoptive siblings than to strangers in the community.
8. Children learn language mostly by instruction and by imitating their parents.
9. Family resemblance in personality and intelligence comes mostly from family members living together in a shared environment.
10. Genetic influence on intelligence gets weaker as individuals get older and accumulate experience in their environments.

On the surface, each of these 10 statements may seem true enough, even self-evident. When asked to decide, students typically find most of these statements reasonable, with 80 percent rating one or more of them as true, and over 50 percent subscribing to a majority of these items. Yet all 10 are mostly if not entirely false, which raises a provocative question: What should one make of a perspective that lends credence to such erroneous statements?

It is not just academic types who seem captivated by social explanations for psychological traits, but also the media. An article in *Reader's Digest* recommended various instructional tasks with young children—for example, look them in the eye, cheer when they learn to drink from a cup, talk to them more often—all this not just to make them happy and secure but to help raise their IQ. There is a desperate quality to this vision of nurture triumphant, as evident in the conflict between the title of the article ("You Can Raise Your Child's IQ") and the first sentence of the concluding paragraph that begins: "Actual IQ scores may not change. . . ." The argument supporting the influence of nurture is shadowed by the inconclusive evidence.

It is not just academics and reporters, but parents who invest in educational boosters: developmental toys for toddlers, flash cards for preschoolers, and special classes or lessons for older children. Such investments have fewer cognitive or vocational payoffs than emotional and social consequences. As expressions of love, however, they can strengthen emotional ties between parents and children, but as expressions of parental power, they can distort or weaken those ties. The belief that parents have more influence than is true—or worse, the belief that they *should* have such influence—makes it possible to rationalize intrusive, restrictive, or overcontrolling behavior, to assume that children can be molded to fulfill parents' fondest hopes and greatest expectations, whether that means being like them or even better. But what about all those children who cannot be either?

Sunday Side: The Remedy of Nature's Ways

Surely one needs no reminding that loving and stimulating environments can have salutary effects, and that abusive or neglectful parenting can leave psychological scars. Why, then, do these effects so often *not* occur or fail to last—why, for example, do most abused children not become abusive parents, while some well-loved children grow up to be monsters? And what about the ugly-duckling child who becomes a swan or the caterpillar child who becomes a butterfly—or that lively child who becomes a melancholy adult, that talented child who proves a failure, or that well-behaved child who winds up stealing cars, writing hot checks, and exploiting people? The inescapable answer is that, if sufficiently strong, inborn potentials can trump parental influence by manifesting in such unexpected and uncontrollable ways that one's child may seem like a perfect stranger.

The power of inborn potential to limit parental influence is evident in anomalous development and in two startling research findings on personality and intelligence: Identical twins reared apart are nevertheless remarkably alike, as if they had been reared together, yet genetically unrelated people reared together are nevertheless remarkably unalike, as if they had been reared apart. These two findings are really quite revolutionary, for they threaten to overturn much of what the Saturday, or nurture, crowd has long assumed.

What, then, are the benefits of exploring the Sunday side of the nature–nurture debate as it applies to parental influence? One benefit is that we discover many interesting things—for example, bright children usually have less bright parents; schizophrenia has nothing to do with parenting; identical twins can't be identical. Exploring the nature–nurture debate also helps us understand why those 10 items that many people think are true, aren't. We also get to appreciate something else, something central to the thesis of this book: that while parenting is essential to psychological development, just as food is essential to physical development, a *particular kind* of parenting may matter hardly at all—at least for some traits.

Is it possible, as one psychologist asserts, that "children would develop into the same sort of adults if we left them in their homes, their schools, their neighborhoods, and their cultural or subcultural groups, but switched all the parents around"? Recoiling from the implications, one woman countered: "I find myself having trouble accepting this, not because I think it might be false, but because I suspect it might be true. The idea that my neighbor could do just as good a job raising my children as I could do is offensive to me, but why? In some ways it is liberating (as a parent, it's good to know I shouldn't screw up too badly), but in some ways it is threatening (my children should *need me*). I guess it comes down to: Why do parents feel so invested in their children if in fact the children don't need them very much—'them' specifically—if just anyone could raise just any child?"

The point is not to deny the importance of family attachments and the power of social influence, but to see where parenting effects are weakest and what all this means for us. The proposed exploration can bring comfort, for example, to adoptive parents whose high expectations and great capacity to love were doomed by an adoptive child whose antisocial personality made him a stranger in the nest, and whose antisocial behavior transformed a happy family into a dysfunctional household.

These parents can readily accept a biological solution—that antisocial traits are highly heritable—if only because they sense that good old-fashioned efforts at self-control and character-building simply haven't worked and that conventional social explanations don't seem to apply. These parents can readily identify with the poignant imagery offered by Samuel Butler in his novel *Erewhon*:

> *Imagine what it must be to have [a child], who is of an entirely different temperament and disposition to your own; nay, half a dozen such, who will not love you though you have stinted yourself in a thousand ways to provide for their comfort and well-being—who will forget all your self-sacrifice, and of whom you may never be sure that they are not bearing a grudge against you for errors of judgment into which you may have fallen, though you had hoped that such*

had been long since atoned for. Ingratitude such as this is not uncommon, yet fancy what it must be to bear! It is hard upon the duckling to have been hatched by a hen, but is it not also hard upon the hen to have hatched the duckling?

Parents need to understand the futility of guilt over their supposed failures or anger over *their* parents' supposed failures. Also, they must understand that despite the best parenting and family life, a child can still grow up to be vulnerable, irresponsible, moody, unambitious, or even suicidal. Likewise, despite the worst parenting and family life, a child can still grow up to be resilient, responsible, secure, ambitious, and optimistic. Parents can help a sensitive child to be more secure, a hyperactive child to be more self-controlled, even a talented child to be more fulfilled—but only when the biological imperative underlying these traits isn't so great as to counteract the effort to persuade and instruct.

How great, then, is the rearing effect when a child matures into a young adult and the parents are increasingly out of the picture? Overestimating the strength, duration, and direction of parental influence—assuming it is strong, lasting, and predictable—means ignoring not just everyday experience but striking evidence to the contrary, all of which raises the question of parental responsibility.

Who Is Responsible?

In triumph or failure, the question's the same: Who gets the credit and who gets the blame? The popular social-science answer—parents—is as harmful as it is misleading for promoting the illusion that parenting has the paramount influence and therefore responsibility for a child's personality, intelligence, and character. Also, it engenders in the solicitous, child-centered parent an unrealistic sense of responsibility and destructive feelings of guilt over a wayward or mentally ill child, while it engenders in the willful, self-centered parent a nagging disappointment or even a sense of betrayal when, for example, a child groomed for the family business becomes an artist or a professor.

Then how should we take the comment by archbehaviorist John B. Watson, who in 1924 offered this now notorious bit of bravado: "Give me a dozen healthy infants and my own specified world to bring them up in and I'll guarantee to take any one at random and train him to become any type of specialist I might select—doctor, lawyer, artist, merchant-chief and, yes, even beggar-man and thief. . . ." Watson believed he could do this, as he said, "regardless of [the child's] talents, penchants, tendencies, abilities, vocations, and race of his ancestors."

Watson wasn't denying inborn dispositions, just their power. Yet Watson's claims were extreme and, given the absence of factual support, oversimplified and naive. He did not understand that what children learn, what children *become*, need not follow what parents strive to teach them—that their psychological development, whether normal or abnormal, ordinary or extraordinary, would be full of surprises even if parents achieved total control over their educational environment.

Over the years, however, Watson's influential view was reincarnated in an assumption that even severe mental illnesses originate in defective rearing. For decades, psychologists, social workers, and educators have convinced millions of parents of their primary responsibility for determining a child's destiny, as if a child were so much malleable clay. Millions of mothers and fathers have internalized this message with a consequently deep sense of responsibility for things gone wrong. This readiness to internalize reflects a powerful disposition to see family life as having paramount control over a child's psychological development. Most people feel a warm nostalgia about their childhood; others feel anger and resentment. Such deep and abiding sentiments often arise from years of shared experience and the commonly held belief that what one has become must have depended mightily on how one was reared.

Then how is it that extraordinary children can come from ordinary parents, ordinary children from extraordinary parents? Why, despite years of shared experience, can family members be so different in intelligence, personality, and other psychological traits, as if strangers in a nest? How come decent, well-adjusted parents can have neurotic or nasty children, while neurotic or nasty parents can have decent, well-adjusted children? And why do life events so often confound expectations, fears, or hopes as they frustrate efforts to make things happen a certain way?

Such indispensable questions can be answered only by acknowledging evidence that parents have much less influence on a child's psychological development than is commonly assumed. Without parents, we could never have been, but with our own *or any other* parents, could we have been otherwise? And to the extent that the answer is no, then the notion that parental influence determined our development is more illusory than realistic.

Chapter One

Within the Nest

The gods were once disputing whether it was possible for a living being to change its nature. Jupiter said "yes," but Venus said, "no." So to try the question, Jupiter turned a cat into a maiden and gave her to a young man for a wife. The wedding was duly performed and the young couple sat down to the wedding-feast. "See," said Jupiter to Venus, "how becomingly she behaves. Who could tell that yesterday she was but a cat? Surely her nature is changed."

"Wait a minute," replied Venus, and let loose a mouse in the room. No sooner did the bride see this than she jumped up from her seat and tried to pounce upon the mouse. "Ah, you see," said Venus, "nature will out."

—Aesop of Samos

Many people resist the Sunday perspective (see Introduction), which is understandable, given that biological mechanisms often can't easily be seen, felt, or imagined. They aren't personal in that they can't easily be seen as relevant to the self. They aren't social, for they don't offer the familiar characters of family and community that we can readily cast in stories of good guys and bad guys, perpetrators and victims. And they don't seem remediable as an educational problem to be solved socially. Lacking these personally satisfying qualities, biological mechanisms are at a disadvantage. Also, they discomfort us by suggesting that much of what we care about is out of our control.

Nevertheless, others are not strictly pronature or pronurture, assuming quite rightly that nature as well as nurture affects personality. As a result, the debate would seem to be over, the controversy resolved, and therefore, so what? But the more interesting question is rather *how much* does biology constrain rearing? And beyond the question of how much is it nature,

8

and how much nurture is another: *What practical and moral implications for parenting and social policy follow from the answers?* Surely it does matter exactly why some individuals are relatively bright, more sociable, more clever, more decent, more talented, more civilized, or more vulnerable to mental illness. If the bigger influence proved to be mostly nurture, that would fall in line with majority opinion. But if it proved to be mostly nature—worse, if nurture had just about nothing to do with it—what then?

A look at the evidence yields surprising answers that are both objectively valid and personally useful, answers that banish misconceived notions while illuminating our behavior, our experience, and our humanity. One might ask—one *should* ask: What if *Stranger in the Nest's* biological take on psychological development proves wrong? Not likely, but granting the worst, let us at least agree with anthropologist Napoleon Chagnon: better to have been wrong about something important than right about something trivial.

Guiding Hypotheses

The central theme of this book can be boiled down into three guiding hypotheses about personality, intelligence, character, and mental health:

1. The influence of heredity and prenatal life (nature) is surprisingly strong.
2. The influence of rearing and family life (nurture) is surprisingly weak.
3. The effects of nature and nurture are surprisingly perverse.

The first hypothesis speaks to pervasive genetic influence on capabilities and dispositions. As columnist Ann Landers has written:

Some children turn out to be champions in spite of parents who provided precious little emotional nourishment, while other kids—loved, wanted, tenderly nurtured, with all the supposed advantages—turn out perverse, estranged, and unable to cope. I have come to believe in the genetic factor which has been ignored by many behavioral "experts." We all inherit our nervous system and if our nervous system is fragile, it places severe limitations on what a person can tolerate. Certain people are born survivors. They can withstand life's harshest blows and emerge the stronger for it. Others crumble in the face of minor adversity. The same fire that melts butter can make steel stronger.

After a lecture on using adoptees to study the genetic basis of individual differences, a student showed up at my office. He wanted to talk about something mentioned in class about the genetic influence. All his life he had felt different, as if he didn't fit in. An adoptively reared person, he was nothing like his brothers and sisters. Unlike them, he liked to tinker with electronics. Indeed, despite years of sharing the same parents and family experiences with his adoptive siblings, he was the odd man out, but only until he discovered his biological family and two brothers who were tinkerers just like him. His obvious delight was with himself, his discovery, and its meaningful connection to the lecture he had just heard. He wasn't merely corroborating an idea about the genetic influence on individuality. He was sharing the pleasure of experiencing a personal and universal truth.

The story of sudden self-discovery in one's close biological relatives is never more dramatic than with identical twins who, meeting each other for the first time as adults, find many similarities and singular coincidences in their personalities and preferred behavior. In June 1961, for example, two poultry trucks collided in Miami, Florida, and the drivers discovered they were identical twins reared apart. At the time, each had the same job, a similar life style, and even similar dogs. Stories like this make us appreciate how much our genes can influence our unique ways of being, from the most general, for example, being thoughtful or kind hearted, to the most specific, say, a preference for certain colors and decorative patterns, a fear of elevators, or a nervous way of laughing.

Until recently, such stories about twins reared apart were collected in haphazard fashion, and with little effect on psychological theorizing. Similar stories are now being collected systematically, in particular at the University of Minnesota in Minneapolis—which, incidentally, is one of the Twin Cities. Psychologist Tom Bouchard and his colleagues have described remarkable coincidences among reared-apart identical twins that include using the same kind of toothpaste, shaving lotion, hair tonic, and cigarettes, having the same kind of job, and enjoying the same hobby. Coincidences also occur for idiosyncratic behaviors, for instance, preferring to enter the ocean backwards, but just up to the knees, while at the beach.

One of the most spectacular set of coincidences surrounds Jim Springer and Jim Lewis, identical twins adopted as 1-month-old infants into unrelated working class families, and first brought together at age 39. The researchers found the usual high resemblance for IQ and personality traits as well as similar medical histories, and a lot more. Both twins liked math and enjoyed carpentry. Both were compulsive fingernail biters and had tension or migraine headaches, experienced generally in the afternoon. Both drank Miller Lite, chain-smoked Salem cigarettes, drove Chevys, and vacationed in Florida.

Many people drive Chevys or vacation in Florida, so these coincidences may not seem that impressive. But what about a string of more idiosyncratic coincidences? For example, both twins had training in law enforcement and experience as part-time sheriff's deputies. Both had married and divorced a Linda, then remarried a Betty. Both had sons named James, one James Allan, the other James Alan. Each had dogs named Toy. Each enjoyed mechanical drawing and stock-car racing. Each had built a circular bench painted white that surrounded the base of a tree trunk in the yard.

A hereditary explanation for such coincidences does not necessarily mean there are genes for smoking Salems, building circular benches, or naming dogs Toy. Rather, it means that genes bias people. A strong genetic potential can bias people in rather narrow ways that make it likely they will wind up behaving the same way. A taste for nonirritating cigarettes may limit one's choices, thereby increasing the chance that someone with the same biases will discover and commit to the same brand.

Strong genetic dispositions tend to restrict the range of likely or even possible behavior. Identical twins are much more likely than others to share potentials and therefore to make highly similar if not identical choices. So it seemed with a pair of identical twins separated 5 days after birth and adoptively reared in different settings. One went to college and got a degree in forestry, but wound up as an installer of fire alarms. The other planned to get a degree in forestry but didn't, and wound up as an installer of sprinkler systems. Thus, while many details of their behavior differed, the general outline of their lives was strikingly similar.

How remarkable that these kinds of unlikely coincidences occur at all when common sense tells us that some of them ought to occur rarely or never. It is not that all identicals display many such coincidences. Many don't, and some identicals are quite different from each other. Rather, it is the *relatively* higher rate of coincidences for identicals compared to the rate for more ordinary siblings, a difference that illuminates an otherwise obscure genetic influence. However useful, such coincidences can nevertheless mislead if, on average, identical twins raised apart are for many measures only 50 percent similar. Yet the coincidences remain, sparking debate as they stir imagination.

Of course, one could ask, how similar would identical twins be if they were reared apart in radically different conditions? Imagine, says geneticist Charlotte Auerbach, a set of identical quadruplets, one reared in a Fifth Avenue apartment, another in an Indian wigwam, a third in a Moscow orphanage, and the fourth in an Eskimo igloo. Or imagine one twin raised by Nazi sympathizers, the other by orthodox Jews—or for that matter, one normally, the other in a barrel! Surely there would be differences, big ones, but who would be surprised at that? More important is rather how much identicals continue to show their striking psychological similarities in talent, intellect, temperament, and quirks—also their striking coincidences—all despite having been reared in markedly different cultural settings.

Strong genetic potentials can reasonably be inferred where identical twins display such coincidences, especially when these involve relatively unusual motives, feelings, and behaviors; and with the same weak genetic potentials, they will likely show much less psychological similarity. *A genetic potential typically varies from weak to strong*, so that in each of us its manifest expression is neither inevitable nor, when weak, even likely. All of which explains why some identical twins can in many ways be quite different, even if they haven't experienced major differences in social influence. *Yet genetic influence over psychological life is generally quite powerful*, given the striking psychological resemblance and behavioral coincidences even if identical twins are reared apart.

Genes influence our intelligence, personality, and psychological adjustment. They can influence our attitudes, religious values, vocational choices, and leisure-time interests—even such things as values regarding the death penalty, censorship, jazz, and divorce. They can influence the smallest details of our behavior, little quirks or habits—for example, a curious way of sticking out the tongue, just a little, at the corner of the mouth while we concentrate on some difficult task, or perhaps an idiosyncratic way of behaving that our child has inexplicably acquired, just like us when we were that age: a persistent disinclination to try something new or a passion for building model planes, a preoccupation with mazes or a penchant for collecting buttons, stamps, or post cards—perhaps a subtle way of hiding pieces of detested broccoli.

About her father who died when she was 7, author Mary Gordon writes, "It startles me to see that my father and I share stylistic tics. He couldn't have taught me to write, and I was well formed as a stylist before I read any of his prose. Why is it then, that we both love the colon and the semicolon? Why do we both go in for the long, argumentative paragraph that ends in a punchy accusation. Why do we both have a taste for parallelisms? Did I hear them in his speech? Or is style something imprinted, like the color of the eyes . . . ?"

Genetic influence affects more than just our quirks, more than our dispositions and habits, or our deficiencies and neuroses. It affects our resiliency, our ability to resist as well as to recover from early-life adversity, and our self-determination, our ability to create as well as react to environments, including family environments. If we are the author as well as the character in the play that is our life, then environments must be more than mere external influences imposed on hapless individuals; they must be expressions of a unique self. *To the extent that our resiliency and self-determination are in many important ways genetically determined, the worlds we create—our environments—are also partly genetic.*

But genetic influence is only part of the inborn potentials that determine what we are and what we will be. It is simply not true that if something is *genetic* it must be inevitable, inflexible, and irremediable. How else can one explain why identical twins are often discordant—the one ill, the other not—even for highly heritable disorders such as schizophrenia and manic depression, even Alzheimer's.

So, imagine going back to the beginning of our development as a fertilized egg, in effect recreating ourself as our own identical twin. For genetic reasons, we would surely turn out to be similar, as is evident in the sometimes striking psychological resemblances and spooky behavioral coincidences often found for identical twins reared apart. But even with the same genes and the same rearing, for prenatal reasons alone we would still wind up at least a little different. This is evident in the sometimes surprising differences at birth displayed by identical twins. Thus, traditional explanations of rearing and shared experience will not suffice. Neither genes nor rearing alone can fully account for why individuals differ more or less in their talents, temperament, character, and preferred behavior.

The second hypothesis, that *the influence of rearing and family life (nurture) is surprisingly weak,* may not be as evident but it is surely more controversial. Can it be that parenting does not explain, at least not very well, the resemblance that siblings normally show in many psychological traits?

And is it possible that parenting also does not explain, at least not very well, the many differences that siblings show? If good evidence suggests an affirmative answer to these questions, then we must consider that at least some of our dearest, most passionately defended assumptions about parental influence are faulty if not dead wrong. Evidence bearing on these points will be explored throughout this book. Here, consider an instructive anecdote.

Two identical twins, separated during infancy, grow up in different adoptive homes. While Beth is reared by well-off adoptive parents who emphasize fun and material possessions, Amy is reared by lower-middle-class parents who emphasize the traditional values of self-restraint and education. Amy's adoptive mother is socially awkward, overweight, and insecure. Threatened by her daughter's blond, blue-eyed, delicate attractiveness, she and her husband consider Amy a problem child and an outsider.

Right from infancy, Amy had psychological problems. Anxious and demanding, her insecurity showed up in a variety of symptoms, including bed-wetting, fear of the dark and of being alone, frequent nightmares, and clinging to her blanket. By late childhood she was in serious trouble, reportedly "shy, socially indifferent, suffering from a serious learning disorder, pathologically immature." She was a classic example of a rejected child.

Amy's history of parental neglect appears to imply that one's psychological destiny has to do with the nature of one's rearing, but wait. Her identical twin grew up with self-confident and loving adoptive parents who doted on and delighted in her. Yet in most ways Beth's personality followed Amy's development. "Thumb-sucking, nail-biting, blanket-clenching, and bed-wetting characterized her infancy and early childhood. She became a hypochondriac and, like Amy, was afraid of the dark and of being left alone. She too became lost in role-playing, and the artificial nature of her personality was even more pronounced than Amy's."

The more compelling implication of this story is the comparable unfolding of inborn potential in two children despite very different social circumstances that would seem to predict major differences. Such anecdotes reinforced by research evidence make clear just how much parental influence is limited even where it seems to be paramount.

Now, if parental influence doesn't explain the resemblance, why assume it explains the differences? Consider three neighbor boys grown up, each 2 years removed from the other. Says a friend of the family:

From day one, each exhibited strong individuality. The oldest is still shy and introspective, always concerned with doing the right thing. The middle son is still outgoing, with a take-charge attitude about everything. The youngest is still an observer, going about his business with calm resolve and a matter-of-fact-attitude.

When the boys were 10, 8, and 6, the family returned to their car in a Kmart shopping center parking lot, only to find the tires flat. It was midnight and deserted, as mom and dad argued over what to do. Embarrassed, the oldest son begged them not to cause a scene. The youngest son got into the back seat of the car and went to sleep. The middle son, at age 8, walked a few steps to Lamar Boulevard and hailed a taxi!

Same family but totally different personalities. Is it really credible that such profound differences come from differential parental treatment, and if so, where is the *definitive* evidence?

What do we know—what do we *think* we know—about the sources of sibling differences? Psychologist Frank Sulloway argues that

Many important environmental factors, including age, size, and power, as well as status and privilege within the family, are dissimilar for siblings. Families are best seen as containing an array of diverse niches, each occupied by a different individual and each presenting differing vantage points on life. From these different perspectives, family members experience the same events differently. Families do share interests and social values. But siblings differ even in their interests and values, and these differences are caused, in substantial part, by differences in niches within the family.

When responding to questions about family life, parents tend to emphasize their similar treatment of each child, while each child tends to emphasize the differences in perceived treatment. But even if parents were scrupulously evenhanded and family environments were truly uniform, each child would still perceive differences. Perhaps parental behavior does not adequately explain sibling differences, at least no more than it explains sibling resemblances.

Psychologist Stanton Samenow tells of a conscientious mother who tried to establish certain requirements, such as homework before play and good conduct, that would continue to apply to her two boys while she was at work. "One of the boys never posed a problem. The other regarded the freedom inherent in the situation as a license to do whatever he pleased. So here was a situation of two boys who grew up with the same mother, in the same home, in the same neighborhood, and who had the same opportunities and temptations. But each chose to react to his environment in a different manner." Samenow's view is reinforced by another point: "We sometimes mistakenly judge parents based on the actions of their children," writes columnist E. J. Montini. "Parents should be judged for what they do, not for what their kids do. Theodore Kaczynski, the Unabomber, has a good mother. Her name is Wanda, and before you condemn her for having produced a monster you should remember she also reared another son, David, who had the courage to turn in his murderous brother."

Is family life then really so influential, as Sulloway argues, or is it much less influential, as Samenow suggests? It may seem that all those expectations, standards, and demands that parents impose on each child must count for something, but in what way and how much? What if future research proves that parental influence is actually mostly nonshared—different for each child, interacting with inborn tendencies to yield different developmental pathways? "Parents do affect their children," says psychologist David Rowe, "but the direction of that 'nudge' is often unpredictable. Encouraging one child to study hard may make that child get better grades, whereas a brother or sister may rebel against being 'bossed' by the parents."

Perhaps children really would develop into the same sort of adults—in many ways *the same* adults—if we left them in their homes, their schools, their neighborhoods, and their cultural or subcultural groups, but switched all the parents around. Of course the new set of nonshared environmental influences associated with a new set of parents would yield differences. The question is not so much that, but whether those differences would be all that impressive and all that permanent. After all, parental influence strong at one stage in a child's development may weaken or disappear in another. The evanescent quality of such influence is evident in parental influence on IQ that decreases from substantial when children are young, to virtually nil when children are grown up.

Parenting is essential to a child's survival as a person, but it has much less impact and even less predictable effect than we have imagined on the development intelligence, personality, and character, all of which makes a child unique. The stunning implication: if our parents' influence on us is less than what they thought, our influence on our children must be less than we think. And if we are often mistaken about our parents and our children, might we likewise be mistaken about ourselves?

The second hypothesis regarding the limits of parental influence reflects something else: a natural resiliency of human nature that protects from abusive conditions. Such resilience has been celebrated by survival fables that forever enchant and inspire us, for example, the classic tale of Hansel and Gretel who triumph over loathsome rearing conditions. As the Brothers Grimm narrate:

> *"I'll tell you what, husband," answered the woman, "early tomorrow morning we will take the children out into the forest to where it is the thickest. . . . They will not find the way home again, and we will be rid of them." . . . The two children had also not been able to sleep for hunger, and had heard what their step-mother had said to their father. Grethel wept bitter tears, and said to Hänsel, "Now it is all over with us." "Be quiet, Grethel," said Hänsel, "do not distress thyself, I will soon find a way to help us."*

It's not just storybook characters that teach us much about how the capacity for resistance and resiliency illuminates the limits of parental influence—remarkable historical figures whose heroic achievements despite crushing circumstances teach us the same. Born to slaves living in Missouri during the Civil War, George Washington Carver experienced a catalog of appalling misfortunes and deprivations. His father died before Carver was born and his mother was abducted while he was still a baby. Brought up by barely literate, impoverished whites, he was denied decent schooling, he was forced to take menial jobs, and he constantly suffered hunger, bad health, a stammer, and racial discrimination. Despite all this, he managed to become an educated man. Initially, he succeeded through his own efforts, then through formal schooling, winding up with a bachelor's degree in agriculture. Eventually he became a leading biologist of the nineteenth century and a celebrated pioneer in the field of agricultural chemistry.

According to psychiatrist Michael Stone, "Where the [inborn] factors are unfavorable *and* the [parenting] factors were clearly horrendous—and *still* the personality emerges whole, or even unusually courageous—the explanatory powers of psychiatry fall to just about zero. Normality eludes us. Instances of this latter sort are a great challenge to psychiatry. But until we can explain why some people become whole who, according to theory, should have been 'basket cases,' our work is only half done." None of this denies that especially vulnerable people can be hurt by abusive conditions or traumatic events, or that they want to believe that their emotional problems come from being a victim rather than from being a bad person. It merely suggests another, too-often unsung side to the story of limited parental influence, namely the resiliency, courage, and virtue that characterizes even ordinary people.

The second hypothesis reflects not only the resilient but the proactive qualities of childhood—the self-generating and creative qualities which mean that children, far from passively experiencing their worlds, actively create them in mental life and in the social arena. Rearing itself is an effect, reflecting a child's personality, and it therefore must have limited causal significance. Ignoring the resilient, proactive, and self-determining elements of personality—thinking of individuals primarily as products of their environment—can never explain a Beethoven who, after all, was a product of his environment. And if it can't explain a Beethoven, a Gauss, or an Einstein—if it can't explain a Mozart, a Helen Keller, or a Jackie Robinson—why should it reveal much of anything interesting about anyone else?

The second hypothesis reflects another related observation: that despite supportive and loving rearing, despite shared experiences and mutual respect, even despite their parents' fondest hopes, expectations, and efforts, children go their separate ways. Sometimes these developments are nothing short of dramatic, as the case of a 15-year-old who shot and killed 2 fellow students and wounded 18 others after killing his parents.

And what kind of parents—disturbed, neglectful, abusive? No: loving, supportive, patient, dedicated, involved—the best parents imaginable. A longtime friend of the slain couple put it this way: "If there was anything possible a parent could do, they did it. If, for some reason, I had been unable to raise my own four children, I would have had no problem saying, 'We'll give them to Bill and Faith.' " Clearly, the problem was not the parents, but a deeply disturbed child—more than a stranger in the nest, an alien creature with a terrible temper, murderous fantasies, delight in torturing animals, obsession with guns, and an idolatry of the Unabomber and the Oklahoma City bombers.

A haunting philosophical implication of hypotheses 1 and 2 will not go away. That identical twins so differently reared apart have become in so many ways the same person surely challenges conventional assumptions about power of a particular rearing to determine the direction of a person's psychological development. But more, it challenges the assumption that, unencumbered by biological and social determination, one can freely choose how to be and what to do.

The resemblance of identical twins reared apart speaks to our bondage as well as to our freedom: *freedom from* social influences that would shape us in personally unsuitable ways—the message in resiliency, reversion to type, proactivity, and creativity—yet *bondage to* genetic and environmental forces that determine the unique person that we are bound to become. We may be the only species capable of arguing with our genes—but capable of escaping genetic determination? *Not if the part of us that argues is as genetically determined as any other part.*

Psychologist Viktor Frankl has written about seemingly ordinary people who, despite the horrors of the Nazi concentration camps, showed their courage and compassion in offers of comfort or even a last crust of bread. "They may have been few in number, but they offer sufficient proof that everything can be taken from a man but one thing: the last of the human freedoms—to choose one's attitude . . . to choose one's own way." Yet we can ask: Exposed to similar challenges in other concentration camps, would the identical twins of such courageous and compassionate people likewise behave courageously and compassionately, maybe to the last detail? If so, in what sense were the heroes of Frankl's story really free to choose?

Then does genetic evidence rule out free will? A reasonable scientific answer in the affirmative won't be fashionable or agreeable; it may be disturbing or even be objectionable. Nevertheless, it should be considered if the evidence of genetic determinism that we get from adoptees, especially identical twins reared apart, suggests that the concept of free will may be obsolete.

The dentist says we don't have to clean our teeth, just the ones we want to keep. In like manner, we don't have to test our assumptions, just the ones that matter—for example, the assumption that we can be whatever we want, if only we put our minds to it and work hard. Yet how true can this flattering message be when the evidence suggests the converse, that we want whatever we can really be—that our personalities, ambitions, and achievements are determined mostly by forces that exist outside our conscious control?

The third hypothesis says that *the combined influence of nature and nurture is surprisingly perverse,* causing unexpected behaviors that contradict parental expectations or that embarrass scientific theories. People want their world to make sense, to be reasonably systematic, explainable, and predictable. Yet the sheer number of possible biological and social causes, both past and present, can make it impossible to predict what will happen or to explain what *has* happened—why, for example, this child became that kind of adult or why someone committed suicide. The complex and chancy aspects of psychological causation make some behavior quite unpredictable or uncontrollable, reminding us in yet another way of the limits of parental influence.

A poignant real-life example is that of a bright young man who enters college with lifelong ambitions to become a doctor. Yet he earns poor grades in premed courses, even ones he is tutoring others to pass. Why? It can't be ability, for he is getting A grades in courses unrelated to medicine, and he has a genius-level intelligence, an IQ over 150. The more likely answer is motivation, an unconscious conflict between a boy's true needs and those of an immigrant father whose aspirations to become a doctor had been frustrated by social and economic circumstances beyond his control. The father's dream would therefore be achieved vicariously, that is, until his son's inner rebellion and self-assertion derails a lifetime of conscious expectations and planning engendered by unremitting pressure. Eventually, the son goes on to do graduate work in literature.

A major reason for this seeming perversity of psychological development is that a child inherits a random half of each parent's genes, and these will interact differently with the different prenatal environment of each pregnancy. The resulting unique pattern of inborn tendencies, along with a unique way of perceiving the world, guarantees that despite family resemblance of the physical and psychological kind, any child will differ from a parent or sibling, even from an identical twin, sometimes in striking and surprising ways.

It is not just a unique pattern of inborn tendencies that defies parental hopes and expectations. Unpredictable circumstances, social as well as neurological, can also cause surprising behavioral changes. Some changes are predictable, as is evident in common observation and psychological studies. An otherwise ordinary person in a position of power, say, a spouse, an employer, a therapist, or a bureaucrat—especially when that power is absolute and without accountability—may prove overbearing, even monstrous. Psychological research on conformity to authority always reveals just how readily people will do even hateful and destructive things that they would never have believed themselves capable of doing.

Even profound changes can occur under other stressful conditions. A talented but undistinguished person might prove heroic under certain challenging conditions—an Oskar Schindler, for example, who by employing them in his munitions factory rescued 1,200 German Jews during the Holocaust. And so, if circumstances warranted extraordinary behavior, how many ordinary people would likewise rise to the occasion—and in what way?

Dr. J. was an enthusiastic Nazi functionary, whom Viktor Frankl characterized as a Mephistophelean being, a satanic figure, and notorious as the mass murderer of Steinhof, a large mental hospital located in Vienna. Years after the Holocaust, Frankl learned that Dr. J. had been confined by the Soviets to Moscow's Lubianka prison. Before he died of cancer, according to a diplomat who had also been there, "He showed himself to be the best comrade you can imagine! He gave consolation to everybody. He lived up to the highest conceivable moral standard. He was the best friend I ever met during my long years in prison."

The stories of Schindler and Dr. J. suggest that no amount of digging into the formative years, no dwelling on the quality of upbringing or the experiences of childhood, will satisfactorily explain behavioral outcomes, for deeper explanations lie rather in the resiliency, proactivity, autonomy, inventiveness, and unpredictability of personality—all qualities that point to the limits of parental influence.

Getting Perspective

A horse can be led to water and made to drink. Rats can be induced to press bars and dogs to dance on two legs; a psychopath can be made to do a good deed. So what? So this: Focus on what people or animals can be induced to do, and learning is revealed as accommodations guided by instruction and modeled behavior or as habits shaped by rewards and punishments.

With this *Saturday perspective* on behavior, one can understand just how much the external forces of family, society, and culture collectively press for self-control, conformity, and civility. One can also understand how a cruel and abusive upbringing may damage emotional life and promote antisocial and self-destructive behavior. The point, however, is not that children can be made to comply with social pressure, but rather why, despite years of learning what parents expect and require, children grown to adulthood nevertheless revert to their own inclinations, which can sometimes make them seem like strangers in the family nest.

Now focus on what people or animals *prefer* to do, what their intuition and imagination inspire them to do with ease and grace. It can be understood just how much learning is guided by inborn abilities and vulnerabilities that drive a person's achievements, personality, and mental health. This *Sunday perspective* on behavior that is preferred or inventive rather than coerced or traumatic makes more evident what the study of twins and adoptees can tell us about the limits of parental influence.

Evidence from that perspective takes us beyond heated debate on two competing visions of human nature, and provides answers to fundamental questions that capture these visions—in particular, *what power does nature have relative to nurture*, and *what responsibility do parents have relative to children?* The first is a statistical question about individual differences, the other a moral question about family relationships. Seeing the connection between these two means addressing a psychological question about the limits of parental influence on a child's development.

Arguments and evidence bearing on all facets of parental influence are fully treated in *Stranger in the Nest*'s two parts. Part 1, "Saturday Side: The Nature of Nurture," makes clear not only the limits of a parent's influence on a child's unique psychological development, but the inability of social science research to illuminate those limits. Those limits are also addressed in Part 2, "Sunday Side: Blueprints for Life," which explores the most compelling evidence of inborn influence, genetic and prenatal factors that strongly determine psychological traits.

Part One

Saturday Side:
The Nature of Nurture

*W*e *must respect the other fellow's [theory], but only in the
sense and to the extent that we respect his theory that his
wife is beautiful and his children smart.*

—H. L. MENCKEN

Chapter Two

Making Connections

Alice laughed: "There's no use trying," she said; "one can't believe impossible things." "I dare say you haven't had much practice," said the Queen. "When I was younger, I always did it for half an hour a day. Why, sometimes I've believed as many as six impossible things before breakfast."

—*Lewis Carroll*

Back in 1980, the Schlitz company tried to convince people that its beer was better than the major rival brands. The company raised prices while using more corn syrup and less barley malt, the ingredient that gives beer its flavor and body. Offering customers a less tasty, more expensive product backfired, with sales going down dramatically. The disastrous course could eventually be reversed, but only if the public were convinced that Schlitz had become not only comparable to, but better than, the competition.

The key to commercial redemption lay in clever advertising, specifically a razzle-dazzle TV extravaganza involving blind beer-tasting tests done in what appeared to be a football stadium with cheering crowds and a referee. Seated at a table were either confirmed Bud or Miller drinkers, people who drank at least two six-packs of their preferred beer weekly. In front of them were two identical opaque mugs, one containing Schlitz, the other either Bud for Bud drinkers or Miller for Miller drinkers.

The results? In just about every test, roughly half the Bud or Miller drinkers picked Schlitz. It would seem that Schlitz must be the better beer. What else explains why so many loyal Bud or Miller drinkers switched to Schlitz? Well, the conclusion is questionable because the so-called beer-tasting test left out a key element: Schlitz drinkers. What if roughly half of *them* had switched to Bud or Miller? That would have confirmed the alternative hypothesis that Schlitz was now essentially no different from the other brands. By leaving out Schlitz drinkers, the Schlitz taste test was really only half a test—the hypothesis was only half-asked—and therefore no test at all because the hypothesis of Schlitz's superiority was never in danger of refutation.

Likewise, by ignoring certain kinds of evidence, social psychological theories often avoid the danger of refutation. The usual parent-child correlations, no matter how consistent with social theorizing, leave out much information that supports alternative explanations of a person's behavior. Given that parents P are a dominant presence, while children C are little and impressionable things, how readily we assume that parenting explains much of the unique psychological development of a child—that P explains C. Unfortunately, such PC theory ignores or minimizes new, more definitive evidence of critically important genetic and other inborn factors (X, Y, Z) that have little or nothing to do with parenting.

The power of such PC theorizing is evident when otherwise sensible people seem oblivious to the obvious, for example, when the usually sensible historian Will Durant suggests quite inexplicably that, "Henry Purcell's genius was in large part a product of social heredity—i.e., adolescent environment. His father was master of the choristers at Westminster Abbey; his uncle was a 'composer in ordinary for the violins to his Majesty'; his brother was a composer and a dramatist, his son and his grandson continued his role as organist in the Abbey." Is it not just as obvious—and, given the evidence, most likely true—that Purcell's genius was the product of genetic heredity?

The Nature of the Evidence

For novelist John Irving, "It's a no-win argument—that business of what we are born with and what our environment does to us. And it's a boring argument, because it simplifies the mysteries that attend both our birth and our growth." Irving is surely right that the argument, being essentially statistical—applying to the generality rather than to any one person— must render human experience less real, less complex, less poignant; most arguments over nature and nurture really do seem rather boring. Irving is also right that the usual evidence, being essentially correlational— confounding cause and effect, nature and nurture—must render scientific explanations less clear, less certain, less definitive.

However, research with twins and adoptees really *has* moved us beyond sterile debate, allowing us to test hypotheses that lead to interesting findings. Such testing has yielded results whose implications are rather clear for certain traits, and interesting not just for showing the strength of genetic influence, but in raising serious questions about the power of parental influence. The key to all of this is the quality of the methods and the credibility of the findings, and this is as true for behavior genetic research as for the social science kind.

Strictly speaking, the behavior genetic method isn't truly experimental, for like the rest of us, twins and adoptees don't get randomly assigned to rearing environments. Most twins are reared by the same parents who have given them their genes, which confounds the influences of nature and nurture. With adoptees, including identical twins reared apart, there are other potential problems, for example, they generally get placed with parents who are above average in many ways intellectually and emotionally, and who are unlikely to be abusive. All this violates the experimental ideal of having newborns randomly assigned to homes representing the full range of rearing environments, from the healthiest to the most abusive. Adoptees may even be selected on the additional grounds of having ethnic, religious, social, intellectual, or even physical characteristics that match those of the adoptive parents—nothing random about this. Finally, twins reared apart are sometimes brought up by different relatives, and there's nothing random about this, either.

This narrowed range of environments experienced by the twins and adoptees limits what can be said about family influence from such research. No doubt, greater emotional differences than are usually found for identicals would be found if one twin were reared by loving parents, the other by abusive parents. Bigger psychological differences would mark twins reared in radically different cultures, but again, the interesting question is rather how much some of the psychological similarities expected for identicals would yet survive such environmental differences.

While we can't answer that question, we can answer the more realistic one about differences for identicals reared apart in social environments that differ in the usual, still quite divergent ways that mark ordinary families in a multicultural society. Twin and adoption studies may each be flawed, but they are each flawed in a different way. Each has holes, but stacked one on top of the other, the holes don't go through. What does come through, though, is consistent evidence of genetic reasons for individual differences. And the evidence is convincing because it comes from studies that disentangle the relative influence of heredity and environment. It is the difference between observations that two things go together and *controlled* observations that really tell us if one of those things *causes* the other. This is why even one flawed adoption study is worth more than countless conventional family studies.

The power of adoption research can be illustrated here with the so-called birth-order effect on personal development. The question is this: Why might first-borns be brighter, more conservative, and less radical than second borns? Social science offers three explanations. One is that during their earliest, most formative years, first-borns get higher-quality intellectual stimulation. After all, first-borns have just their parents, who are smart adults, while second-borns must contend with parents and a sibling. Another says that first-borns become intellectually more sophisticated by acting as teachers of their second-born siblings. A third says that conflicts inevitably arise when a second-born sibling must compete for parental favors already acquired by the first-born child. Out of these conflicts comes a more liberal personality, one that is relatively more open to new experiences.

Such theorizing about family influence seems reasonable enough, but only by ignoring that birth order is as much physiological as social, that it reflects which sibling is senior in the family (social standing), but also which came from a first or later pregnancy. Psychologists Jeremy Beer and Joe Horn have disentangled the effects of these two normally confounded factors by comparing first-born adoptive children reared either as a social senior with a younger sibling or as a social junior with an older sibling. Thus, they compared first-born social seniors with first-born social juniors.

With such a comparison, *none* of the expected IQ and personality differences showed up; the expected connection between psychological differences and social seniority simply wasn't there. The clear implication is that the birth-order effect is uterine rather than social, physiological rather than familial. And so it may be asked, with the application of a more definitive scientific method, how many other presumed social influences, including those involving rearing, would likewise prove to be biological? The answer, we will see, is as sobering as it is illuminating.

Parenting, Intelligence, and Academic Achievement

Good parents care about their children's academic achievement, but where does academic achievement come from? The usual answer, rearing, really can't explain why children's academic achievement correlates more strongly with their parents' intelligence than with their parents' attitudes and rearing styles. In experimental fashion, hold parenting constant— select parents with similar parenting styles—and variation in parental intelligence still predicts their children's academic achievement in adolescence. Now hold parental intelligence constant—select parents with similar intelligence—and variation in parenting *doesn't* predict that achievement. Here, then, is a good example of how one salient thing (parenting style) can seem so important, when a more subtle thing (intelligence) is the real influence.

But why does intelligence rather than parenting style predict a child's achievement? One social explanation is that intelligence translates into educational practice; for example, brighter parents stimulate their children more, increasing their abilities and therefore their ultimate achievements. Sounds perfectly reasonable, as do many social explanations, but here is a simpler one: Parents transmit their genetic potential to their biological offspring. Even within the same family, children who get the genetic potential for higher intelligence score higher on IQ tests and show greater academic and socioeconomic achievement. In short, intelligence predicts intelligence, whether it is parents' IQ and their offspring's IQ, parents' IQ and their offspring's achievement, or, for that matter, a person's IQ and achievement.

A headline announces that more breast-feeding may facilitate eventual academic achievement. But does a correlation between the number of months children are breast-fed and their academic achievement really mean that breast-feeding has a salutary effect on academic motivation and capability? If so, then mothers should breast-feed longer; but if not, what then? Reading further reveals that the mothers who breast-fed longest were better educated and wealthier—two good indicators of relatively high intelligence. If brighter mothers breast-feed longer, then their children's higher achievement is likely a matter of heredity more than of breast-feeding.

The media are replete with such ambiguous and misleading findings, which often suggest that rearing profoundly affects a child's intellectual development. Yet closer inspection suggests the opposite, that the correlation represents a child's inborn potentials and a parent's limited influence. According to one headline, for example, "Harsh Discipline Hurts IQ." The implication is that, because harsh discipline goes (correlates) with a 12-point IQ disadvantage, punishment *causes* lower IQ. But what if low-IQ children cause their parents to punish them more? Or what if low-IQ parents tend to be more aggressive and therefore to have more punitive relationships? In either case, less punitive discipline will not appreciably increase a child's IQ.

According to another headline, "Poverty before Age 5 Leaves Children with Lower IQs." The implication is that, because poverty goes (correlates) with low IQ, poverty *causes* lower intelligence. But what if poverty mostly reflects the low intelligence of parents whose low-IQ children would grow up to be relatively low-IQ adults, poverty notwithstanding? Then reducing poverty will not make low-intelligence kids score appreciably higher on IQ tests.

We read that the number of words an infant hears each day predicts later intelligence, academic achievement, and social competence. Researchers looked at 42 children born to professional parents, working-class parents, or low-income parents. During their first 2½ years, the children's every word and interaction with a parent was recorded for an hour each month. At age 3, standard intelligence testing showed that children of professional parents scored highest, and that spoken language seemed to be a key variable. But was it?

Rather, spoken language may have been an outward expression of what was the actual key difference, a genetic one. Professional parents talked three times more to their infants and gave much more positive feedback to their children than was the case for the low-income parents, but can there be any surprise in this? We are informed that affirmative feedback is important, that a child who hears "What did we do yesterday?" or "What did we see?" will listen more to a parent than will a child who always hears "Stop that!" or "Come here!" Yes, but which parent likely has the higher IQ, and therefore which one will transmit more genes for IQ?

Animals reared in enriched environments have larger brains with more neurons and more connections. Surely this fits what many people have always suspected: that good parents enrich their children's lives, right from infancy, that they provide as much cognitive stimulation as possible along with loving-kindness and emotional support. But do such findings with animals really apply to humans? Even poor households in modern societies may be the psychological equivalent of enriched environments that make laboratory animals develop more brain cells. If so, then most children are already about as stimulated and big-brained as they are likely to be.

Now suppose the findings really did indicate that the more stimulating the human environment, the bigger the effect on a developing brain. What, in the practical sense, would all those extra neurons and new connections really mean? There might be no noticeable effect on potentials and on behavior. On the other hand, children might be brighter for a short while, after which the gains might disappear as inner-directed brain reorganization occurs during puberty, with millions of neurons pruned and billions of neural connections lost or rearranged. Extra growth of neural tissue in animals exposed during infancy to enriched environments disappears when they are transferred to ordinary environments. So it seems fair to question the permanence of early-enrichment effects.

Let's say that the extra stimulation imposed early in life really did translate into reliably brighter kids who could go on to be more successful adults. Then would the effect be big or small relative to other influences? What if the effect explained only 5 percent of all the variation in adult achievement compared to, say, 75 percent from genetic differences? Would the effort justify the financial and emotional cost of a new educational push that would inevitably be demanded by parents, politicians, and the education industry?

Despite the strong impression suggested by magazine articles, not a shred of evidence supports the notion that vigorous efforts to promote psychological enrichment, especially during the so-called critical period, will make an otherwise normally reared child bigger brained and, therefore, brainier.

Parenting and Personality

Fifteen centuries ago Saint Augustine challenged the belief that personality comes from the planetary alignment at a person's birth. The great fifth-century theologian had his hands full, for as historian Will Durant notes, people accepted, for example, that "persons born under the ascendancy of Saturn would be cold, cheerless, saturnine; those born under Jupiter, temperate and jovial. . . ." Thus, to have a proper horoscope, to observe the hour, required knowing the precise moment of birth and the precise position of the stars.

Nonsense, countered Augustine, for if astrological alignments were truly important, how can fraternal twins born at almost the same moment be as different as any two siblings born in different seasons? Citing the biblical case of Esau and Jacob, he wrote: "Now there was such a difference in their lives and characters, such divergence in their actions, such disparity in the affection of their parents, that these discrepancies turned them into mutual enemies. [Furthermore,] one of those twins was a paid servant, the other was not; one was loved by his mother, the other was not; one lost that position which in those days was counted a great honor, while the other acquired it. Besides, what a vast difference between their wives, their sons, the whole setting of their lives!"

The moral of the story: Even if we can't do experiments—even where there are no experimental data—we can at least *think* experimentally, for example, about parent-child correlations, some of which are as misleading or illusory as are personality-astrological correlations.

Media stories about parents and children are legion, but what do they really tell us about parental influence? A headline says that "Family Rituals Promote Better Emotional Adjustment." Apparently, because reading bedtime stories and other family rituals go (correlate) with good feelings, such family rituals *cause* better emotional development. But what if family rituals merely reflect happier, better adjusted family members who like to be with each other? Then adopting more family rituals will not appreciably affect the emotional adjustment of children as they grow up.

A second headline says that "Teens Who Feel Loved Do Better." Apparently, because feeling loved goes (correlates) with doing well socially—say, in the sense of not using drugs—love *causes* teens to do better. But what if lovable teens who grow up to be lovable adults are simply loved more? Then trying to love teens more will not make them do appreciably better.

A correlation in social behavior has been found, but only for parents and their biological children. Biological children with fewer behavioral problems tend to have more supportive parents; the correlation is a modest 23. It is, however, only 7—just about nonexistent—for adoptive children and their adoptive parents. Apparently, without the usual 50 percent genetic overlap that permits parent-child resemblance, almost no correlation exists between typical parents' behavior and their children's emotional adjustment.

Lacking adoption methods, social scientists are typically reduced to using less definitive methods. With one, they classify parents' self-reported attitudes and approaches to rearing their children—for example, as warm or hostile, restrictive or permissive. They also ask parents to categorize their children as healthy, neurotic (anxious, sensitive), or antisocial. Healthy children are outgoing, independent, friendly, and creative. Neurotic children are quarrelsome, unhappy, timid, and socially withdrawn. Antisocial children are immature and aggressive, noncompliant, or delinquent. Not surprisingly, the expected parent-child associations are found: Parenting associated with healthy children tends to be warm, authoritative, and permissive while parenting associated with neurotic and antisocial children tends to be hostile, authoritarian, and either restrictive or overly permissive.

Good parenting does tend to *go with* good outcomes, bad parenting with bad outcomes, but does "go with" represent causality from parent to child? If so, why are there so many normal children with neurotic parents or antisocial children with nurturing parents, and why are such questions so often not asked? Even a strong connection between rearing and traits would support various interpretations, in particular, the usual one that parents determine their child's development, and a variant of this, that children determine their parents' behavior. We need only ask ourselves this: Where do parenting practices come from? The obvious answer is *parental personality*. Regardless of a child's behavior, parents tend to express themselves in certain ways that, we will see, are substantially heritable. We are also responsive to situations and react accordingly, which means that children's traits can drive their parents' behavior. And this includes parents reacting maladaptively to the eccentric or socially disruptive behavior of their own or another parent's child.

Thus, causation can go from child to parent, as when a hyperactive, autistic, or excessively timid child makes a parent aggressive, intrusive, or withdrawn. The parent of a highly active child is in some danger not only of being blamed, but of accepting blame. After all, conflict and family strife seem almost inevitable when even a temperamentally normal parent interacts with a highly active child. Parents of active children are likely to engage in power struggles that can make for disruptive, unsatisfying relationships. Unfortunately, such parental reactions—such parent-child correlations—are often mistaken for causes. When tempted to conclude, no wonder little Billy is so neurotic; just look at his parents, we should consider the reverse: No wonder his parents are so neurotic; just look at little Billy.

Clinical research on infants reinforces the point. Roughly 4 percent of children have extremely difficult temperaments. Their sleeping, eating, and energy levels are markedly irregular, unpredictable, and frustrating to parents. So, too, are their anxiety and irritability, and their tendency to withdraw from or react against new stimuli. Their reactions are unusually intense and have an all-or-nothing quality.

As temperament researchers Thomas, Chess, and Birch explain it, "such a child will tend to cry loudly when he is hurt whether he has a minor scratch or a deep and painful gash. . . . He may fuss as intensely when he makes a spelling mistake in a minor bit of homework as he may when he makes an error in an extremely important project in which he is engaged. When frustrated, such children may destroy whatever they are working on whether it be a minor construction with tinker toys or a complicated model which has been worked on for several weeks."

Not surprisingly, the parents tend to be irritable, anxious, punitive, or distant, but also guilt-ridden, frustrated, and helpless. Yet before the birth of their difficult child, they no more readily experienced such emotions than did a comparable group of parents whose children turned out to be normal. Rather, they had the usual positive expectations about being a parent and positive attitudes about how to rear children. The drastic change embarrasses the usual assumption that a parent's attitudes and behavior strongly influence not only a child's temperament, but that child's eventual development. Rather, it suggests just how much children are in charge of their own socialization.

A newspaper story has reported that parental use of corporal punishment actually made children more antisocial in later years. The actual finding was that the self-reported number of spankings parents used on their 6 to 9-year-olds correlated with the amount of lying, cheating, and disruptive behavior the children displayed in school 2 years later. Spanking can aggravate bad behavior in specific situations, but does it really increase the *disposition* to bad behavior that, for reasons of inborn potential, might get worse regardless of what parents do? Perhaps spanking is as much an effect as a cause, a reaction to socially disruptive behavior that a frustrated parent cannot imagine controlling in any other way.

The parent–personality connection can be looked at profitably by asking about sources of self-esteem. Many people with low self-esteem were exposed to parenting that stressed how much they were inferior to others. A child's self-esteem could be undermined by a mother's constant criticizing, while his or her sense of self-importance could be injured by a father's emotional distance. People can thus come to see themselves as unworthy and unlovable.

Well then, does self-esteem come from how people think about themselves, or does how they think about themselves come from their self-esteem? Either view could be argued from standard social science correlations. Perhaps the better answer is that self-esteem simply depends on how good one feels, which depends on one's temperament more than upbringing. After all, with no special change in external condition or personal history, a few little pills of serotonin booster can cause lighter mood and greater self-confidence.

Does the pill create in some people what comes naturally to others because of their sunnier temperament—that is, self-esteem and thoughts about one's self therefore normally arise from an inherited tendency, regardless of circumstances, to feel good or bad, happy or sad, secure or insecure? This idea can explain people who have low self-esteem and a tendency to feel unhappy despite good luck and fortunate circumstances. It can also explain all those people with high self-esteem and a sense of well-being despite bad luck and difficult circumstances.

An even better question: What would happen if newborns were separated from their biological parents and reared by adoptive parents? Would the adoptive offspring born of high self-esteem adults develop the active, self-assertive, high self-esteem qualities of their biological parents? And is it not likely that their active, self-assertive (high self-esteem) traits would cause the adoptive parents to be more active and assertive?

We need no reminding that parents and their biological children show the kinds of modest correspondences called family resemblance. Parents who are characteristically warm, demanding, respectful, and authoritative might simply pass the genes for these admirable qualities to their children—no surprise, then, that these children wind up with the relatively high self-esteem that *their parents showed as kids* and who, when they, too, become parents, are similarly warm, demanding, respectful, and authoritative with their children. Parents surely influence their children's self-esteem, but just how much and to what extent does that influence carry over into adulthood? On this question, social science correlations, being fundamentally ambiguous, are merely arguable.

Divorce, Child Abuse, and Personality

Compared to children of single-divorce parents, children of parents who divorce and remarry more than once experience more anxiety, depression, and a sense of vulnerability. They have elevated risks for engaging in precocious sexual behavior, for alcohol and drug abuse, and for committing suicide. They also have more problems with school adjustment, including lower academic achievement and a relatively high risk of falling below the poverty line. Eventually, they have more troubled marriages and a higher divorce rate.

No doubt multiple divorce adversely affects children, especially in the short run. Many will experience apprehension, resentment, alienation, and loneliness, and many will have abandonment fears and fantasies. In some children, many of these psychological changes, like physical scarring, will last a lifetime. Yet an association between the behavior of parents and the personality of their offspring does not prove that one is an important cause of the other. Each may reflect something common to both, which would explain why the parents of temperamentally difficult children have an elevated risk of divorce.

That divorce is an outward indication of hidden dispositions shared by parents and children comports with what twin research suggests, namely that genetic influence partly determines whether marriages succeed. Parents can transmit to their children the genetic qualities of troubled temperament, poor judgment, and self-centered immaturity that figure in the psychology of multiple divorce. It is therefore no surprise that men who divorce their spouses are many times more likely to have a diagnosable antisocial personality, which is a highly heritable personality trait. And the converse: The children of divorced parents are likely to be genetically different from the children of parents who do not divorce. All this can explain the children's emotional and academic problems, even those they display many years before their parents divorce, and eventually their own elevated divorce rate.

Genetic factors controlling parental dispositions are likely transmitted to children, who then express these dispositions in their own way and when grown up are likely to behave with their spouses and children as their parents did with them. Can it be assumed that the cycle of family violence from generation to generation is strongly genetic rather than merely shaped by upbringing? No doubt the behaviors of parents and children interact, but the *relative power* of the underlying dispositions—in particular, the child's disposition—can be resolved only by adoption studies that have yet to be done.

Adults who report having been abused as children often have problems of aggressiveness, antisocial behavior, drug abuse, sexual promiscuity, depression, and poor self-esteem. Many seem to wind up abusing their children or spouses, but why? Perhaps it stems from personal experience with abusive rearing.

Child abusers often report that they themselves were abused as children; estimates range from 7 to 70 percent. We can take the average to be approximately 40 percent, but what does any such figure really mean? Conventional social theorizing offers two possibilities. One is that abusive parents model socially undesirable behaviors, through which their children become badly educated about what is permitted—about violence toward loved ones being a normal part of parenting. The children, as parents themselves, apply that lesson with their own family members.

The other possibility is that abusive parenting creates an antisocial personality that itself causes abusive behavior not only with spouses and children, but with non–family members as well. Through neglect, punishment, and traumatic experience, children learn that the world is a dangerous place. They become vigilant and sensitive, even to the point of minor paranoia. They have problems of aggressiveness, antisocial behavior, drug abuse, sexual promiscuity, depression, and poor self-esteem.

One problem with all this theorizing is that most abused children grow up to be nonabusive parents, and many abusive parents were not abused as children. Another problem is that the child abuser's telltale personality traits and behavior problems are heritable, meaning that, at least for some people, an abusive disposition may express one or more genetic potentials that can develop in many rearing environments, not just the abusive kind. If the abuser potential is at least partly inborn, the pertinent question is this: How much does experiencing suboptimal parenting, including the abusive kind, enhance the risk of becoming a child abuser *beyond what comes from inborn potential?*

Until we have a definitive answer, anyone's assumption is as good as any other's—for example, the skeptical position taken by neuroscientist J. Allan Hobson, who argues that hundreds of thousands of people have "troublesome problems like anxiety, depression, and neurosis. Society readily assumes that all these people must have had some history of psychological stress or trauma that has caused them to be this way. I say no. They rant and rave, or flit about nervously, or fail to show up for work, or carry Valium in their purses because there is a functional disorder of the state of their brain-mind. They may well have been abused as children or have lost their self-esteem, and this can cause real emotional distress. But it does not cause their actual anxiety, depression, neurosis, or any other of a long list of problems."

Definitive answers to such questions won't come from mere comparisons of parents and children because, as we have seen, correlations cannot disentangle the influence of genes and rearing. Currently, the only way to get something like a definitive answer would be with adoptees, because the correlation of adoptive children with their adoptive parents can estimate influence of rearing, while the correlation of those same adopted children with their biological parents can estimate the influence of heredity.

A simple study would compare two groups: the adopted-away offspring of divorced parents or child abusers and the adopted-away offspring without such biological parents. All the adoptees, of whatever genetic background, are reared from birth by normal parents. Upon reaching adulthood, all become parents, but what kind? Here are two scenarios, each supporting a different view.

In the first, the adoptees of both groups wind up with a comparably low rate of divorce or of abusing their own children. Apparently, a normal rearing prevents either potential, which implies that divorce or abusive rearing engenders the potential. But wait. In the second scenario, only those adoptees born to divorced or abusive parents have the elevated rate usually observed for people who have experienced divorce or who were abused by their natural parents. Now the opposite conclusion must be drawn: A disposition to divorce or abusiveness reflects a genetic potential that, when sufficiently strong, resists the influence of normal upbringing.

Parenting, Smoking, and Obesity

Cigarette smoking is 2 to 4 times greater in the offspring of smoker parents than the offspring of nonsmoker parents. Conventional social explanations invoke modeling, the promotion of behavior by example, and who provides more salient and compelling examples than a parent? Peers do, but can peer pressure, as parenting, really explain why just some children graduate from the experimental to the habitual use of cigarettes?

Children choose, and are chosen by, peer groups. People with the inborn potential to become smokers may prefer and be preferred by others with the same potential. In this way, inborn potentials could be the real prime movers that shape social conditions. Therefore, why not assume that inborn potential rather than parental modeling or even peer pressure is the fundamental reason for who becomes a smoker and who does not?

A comparison of twins suggests that over 40 percent of the smoker-nonsmoker difference is genetic. Furthermore, *the parent-child correlation for smoking is just about 0 if the genetic connection is 0, as when the parent-child relationship is adoptive.* When it comes to smoking, it seems that inborn potential strongly constrains not so much who will experiment with smoking, for this is largely a matter of peer pressure, but who will become a smoker, and that parental influence has little or nothing to do with it.

The same argument can be made for body weight. Children and their parents correlate about 25; siblings about 40. Clearly, body weight runs in families, but why? Many people believe that the answer lies in how parents manage food and eating during the formative years, and also what children perceive in their siblings. If that is so, why does body weight correlate *0* for adoptees and their adoptive siblings, while it correlates over 70 for identical twins reared apart? Why is the correlation for parents and biological children the same even if those children are adopted away at birth?

If the body weight of siblings and children can indeed be predicted from the weight of biological relatives but not from the weight of adoptive relatives, then body weight runs in families largely for genetic reasons. Turns out, the heritability of body weight is about 70, meaning that about 70 percent of individual differences from thin to fat comes from genetic differences.

Such findings question conventional assumptions about parental influence. They suggest that, to a greater extent than is often assumed, the usual parent-child resemblances reflect a common genetic quality often more than shared experiences. This could explain why children's psychological problems are more reminiscent of problems their parents displayed *as children* than of problems the parents display as adults—why, for example, preadolescent behavioral disorders are even more strongly correlated with a father's childhood behavioral disorders than with his adult substance use. Likewise, an 8-year-old child's aggressiveness correlates better with the aggressiveness his or her parent displayed at the same age than the aggressiveness the parent currently displays. Rather than imitation of parents and others, a heritable aggressive self-expressiveness running through the family seems to be the rule.

The idea that certain traits run in families for strong genetic reasons has enormous implications, one of which concerns the historical tradition of blaming parents, especially mothers, for their child's emotional problems and mental illness. Parent blaming reflects a common inclination to exaggerate parents' responsibility for a child's ways of being—likewise parents' inclination to accept responsibility—even where such inclinations are scientifically unjustified. Recognizing the genetic factor in behavior provides a much-needed antidote to this inclination.

Chapter Three

Blaming Parents

My mother used to say to me, if a strange man comes up to you and offers you candy and asks you to get in his car . . . go!

—Woody Allen

Actress Lauren Bacall once explained how her relationships with men were conditioned by having to cope with the loss of a father who disappeared 2 years after her parents divorced, when she was 8.

My mother put out everything for me, and he gave nothing. Somewhere, unconsciously that must have affected my feelings about men, my basic distrust of a relationship with a man being able to last any length of time. . . . I felt deserted by my father, certainly, which was an actual fact. We all grow up with scars, and that scared me when I was young, and from that time on I always dreamed of all these wonderful fairy tales, those wonderful stories of when the prince comes along, and saves you, and I was very, very insecure. . . . Maybe that has to do with having an incomplete family, being an only child.

No doubt a young child can be deeply affected by divorce and desertion: the sense of betrayal, the insecurity, the searching for relationships to put things right, and the lingering self-doubts. But does this necessarily explain the subsequent psychological development? Say another woman discloses the same insecurities, difficulties with men, and early-childhood love of fairy tales and fantasies of rescue, all this even though she was raised by two loving parents and supportive siblings. Must it then be concluded that a healthy family life promotes insecure personality development? Surely not. Where, then, does a reasonable explanation lie? What if the two women were identical twins separated at birth—what if, reared under different circumstances, they nevertheless turned out to be similar in personality and behavior—what explanation would *that* suggest?

Guess Who's to Blame? Mom's the Word

Social psychological explanations have all too often blamed parents, mothers in particular, for messing up their children's lives. "Talk shows," says neuropsychiatrist Sidney Walker III, "regularly feature psychiatrists who explain why John suffers from anxiety (his father was overprotective), why Jane abuses drugs (her parents subconsciously rejected her), or why Tom is a mass murderer (his father was cold and unfeeling—or perhaps overaffectionate and threatening). . . . What's more, according to many psychiatrists, even the most minor of parental faults—cutting the apron strings too late, assigning too many chores, or attending too few Little League games—can lead to disastrous consequences." Of course, as Walker trenchantly observes, it's all baloney, this blaming little things for big problems, when most children exposed to much worse do much better. But it is big business, for it seems that all too many people can't get enough of it.

Most notorious of the parent bashers was Bruno Bettelheim, a one-time influential and widely quoted child therapist who apparently was given to misdiagnosing and physically abusing his young charges and blaming parents for making their children mentally ill. In a revealing book, journalist Richard Pollak describes the frustration of being deceived and insulted by an apparent psychiatric charlatan. "My father dismissed [Bettelheim] as crude and somewhat simple-minded. . . . My mother was the villain . . . almost entirely responsible for my brother's problems. With astonishing anger, he said she had rejected Stephen at birth and that to cope with this lockout he had developed 'pseudo-feeble-mindedness.' "

Most astounding is that for so long so many people thought Bettelheim was an authority on how parents cause their children to become autistic or schizophrenic. When Bettelheim committed suicide in 1990, the *Washington Post* celebrated "the originality, warmth and wisdom he brought to the study of the minds and emotions of children," while the *New York Times* noted that "he was widely admired as a practicing therapist and as a profound and original thinker in psychoanalysis." *Parenting* magazine suggested that Bettelheim "left to the world—and especially to parents and children an enduring vision of love, innocence, and idealism." Yet as columnist Joan Beck wrote, "The need to set the record straight about Bettelheim goes far beyond the fact that the famous guru who preached love and supportive care for children often beat them . . . and emotionally undermined them in ugly ways. It is important to discredit permanently

Bettelheim's conviction that mental illness in children—especially autism—is caused by emotional factors, especially maternal feelings and behavior."

According to Sidney Walker, the parent-bashing spirit of Bettelheim is reincarnated in Peter Breggin, author of *Toxic Psychiatry*, who promotes the idea that parenting rather than genes explains why someone becomes schizophrenic, suicidal, bipolar, or hyperactive—this even while the scientific evidence clearly shows that just the opposite is true. "But then," says Walker, "scientific evidence is not Breggin's forte." And, he says,

> *[T]he only practices Breggin seems to endorse . . . are "love and compassion," which have never—in any era—cured syphilis, tumors, endocrine dysfunction, meningitis, or other disorders affecting the brain. Furthermore, it is difficult to understand how a doctor who ignores the biological roots of behavioral and emotional disorders—thereby potentially endangering the lives and sanity of his patients—can be more loving or compassionate than a doctor who successfully diagnoses, treats, and cures his patients. And it is hard to understand how Breggin, a psychiatrist who prides himself on being compassionate, can lay such terrible guilt on parents who have played no role—except in some cases, an unwitting genetic one—in causing their children's tragic disorders.*

Many notions percolating from the parent-blaming tradition are not only unlikely on the face of it, but either are untestable or, when testable, are unverified. Why, then, do these beliefs endure? One reason is educational: Many people simply do not know the evidence. Another is personal: Blaming one's parents rather than one's biology is easier to accept if it means that at the deepest level, one is not a bad person, just a victim of bad persons. A third reason is experiential: The power of parenting is evident in the perception that parents *can* influence psychiatric symptoms, from the mild to the severe. And through their own educational efforts, parents *can* help a sensitive child to higher achievement or a hyperactive child to greater self control, all of which can enhance self-esteem. On the other hand, dysfunctional parents can make things worse, make the sensitive child more anxious and depressed, the hyperactive child more disorganized and antisocial.

Given these effects, observers assume that the power of rearing is greater than it really is, which implies that parents must not only be blamed for negative behavior, but also be credited with felicitous outcomes. Yet such categorical thinking—parents are either responsible or not—conceals the fact that parental influence and responsibility are matters of degree: the greater the power of the potentials, the weaker their influence.

A strong genetic potential is not always evident, for the manifest behavior that expresses even a strong genetic potential can be subtle—for example, cyclothymic disorder sufferers' modest mood swings between euphoria and melancholy, which can affect their personal achievement and interpersonal life. One may not think of such mood swings as a manifest expression of a strong genetic potential. But what else could explain why their relatives have the *same* high rate of manic-depressive disorder and suicide as do the relatives of people who suffer full-blown manic-depression? Apparently, cyclothymics carry the same genetic load as do manic-depressives, though this is not evident in their relatively mild behavior and fewer psychiatric problems.

Though familiarity with recent research findings means most people are no longer inclined to blame parents for their offspring's manic-depression, how many are still tempted to blame them for lesser mood swings and other problem behaviors, including hyperactivity? Even researchers friendly to the biological point of view are still compelled to say that hyperactivity and other childhood psychiatric disorders may stem, albeit in part, from the practices of parents. Yet one cannot justifiably assume that hyperactivity is caused, even in part, by dysfunctional rearing when the evidence points to genetically based abnormalities of brain chemistry. And this is true whether the hyperactivity (or other disorder) is mild or severe. *Mild symptoms that blend into seemingly normal traits may be as genetically determined as any other traits.*

Parents are blamed in part because of the difficulty people have in accepting bad luck. Psychiatrists Michael and Mona Bennett say:

> In the absence of scientific evidence to the contrary, it is tempting to regard the cause of an emotional problem as human in origin in order to make it seem more controllable and treatable; it is more frightening to be the victim of bad luck. Most theories of psychotherapy provide fertile ground for this temptation by positing causative relationships between emotional problems and . . . bad parenting, intolerable trauma, or weak character. Any theory that places primary responsibility on a factor that is responsive to human efforts may be misused to preserve excessive expectations for change and cure.

It is easy to visualize a social explanation with villains to blame and broken spirits to repair. "We destroy our children," writes an anonymous, self-styled former psychotic. "We cut them down to our own level. We negate their god-hood in the interest of our own impotence, as we ourselves were once denied our divinity, and as our creative and intellectual presumptions were once permanently embarrassed by an enforced obeisance to the conditions of life and social order into which we were born."

How can anyone resist such feverish imagery when people search for any reason to find blame and point to the parents for the nasty influences that molded a child's personality and sabotaged the child's potential? It is much more difficult to replace imagery with the cold, mechanical terminology of biological explanation. When reflecting on why we did or didn't do something, how often do we slip into thinking about parent-child conflict during the formative years and subterranean meanings rooted in earliest childhood?

Schizophrenia: The Classic Case of Parent Blaming

Even more than other social theories, psychoanalytic theory, like any good theory, speaks to what many sense is true about their own lives—and what they sense to be true, they see rooted in a personal history involving family, friends, and, in particular, the mother. This assumption, heretofore often made by people trained in medicine, meant separating the patient from the mother and applying reeducational therapy to cure the patient. Such treatments were failures, and newer research has demonstrated a biological basis for the disorder and shown that powerful brain-altering drugs are the only hope. But why have even the brightest, best-educated people so readily come to believe that parenting is a major cause of severe mental illness? One answer lies in the textbooks.

To explain schizophrenia, for example, textbooks still emphasize social factors, including intrusive or indifferent mothers, aggressive or distant fathers, and parental conflict. Also included is a family environment that is neglectful, intrusive, demeaning, belittling, and generally lacking in models of appropriate behavior. This social roundup typically appears after a discussion of genetic findings implying that parental influence *cannot* explain why one person develops schizophrenia while others do not. One of the most compelling of these findings involves the offspring of people with schizophrenia. Whether reared by the ill parent or adopted away at an early age—*either way*—such "high-risk" offspring have *the same* elevated risk of developing schizophrenia, about 10 percent. That same 10 percent risk applies as well to children reared by a psychologically normal parent whose identical twin has schizophrenia.

A bias toward blaming the rearing environment is also evident in the imprecise language used to convey social science findings, such as those implicating the rearing practices of parents in severe mental illness. Thus, a textbook might say that because it precedes the development of schizophrenia, abnormal rearing *plays a role* in the illness. The phrase "plays a role" implies that deviant parenting causes the illness in offspring. Yet the actual research finding is merely a weak tendency for parental deviance to go along (correlate) with the illness in offspring. And what does "go along with" really mean, when parental deviance might be a reaction to, not a cause of, an offspring's odd behaviors?

Textbook authors and reporters strive for something called *balanced coverage*, which is a fine idea, except when it includes two things that are not so fine. One is what historian and author Henry Adams described as a mania for handling all the sides of every question, looking into every window, and opening every door, which he said is fatal to their usefulness. The other is a tendency to treat all conventional views as being equally reasonable or having equal scientific merit. That's often not the case, though it probably explains the frequent use of those tell-tale euphemisms whose effect is to minimize or deny both the strong influence of biology and the weak influence of rearing. About a theory, for example, that bizarre or even just eccentric parental behavior increases the vulnerability to schizophrenia: Why say there is little evidence that it is true, when there is much evidence that it is false? A physicist would not say that there is little evidence that the world is flat.

Saying that, compared to the offspring of a schizophrenic, the *adopted* offspring of a schizophrenic have an *elevated risk* for schizophrenia doesn't rule out the strong influence of rearing. Saying that the adoptive offspring have the *same* elevated risk *does* rule out the strong influence of rearing, properly suggesting that any environmental causes are likely to be prenatal. That 10 percent risk for adopted children reared under schizophrenia-free conditions is increasingly recognized in textbooks as convincing evidence of a strong genetic factor in schizophrenia, and rightly so. But it is even more convincing evidence against rearing factors. After all, if schizophrenic behavior of a parent doesn't affect a child's risk, why assume that some other parental behavior does?

We are told about the importance of nurture (parenting) *as well as* nature (genes); it is the standard cliché, and, of course, it is true for any person. Yet what is the meaning of "as well as," given evidence that a particular rearing has little or nothing to do with schizophrenia? Surely the public is better served by more precise language that makes clear just what is known and what is not known.

Imprecise or misleading language is one source of confusion for consumers of social scientific findings; poor understanding of numbers is another. After the usual cursory review of evidence for a genetic factor in schizophrenia, a textbook offers the following argument: Because fewer than 10 percent of people with schizophrenia have a schizophrenic parent, genes can't play a powerful role in the disorder. But why not? After all, fewer than 10 percent of very tall people, say, over 6 feet 7 inches, have very tall parents, yet no one doubts that tallness is mostly genetic. Fewer than 10 percent of the parents of elderly people with Alzheimer's disease showed signs of the disease, yet no one suggests we look to rearing for explanations of dementia.

Virtually *none* of the parents or siblings of an autistic child is likewise autistic; the rate of childhood autism in the siblings of autistic children is 3 to 6 percent. Such a measly rate, except that it is at least one-hundred times greater than the expected, or population, rate of 0.03 percent, which strongly suggests that the vulnerability to autism has a strong genetic component. And this is confirmed by evidence that identical twins are at least 60 percent concordant for autism, meaning that in 60 percent of pairs with at least one autistic twin, both twins are autistic; that's a *two-thousand* times greater rate than expected, which suggests a heritability of roughly 90 percent, meaning that almost all of the vulnerability to autism from the weakest to the strongest reflects a genetic difference.

Evidence of strong genetic influence ought not to be toned down to accommodate the gratuitous cliché that genes aren't everything. As one textbook notes, identical twins are "only 40 percent" concordant—in 40 percent of the cases, when one twin has schizophrenia, so does the other—which means that environmental influences must be important. Indeed, but why assume that those environmental influences are mostly parental, when good evidence suggests that they are mostly prenatal?

The question is especially pertinent given that the 40 percent concordance also applies to identical twins reared apart—well, sort of. Our best estimate, based on sporadic cases, is an even higher 58 percent, the most conservative estimate being 50 and the most liberal, 75. A recent estimate of 64 percent is based on 14 pairs of reared-apart identicals, at least 1 of whom had schizophrenia; in 9 cases the other twin also had schizophrenia.

Then how does one understand the suboptimal conditions that may characterize the families of mentally ill people? Parents of a child with schizophrenia are mostly normal, though some tend to be relatively more eccentric than the parents of normal children, communicating more deviantly and acting more intrusively. However, these observations do not conclusively indicate significant parental influence on vulnerability. Rather, what looks like parental influence may in fact be a reflection of shared genes.

On a midterm examination, a student got right to the nub of the issue with this pithy observation: "How many times has someone proposed that a biological mechanism caused a mental disorder and then later it was conclusively determined that poor mothering actually was the cause. As far as I know, that has never happened. The opposite case has happened many times, and most likely will continue to occur as time and knowledge progress."

Compulsive Behavior: Another Classic Case

People burdened by what is now called obsessive-compulsive personality disorder are preoccupied with details, rules, schedules, and the like. Often so engrossed in details, they may never finish projects. They are work oriented rather than pleasure oriented and have inordinate difficulty making decisions (lest they err) and allowing time (lest they focus on the wrong thing). Their interpersonal relationships are often poor because they are stubborn and demand that everything be done their way. They are generally serious, rigid, formal, and inflexible, especially regarding moral issues. They are unable to discard worn-out and useless objects, even those with no sentimental value, and are likely to be miserly and stingy.

What are the central traits that give the pattern its pathological stamp, and how do they come to be? Freud focused on three traits: orderliness, obstinacy, and frugality—a so-called anal triad that he considered to be the irrational residual of a mostly unconscious conflict over toilet training. In Freud's view, orderliness defends against dirty impulses; obstinacy defends against being controlled. Parsimony in saving money or hoarding collectibles indirectly satisfies the desire to retain feces.

Yet Freud never said exactly how toilet training has its negative effect. Is it a matter of being enforced too early, too late, or too strictly? In any event, he assumed the main culprit to be an insensitive or abusive parent who mismanages a young child's urge to experience bodily pleasure and the child's need to be free from external restraint. Freud characterized such mismanagement as an education designed to break a child's will and make him or her submissive. In short, personality traits are the surface expressions of deeply repressed, conflict-ridden memories forged by early rearing that clashes with infantile willfulness.

Was Freud right about toilet training, personality, and, therefore, parental responsibility? There is no clear relation between the traits and any preoccupation or problem with things excremental, such as constipation. Moreover, self-reports show no clear relation between toilet training and compulsivity. The severity of the one simply doesn't correlate with the strength of the other. Even compulsive mothers aren't especially severe toilet trainers, but what if they were?

It is likely that toilet training is merely the first of many battles over a child's inborn need to be autonomous and to resist intrusion, to say "No!" And what of a child for whom these needs are particularly strong? Such a child can make a mother's work that much harder, not only at toilet training but also at just about anything requiring conformity to social standards. In this view, severe toilet training is mostly an effect, not a cause, of a child's obstinate behavior.

Another, often overlooked, possibility is that a mother and her offspring share genes for a disposition, like any heritable trait, which can express itself differently in a child (obstinacy) and in an adult (orderliness and frugality). This possibility is more than just reasonable. It has the additional virtue of conforming to the evidence that identicals are generally more alike than fraternals in compulsivity.

Like so many parents of children with problems, parents with compulsive children have no reason to feel guilty about what they presumably did or failed to do—likewise, the parents of children with obsessive-compulsive disorder. Though it has a similar name to that of obsessive-compulsive personality disorder, obsessive-compulsive disorder (OCD) involves strong anxiety, obsessions, and compulsions that may require psychological as well as pharmacological treatment, even hospitalization.

The anxiety of OCD comes in many forms, including, for example, doubt about whether one turned off the stove or locked up the house. Or there may be phobic fearfulness—for example, about having a dread disease or having been contaminated. The obsessions of OCD are intrusive and often antisocial—for example, thoughts about acting in an embarrassing manner (shouting obscenities) or doing violence to a loved one. The compulsions of OCD are mostly involuntary, all-consuming, often ritual-like behaviors involving grooming, cleaning, checking, counting, and self-control. These include endless washing of the hands, touching door jambs, cleaning the house, arranging objects, or checking lights and locks.

Obsessive-compulsive personality disorder is different from OCD. People with the personality disorder rarely go on to develop OCD, and while they typically have a personality disorder, is it not likely to be the obsessive-compulsive type. Finally, OCD is far more debilitating than obsessive-compulsive personality disorder. Despite these differences, traditional psychoanalytic theory nevertheless held that OCD, too, is rooted in struggles between parent and child. "It was originally carried on in an atmosphere of toilet training . . ." says a popular and influential textbook used extensively in the 1960s. "The merely insistent parent seems a relentless persecutor. A determined parental face, seen by a small child who is filled with fury and frustration, may be seen as the cruel face of a monster. It is clear that the angry child himself contributes to the hostility that he experiences. *The parental contribution, however, is often much greater than the parent realizes. In some of our cases, the parental contribution was decisive.*"

Despite what is italicized for emphasis, no scientific evidence supports any element of this statement regarding parental culpability, nor could a clinical psychologist ever prove scientifically that a parent's behavior was decisive in causing a patient's symptoms or disorder. Similarly, research has found that the way parents raise their child is mostly irrelevant to many disorders, including OCD.

OCD involves abnormal activity of the frontal lobes and connected structures—in particular, one called the caudate—that lie deep within the front part of the brain. When people with OCD experience their obsessions, the caudate becomes abnormally active. When they successfully complete cognitive-behavioral therapy, caudate activity looks more normal, and with that come other changes suggesting brain activity closer to the norm.

A relatively high rate of OCD occurs in people with Tourette's syndrome, a genetic disorder marked by tics that runs in families and is observed worldwide in all racial groups. Tourette's sufferers and their relatives have an extraordinarily high rate of OCD—over 50 percent for the afflicted and over 20 percent for their relatives. More important, however, is that *regardless of whether Tourette's sufferers have OCD*, their close relatives still have that same extraordinarily high 20 percent rate of OCD.

This observation suggests that OCD and Tourette's may be different expressions of a brain abnormality that probably involves the caudate.

Furthermore, research has discovered that OCD can be caught like a cold. After recovering from a strep infection, psychologically normal children can develop severe OCD. One intriguing clue to this enigma is this fact about virtually all OCD children: *Even if they've never had strep*, their immune systems are especially reactive to an antibody—a specific protein called D8/17. The protein is created by the immune system of mice after having been injected with the white blood cells of humans who once had rheumatic fever, *which is a complication of strep.*

Could it be, then, that when the immune system attacks a strep infection, it also attacks the caudate, whose surface is chemically similar to strep? That would make some cases of OCD an *autoimmune disorder.* The same scenario holds also for Tourette's, which is likely to affect certain vulnerable children who have had strep. Here is further evidence of a biological connection between Tourette's syndrome and a variant of OCD. No one claims that Tourette's comes from defective mothering, and given the Tourette's–OCD connection, the same should be said for OCD.

OCD thus represents yet another example of a neurological disorder once believed to be caused by rearing conditions, mom's behavior in particular. Nevertheless, the social explanation, especially mom-blaming, remains as popular as ever and is often the default view taken unless a compelling biological alternative suggests itself. Here's one, in the form of a clinical observation. Two 30-year-old identical twins separated at birth and raised in different countries were asked about their personal habits. Interviewed separately, they both proved to be compulsively neat, precise, meticulous, punctual, and obsessed with cleanliness, all to pathological excess. Asked for an explanation, one twin answered, "My mother. When I was growing up, she kept the house perfectly ordered. She insisted on every little thing being returned to its proper place. . . . I learned from her. What else could I do?" Convincing enough, except that when asked the same question, the other twin answered, "The reason is quite simple. I'm reacting to my mother who is an absolute slob."

This anecdote, described by Peter and Alexander Neubauer, yields two credible, even self-evident, explanations about maternal influence, yet each is questionable when placed in context with the other. And such placements *ought* to be made lest we miss the deeper explanation: that normal personal development unfolds along inborn trajectories, and would unfold more or less the same way regardless of parenting.

Other Mental Diseases: An Ongoing Case of Parent Blaming

There is a venerable tradition of blaming parents for all sorts of psychiatric disorders reflecting brain abnormality. J. Allan Hobson describes how, in the 1960s when he was in psychiatric training, his mentors simply assumed that mental illness was caused by an overprotective mother, one whose behavior was so psychologically toxic, so confusing, that she was labeled schizophrenogenic. Well, this convenient fiction meant that separating the patient from the mother and applying some sort of reeducational therapy would do the trick—never mind that such treatments were abysmal failures, that powerful brain-altering drugs were the only hope, and that new research was demonstrating a heritable basis for brain abnormalities associated with psychosis. Hobson says:

> *Many human problems are caused by brain abnormalities masquerading as mental illness. There are hundreds of thousands of [people] who have less dramatic but troublesome problems like anxiety, depression, and neurosis. Society readily assumes that all these people must have had some history of psychological stress or trauma that has caused them to be this way. I say no. They rant and rave, or flit about nervously, or fail to show up for work, or carry Valium in their purses because there is a functional disorder of the state of their brainmind. They may well have been abused as children or have lost their self esteem, and this can cause real emotional distress. But it does not cause their actual anxiety, depression, neurosis, or any other of a long list of problems.*

Behavior once taken to be all in the head can often be explained in a much better way when we assume that in the head is a brain as well as a mind, and that the brain is shaped by a unique genetic inheritance and prenatal life, not just by social influences. This is evident in mental disease, and not just in schizophrenia, manic depressive, or other severe kinds, but in so-called neuroses involving depression, anxiety, and hysteria. Depressions once thought to stem from poor parenting, childhood loss, or defective character are proving to be biological conditions, some signifying a highly heritable psychological vulnerability, others a medical condition.

Imagine a patient initially diagnosed with depressive disorder, based on classic symptoms involving blue mood, poor sleep, low energy, no appetite, and sluggish thinking. She has been in psychotherapy and has been taking antidepressant medication, which she once used in an effort to kill herself by overdose. Careful examination reveals hypothyroidism, a disease of the thyroid gland that causes hormone deficiency. Apparently, during thyroid-replacement therapy, her depression gradually disappears. A psychiatric disorder can arise from too much rather than too little thyroid activity. Hyperthyroidism can cause nervousness, anxiety, mood swing, even psychosis, as well as many physical symptoms, including fatigue, rapid heartbeat, breathing difficulties, and weakness.

Diabetes can cause psychiatric symptoms; so can Lyme disease. A previously healthy college student experiences panic attacks, insomnia, and loss of appetite; an initial examination fails to reveal anything medically significant. The problem seems to be entirely psychological: some kind of adjustment reaction. Her symptoms worsen to where she believes she is going crazy. Only then does a closer examination reveal the real culprit: a tick-borne bacterium similar to the one that causes syphilis. In time and without treatment, such an overlooked infection can lead to many physical, neurological, and mental symptoms.

Medical disease is often unrecognized or misdiagnosed. It might be a brain tumor diagnosed as anorexia nervosa or Huntington's disease diagnosed as schizophrenia. It might be Alzheimer's disease diagnosed as depression. In one study of people referred for psychiatric treatment, *almost half* proved to have a medical condition. In the majority of these cases, that condition probably caused or complicated the psychiatric problem. Failure to identify medical disease occurred in a third of those referred by nonpsychiatric medical professionals. It occurred in about half of those referred by psychiatrists, and in over 80 percent of those referred by themselves or by social workers.

Such observations challenge the traditional separation of psychiatric illness (for which parents have often been blamed) and medical illness (for which they have not). Separating the two merely promotes the false idea that a psychiatric disorder, like personality or intelligence, is somehow not biologically determined. Even the so-called hysterias, those most psychological of disorders, may prove to have a biological basis. For example, some women had been called hysteric for complaining about chest pain that could not be explained until better diagnostic techniques proved they had *microvascular angina*, pain from abnormally small arteries of the heart.

Hysteria may be suspected when a patient feels touch but neither pain nor temperature. This unusual complaint might seem purely imaginary, yet it, too, can have a medical explanation. A spinal cyst can block the flow of sensory information regarding pain and temperature, yet allow information about touch to reach the brain.

The moral of the story is twofold. First, anomalous, inconsistent, and unpredictable behavior may very well have a biological explanation, even when a social psychological explanation seems much more reasonable. Clearly, parent blaming should not be the default explanation when so much evidence points to medical conditions, to brain abnormalities, and to genetic determination rather than to rearing as the primary causes of many psychological problems. It may be difficult to make the distinction, but then that is the responsibility of the physician or psychiatrist. Second, psychotherapy may be hazardous, even lethal, if used for emotional problems that are actually symptoms of brain disease—such as depression caused by undetected diabetes, hypothyroidism, or brain tumor.

Child Abuse: A Contemporary Case of Parent Blaming

Little girls are given a "medical exam" that includes just measuring the wrist with a ribbon, putting a label on the stomach, and tickling the foot with a stick. Afterward, they are asked about the exam, for instance, did the doctor touch their vagina? Initially, children usually answer negatively to such questions, for their memory is quite good. With some of them, however, and even without suggestion or prodding, their stories can change radically. For example, a few days after the examination, a father gives an anatomically correct doll to his daughter and asks about the visit. "So what did he do?"

At this point, the child describes how the doctor strangled her by wrapping the ribbon around her neck and pulling "real tight." Next she picks up the doll, lays it out, and places a stick between its legs to show how the doctor put a stick in her vagina. To emphasize the point, she bangs the stick with a hammer. Then she picks up the doll, flops it over, and looks between the legs to show how the doctor had looked into her hiney. According to the investigators, about half the children in their studies make up such stories.

These observations dramatically underscore how tenuous is the connection between the actual environment and what a child—even an adult—really knows. The imagination of a child, so perverse, so charming in its own right, can nevertheless be a problem when, taken for reality, it is used to blame parents or prosecute parent-surrogates for nasty deeds never done. Likewise the imagination of an emotionally immature adult, whose fantastical memories of child abuse can be encouraged by so-called repressed-memory therapists, and whose accusations hurled at an innocent parent or parent surrogate can have tragic consequences for everyone concerned.

"What starts as a guess about what type of abuse might have caused their present emotional problems," say researchers Ofshe and Watters, "grows into guessing which relative committed the abuse. Repetitive retelling and reshaping of this account can transform a 'perhaps' into a 'for sure' and can thereby create a sense of certainty." And the result of such so-called therapy? Says Sidney Walker, just about all the patients, even those who began therapy with relatively minor problems, get a lot worse; frequently "they wind up bitter, withdrawn, distrustful . . . [and the] consequences have been tragic for thousands of families. Relationships have been irretrievably ruined, careers and marriages ended, fortunes spent on legal defense, and jail terms served by innocent family members convicted of crimes that never occurred." According to Ofshe and Watters, repressed memory patients get "the closest thing to the experience of rape and brutalization that can ever be done without actually touching them."

One physician, commenting on the validity of such child-abuse accusations, says: "I have no doubt that child abuse is a serious public health problem." Nevertheless, he continues, "my concern is the lack of verification that the events in question even occurred. It doesn't take much clinical experience to realize that such histories obtained from patients and informants often vary remarkably. It may be argued that there was no reason to doubt the subjects, but no court would uphold such unsubstantiated claims."

A readiness to imagine the worst about parents is evident in modern reincarnations of witch-hunt hysteria directed against parent surrogates. Day care workers have been prosecuted for child abuse even when the absolutely fantastical nature of the evidence is obvious to impartial observers. How ironic that parents, who have been the object of unjustified blame by therapists for their offspring's emotional problems and neuroses, are so ready to believe the worst about parent surrogates. A case in point, described by journalist Dorothy Rabinowitz, was the trial of 60-year-old Violet Amirault, proprietor of the Fells Acres Day School in Malden, Massachusetts.

Along with her son Gerald and daughter Cheryl, Violet was charged with "having perpetuated monstrous sexual crimes against children ages three to five . . . children had supposedly been raped with knives—these miraculously failed to leave any signs of wounding or other injury—and sticks, and been assaulted by a clown (allegedly Gerald) in a 'magic room.' Some children told—after interrogation by investigators—of being forced to drink urine, of watching the Amiraults slaughter blue birds, of meeting robots with flashing lights. Violet Amirault was accused of shoving a stick into the rectum of a child while he was standing up, and of raping him with a 'magic wand.' " Other incredible horrors were alleged, and the more bizarre they were, the more convincing they seemed to the jurors.

Initially, the children earnestly reported that nothing untoward ever happened; there had been no disrobing, no magic room, no bad clown. Yet the children were neither believed nor dismissed until they confessed to what the investigators "knew to be true." The interrogators would persist, bribe children with candy, and tell them their friends had described the bad things. Rabinowitz continues: "At one point the interviewer [a nurse] tells the child that her friend Sara had said 'the clown had you girls take your clothes off in the magic room.' Child: 'No, she's lying.' Nurse: 'She's lying? Why would she lie about something like that . . . ?' Child: 'We didn't do that.' " And so on.

Tired and hungry, the resistance of the brainwashed children finally broke down. What followed, as with any successful brainwashing, was false testimony whose features were as irrational and bizarre as the behavior of the torturers was malignant and sadistic. Nevertheless, the three accused were eventually convicted, languishing in prison 8 years for Violet and Cheryl, longer for Gerald.

According a *Wall Street Journal* editorial,

> *By now, most of the rational world acquainted with the facts of this case understands that three innocent people were convicted in the Fells Acres prosecution—with its patently incredible charges. . . . This comprehension of reality, needless to say, did not extend to exterminating angels who preside over the system of justice in Massachusetts. While the state no longer burns witches at the stake, some quite similar impulse explains how it came to pass that Violet Amirault*

has spent most of the last decade of her life in prison—and the remaining two struggling to survive the district attorney's determined efforts to get all the Amiraults back into prison and preserve their convictions.

In a letter to the editor of the *Journal*, a reader wrote: "Such evils as lynch mobs, red-baiting and rigged trials dot our history. But there is something very ominously sinister when the full mechanism of justice wreaks havoc for its own sake on an innocent family, while elected leaders watch in silent indifference"—and we might add, while they participate with cruel and craven avidity.

This is no isolated incident. Consider the equally notorious case of Kelley Michaels, 23-year-old teacher at the Wee Care Nursery School in Maplewood, New Jersey. Convicted of 115 counts of child abuse, Michaels was sentenced to 47 years in prison, as one observer put it, "on patently ridiculous charges of sexually molesting virtually all the 3- to 5-year-olds at the Wee Care Day Nursery unnoticed by any of her fellow workers." According to the so-called testimony, she had taken her charges to either of two special rooms. There she made them urinate and defecate on the floor and on each other, had them smear peanut butter on each other and lick it off. She stabbed them with knives and forks, inserted leggo blocks into various orifices, and had forced sexual intercourse with the boys. Of course, all this happened before getting everyone dressed, cleaned up, and back to the main room, and with nary a scratch on the children or microscopic residue of bodily products on the floor or furniture.

As in the Amirault case, testimony was forced from tired, hungry, reluctant children. Interrogators used all the tricks: promises (of relief or rewards), insinuation (Kelley's caught and is in a lot of trouble), lies (I am your friend and want to help you), and threats (I'll stay here all day till you tell me).

Similar horror stories can be told about parents suddenly blamed by their grown-up children for all sorts of "repressed" outrages. Psychologist Elizabeth Loftus tells about a woman who during psychotherapy sessions was induced to remember experiences of "having been in a satanic cult, of eating babies, of being raped, of having sex with animals and being forced to watch the murder of her eight-year-old friend." There were other such memories, the only problem being that they were all false, fabricated under hypnosis and other forms of heavy suggestion by a gullible person.

How can presumably sensible people believe what common sense, decency, and good judgment show to be manifestly arrant nonsense?

Why, then, are we so taken by the idea that children repress, then as adults suddenly regain, traumatic memories of having been sexually abused or in other ways outraged—why, indeed, when there is no scientific support for such a mechanism? And how sad—how ironic—is such naive credibility.

One observer was moved to ask, "How can a nation ever apologize to these victims of 'repressed memory hysteria'?" Indeed, how can they after the recent 300th anniversary of the Massachusetts Day of Repentance (January 14, 1997), which offers an official apology for the Salem Witch Trials? And who will apologize to the legions of parents, especially mothers, whose personality and behavior supposedly caused their offspring's mental illness and whose family life was disrupted or destroyed?

There is a deeper implication in this tragic story of the irrational and malignant blaming of parents and parent surrogates. When emotionally stirred, the preference for good stories over critical thinking—for arrant nonsense over objective evidence—becomes all too evident, and someone always pays a heavy price. Some parents who suspected that their children were being sexually abused by day care workers were even more convinced when the stories grew more complex and bizarre, with secret rooms, satanic rituals, and sexual abuse in space ships.

But what does it mean that day care workers could be prosecuted and convicted for abetting the diddling of tots in outer space and other such flapdoodle? It is more than a mere perversion of justice, more than political corruption—even more than the cruelest and most tragic replays of Salem-like hysteria in the annals of American history. In this presumably sophisticated day and age, it would seem no exaggeration to call it triumphant stupidity—stupidity, says writer Milan Kundera, representing a dark aspect of human nature. For as he says, "stupidity does not give way to science, technology, modernity, progress; on the contrary, it progresses right along with progress!" Will Durant put it more poetically: "Underneath all civilization, ancient or modern, moved and still moves a sea of magic, superstition, and sorcery."

A Proper Humility Regarding What We Know

Various psychological conditions, each involving a genetic or otherwise inborn abnormality, have been attributed to neglect, abuse, lack of opportunity, or some deficiency of character: childhood autism and schizophrenia to cold, neglectful mothering; manic-depression to frustrated dependency needs; obsessive-compulsive disorder to severe toilet training; pathological obesity to overfeeding during infancy and food accessibility during childhood; Down's syndrome to maternal stress during pregnancy; Tourette's syndrome (uncontrollable tics) to childhood trauma; and narcolepsy (excessive daytime sleepiness plus intermittent sleep attacks) to poor parenting or just plain laziness.

Apparently, such conditions have little or nothing to do with rearing. Yet for years social explanations have been avidly embraced to the detriment of innocent victims and their families. Enthusiasm for gratuitous social explanations can infect even the most intelligent and sensible people. For example, Will Durant explains that Leonardo da Vinci's mother, a peasant girl named Caterina, had been seduced by the Florentine attorney Piero d'Antonio. When Leonardo was born, Piero married a woman of his own rank, and Caterina, newly married to a peasant husband, gave up her child to Piero and his wife. Perhaps, says Durant, Leonardo's homosexuality came from having been reared in semiaristocratic comfort but without maternal love.

How many bright, sensitive boys are reared without maternal love— even assuming this was Leonardo's fate—yet *don't* develop a homosexual disposition? Is it then appropriate to hypothesize that the absence of maternal love helps promote heterosexuality? After all, lots of homosexuals have loving parents, and even more heterosexuals have neglectful or abusive parents.

The lesson is that we need to adopt a proper humility about what we know and what we think we know, for only then will we be less inclined to promote theory without due consideration to its scientific basis. Likewise, only then will we be less inclined to blame parents for things over which they have little control.

"In the old days," says geneticist C. C. Li, "girls used to sew and embroider with colorful threads. They have early contacts with color, upon which their beauty depends so much. The boys used to ride on horses, play ball, practice fencing, or engage in some other physical activities, none related to color. The difference between boys and girls in their early contacts with color and the difference in value they attach to color exists and is real. Hence there are more boys than girls who never learned to distinguish certain colors."

This social explanation may at one time have seemed perfectly reasonable, except that it is false. Color blindness has nothing to do with early opportunities or rearing conditions. Rather, it is a sex-linked recessive trait that males inherit from their mother. The case of color blindness reminds us that social explanations, however compelling and complex, can always be invented for just about any behavior, normal or abnormal. And so it seems reasonable to ask, what other more familiar traits are likewise mistaken for socialized residues of early opportunities or rearing conditions?

Philosopher Bertrand Russell asks,

How many once universal beliefs are now discarded? It was held that there could not be men at the antipodes, because they would fall off, or at least grow dizzy from standing upside down. Everybody believed that the sun goes round the earth, that there are unicorns, and that toads are poisonous. Until the 16th century, no one questioned the efficacy of witchcraft; of those who first doubted the truth of this superstition, not a few were burnt at the stake. Who now accepts the doctrine, once almost universal throughout Christendom, that infants who die without being baptized will spend eternity in hell because Adam ate an apple? Yet all these now obsolete doctrines could formerly have been upheld by appeal to the wisdom of the ages.

How many current views about human behavior—including the influence of parenting on children's psychological development—will wind up on a future Russell's list? That historian, looking back at us, may indeed find our ignorance amusing if not appalling. Granted, this is not a felicitous idea. Yet, it *is* a useful way to think about theories that presume to explain human behavior, for it is certain that with an increase in scientific understanding, much of the so-called conventional wisdom of today will become the fables of tomorrow.

Chapter Four

Forging a World

You can have a terrible childhood, and you can make something really good out of it.

—Louie Anderson

In 1971, a pair of identical twins were rescued at age 7 after living most of their lives under almost inconceivably abusive conditions. Their biological mother had died shortly after their birth, so the twins had initially been placed in a children's home. About a year later, they were retrieved by the newly remarried father, who was an aggressive and physically abusive person. His new wife was worse: eccentric, paranoid, and physically abusive toward her newly acquired stepchildren. For over 5 years, the cruel couple kept the twins isolated in a small, unheated closet or locked in a cellar. With bad food, no bed, no sunlight or fresh air, no toys, and no love, they struggled to survive.

At the time of their rescue, the twins had the bruised and battered look of severely abused children. Stunted and suffering from rickets, they were the size of 3-year-olds. Not surprisingly, they were distrustful, timid, and seemed mentally retarded. Their impoverished speech was composed largely of gestures and grunting. After hospitalization followed by a stay in a group home for preschool children, the twins were eventually placed with a family. Initially difficult to reach emotionally, they gradually developed into cheerful, ambitious, inquisitive, confident, well-liked adolescents. They excelled in arithmetic, showed creativity and technical talent, and enjoyed reading. Initially, their IQ was all but impossible to assess. By adolescence it was roughly 100, which is what would be expected, given three facts: The average IQ of the Czech population is 100, the twins' biological parents had average IQs, and the twins showed no evidence of brain damage.

This clinical research, reported by psychologist Jarmila Koluchová, dramatically illustrates an amazing resiliency in the face of seemingly impossible odds. While more anecdotal than experimental, the finding nevertheless reminds us that many children have adaptive powers and autonomous ways that, among other things, severely limit the long-term impact of even suboptimal parenting. Yes, children can be beaten down, knocked off their developmental trajectory, bullied into ego-alien behaviors. But as soon as the pressure is off, after they are rescued or get into more benign environments, their natural ways will reappear—assuming, of course, that there is no clinically significant brain damage. And this point goes directly to the limits of a parent's influence on a child's psychological development.

Such limits are especially evident in four psychological characteristics of the child. Three explored in this chapter are *resiliency*, or the capacity to resist ego-threatening conditions; *reversion to type*, or the tendency toward preferred ways of being even after years of accommodating to ego-alien influences; and *proactivity*, or the disposition to select and create environments suitable to the self. A fourth, explored in the next chapter, is linguistic *creativity*, the capacity for inventive thinking that is evident in language learning, a type of learning that occurs without benefit of instruction. These universal characteristics of resiliency, reversion, proactivity, and creativity are essential to understanding, from a psychological perspective, the limited influence of parenting. They can also be thought of as the sources of a child's autonomy, individuality, and dignity.

Resiliency: Surviving the School of Hard Knocks

Psychiatric files brim with outrageous yet sadly familiar stories about neglect, physical and sexual abuse, belittling, and shaming, and all this must have at least some effect. Psychic wounds are often reported for eating disorders, drug addiction, domestic violence, suicide attempts, self-mutilation, or other forms of self-destructive behavior. For some psychiatric disorders involving depression, anxiety, or antisocial behavior, there may be up to a 30 percent chance that child abuse was involved. The highest figures, over 50 percent, are found for people who suffer dreamlike states, sensations of unreality, spells of forgetfulness, altered bodily sensations, self-abuse, and multiple personality.

The rearing environment does influence children, with truly abusive social conditions turning the most vulnerable into emotional wrecks, others into antisocial brutes. In an indifferent and hostile world, even the strongest may knuckle under. Even the most decent may be driven into sullen accommodation, if not alienating anger and brutish aggressiveness. Then how do so many children nevertheless survive and even thrive, while other children, though loved and given all the advantages, nevertheless fade and fail? Can the latter really be explained if not the former? Consider a few telling observations from clinical research.

Of the many children separated from their mothers during World War II, the vast majority made normal adjustments. Despite deprivations and separation from their mother, the children didn't seem to suffer greatly in terms of intelligence, personality, or character development. Such findings prompted one observer to comment that, "If orphans who spent their first years in a Nazi concentration camp can become productive adults and if young children made homeless by war can learn adaptive strategies, after being adopted by families, then one can question the belief that the majority of insecurely attached 1-year olds are a high risk for later psychological problems.

Psychologist Manfred Bleuler describes the offspring of schizophrenic patients he has followed for over 20 years. As expected, some of them are likewise disabled by the disease. Nevertheless, most were doing better than that, which is no doubt remarkable, considering their emotional suffering and social ostracism. Bleuler says he is impressed with how pain and suffering can have a steeling effect that allows some children to master life as if spiting their disadvantages. It is as if, for some people, early stress inoculates against later stress. Animal studies lend support to these ideas. Adult rats handled or otherwise stressed during infancy grow up to be less fearful adults than rats reared under normal conditions. They also display fewer memory impairments associated with aging. Apparently, their increased hardiness comes from neurological changes that make the brain better able to inhibit stress hormones or their effects.

Abusive conditions that scar the vulnerable while leaving the thick-skinned comparatively unscathed would give the average child bad memories of mostly little consequence. At worst, it would engender islands of pathology in a sea of normal personality. Later, if faced with a situation reminiscent of earlier experience, and with defenses and self-confidence weakened, this otherwise well-adjusted person might act in an irrational or even disorganized manner. A successful business woman once revealed to me the emotional effects of child abuse she was forced to endure for many years. A psychotic mother had terrorized her throughout childhood, beating her for minor or imaginary infractions, or dragging her out of school and then screaming about why she was home on a school day.

At age 50, she was only then confronting the effects of this abuse and working them out with the help of an older sister who had corroborated her worst memories. What struck me about her story, besides the obvious pain and awful sadness of such things, was her strength of character. Call it courage, a capacity to do well and good despite all the nasty conditioning, the haunting memories, and any genetic vulnerability she might be carrying. The telling point is thus not so much that a person had been deeply affected by an abusive experience but that, like so many others, she wound up doing so well for so long when so much social theorizing would have predicted otherwise.

The limits of even abusive parental influence illustrated in these examples makes evident that deep within a personality crippled by mental disease or obscene conditions lie certain constants that, in the deepest sense, define each person. With identical twins discordant for schizophrenia, the personality of the ill twin is in many ways congruent with the well twin's personality. Psychiatrist E. Fuller Torrey and his colleagues have described how "examiners experienced frequent flashes of déjà vu as the second twin of the day responded to an interview question with the same posture, gesture, intonation, expressive style, and response as had the earlier twin."

These and other examples of extraordinary resiliency and inventiveness—recall Koluchová's study of twins rescued and recovered from excessive abuse—reinforce more conventional evidence regarding children rescued from dysfunctional homes. After 5 years of noxious rearing, most children forced to endure such conditions do surprisingly well after a time of healing and readjustment in adoptive settings. Child welfare workers are as heartened as they are baffled by how often children removed from terrible circumstances can develop a normal and happy life, with a capacity to give and receive affection.

Reversion: The Biology of Self-Fulfillment

It is not that children are unaffected by their place in the family or their sense of how much they are valued and loved. It is not that they haven't learned what their parents intend or have not conformed to those expectations, whether through love or coercion. Parents can impose behavior, but does being forced to clean up one's room make a child a neat person? Parents can provide various opportunities, but does a decade of dance lessons make a child a graceful dancer? Parents can use their influence to secure advantages for a child, but does securing a slot in a top school or a highly paid position in a top corporation make an ordinary child into a socially successful, high-achieving adult? Behaviors can be forced, promoted, encouraged, and changed by parents and peers. But what effect does any of this have on intellect or personality—how much of it is mere imitation without conviction, conformity without identification, performance without persuasion?

Hollow accommodations tend to fade as inner potential ripens; if forced on an unwilling or ill-equipped child, such accommodations lead to failure, or worse. Most children can be taught to control themselves, but they cannot be taught to *be* themselves, which is why parents probably do best when they insist on self-control and civilized behavior while providing as much educational opportunity as possible. Nevertheless, trying to make children much more intelligent, considerate, and sociable or much more assertive, graceful, accomplished, or content with life: Any of these will likely fail, if not backfire, at least in the long run.

As novelist Theodore Dreiser wrote in *Sister Carrie*, the needle of our ways of being will yet aim steadfast and unwavering to a distant pole of an inner compass. Despite even strong parental influence, we tend to follow our heart—if not now, then eventually. Yes, we can learn to do and believe things that are incompatible with our deepest self, but to what end? So, too, with educational influences: Indifferent students can be exposed to literature and science. They can be made to study, pass tests, and graduate, but again, to what end—to what extent does this education sink in? If we are interested in more than the new tricks old dogs can learn—if we are interested in something more akin to personal traits, individual potential, and self-fulfillment than to conditioned behavior—we must ask how people reared with genetically unrelated others develop psychologically? The question is about adoptees; the answer is about all of us.

Young animals can be reared by adoptive mothers of another breed, or even species. Mice bred to be aggressive remain so even if reared by nonaggressive foster-parent mice. Tenacious and combative terriers likewise retain these traits even if reared by placid beagles. Finally, monkeys bred to be uninhibited remain fearless and active despite being raised by inhibited mothers.

If an expansive nature is relatively impervious to change, what about the opposite, an apprehensive and timid nature? Uptight rhesus monkeys are fearful and withdrawn in novel, depressing, or otherwise challenging situations. During a brief separation from the mother or from peers, uptight monkeys show poor adjustment. Unlike their aggressive or easy-going brethren, they continue to have problems eating and sleeping. They stay put, showing no inclination to explore in hopes of undoing the isolation. Even after reunion, these changes in behavior tend to persist. Some of the uptight monkeys even show withdrawal and other signs of depression.

About 15 percent of rhesus monkeys are born uptight, mostly from uptight parents; and they remain uptight for a lifetime, even if they are adoptively reared by easygoing and protective mothers. These two observations suggest that the trait is highly heritable. The behavioral expression of the trait, however, is another story. During adolescence, rough-and-tumble competition from less inhibited peers can bring out the timidity and anxiety of uptight monkeys, yet such reversion to type is not inevitable.

Uptight infants can be reared by nurturant foster mothers, then transferred to an older caretaker couple that keeps watch over them as they play together. Under these safe conditions, those uptight monkeys seem confident; they may even wind up dominating most of their peers. In contrast, uptight monkeys reared by punitive foster mothers seem timid, often winding up at the bottom of the dominance hierarchy, where they are readily bullied by everyone. *Apparently, the same genetic potential can show up in different, even opposite, ways.* It all depends on the situation: confident and expansive behavior in safe situations, timid and avoidant behavior in challenging environments.

As with rhesus monkeys, approximately 15 percent of children are uptight or inhibited from infancy. This temperamental difference is evident in their timidity and shyness, and in their readiness to develop phobias by 7 or 8 years of age—a difference of 32 percent for timid children versus 5 percent for other children was observed in one study. The temperamental difference is also evident in their generally elevated heart rate, blood pressure, muscle tension, and stress hormone levels, even the larger diameters of their pupils. Inhibited temperament is most evident in situations involving unfamiliar children or adults. It is also evident in fearfulness, for instance, about being alone or speaking up in class. Siblings of inhibited children also tend to be apprehensive, suggesting, as with rhesus uptightness, that the trait is highly heritable.

The similarities of the two species go further. Like their rhesus counterparts, uninhibited children are uninhibited regardless of situation. In contrast, but again like their rhesus counterparts, inhibited children are confident in secure circumstances but apprehensive in insecure situations, reverting to their timid ways when conditions become stressful. Such observations show just how much the impact of rearing depends on inborn tendencies, how temperament (nature) can limit or exaggerate the impact of rearing (nurture). With some traits, differences in rearing may have a relatively small effect on a child's development; with other traits, differences in rearing can make a big difference.

The sometimes subtle interacting influences of inherited temperament and rearing is illustrated by research on pairs of young adopted children reared together with either another adoptee or with a biological child of the adoptive parents. Adoptive mothers rated her children for three general personality traits: *extroversion*, meaning warm-hearted, outgoing, talkative, happy-go-lucky, socially adventurous, and zestful; *good socialization*, meaning conscientious, moralistic, self-disciplined, rule following, and realistic; and *emotional stability*, meaning calm, relaxed, self-assured, secure.

These and other ratings typically suggest that better adjusted children generally have better adjusted mothers. Yet in this study, it appears that the better adjusted adoptees tended to have a more maladjusted birth mother, one who reported she cried easily and was more sensitive than most people. What can such a surprising observation mean? The investigators suggest that good-quality adoptive rearing can, *at least for a time*, bring out desirable qualities in sensitive, environment-responsive adoptees who might otherwise have been inhibited if not maladjusted.

I say "at least for a time" for this reason. There was a 10-year follow-up period during which the adoptees were moving into the wider, rough-and-tumble competitive world of friendships and school. At this time, the adoptees who had done surprisingly well—the ones who tended to have poorly adjusted birth mothers—were faring less well. They weren't doing badly—good parenting can have salutary effects on at-risk children—just worse than one might have expected from their earlier ratings. Apparently, their new adjustment was more consistent with what would have been expected from their birth mother's adjustment.

Reversion to type—a slipping back to personal, largely inborn ways—illuminates the obligatory quality of the instinct to self-preservation and self-expression. And this is true for all children who, despite their emotional dependency, exposure to behaviors modeled by parents, and years of social conditioning, resist or outgrow influences that are incompatible with their preferred ways of behaving.

The classic scientific investigation of reversion was reported by psychologists Keller and Marian Breland. In return for food, hungry pigs learned to carry wooden coins to a piggy bank. In time, however, the animals reverted to their piggy ways, rooting the coins with their snouts rather than depositing them in the bank, even though it delayed getting food. Such seeming perversity in hungry animals prompted the Brelands to comment on what they described as instinctive drift. "After 14 years of continuous conditioning and observation of thousands of animals, it is our reluctant conclusion that the behavior of any species cannot be adequately understood, predicted, or controlled without knowledge of its instinctive patterns, evolutionary history, and ecological niche."

Laboratory results fit nicely with naturalistic observations of how nature limits and channels nurture. According to ethologist and Nobel laureate Konrad Lorenz, a newly hatched Greylag gosling quickly learns to follow the first object it lays eyes on. Such instinctive learning, or *imprinting*, requires only that exposure to the object occur during a critical period lasting just a few hours. Once imprinted, the animal will seek out and remain close to the object that, in this case, is Lorenz. Despite the Greylag's strong attachment to the human, it has an even deeper preference for goosey ways. Says the researcher, "While being completely indifferent to any fellow-member of the species and most intensely and affectionately attached to its keeper as long as it stays on the ground or on the water, it will suddenly and surprisingly cease to respond to the human in any way whatsoever at the moment it takes to wing in pursuit of another Greylag." Lorenz believes this reversion to be a complete mental transformation.

Reversion to type, or instinctive drift, represents inborn biases in the way individuals perceive, learn, remember, and feel about experiences. This is why preferred habits, even messy, fractious, addictive, wasteful, self-indulgent, or otherwise harmful habits, resist change and why, after being suppressed, such habits reappear as if following some inexorable principle of self-determination.

We can learn to socialize like macaques and to quack like ducks. In the end, though, no amount of monkey business will make us macaques; no amount of quackery will make us ducks. Children's behavior, even if incompatible with temperament, can be shaped by parental example and reinforced by physical and moral suasion; civilized conduct and educational achievement can be promoted even when learning self-control and good conduct is as daunting as learning to multiply by 7.

But what does the learned behavior represent: something deep and abiding or something superficial and evanescent? As professor Robert Hutchins once observed, "a student . . . can learn how to read, but if he does not read anything thereafter, or if he has no judgment about what he reads, if the ability to read does nothing to civilize him, we should be hard put to it to say that any education had taken place." As it is with a child's cognitive education, so it is with his emotional education. Marionette accommodations, often acquired at great psychological cost in rebellion and unhappiness, have a way of unraveling as children diverge from their siblings and from what, over many years, their parents expected and required.

Truth is, for better or worse, individuals learn best in their own way, assimilating information as they assimilate food, by breaking it down into elements that are recreated in their own fashion. It is why, even when exposed to the same conditions, biologically different people wind up different, and also why, even when exposed to different conditions, biologically similar people wind up similar. It is what limits the influence of parents.

Proactivity: Making Our Own Environment

A student once confided that 7 years earlier he decided to have himself killed, but in such a way that no one would suspect a suicide. He had come to experience life as meaningless and felt that he was somehow responsible for his unhappy state. The macabre plan was to first get thrown in jail where there would be no possibility of escape, then to provoke an inmate mean enough to kill him.

Unexpectedly, he was savagely attacked by the provoked inmate, who wielded a metal-tipped broomstick. After a month in a comatose state, during which he had a stroke, he awoke to a life of brain damage that left him with attention deficits, slowed thinking, labored speech, and a general weakness on his right side. For a while, his feelings of meaninglessness and self-loathing were compounded by a residual anger and depression. In time, through rehabilitation and an almost miraculous degree of healing, he attained some peace of mind. Nevertheless, permanent cognitive disabilities would forever frustrate and limit his now unrealistic ambitions.

On one level, this person was done in by his environment, yet one orchestrated by him. Social philosopher Ortega y Gasset observed that circumstances don't so much decide our fate as test our character, for how are people creatures of circumstance when a situation may well be of their own making? This was the conclusion of a review of 40 years of research testing the hypothesis that early social experiences, especially those related to maternal behavior, have a powerful influence on the development of mental illness. The review turned up much evidence that was inconsistent with this hypothesis. Although indeed associated with the sufferers of mental illness, disturbed social environments were often found among normal people as well. Furthermore, no special environmental abnormality was reliably associated with one or another type of mental illness.

The review ends with a penetrating distinction between what the family does to the child and what the child does to the family. "The important variables in the development of psychopathology might be factors which the child brings to the family, the functioning of the nervous and metabolic systems and the cognitive capacity to integrate stimuli," Frank says. He then asks "whether the proclivity towards fantasy distortion of reality might not be the factor in the development of psychopathology. . . ."

Far from being passive victims, then, we select, evoke, and manipulate our environments, which gives us a modicum of control and therefore responsibility for what happens to us. *Selection* means approaching or avoiding people and situations, whether this be geographical (choosing to live in the country rather than the city), recreational (buying a sports car rather than a sedan), intellectual (selecting this rather than that course of studies at college), or interpersonal (choosing one or another kind of person to be a friend or mate). People at greatest risk for posttraumatic stress disorder, for example, not only have prior psychiatric problems, but may also seek out dangerous environments and situations that aggravate their vulnerabilities.

Selection also means that genetically similar people will wind up being environmentally connected. Thus, talented people will gravitate toward similarly talented others with whom they can then create intellectually stimulating conditions. Neurotics will embrace troubled partners with whom they create conflict-ridden, painfully unhappy relationships. Psychopaths will gravitate toward antisocial companions and exploitable victims with whom they create antisocial conditions. Kindred souls will tend to seek out each other for romance and procreation.

Sexual partners typically pair up in ways that are anything but random. Despite some recent trends, including marriages across racial or ethnic groups, long-term mates are mostly alike in age, race, and socioeconomic background. They also share similar attitudes for religious beliefs, political values, and ideas about tradition, civility, and piety. In some ways, spouse resemblance may rival that shown by first-degree relatives. Indeed, many couples even look like brother and sister.

The mostly unconscious tendency to seek one's own kind in a spouse (environmental selection) is called *assortative mating*. In the short run, opposites may attract. In the long run, however, the tendency is for birds of a feather to flock together. Attractive people pair off, as do the well off, the bright, and the normal. In like manner, the unattractive, the poor, the dull, the vulnerable, and the antisocial tend to pair off.

In assortative mating, people create their own environments by selecting them ready-made. Regardless of its initial magnitude, spouse resemblance does not change much, and mutual attempts to make over typically fail, while causing much interpersonal conflict. Spouses do adjust to each other's needs. A wife may watch a lot more sports than she would prefer, but such accommodations don't represent convergence of personality. After 20 or 30 years of shared experience, spouses are no more alike in personality than they were at the outset. It is not true that the longer spouses live together, the more they resemble one another. Rather, spouse resemblance has little or nothing to do with having shared a common environment. In this, spouses are like siblings whose family resemblance fails to increase despite years of shared exposure to the same discipline, attitudes, and values.

Look at spouse resemblance or parent-child resemblance. Compare the resemblance of adoptees with that of their genetically unrelated relatives. Even compare identical twins reared together or apart. In each case, the results are the same: *The psychological resemblance displayed by siblings and spouses comes mostly from sharing genes; just about none of it comes from sharing environments, including rearing environments.*

That people orchestrate their environments is evident with evocation and manipulation. *Evocation* refers to the ways individuals unintentionally and often quite unconsciously elicit events in the physical world (clumsiness causes accidents) or reactions in the social world (impulsivity or arrogance provokes power struggles with others). *Manipulation* refers to ways that individuals intentionally exploit, alter, or impose control over the physical world (designing living conditions) or the social world (intimidating, seducing, or conning others through tactics involving charm, coercion, reason, debasement, shunning, or shaming). All three characteristics—

selection, evocation, and manipulation—become more evident as inborn potentials strengthen, as the opportunity to express them in the wider social world increases, that is, as the influence of rearing wanes.

Consider an impulsive young man with strong needs for excitement and adventure. His behavior often clashes with demands for good conduct imposed by religiously observant parents. While still a child, he occasionally gets into fights or other trouble. Nevertheless, he has limited ability or opportunity to express his antisocial traits, limited opportunity for self-fulfillment. The effect of the rearing environment is to suppress the antisocial expression of his temperament. However, high school affords him more freedom to exploit various opportunities to socialize with rebellious, risk-taking, drug-using peers, and he becomes increasingly antisocial.

Clearly, some situations better serve our needs for self-expression and self-fulfillment, which is why individuals actively select and create them. This principle of self-determination is illustrated by research answers to an enduring question: Why are some people prone to accidents or to creating distressing or traumatic situations? Are such dispositions rooted mostly in rearing conditions that mold personality, more in some than in others—this would surely threaten our thesis about the limits of parental influence—or are they rooted mostly in genetic inheritance? Before deciding, consider another question: Why are identical twins more alike than fraternal twins in experiencing stressful life events that involve, for example, personal injury or financial difficulties?

Identicals' greater coincidence of misfortune suggests at least some genetic tendency in all of us to create certain conditions and react to them in certain ways. This idea is supported by a study of separately reared identical and fraternal twins whose average age was roughly 60 years. The twins reported on any stressful life experiences, choosing from a list of 25 alternatives—for example, retirement, the death of a spouse or friend, serious conflicts with a child, loss of sexual interest, divorce, and the like. Each alternative was also rated for its emotional importance, using a scale from 1 (little importance) to 3 (great importance), with overall importance, or weight, its average rating. A total life-events score for any twin was therefore the sum of the alternatives, each weighted according to its average importance.

Identical twins were generally more alike in experienced stress than were fraternal twins, who showed almost zero resemblance. But what can explain why people reared apart wind up at age 60 resembling each other more than others in their living conditions? One answer is that identical twins reared apart nevertheless experience similar social and educational conditions, especially if, as sometimes happens, they are reared by relatives. Yet cousins who in like manner are reared by relatives and who are reared in at least as similar conditions show almost no resemblance. For example, adult identical twins reared apart show strong resemblance for IQ, correlating about 75, while cousins reared together show relatively little resemblance, correlating roughly 15.

The more likely answer to the question of family resemblance—shared genes—comes from a look at what caused the variation in living conditions reported by the twins. First, none of it came from the shared kind, say, of having the same parents and same peers, that makes people alike. Rather, about 60 percent of it came from the nonshared kind, unique environmental influences that make people different. The rest of the variation was due to genetic influence, which makes identicals maximally alike and genetic unrelateds maximally different.

Let's say that twins are asked about social support from friends, confidants, and relatives—specifically, about the number of contacts with others and how supportive, caring, or critical they are. Identicals are far more similar than fraternals in perceiving social support. Apparently, genetic influence strongly influences the quality of a person's social environment, its complexity, and its supportive or stressful elements. The upshot is more than that we just select environments ready-made or even fashion them to fit our needs, dispositions, and competencies. The point is that, insofar as these qualities are heritable—and in Part 2, we will see just how heritable—*our environments will also be heritable.*

One way to test this idea is to see if something in a biological parent's behavior or personality predicts his adopted-away child's environment. A bright adult's adopted-away offspring will tend to be a reader, and this will elicit book purchases by the adoptive parent. In like manner, a hyperactive adult's adopted-away offspring will tend to be socially disruptive, and this will elicit controlling behavior by the adoptive parent. To the extent that people determine their environments, they cannot justifiably explain away much of what they do as being caused by social influences imposed from the outside. That this is true, especially when it comes to parental influence, is especially evident in the way that children learn language.

Chapter Five

_____

A Mind of One's Own

*We start by living, each one of us, in the solitariness of our own
minds and from the data given us and our communications with
other minds we construct the outside world to suit our needs.*

—*Somerset Maugham*

Get close to a newborn infant and wiggle your tongue from side
to side. Staring with rapt attention at an adult's wiggly tongue, newborns
as young as 1 hour can imitate the gesture, however awkwardly. It is wondrous to see a newborn and an adult thus communicating without words,
but how can a newborn do this without benefit of prior experience or
instruction? Such imitation suggests the newborn intuitively knows the
meaning of tongue movement—that the sight of a moving tongue is in
some sense the same as the inner feel of a moving tongue.

Just getting close to the infant in itself won't suffice because the
response isn't merely joy or anxiety, but a reaction to something specific.
The adult's wiggly tongue seems to be an environmental key that unlocks
an otherwise hidden potential. When again faced with the adult, who no
longer makes the gesture, infants will stick out their tongues, which
implies a kind of learning guided by a deep, inarticulate knowledge that is
likely inborn. As a model for thinking about the development of personality and other potentials, this point has direct bearing on the nature of a
parent's limited influence on a child's psychological development.

Inborn Knowledge?

Intuitive knowledge can prevent as well as promote new learning. The
3½-year-old child who made the smiley-face drawing on page 75 has had
countless experiences with human forms, none of which looks like what he
has drawn. His drawing thus violates everything he has seen. Deep down,

he may know the proper proportionality of human heads and bodies; suddenly confronted with a huge-headed human, he might well be disturbed as when an expectation is violated. Why, then, does he draw a big head on a small body? If heads are most important, with their faces that reveal so much vital information about emotion and intention, then heads must get special attention.

Can we really attribute to a parent's behavior the singular direction of a child's psychological development when so much depends on the child's perception and understanding rather than the objective facts? How else can we explain a string of nightmares that makes no sense to guilty parents fretting over their child's fearful imagery and overwhelming anxiety, but that makes a lot of sense if dreams explore subjective worlds that might not be so comfortable, caring, and safe? In short, fantastic preoccupations and apprehensions can come from an inventive mind capable of dreaming up various things that need have nothing to do with the way the world—including the world of parenting—really is, yet must have everything to do with the way the self really is.

Children draw what they know to be important, what is subjectively true rather than objectively accurate; but is this fundamentally different from the case of the adult? All adults have had countless experiences of seeing liquid in a container, yet many haven't properly learned that regardless of a container's tilt, the water inside remains horizontal. These adults, some college educated, draw a tilted water level in a tilted glass, as in the drawing below, which violates every experience they have ever had.

Bartenders and waitresses are experienced with glasses filled with liquid. Surely they do better than others when tested. Not so. One study found relatively few of them correctly drew the water level (33 percent) compared to less experienced people, such as bus drivers and housewives (53 percent). Many who failed the test were surprised when the principle of horizontal water levels was explained. Without proper understanding, the assimilation of information is difficult, the resulting accommodations awkward, artificial, and short lasting.

Over 2,000 years ago, Socrates argued that learning is recollection, a recovering of tacit, inarticulate knowledge that comes from the soul. How can knowledge exist even before birth—how can one know things before one learns things? Knowledge can exist prior to any learning. For example, people born without an arm or leg can nevertheless move phantom fingers or toes and can feel pain in the nonexistent limb. Is the brain equipped at birth with a body image, a representation of bodily knowledge that can be activated at will or by circumstances? Presumably, experience with real arms or legs or with seeing others would be a reminder, a remembering, activating and modifying what is essentially an inborn mental representation.

Do newborns really know specific things before they learn them or because they have a more general capacity to develop knowledge quickly by interacting with the environment, a capacity that needs no systematic instruction by parents and that occurs so quickly it seems more inborn and ready-made than interactive and learning based? If phantom limbs in congenitally limbless people suggest inborn knowledge, they also support the less radical notion of a biological preparedness to quickly recognize faces, understand emotional expression, walk erect, acquire language, fantasize and dream, fashion tools, invent stories, create gods. Insofar as variation exists in either inborn knowledge or inborn readiness to learn certain things, the environment's seeming power to shape development depends on the readiness to be shaped, which in turn depends on being unique genetically.

Biological preparedness is seen in young children learning quickly to extract certain linguistic rules mostly on their own. Psycholinguist Peter Gordon discovered that children respect a certain rule about compound words, which may be constructed with irregular plurals—thus, mice-eater—but not with regular plurals; rats-eater is incorrect. Likewise, you can say teeth marks but not claws marks. When speaking, the parents of young children hardly if ever use many compound words that children readily figure out, which suggests that children express their natural geniuses for intuiting linguistic rules.

It appears that parents have limited ability to determine language learning as they have limited ability to determine personality development. But to understand better these limits of parental influence we shall have to explore the nature of learning, starting with the linguistic kind.

Charming Errors: Learning as Perversely Imaginative

Under normal conditions, much personal development involves a kind of self-generated learning that occurs without the benefit of explicit instruction, rewards, and punishments. Consider what happens when information given to children violates rules they have learned on their own. As 2-year-olds learn to say "walked" to indicate a past event, they learn "came" and "went." Yet after some time and despite much exposure and practice with correct usage, even bright children will start saying "comed" and "goed." Why? Because they comprehend the *-ed* rule that indicates the past tense of a verb. Says psycholinguist Dan Slobin: "One cannot help but be impressed with the child's great propensity to generalize, to analogize, to look for regularities, in short, to seek and create order in his language." More important, their rules prevent children from understanding errors even when those errors are repeatedly pointed out. After a year or more, children do arrive at a working idea of irregular verbs as exceptions to the rule. It is thus evident that perception and behavior are dominated by internal rules extracted by the child.

Another example of self-learning involves line drawings. Average 3-year-olds can copy a circle but not a square. Trying to get 3-year-olds to copy a square is pointless when those very children, at age 5, will be able to do it without either instruction or guidance. Yet these 5-year-olds can't copy a diamond created by merely rotating that square 45 degrees. Trying to teach diamond-copying is gratuitous because, as 7-year-olds, the children will succeed with neither instruction nor guidance. Clearly, children cannot be taught, at least not easily or well, what they will later learn effortlessly on their own. How else to explain this conversation between a mother and her son who asserts that when he grows up he will be a writer and a sidekick: What's a sidekick, she asks? "It's a detective that looks into the future," her son replies. "No," she answers, "you mean psychic." "Yes," he replies, "a sidekick."

Much of learning is self-directed and motivated from within, meaning it is promoted but not imposed by parents. Infants learn to walk because they are bipedal organisms, not because of instruction. Try teaching an infant to walk and the process will likely take longer. Try teaching a 2-year-old how to talk, and who knows what emotional trouble you'd create? So too with teaching a child to speak in grammatically correct fashion, as evident in this bittersweet example offered by psychologist David McNeill:

CHILD: Nobody don't like me.
MOTHER: No, say "nobody likes me."
CHILD: Nobody don't like me.

This pathetic interaction continues for a total of eight repetitions until the following:

MOTHER: No, now listen carefully; say "nobody likes me."
CHILD: Oh! Nobody don't likes me.

The child's difficulty makes good sense for two reasons. First, his speech follows an intuitive grammatical rule. The mother's instruction fails because it is unnatural to the child. Second, the word "likes" is just the opposite of what the child is trying to communicate, which is that people *don't* like him. In short, the child hasn't figured out the conventional adult rule without which parental instruction is fruitless. Yet with that rule, which the child will acquire on his own, parental instruction is gratuitous. In any case, such instruction is far from the rule, for parents usually respond to (reward, punish) the content more than the form of a child's speech. They respond to its truth value rather than its grammaticality, which means that grammatically incorrect statements will often be approved, grammatically correct statements disapproved. Someone once said most adults are either charmed by children's errors or too busy to correct them.

Any normal infant can learn any language even without formal schooling. All that is needed is exposure to linguistic sounds, the usual give-and-take with linguistic speakers, and the freedom to explore the ruleful patterns that characterize the native language. Some researchers believe human brains are prewired for universal rules of grammar, that rules are biologically biased. This can explain why some linguistic forms are more readily learned while others are learned with great difficulty or not at all.

Consider the common grammatical errors of the nobody-don't-like-me kind. These are universally observed where children of different cultures work and play together. Initially, the children communicate in a primitive, grammatically limited *pidgin.* (Adults working together with no common language do this too. An example: "I only church go pray, other things I business is-not," which means, "I just went to church to pray; other things were not my business.") Soon, and without benefit of adult intervention, the children inevitably create a grammatically more sophisticated *creole* language, for example, "Nobody don't have this." Even deaf children do this. After 1979, deaf Nicaraguan children placed in special schools were soon inventing language. First came a pidgin expressed in signs based on gestures the children were using earlier when isolated with their hearing families; later, in the youngest children, a fully grammatical creole appeared.

The instinctive readiness to invent a grammatically structured creole suggests a bias in language ability—what some psychologists call an instinct for language. "My wife and I," says evolutionary physiologist Jared Diamond, "have been barraging my sons from early infancy onward with grammatically correct English questions as well as statements. My sons quickly picked up the correct order for statements, but both of them still use the incorrect creolelike order for questions, despite hundreds of correct counterexamples that my wife and I model for them every day. Today's samples from Max and Joshua include, 'Where it is?' 'What that letter is?' 'What the handle can do?' 'What you did with it?' It's as if they're not ready to accept the evidence of their ears, because they're still convinced that their preprogrammed creolelike rules are correct."

It is not just creolelike universals but idiosyncratic inventions that mark a child's instinct for language. As a 2-year-old, my son Jason enjoyed having a book read to him while we sat on the *dat'n'a.* The correct word may be preferable, but *rocking chair* simply lacked the intuitive appeal of *dat'n'a*—for him and, I must admit, for me. *Dat'n'a* meant a rhythmic movement, given that Jason used it to describe the back and forth movement of the vacuum cleaner and our car's windshield wipers. So we sat in the *dat'n'a* and every so often Jason would invent a word that became part of the *flammy's* vocabulary, like the time we rode on the *pluggett* (public) bus, which wasn't all that *comftaful*, but was very fun. Didn't you ever eat *pisghetti* or read a *mazagine?* "The darling mispronunciations of child-hood!" says Mark Twain. "Dear me, there's no music that can touch it; and how one grieves when it wastes away and dissolves into correctness."

If children learn language mostly by imitating parents, how, asks psycholin-guist Steven Pinker, can one explain "I goed" or "Don't giggle me," phrases commonly uttered by children but never by a parent? Language learning thus reflects a charming if sometimes troublesome inventiveness of mind that makes for a tenuous relation between what is given by the environment, including the rearing environment, and what is learned by the child—likewise with the song learning of certain young birds. In one study, swamp sparrow nestlings 2 to 10 days old were taken from the field and reared in the labora-tory. Beginning at about 20 days of age and for 40 days thereafter, they were exposed to the elements of bird song typical of their species.

Not until about 8 months of age did the birds begin singing sponta-neously in the adult manner. Remarkably, the content of that song was a half-and-half mixture of bird song elements heard during infancy and novel elements never heard. About this, researchers Peter Marler and Susan Peters observed: "Only 59 syllables—less than a third of those pro-duced—were judged to be accurate copies of the models. Of the remain-der, 36 were construed as poor copies modified by improvisation. This left 104 syllables unaccounted for. We conclude that these were inventions. Four of the birds sang only invented and improvised syllables and 12 sang a mixture of imitated syllables. Invented and copied syllables mingle freely in plastic song, and a facility for syntactical rearrangement is evident in the many syllabic recombinations that occur."

Here then is an example of how information is taken in, rearranged, and explored in novel ways to yield something highly individual, and in some ways totally unpredictable. It is a model of what happens with humans in the face of social influences. Exposure to those influences is as necessary for intelligence and personality as exposure to bird vocalization is necessary for normal song development. Still, the singular effect of that exposure—*the very way the self invents itself through a process of self-determined learning*—depends a lot on a receptivity, competence, and inventiveness rooted in the biological preparedness of the species and, in unique ways, of the person.

Bright-Noisy Water: Learning as Self-Invention

"Language," says Steven Pinker, "develops in the child spontaneously, without conscious effort or formal instruction, is deployed without awareness of its underlying logic, is qualitatively the same in every person, and is distinct from more general abilities to process information or behave intelligently. For these reasons, some researchers have described language as a psychological faculty, a mental organ, a neural system, and a computational module. But I prefer the admittedly quaint term 'instinct.' It conveys the idea that people know how to talk in more or less the sense that spiders know how to spin webs."

That quaint term, *instinct*, may not be quite appropriate, for language ability seems to involve a lot more interaction with the environment than what instinct in the strict sense of that word implies. Well then, call it *instinctlike* and apply it to personal development: to the question of why children do not—why they simply *could not*—acquire their intelligence and personality mostly through exposure to parental behavior and why major differences must occur among parents and siblings despite sharing genes, environments, and experiences.

Protected, loved, and left mostly to their own devices, children will learn and invent not just new things, but themselves. Nothing short of abuse or other trauma will make them what they're not biologically prepared to be. They listen and learn best when what they hear makes sense, that is to say when new learning is preceded by a prior understanding that is intuitive and instinctive.

Without such understanding, learning is arduous and evanescent, a clumsy, sometimes grotesque caricature that depends on powerful external conditions. To avoid starvation or pain, rats will learn to press bars and do other rat-alien things. Apes or lions reared by humans can learn domestic ways that are inconsistent with their preferred simian and leonine ways.

In like manner, children can learn things from parents, peers, and teachers that they otherwise wouldn't bother with, *things they will mostly slough off once they are independent adults*. A real-world illustration is offered by professor Robert Hutchins, one-time master in a preparatory school whose students had failed at other schools and had only one more chance to get into an Ivy League school. Toward this goal, the parents were willing to invest a lot of money, which the instructors were just as willing to earn. "We accomplished this highly measurable result by deliberately refusing to educate these children—we did not want to confuse them." In other words, the students were drilled with no concern for understanding or appreciating what they were learning. "We made sure they could answer every question that had been asked on the College Boards since those examinations were instituted in 1909. As I remember it, our pupils all got into college and all of them flunked out at the end of the first semester. But we had performed our contract. A good deal of learning went on in that school, but very little education." Analogously, a good deal of learning goes on in homes, but rather little that goes into shaping a personality, even during the so-called formative years.

Some things are learned with great difficulty or not at all, no matter how hard the effort. The point is neatly illustrated by still another impressive observation, this one from the work of psychologist John Garcia. In his classic study, thirsty rats learn to drink water by licking the end of a tube. Half of them get water sweetened with saccharin. The other half get water made bright and noisy with a flashing light and clacking, both of which occurred whenever the rats drink.

After the rats have learned to drink either the bright-noisy or saccharin-sweetened water, a punishment is introduced. For half the rats, drinking is followed by electric shock. For the other half, drinking is followed by nausea induced by drugs or by x-irradiation. We thus have four groups of rats: (1) sweet-water, shocked; (2) sweet-water, nauseated; (3) bright-noisy water, shocked; (4) bright-noisy water, nauseated. Just two of the four groups learn relatively quickly to avoid drinking: rats made nauseous after drinking saccharin-sweet water (Group 2) and rats shocked after drinking bright-noisy water (Group 3).

This readiness for the rapid learning of certain connections is an inherited, evolutionary characteristic of the brain's wiring. Taste information from the mouth goes directly to the same area of the brain that receives information from the stomach, somewhat like a nonstop flight with no intermediate connections. In contrast, information from the eyes and ears goes directly to a different area, one that handles sensations from the skin, again somewhat like a nonstop flight. However, because these two areas are neurally distant from each other, information flow from one area to the other traverses more than one neural link, like an indirect flight with more than one connection where baggage has a greater chance of getting lost. Here then is an ancient physiological reason for some connections (learning) to come easier, but for others to come harder or not at all.

It follows, says Steven Pinker, "when children solve problems for which they [are biologically prepared], they should look like geniuses, knowing things they have not been taught; when they solve problems that their minds are not equipped for, it should be a long hard slog." Genetic variation in the quality of these modules explains why individuals differ in their ability to learn, but also in their talents, intelligence, personality, interests, and vulnerabilities. All this makes tenuous the connection between environment and person, between the rearing environment and the developing child. And it illuminates in yet another way that parental influence must be much more limited than generally thought.

The Charming Ambiguities of Language: What Does a Child Really Learn from Parents?

Psychologist Selma Fraiberg tells about a bright 2½-year-old boy who will soon be flying to Europe with his parents. Initially David was excited about the trip. Then, gradually, he became subdued, even despondent. When pressed for an explanation, the tears come as he blurts out his secret. "I can't go to Yurp. I don't know how to fly yet!"

Notice that while his parents speak of *Europe*, David hears *Yurp*. It is another example of the nobody-don't-like-me kind, of how different instruction and learning can be. Furthermore, David is confused about a couple of other things. First, he assumes his parents can fly but have not yet taught him this advanced skill, that his parents will fly off leaving him stranded on the front lawn. Second, while he knows about airplanes as little things that move in the sky, he hasn't figured out people fly *in* them. "Here is a little boy," says Fraiberg, "who speaks our language so well that we can confidently discuss European trips and travel plans with him, but we discover that, after all, we are not speaking the same language. In the fantastic world of a two year old all things are possible, and a mother, a father, and a little boy will assemble on their front lawn one morning, flap their arms and take off for a continent across the sea."

Older children too can have fantastic misperceptions. Psychologist Steven Ceci and colleagues discovered how children who otherwise tell the truth will under certain conditions make up stories that, while utterly false, may yet seem credible to adults. In one scenario, preschoolers are told a clumsy man named Sam Stone will visit their classroom. Shortly afterward, the man comes in, stays for just a few minutes during which he does nothing, and leaves. Four times during the next few months some of the children are asked leading questions. These might be about the man who came into the classroom and broke a toy. Did he do it on purpose or was it an accident?

Initially children usually recount the events accurately, but this can change. After repeated questioning, one child came to insist in all earnestness that Sam Stone threw dolls and books in the air. Over 70 percent of the children reported imaginary events as real, and with much detail—for example, Sam Stone had gone to the corner store to buy chocolate ice cream. More important, after seeing the videotapes of the children's accounts, hundreds of experts could not distinguish the true reports from the false ones.

In one study, 4- or 5-year-olds were asked, "Have you ever gotten your finger caught in a mousetrap and had to go to the hospital?" Initially, almost all children correctly answer negatively. The same question is asked again, once a week for 10 weeks, and with no prodding or leading questions. By the 10th week, many children are answering affirmatively, weaving elaborate, highly detailed, and in many cases altogether credible stories earnestly told with deep conviction. They might describe exactly where in the basement the mousetrap was located (next to the woodpile), which finger was damaged (the index finger of the right hand), and exactly who went along to the hospital (the mother and all the siblings). The children are reminded that initially they denied the incident ever happened and that recently they had been reminded that the whole incident was imaginary. Even then, the children insist it wasn't just a story, but that it really *did* happen.

With all these various examples, we can easily appreciate the often great chasm between the rearing or school environment and the mind of a child—what parents or teachers offer and what a child's psychological digestion of experience creates: knowledge, certainly, but also personality and a sense of self. Despite the often tenuous relation between children and their environment, left to their own devices they somehow learn to speak grammatically, to dream narratively, to draw accurately, and to think more objectively. Yes, they can be pushed, prodded, and shaped by circumstances, even cruel circumstances, but molded willy-nilly? Not likely, for they, not the external forces of parenting and society, are responsible for much of what they are and what they become.

Chapter Six

Random Elements

It is not every truth that recommends itself to the common sense.

—*Henry David Thoreau*

The limits of parental influence will be difficult for many people to accept when the correlations reported in the media and so much parent-child interaction suggest that strong parental influence is a sure thing. Yet consider another sure thing: a stock market adviser who sends us a letter saying that he can predict the direction of the stock market. Apparently, the adviser uses special skills, computer programs, and inside information, and he can prove his claim. Once a week, for a total of 6 weeks, we receive from him a letter that correctly predicts the direction of the stock market during the following week. A sixth and final letter asks if we are willing to pay a mere $500 for next week's prediction. It appears to be a sure thing, but is it? Here is what actually happened.

The adviser began by sending out 32,000 letters, half predicting the market would be higher, half predicting it would be lower during the following week. Naturally, half of these predictions were on the money: To those who received them, another letter was sent. Half these 16,000 letters contained the correct prediction, and to the 8,000 people who received one, a third letter was sent. Again, half of these received a letter with a correct prediction and these people were then sent a fourth letter, and so on, until a fraction of the original, including us, received six letters, each with a correct prediction. The system seems like a sure thing, and it is—for the con man who uses a random process to exploit our gullibility for illusory things that flatter egos and reinforce hopes, not to mention the penchant for single-minded focusing on one aspect of a problem, usually the most dramatic and self-relevant.

Resisting that temptation, however, means asking three somewhat personal questions that form a touchstone for critical thinking. Could my assumption or theory be false? If so, how would I ever know—what test results would convince me? Assuming I were convinced right now, would I really change my view? These three questions are about imagination and intellect, but also character, for they reflect a steadfast willingness, despite bias and prejudice, to recognize that many of our assumptions will prove incorrect and that much of the evidence for those assumptions will prove inadequate or even illusory. This is certainly true about assumptions that we make about the power of parents to shape their children's psychological development; some of that power will prove not just limited but illusory.

A Second Chance:
What Can We Predict about a Person?

Parents use rewards and punishments to make their children conform to their standards and expectations. But what if apparent rewards do not actually reinforce, and apparent punishments do not actually inhibit, either a current behavior or psychological development? Consider an important but little appreciated statistical fact of life: *Bright parents have less bright children and dull parents have brighter children.* How could this be if children are as greatly influenced by their rearing environment as we commonly suppose? To answer this question, we start with the parents themselves, for they, like their children are subject to a little-known but powerful statistical fact of life that must change everything about our theories of parental influence.

Imagine that we have selected two groups of people. One group includes those with extraordinarily high IQ scores that average 130, the other people with extraordinarily low IQ scores that average 70. Notice the average, or *mean*, score for each group deviates 30 points from the population mean of 100; one is 30 points higher, the other 30 points lower. Question: What happens the next time all those people retake the IQ test?

We typically assume that the brights will score as high as before, averaging 130, while the dulls will score as low as before, averaging 70. But that is not what happens. In fact, the brights tend to score somewhat lower, averaging maybe 125, while the dulls tend to score somewhat higher, averaging maybe 75. Notice the average for each group is now closer to the population mean of 100, which is why the apparent shift is called *regression toward the mean*. Did the bright group really get duller, the dull group brighter? No. Then what explains the regression, and how does this illuminate the limits of parental influence? For an answer, consider a scenario with many people, each of whom rolls a pair of dice.

For any roll, the maximum number is 12 (6 and 6, or "boxcars") and the minimum is 2 (one and one, or "snake eyes"). On average, the most likely, or expected, number is 7. Let's call any roll above 9 extraordinarily good, and any roll below 5 extraordinarily bad—simple enough. The dice are now rolled, and those who roll better than 9 are placed in a super-high group whose average is 10. Those who roll less than 5 are placed in a super-low group whose average is only 4. Question: On the next roll, how well will those extraordinary performers do—will the super-highs again roll high numbers averaging 10? And will the super-lows again roll small numbers averaging 4?

The obvious answer is no, because whatever the number thrown before, each group will now average roughly 7, the expected value, or mean, for dice on any throw. Given that the initial performance was due 100 percent to luck, regression will not just be *toward* the mean, it will be all the way *to* the mean. And this would be so even if the high rollers were praised for performing so "well" or the low rollers criticized for performing so "poorly," or even if the low rollers were praised and the high rollers criticized. And of course it would be true even if nothing had been said to either.

A Second Generation: What Can We Predict about a Person's Offspring?

How does all this relate to the limits of parental influence? Well, insofar as some extraordinary behavior is a fluke, or chance event, any rewards or punishments applied will be ineffective, no matter how effective those rewards and punishments may seem and no matter how convincing the belief in their application.

Let's say your child performs extraordinarily well on her exam or extraordinarily poorly on his bicycle, falling off too soon. The word *extraordinarily* is the key for suggesting an element of chance. Thus, praise her extraordinarily good performance or criticize his extraordinarily poor performance, and what will happen the next time around—will the behavior, if repeated, be as extraordinary as before? Typically, it will not. Regardless of praise, our happy test-taker will likely do less well on the next test; she'll perform more as she usually does. So, too, regardless of criticism, our hapless bike rider will likely stay on his bike longer the next time, performing more as he usually does. How strange for parents that their praise is often followed by a child performing worse while their punishments are often followed by a child performing better—that their praise tends to be punishing while their punishment tends to be rewarding! According to conventional doctrine, this difference should incline parents, however unconsciously, toward relying more on punishments than on rewards.

With practice and increasing skill, a child's performance will gradually improve. The mean to which behavior regresses can thus be thought of as a moving target that reflects the true accumulation of experience. But real learning, much of it autonomous, is a different question from the statistical one of regression toward the mean, wherever that mean happens to be at some point in time. All this suggests that parents won't be able to reinforce or discourage what is reliable, what reflects inborn dispositions and even growing skills. In like manner, parents won't be able to reinforce or discourage what is unreliable, or chancy, and this will be true no matter what the behavior and no matter how effective such efforts may seem to be.

Why are the offspring of great men so often mediocrities? asks Will Durant, who then suggests an answer consistent with regression toward the mean. "The gamble of the genes that produced them—the commingling of ancestral traits and biological possibilities—was but a chance, and could not be expected to recur." This answer is interesting and its implications are even more so. Consider.

The first scenario is about people who did well or poorly on an IQ test retaken on a second occasion. The next is about how the *children* of bright or dull people do on the IQ test, and why. Not surprisingly, the children of bright parents score high and the children of dull parents score low. Yet those bright children tend to score lower than their bright parents, meaning they score closer to the mean of 100; the dull children tend to score higher than their dull parents, likewise closer to the mean. The children of IQ-130 parents might average roughly 120; that's bright, but less so. The children of IQ-70 parents might average roughly 80; that's dull, but again, less so.

In the real world, men of the highest socioeconomic class average about 115 IQ, while their sons average about 110, which is closer to the mean. Men of the lowest class average about 81, while their sons average 92, which is closer to the mean. The two father groups differ by 34 points, while the corresponding son groups differ by 18, which is less though still a big number. This father-son difference is a clear-cut case of regression toward the mean, but is it not strange that sons reared in the highest, presumably most advantaged, class nevertheless average 5 points lower than their fathers (115 versus 120), while sons reared in the lowest, presumably most disadvantaged class nevertheless average 11 points higher than their fathers (92 versus 81)? The most likely answer is simply that element of good or bad luck inherent in life's roll of genetic and nongenetic dice.

To make the parent-child connection clearer, let's take another look at regression, this time with a slight alteration of the dice-game imagery. In our initial scenario, the dice were unbiased, meaning that, on average, the most likely number on any roll is 7. Now imagine a scenario with biased dice. Being weighted, these dice tend to wind up with one or another side more likely to face up. Unlike fair dice that average 7, high-biased dice average 9, low-biased dice 5. People with high-biased dice will obviously outperform people with low-biased dice. As before, call any roll above 9 extraordinarily good, any roll below 5 extraordinarily bad. The dice are rolled and each player's number is noted. Those with high-bias dice who roll better than 9 are placed in a super-high group that averages 10. Those with low-bias dice who roll less than 5 are placed in a super-low group that averages 4. What happens on the next roll? Will the super-highs roll high numbers that again average 10; will the super-lows roll small numbers that again average 4?

The answer is yes and no—yes, because the dice are biased, the super-highs will again roll relatively high numbers, and the super-lows will again roll relatively low numbers; no, because any dice roll is chancy, some regression must occur. Thus, on the second roll, the high-bias dice rollers will average 9. That's better than normal (7), reflecting the high bias, but it is worse than what was rolled before (10), which reflects regression toward the mean. For the same reasons, the super-lows will average 5. That's worse than normal (7), which reflects low bias, but it is better than what was rolled before (4), which reflects regression toward the mean. How does all this apply to parental influence in the face of inborn potential?

Each person's dice represent the genetic influences originating with the biological parents. The reliable aspect of all that influence is in the bias of the dice. The unreliable, or random, aspect is the *roll* of the dice, for example, the random mix of parental genes each child inherits. Achieving an IQ of 130 is therefore like rolling 11, which is higher than expected, even with high-biased parental dice. Conversely, averaging IQ 70 is like rolling 3, which is lower than expected even for low-biased dice. It is likely that 130-IQ people represent high-biased dice—lots of IQ genes and socioeducational advantages—plus good luck in the roll. Conversely, 70-IQ people probably represent low-biased dice plus bad luck in the roll.

In each case, then, there are two elements. Bias makes outcomes predictable so that parents can correctly imagine, at least roughly, how intelligent their children are likely to be. Chance makes outcomes unpredictable, so that parents can never tell exactly how a child will turn out. Bias and chance thus explain why the offspring of the super-highs also have high IQs that nevertheless average lower than do their parents'. They share with their parents the reliable aspect of high-bias dice, but not the random element of the dice roll. In like manner, bias and chance explain why the offspring of the super-lows also have low IQs, though higher than their parents'. They too share with their parents the reliable aspect, but not the random element.

The principle is clear: *Selecting behavior because it is extraordinary means capitalizing on chance.* That is why on the next occasion a behavior tends to be more ordinary, meaning closer to what is normal for the person, the family, or the population. It is why, despite all their advantages, children of the brightest parents tend to be less bright, and why, despite all their disadvantages, children of the dullest parents tend to be less dull. It's also why the children with the best-adjusted parents tend to be less well adjusted, while children of the most mentally ill parents tend to be less mentally ill. It is also why the children of alcoholics, despite their relatively high risk, are likely not to be alcoholics.

The chancy element also explains why extreme IQs don't disappear over the generations, with just about every one of later generations ending up at the mean. The regression we *commonly* get when starting from extraordinary IQ is counterbalanced by a "negative regression" we *occasionally* get when starting from ordinary IQ. After all, the large population of ordinary parents occasionally produces extraordinary children, bright or dull—just enough to replenish what regression appears to have been removed from the population of extraordinaries.

Life's random element is typically ignored in social science explanations of IQ and other traits. Accordingly, it may be argued that bright (IQ-120) children don't get the intellectual stimulation enjoyed by their higher-scoring (IQ-130) parents. It may also seem that those dull (IQ-80) children get IQ-stimulating educational and social programs that their even duller (IQ-70) parents never enjoyed. Yet no evidence supports the first impression, and good evidence contradicts the second, for example, a zero long-term effect of Head Start programs on IQ. The simplest explanation is the random element, and if any doubt remains, remember just this: *Regression to the mean works even when we start with children, then look to their parents.*

History holds many impressive examples of extraordinary genius arising out of ordinary clay and even abysmal circumstances. Johannes Kepler's father was a small-town innkeeper and a drunk whose sorry circumstances forced the boy to spend endless hours at drudge work. Johannes nevertheless grew up to be one of the greatest astronomers of all time. Carl Gauss's father was a small-time, no-account bricklayer who devalued the talents of a child prodigy who would become a prince of mathematics.

Jean-Jacques Rousseau grew up poor and socially rootless, his mother dying and his father deserting him during his infancy. Despite all, Jean-Jacques became one of the best known and most influential philosophers of the eighteenth century. Benjamin Franklin, businessman, statesman, scientist, and one of the great men of the eighteenth century, was the tenth son of a candlemaker. Jesus' awestruck neighbors asked, "Where did he get his wisdom, and the power to do these wonders? Is he not the carpenter's son?" What sort of social learning theory can credibly explain bright, extraordinary children reared by ordinary or even dull parents, or for that matter, dull, ordinary children reared by bright, extraordinary parents? The answer is that parental influence may be more than just limited; some of it may be *illusory.*

But let us be clear that the message in all this is not that parents intervene too much in their children's lives or that the intervention is without influence. After all, rewards and punishments, even when ineffective or even illusory, still signify an emotional engagement essential to healthy family life. They are still a part of the natural fabric that binds family members together in mutual respect and love. No, the message is rather that while acknowledging and appreciating what parents do, one must neither overestimate the power of their influence nor underestimate the power of inborn potential. And this means recognizing another aspect of family life that we may often overlook but that is real and that further underscores the limits of parental influence over a child's psychological development.

Stranger in the Nest: Going Our Separate Ways

In all but utopian cultures, parents as creators are in a sense the owners of their children. Even if not their brother's keepers, parents are surely their children's keepers. As such, they are responsible for their children's behavior and achievements.

Parents are bound to their children legally as well as biologically and psychologically. As such, they are custodians and educators whose effects are supposed to make a difference—to make their kids the best they can be. The American tradition in particular promotes a can-do optimism about hard work having big effects and a concomitant sense of personal responsibility. These translate into justifiable pride and joy in children's accomplishments, but also guilt and embarrassment over their failures.

The power of such tradition engenders in parents a deep sense of responsibility. This is especially evident in the blurred distinction between poor conduct that reflects deficient parenting and poor conduct that reflects inherited or acquired brain abnormalities. Countless parents who understand this distinction nevertheless have been allowed, even encouraged, to blame themselves. "Where did we fail?" Yet their child's schizophrenia, manic depression, psychopathy, or hyperactivity is no less a disease than diabetes, and the parents' responsibility no greater.

Cultural traditions reinforce the instinctive need to control events and people. The need for control is most evident where emotional commitments are strongest, as with close relatives and personal possessions. Fitting both categories, children are subject to the greatest efforts at control. After all, children are the most personal of investments. Like any other investments, these have preferable outcomes that will both flatter the parents and corroborate their expectations.

Whatever else it may be, a child's development is thus a kind of experiment for validating parents—for testing what they represent, but more important, what they *are*. A child's resemblance supports the parent's fantasies of personal immortality. Perhaps that is why adoptees more often than natural children are given a parent's first name; it establishes the illusion of a biological connection. The problem is, though, that children have their own agenda; they are not inclined to validate anyone, but to be themselves, all of which can create big problems in the family. It would seem then that parenting is a kind of Faustian bargain. Joy, satisfaction, and 10-odd years of decisive if not absolute power—at least the perception of decisive power—over another human being comes at a cost. In the best of scenarios, that cost is a keen sense that parental influence is fleeting or illusory; in the worst, it is a lifetime of frustration, remorse, or guilt over what was or what might have been.

That each child is destined to travel in a unique psychological direction should be evident early on to any parent with two or more children or to any parent with even one hyperactive or introverted child—or, for that matter, one little genius. With such a child, parents readily appreciate what biographer Robert Massie calls that "strange alchemy which, for no apparent reason, lifts one child out of a large family and endows it with a special destiny." Now, this specialness can be thrilling, as when a child's intellectual, artistic, or other achievements flatter and validate a parent while going far beyond what a parent ever hoped. Yet it can be disappointing or embarrassing—literally, a betrayal—when, for instance, a child reared by loving parents turns out misguided, mean-spirited, or so different in interests and attitudes as to seem a stranger.

Even with decent children who care about their parents and siblings, an inevitable tension, perhaps even a little alienation of affection, will arise when the press for accommodation or conformity on the one hand clashes with the need for autonomy and individuality on the other. "I would not have picked her as a friend," says novelist Ayn Rand of her middle sister, "it was only a family affection. She was my exact opposite: she was not intellectual, and she was very 'feminine'—when the family was in rags, she was interested in her personal appearance, she was more interested in young men than I was, and she had girlfriends in school, which neither I nor my little sister ever had, she was much more conventional."

The alienating effect of individual development on family life is forcefully captured by novelist George Eliot's haunting words from *The Mill on the Floss* about family likeness having a deep sadness to it.

Nature, that great tragic dramatist, knits us together by bone and muscle, and divides us by a subtler web of our brains; blends yearning and repulsion; and ties us by our heartstrings to the beings that jar us at every movement. We hear a voice with the very cadence of our own uttering the thoughts we despise; we see eyes—ah! so like our mother's—averted from us in cold alienation; and our last darling child startles us with the air and gestures of the sister we parted from in bitterness long years ago. The father to whom we owe our best heritage—the mechanical instinct, the keen sensibility to harmony, the unconscious skill of the modelling hand—galls us, and puts us to shame by his daily errors. . . .

What Do We Really Know?

In the chapters of Part 1, we have addressed the assumptions, weaknesses, and limits of a "Saturday" perspective that offers ambiguous correlations while ignoring the qualities of self-determination—resiliency, proactivity, reversion to type, and creativity—and the element of chance (regression toward the mean). Throughout these chapters, the fundamental argument has been consistent and straightforward. In many ways, not only is a parent's influence surprisingly weak or even illusory, but this *must* be so, given the power of inborn potentials. In Part 2, we will address those inborn potentials more directly by exploring the most compelling evidence of genetic and prenatal factors that limit parental influence—factors that explain the predictable but also the unpredictable aspects of personality, intelligence, mental health, and behavior.

As we make the transition, we should consider 14 specific questions about parental influence, individual potential, scientific evidence, and social policy, all of which we have begun to explore and will address more directly in the chapters to follow.

First are questions about parental influence. *On which traits or behaviors does parenting have the least enduring influence?* This question goes to our tendency to blame even devoted parents for all sorts of bad things—such as underachievement, mental illness, antisocial behavior, even suicide—none of which may have been predictable or preventable.

Children can be made to comply with social pressure, but what does this imply about parental influence on a child's abilities and dispositions—what is a parent's long-term effect on a child as a person? This question goes to a compelling fact of family life. Despite years of exposure to models and years of learning what's expected, children grown to adulthood nevertheless revert to their own inclinations. Still, strict parenting mixed with love and support can bring out the best in most children regardless of their individuality, while neglectful parenting can spoil children, allowing their worst instincts—cruel, selfish, narcissistic—to overwhelm their best.

What do the survival and personal development of children victimized by abuse, neglect, or misfortune tell us about their adult behavior? This question goes to differences in moral fiber and social conduct (character), like differences in talent and temperament, that reflect corresponding differences in inborn dispositions more than in rearing conditions.

Next are questions about individual potential. *In what ways are we the result of systematic and therefore predictable influences, and in what ways the result of chancy and therefore unpredictable influences?* This question speaks, first, to the fact that some things just happen—they aren't caused by anything we can predict, control, or take blame or responsibility for—and second, to the biological as well as social reasons that guarantee the uniqueness of each person.

How is genetic influence as much about weak dispositions as about strong ones, about elevated risk for one behavior as much as the sheer inevitability of another? The question goes to a common but false assumption that if something is genetic it must be inevitable, inflexible, and irremediable.

How does the artificial distinction between individuals versus environments obscure just how often we fashion our own environments? This question reminds us that while they influence our social behavior, environments are orchestrated by individuals and thus reflect the genetic qualities of those individuals—*environments are thus heritable*—all of which goes to our responsibility for our own behavior.

Next are questions about scientific evidence: *Why are anecdotes, though perfectly useful for illustrating or developing a theory, totally useless for proving a theory?* This question goes to our preference for individual cases that spark our imagination rather than statistical patterns that leave us cold—for storylike explanations involving social influence rather than scientific explanations involving biological influence.

How are we poorly served by the unexamined assumption that, because two things are related, the one necessarily causes the other? This question goes to evidence that a parent-child similarity may reflect not so much a parent's influence on the child as some genetic potential shared by the two.

Why is one adoption study worth more than any number of conventional family studies? This question goes to the fact that some evidence is simply better than other evidence—more definitive, less ambiguous.

Finally, questions about personal and social implications: *How should the natural inequality of individuals, including siblings, be treated effectively as well as fairly by parents, by schools, and by society?* This question goes to inevitable differences between equal opportunities and unequal outcomes—between educational efforts to maximize a child's potential and the sometimes disappointing, though sometimes delightful, eventualities.

How should we accommodate the personal relevance and social value of scientific evidence? This question goes to the fact that research findings often have social and personal meanings, even political implications, and that such findings may enrich intellectual life, sometimes by threatening complacent assumptions about ourselves and other people.

What do the political extensions of sociology and biology say about individual autonomy and therefore responsibility? This question raises a most difficult and fascinating one about free will: Do we really have it, or is it a useful fiction and comforting illusion?

By addressing challenging questions and accepting the implication of the answers offered in this book, we get a better understanding and appreciation of ourselves and our world—of what we are and where we come from. We are, in the words of microbiologist Jacques Monod, creatures of chance and necessity. That is, we are more than predictable expressions of heritable traits and years of upbringing. An unpredictable element is guaranteed by the random mix of parental genes, the chancy nature of embryological development, qualities that arise sporadically from interacting traits and the complexities of social life.

How strangely inconsistent we are, at once understandable yet mysterious. Yes, we are familiar and even predictable by virtue of our own past behavior and our relatives with whom we share genes and experiences. Yet we are in many ways unique, surprising, and unpredictable because we are partly determined by subtle, complex, even chance occurrences that we can neither control nor even specify. This may seem a little strange or disconcerting, yet it is essential to the story of individuality, its nature, and its origins.

Part Two

Sunday Side:
Blueprints for Life

The [evolutionary] foundation has so much the upper hand over personal accidental experience that it makes no difference whether a child has sucked at the breast, or has been brought up on the bottle and never enjoyed the tenderness of a mother's care. In both cases, the child's development takes the same path.

—SIGMUND FREUD

Chapter Seven

Intelligence and Personality

What a wonderful thing it is that the drop of seed from which we are produced should carry in itself the impressions not only of the bodily form but of the thoughts and inclinations of our fathers. Where can that drop of fluid contain that infinite number of forms? And how do they convey these resemblances with so heedless and irregular a course that the son will be like his great-grandfather, the nephew like his uncle?

—Montaigne

A 40-year-old woman reared by her mother and a stepfather was battling breast cancer. Linda required a thorough medical history, which meant seeking out her biological father whom she had never known. Finding him filled in blanks in her medical history, which contributed to the successful treatment of her illness. Finding him also filled in blanks in her psychological history. Linda discovered in her biological father and his family many elements of herself and her children that were never evident in her stepfather.

There were the expected physical resemblances; her son was the spitting image of her father. There were also surprising psychological resemblances, some evident in his characteristic behaviors and talents; like Linda, he, too, was an artist. Some resemblances were evident in her father's environment, in little things like the precise arrangement and selection of his books or hearthstone utensils. And something more intriguing: Both Linda and her father had a pet named Winston, clearly not a common name. Also, both loved to eat Snickers bars, which is rather more common, but also both couldn't stand peanut butter or chocolate, which is rather unusual. It was, she said, like finding herself in him and his world.

Linda's biological father shared many of her attitudes, sentiments, interests, sense of humor, and energetic way of doing things. Both were on the intellectual side, conservative in their politics, but liberal in their religious philosophy. Linda and her biological father showed the same characteristic energy, curiosity, enthusiasm for details, and perfectionism in projects. On trips, they both checked out every trail, museum, and ruin.

Linda and her biological father loved sports, freely venting their emotions in the heat of the moment. The first time they had met, they had settled down to watch a football game. After one particular play, they both jumped up, waved their arms, and yelled in the same gleeful way. It was as if they had been choreographed. Linda's stepfather watched sports in a reserved, undemonstrative manner, while her mother showed little interest. Linda and her biological father both painted landscapes, she in watercolors, he in oils. Neither her mother nor her stepfather showed more than mild interest in her talent.

Linda observed that while in physical appearance she favored her mother, psychologically she favored her father. "I find it especially intriguing that on my wedding day, my mother commented to me, 'Harry would be proud of you; you are so very much like him.' That comment explained away years of frustration and confusion, living in a household which always seemed to be at odds with my psyche."

Linda's self-discovery in her biological father is a poignant reminder of how much one's characteristic behavior, being inborn and therefore fundamentally self-determined, transcends the influence of a particular rearing. But to show this scientifically, one must address the question of just what is meant by characteristic behavior and how it is measured.

Pattern and Predictability in Measuring Traits

Clues to human potential come from two kinds of behavior. One is the extraordinary, sometimes unforeseeable kind, anything from a stunning achievement to a nervous breakdown. The other is the mostly ordinary, mostly predictable kind. We know someone is intelligent, not necessarily from one bright remark but from numerous examples of sophisticated thinking, good judgment, and elegant solutions to complex problems. We know someone is a skilled ballplayer, not from one good hit or catch, but from the overall quality of play evident in batting and fielding statistics. It is why we don't revise our high opinion of a .300 hitter who strikes out four times during a single game.

The value of averaging applies to tests of any trait. Take the parts of an intelligence test, for example. One could be a task that taps educational knowledge, with questions like, "Who wrote Macbeth?" Another could be a task that taps perceptual knowledge, with pictures of an object, say a playing card—the seven of diamonds—that lacks some part (one of the diamonds). Still another could tap arithmetic thinking, with problems that involve making change or figuring out ratios. Passing one such item means a modest likelihood of passing another, which means that individual IQ test items correlate weakly with each other and with achievement in the real world.

Things change when those items are averaged to predict things. Tests made up of items averaged together correlate moderately well with real-world achievement; an omnibus IQ test made up of many such tests correlates even better. Thus, the more items averaged together, the more reliable and predictive a test. It is true for IQ estimates of intelligence, but also for tests of honesty, self-control, and other social traits, including altruism, or the willingness to go out of one's way to help others even at one's own expense. While the occasional altruistic act may tell us little about a child's reputation for helping others, an average measure of such acts correlates rather well with the child's reputation.

Averaged measures also help explain why people differ in temperament and disposition. Take, for example, the difference between inhibited and uninhibited children. Only a modest correlation exists between this difference and a difference on any one physiological measure, whether it be heart rate, blood pressure, muscle tension, pupil dilation, or stress hormone levels. Yet an average of these measures correlates quite strongly with the trait, suggesting a real physiological difference between inhibited and uninhibited children.

Averaging enables an estimate of central tendency, a dispositional truth beyond the specific behaviors that vary from situation to situation. Anthropologist Francis Galton delighted in what comes from averaging even chaotic elements: "an unsuspected and most beautiful form of regularity [that] proves to have been latent all along." Philosopher Ralph Waldo Emerson likewise wrote that "we ascribe beauty to that which is simple; which has no superfluous parts . . . which is the mean of many extremes." The nineteenth-century Belgian statistician Lambert Quetelet even suggested that "If an individual at any epoch of society possessed all the qualities of the average man, he would represent all that is great, good, or beautiful." Twentieth-century science has given new life to these contentions.

Consider a computerized mean of many extremes, or in this case, an average of many individual faces. As psychologist Judy Langlois has shown, if each is ordinary or even unattractive, the composite face has surprising appeal. The more faces used, the more attractive the composite, as evident in the following photos.

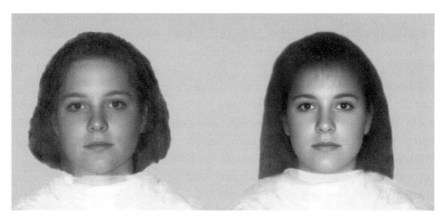

Composite averages of 4 faces (left) and 32 faces (right) like those used in Langlois, Ritter, Roggman, & Vaughan, 1991.

On the left is an average of 4 faces; on the right, an average of 32. An *averaged* face is more attractive than an average, or typical, face, but why? An averaged face need not be seen as more youthful or symmetrical, but as an approximation of an idealized picture, or prototype, of our species. After all, people seem instinctively disposed to perceive and to embrace prototypes, which are familiar even when they have never been experienced personally. This is evident in babies preferring attractive faces that look like averaged faces; they also prefer 32-face composite female faces to individual faces. They stare longer at them, and what they stare at longer, they tend to smile at and, if given the chance, approach and manipulate.

How Comparable Are the Environments of Identicals and Fraternals?

How much do genes influence those prototypelike qualities called *traits?* Ideal estimates of genetic influence come from identical twins reared apart in conditions that vary randomly. Measure their resemblance on any trait—get the correlation—and you've estimated the heritability of that trait. That's all there is to it, assuming that such resemblance can occur only because of identical genes. Unfortunately, finding such twins is no easy matter, so typical studies are done on identical and fraternal twins reared together.

The ordinary family resemblance of fraternal twins comes from sharing half their genes as well as a common environment. The extraordinary resemblance of identical twins comes from sharing *all* their genes as well as a common environment. But can it be that those common environments shared by identicals and fraternals really are comparable, such that any greater resemblance of identicals on some trait reflects their 50 percent greater genetic overlap, and nothing much else? Some people will surely object, pointing out that identicals and same-sex fraternals *don't* experience comparable environments, that identicals are treated more alike by family and friends, which easily explains their extraordinary psychological resemblance.

Identicals *are* treated more alike, but why assume this makes their experiences more comparable and their personalities more alike? Indeed, why not assume just the opposite, that similar treatment is an effect rather than a cause? Physical similarity includes the brain, and brain similarity can explain psychological resemblance, which in turn would explain the similar treatment by others enjoyed by identicals. Is it possible that how they are treated as twins really doesn't much explain the similarities of identicals or differences of fraternals?

The *equal-environments assumption* is about opportunities for learning, not what twins are taught. It is about what they get out of their environment, not what they are given by it—as with the digestion of food. Accordingly, identical and same-sex fraternal twins are assumed to experience roughly comparable rearing, education, and peer pressure. All other twin-specific influences are mostly irrelevant to their unique psychological development. Thus, unusually similar treatment doesn't explain the extraordinary family resemblance shown by identicals, while relatively less similar treatment doesn't explain the ordinary family resemblance shown by fraternals and other siblings.

Imagine identical twins fed the same kind of food, say, American, or French, or Chinese, while fraternal twins are fed different kinds of food— one gets American and the other Chinese, or one French and the other Italian. Assume that all the food is reasonably good, for it is obvious that, just as scarce or poor-quality food can stunt physical development, neglectful or abusive rearing can stunt psychological development. Would similar food explain the extraordinary physical similarities displayed by identical twins, and would different food explain the usual physical differences displayed by fraternal twins? No, for it is obvious that one kind of food will do as well as any other to bring out those mostly inborn characteristics that make identicals look alike and fraternals look different. Identicals reared on different foods would still look alike; fraternals reared on the same foods would still look different. Why, then, not in like manner with social treatment and psychological resemblance?

As food is digested, as it is broken down and built back up according to purely physiological rules; likewise, information from the social environment is digested and reconstructed, but according to psychological rules of perception, thought, and memory. If the mind is like the stomach, then what counts is not so much what goes in but how what goes in gets digested, which means people may have to go through a lot of nourishment to get what they need.

What makes all the difference, clearly, is not how one is treated but how one digests the experience, and how one digests is strongly influenced by genetic endowment. Therefore, similar treatment may be no more relevant to the psychological resemblance of identical twins than being given the same food is relevant to their physical resemblance.

With maybe 20 percent of twins misclassified—identicals as fraternals, fraternals as identicals—comes a good opportunity to test a major assumption about social influence. Identical twins reared as fraternals are presumably treated less alike than other identicals, yet they show the same extraordinary resemblance for personality traits. Fraternal twins reared as identicals presumably are treated more alike than are other fraternals, yet they generally show the same ordinary resemblance.

These observations hold even with more direct measures of social influence. Identicals exposed to similar influences aren't any more similar than identicals exposed to different influences—so, too, with fraternals. For example, identical twins who are most similar in parental attention or major childhood illness are no more alike than identicals who differ in these ways. Identicals who, as children, were dressed alike, had friends in common, and shared the same classes at school show no greater similarity, for example, in their vulnerability to severe depression than do other identicals. Fraternal twins with similar treatment likewise show no greater similarity in such vulnerability than do other fraternals.

Apparently, similar treatment is no more relevant to the psychological resemblance of identical twins than being given the same food is relevant to their physical resemblance; how one digests experience, not so much how one is treated, determines the learning that figures in self-development. Then how much is that digestion determined by genetic inheritance?

Genetic Influence on IQ: How Strong Is It?

Now, the typically greater resemblance of identical twins reflects genetic influence *in a family*, but we want to estimate genetic influence *in a population*. In a population, genetic differences, or variation, can go from 0 (between identical twins) all the way to 100 percent (among unrelated people). In families with twins, however, genetic variation goes from 0 (again, between identicals) only to 50 percent (between any two nonidentical siblings, including fraternal twins). Genetic variation within families with twins (0 to 50) is thus just half what it is in the general population (0 to 100). That is why genetic influence is underestimated by half when comparing the resemblance of identicals and fraternals.

So, to compensate for the underestimation—to estimate heritability—that difference in resemblance is doubled. Here's a simple illustration. On IQ tests, identical twins correlate about 85, fraternal twins about 60. Subtracting the 60 from the 85 yields 25. Doubling that difference yields a heritability of 50, the percentage of IQ variation in the population that is genetically determined.

Based on more than 10,000 pairs of twins from many studies, the heritability estimate of 50 for intelligence measured by IQ test is surely reliable. A comparable estimate appears to hold for elderly people. A study of twins at least 80 years old yielded substantial heritability estimates for different measures of intelligence, including an estimate of 62 for general cognitive ability, which is akin to IQ. A heritability of 60 or even 50 may seem high, yet it is actually *lower* than the over-70 estimate from five studies of identical twins reared apart. The five studies, all done during a 60-year period, used different IQ tests on reared-apart twins from working-class to professional families living in Europe and North America. The reported correlations ranged from 69 to 78, averaging 75; a sixth, reported by the controversial English psychologist Cyril Burt, is an almost perfectly comparable 77.

What then *is* the heritability of IQ—roughly 50, as suggested by comparisons of identical and fraternal twins, or over 70, as suggested by comparisons of reared-apart identicals? The answer may lie somewhere in between, but exactly where may not be so important, because either way, it is a lot. Then again, there may indeed be a more interesting answer. Studies of identical and fraternal twins typically use children and adolescents, while studies of identical twins reared apart typically use adults.

Assuming that the findings of both approaches are correct suggests that the *heritability of IQ increases from 50 during late childhood to over 70 by adulthood*, possibly decreasing somewhat with old age. The idea gains support from this observation: In comparison with most twin studies, research with adult twins suggests a heritability closer to 70 than to 50. That higher figure is consistent with another piece of evidence, a heritability of roughly 60 to 70 estimated by doubling the IQ correlation of young adult adoptees (average age, 18) and either their birth mothers or birth fathers.

This change in heritability may seem odd, but only if all aspects of IQ, including its genetic basis, are fixed and absolute. But they aren't. During childhood, identical twins correlate a little over 80 for IQ, fraternal twins a little less than 60—a relatively small difference. After puberty, while the correlation of the identicals remains roughly the same, about 85, the correlation of the fraternals is only about 40.

The difference—the apparent increase from about 25 percent during middle childhood to over 40 percent by adulthood—means an *increased heritability* (from about 50 to 75 or even higher), which you will recall is estimated by doubling the difference. The change implies that unless one shares all one's genes for IQ with another person, intellectual divergence is likely; a mere 50-percent sharing will not suffice to prevent this. In short, as people get older and accumulate unique experiences, genetic influence on intelligence surely doesn't weaken—if anything, it strengthens.

What, then, is left for environmental determination of IQ? Recall the two kinds of environmental influence: the *shared* kind (sharing the same parents or friends) that supposedly makes people similar; and the *nonshared* kind (being first or second born, having different friends) that supposedly makes people different. For IQ as well as for many personality traits, the shared kind of environmental influence often proves rather weak, as can be seen in the resemblance of identical twins. Remember that for identicals reared together, resemblance comes from their identical genes and shared environments. For identicals reared apart, resemblance can come only from their identical genes; any greater resemblance of reared-together identicals must therefore estimate the effect of sharing an environment.

How powerful, then, is the shared-environment influence? More specifically, just how much greater is the IQ similarity of identical twins reared together versus apart, when resemblance is measured by correlation, which for twins, you will recall, can be thought of as percentage alike? For reared-together identicals who have reached adulthood, the best estimate is about 85—incredibly high, given that identicals normally correlate about 90 for height; for reared-apart identicals, however, the IQ correlation is about 75. That little difference between 85 (reared together) and 75 (reared apart) estimates how much psychological resemblance depends on the influence of shared environments beyond the influence of shared genes.

A 10 percent difference may not seem like much. Still, it is a lot more than the *0 percent* for adult adoptees and their adoptive relatives. Four studies of genetically unrelated siblings have yielded correlations from +5 to −3—essentially 0 correlation and really no different from the total nonresemblance of adult pairs randomly chosen from the same population! The real surprise in all this, then, isn't so much that genetic influence is strong but that the shared-environment influence—and by implication, rearing and peer influence—seems so weak.

Consider additional observations on intelligence as measured by IQ. IQ differences show up between job classifications, such as physicians versus home builders, but also *within* the trades: contractors versus carpenters, for example. IQ predicts job success—in particular, productivity and promotion—better than does the amount of formal education. Of course, many factors go into job success, but IQ is a big one. Higher IQ tends to go with better performance in all known jobs. Other things aside, the brighter police officer is likely to be the better one; the brighter gunner is more likely to hit the target when firing a tank gun. Brighter employees generate more wealth while wasting less time and money. It seems that the more complex a job, the more IQ predicts performance.

From a biological perspective, though, the validity of IQ is even more compelling, and even less arguable as a social phenomenon. The verbal IQ of school-age children is correlated with certain perception tests taken when they are 6 months old—for example, the better the infants are able to sustain attention to novel stimuli while showing boredom with familiar stimuli, the higher their childhood IQ. This kind of observation is important for the simple reason that, at 6 months, the infant has not been exposed to many of the educational advantages or disadvantages presumed to explain individual differences in IQ.

Adult IQ can be predicted from performance on *culture-fair* intelligence tests that depend little on language or educational experience. For this reason, they can easily be used cross-culturally to test for individual differences. A good example involves complex reaction time. The test measures the speed and accuracy of responses to any one of several light bulbs that can be illuminated at random. IQ correlates with such measures, so that the more complex the task—the more bulbs—the higher the correlation. IQ correlates but poorly with simple reaction time, or quick responsiveness to a single bulb.

The implication is that IQ reveals something about how quickly and efficiently a person's brain handles information, especially when there is some degree of uncertainty. This is surely consistent with two more observations. One is that IQ correlates with specific brain waves evoked by light or sound. The evoked EEG of high-IQ people compared to low-IQ people tends to have a shorter reaction time, meaning that it occurs more quickly after the stimulus. It also has greater waveform complexity, or more little bumps and variability and a longer total length. The other observation is that IQ correlates with measures of brain metabolism. On difficult tasks, the brain of a high-IQ person has a *lower* metabolic rate, as indicated by lower glucose consumption, suggesting less expenditure of effort.

Two final observations suggest that IQ does indeed reflect brain differences. The IQs of adult adoptees correlate with the IQs of their biological parents, not with the IQs of their adoptive parents. The brain must be implicated, and sure enough, IQ does correlate with brain size. As of this writing, at least eight independent studies using computer-assisted brain scanning methods have all discovered that people with higher IQs, whether male or female, tend to have bigger brains, the correlation of IQ and brain size being about 40. A brain size–IQ correlation of 40 really is quite impressive, given the widespread assumption that it is 0. One observer even noted that being able to predict the stock market as well as brain size predicts IQ would make a person rich! The correlation is merely a crude marker of the quantity and quality of brain tissue, the machinery of mind, experience, and behavior.

In summary, the observations support a biological view of intelligence as estimated by standard IQ tests:

- IQ correlates with attention measured at 6 months.
- IQ correlates with performance on culture-fair intelligence tests.

- IQ correlates with specific brain-wave patterns.
- IQ correlates with brain metabolism.
- IQ correlates with brain size.
- IQ correlates with the IQs of biological, but not adoptive, relatives.

IQ differences among siblings average about 12 points, which means that *roughly half of all siblings differ by more than 12 points*. This is really quite amazing, given that siblings grow up within the same family on the same side of the tracks, sharing roughly the same rearing and socioeconomic advantages or disadvantages plus a full 50 percent of their genes. Despite all the sharing, however, the 12-point difference among sibs is about 70 percent of the 18-point difference among children randomly selected from the population.

In short, no reasonable argument about the heritability of intelligence is possible if the following two sets of reliable observations previously noted are ignored or denied. First, identical twins reared apart are highly correlated for IQ, even more so than fraternal twins reared together; that difference becomes even more pronounced when identicals and fraternals are compared during adulthood. Second, genetically unrelated siblings reared together are poorly correlated for IQ, despite being more highly correlated with biological relatives they've never met; and as genetically unrelated siblings grow to adulthood, even their poor correlations diminish to zero.

Clearly, then, IQ can't be merely or even mostly a matter of parenting and other social and economic factors, for that couldn't explain such within-family differences listed previously or this simple fact: Siblings who score higher than their family's average IQ tend to rise socioeconomically, while siblings who score lower tend to fall. Within each family, much variation occurs in the abilities to think logically, abstractly, and efficiently, abilities that are heritable. Moreover, these abilities likely reflect the density and organization of neural connections, and how fast and with what fidelity information is shuttled around the brain. Variation across family members in these qualities of the brain are undoubtedly determined in large part by corresponding genetic differences.

Genetic Influence on Personality: More Surprises

A personality trait can be just about anything—for example, a disposition to be ambitious; being articulate, sharp-witted, and versatile rather than apathetic, awkward, and shy; being active and self-centered rather than passive and self-abasing; being serious, honest, modest, and industrious rather than defensive, demanding, and rebellious; or being tolerant, clear-thinking, and resourceful rather than suspicious, judgmental, and aloof. Fortunately, this virtually endless list can be boiled down to five general supertraits called the Big Five:

1. *Extroversion*—the tendency to be sociable, adventurous, and energetic
2. *Agreeableness*—the tendency to be kind and affectionate
3. *Conscientiousness*—the tendency to be reliable and organized
4. *Emotional stability*—the tendency to be calm and stable
5. *Intellectual openness*—the tendency to be insightful and inventive

These five supertraits appear to be universal variants of human nature, for they are found in cultures throughout the world, each with different traditions, world views, and languages. The Big Five pattern is virtually identical in societies that speak German, Portuguese, Hebrew, Chinese, Korean, and Japanese. Evolutionary psychologist David Buss argues that personality traits "provide a source of information for answering important life questions: who is high or low in the social hierarchy? Who is likely to rise in the future? Who will make a good member of my coalition? Who possesses the resources I need? With whom should I share my resources? Who will share their resources with me? On whom can I depend when I am in need? With whom should I mate? Whom should I befriend? Who might do me harm? Whom can I trust? To whom can I go for sage advice?"

In short, traits enable people to communicate and to identify personal qualities that help them survive in the social world. If these traits are part of our genetic heritage, then they ought to be heritable, with genetic differences helping to explain individual differences in extroversion or other major traits. Indeed, resemblance on those Big Five supertraits does appear to be roughly 2 times greater for identical twins than for fraternal twins. Doubling the difference yields conservatively estimated heritabilities of about 40. That's roughly what the correlations of identical twins reared apart yield: comparable if even a little higher (about 50). Such comparable resemblance (correlation) of identicals whether reared apart or together rules out the importance of shared rearing and shared peers.

A closer look at this point will illuminate the highly controversial argument offered by psychologist Judith Rich Harris regarding personality development: that, beyond genetic sharing, peer influence is paramount and "parents count zilch." It's a bold assertion, but questionable for the following reasons.

First, recall the comparable resemblance of identical twins reared either together or apart, which can reflect only the sharing of genes. Such comparability rules out the sharing of *everything else*—peers as well as parents, economic status, neighborhoods, parental networks, school systems, etc. *All of it* must be zero. Thus, if parents "count zilch," peer influence also counts zilch.

Second, if the zero shared-environment effect on personality is generally true—if neither parental nor peer influence explains why we resemble each other—still, one or both of these influences might at least partly explain personality *differences;* that is, parents and/or peers might yet constitute much of that *non-shared* influence—that 50 percent environmental influence beyond the 50-percent genetic plus zero shared-environmental influences—but just how much? About 20 to 25 of the 50 percent is probably *physical*—prenatal, paranatal (birth complications), and post-natal (injuries), all of which can affect brain development. This leaves 25 to 30 percent for parents and sibs, peers, and everything else non-shared, including teachers, romances, traumas, etc.

Again, no definitive evidence indicates, nor does common sense suggest, that peer effects are everything, all others nothing; nor does any definitive evidence indicate that peer influence, so obviously powerful when it comes to behavior and conduct, nevertheless has much if anything to do with long-term personality-trait development. So, even granting, for argument's sake, that peers are the larger influence (say, 10 to 15 of the 25 to 30 percent), parents a lesser influence (say, 5 to 10 percent), and all the rest the least influence (say, 5 to 10 percent), no one of these is all that impressive.

And note that our measurements of all these influences are far from perfect, far from reliable. Measurement error causes us to overestimate environmental influence while underestimating genetic influence, probably by 20 percent or more. Thus, correcting all the numbers—estimating what we would get with better measures—adds about 10 percent to our estimate of genetic influence, which rises from 50 to 60 percent, while it reduces our estimate of all non-shared influence by the same percentage. Thus corrected for measurement error, peer as well as parental influence is even less impressive—together, 12 to 20 percent of all non-shared influences—but surely not "zilch." Is there any empirical evidence for such an assertion?

In 1997, psychologist John Loehlin reported that the resemblance of twins actually correlates with amount of peer sharing and with similarity of parental treatment, for instance, being dressed alike. In his study, personality resemblance correlated with peer sharing .13 for identicals and .19 for fraternals; it correlated with similarity of parent treatment .08 for identicals and .13 for fraternals. These little correlations, *corrected for measurement error*, are in line with the corrected estimates offered in the preceding paragraph, suggesting that peer influence, like parental influence, is modest at best. And consider this: some of the apparent peer effect could really be a parental effect, to the degree that parents determine who their children's peers will be. In any case, we can also imagine how much of this little influence might slough off—the parental kind, as children become adolescents, and the peer kind as adolescents become adults.

One more point: The zero shared-environment effect on personality is only one indication of parenting influence on personality. The other is the nonshared environment effect. And the evidence is clear: Parenting quality can help determine whether a child who has experienced fetal stress or a birth complication develops a disposition to antisocial, criminal, or violent behavior. Thus, good parenting may yet influence the quality of siblings' social conduct or the degree of scholastic and practical achievements. The scientific evidence on this is still ambiguous. Yet the idea, which fits every parent's intuition, cannot be dismissed by focusing merely on a zero shared-environment effect.

In any case, the logic or the arguments and the force of the evidence combine to suggest that, no matter how powerful its effects on behavior and social conduct, peer influence cannot be a major factor in long-term personality development.

Genetic overlap alone can explain the psychological resemblance that individuals show with other people. It surely seems so when it comes to Big Five traits, but it holds for others, too. A good example is sensation seeking, being excited by novel stimuli and taking pleasure in exploring new things, often without the usual concern about possible harm. Identical twins, even when reared apart, are highly similar, correlating over 50; fraternals correlate much less (about 20), which makes the heritability of the trait at least 50 percent.

Until 1996, evidence for genetic influence on psychological traits was mostly the indirect kind from twin and adoption studies. Then, apparent connections were discovered between single genes or even just DNA patterns and personality traits, for example, neuroticism. Neuroticism involves the tendency to be anxious and depressed, as measured by personality questionnaires in which subjects note how much they agree or disagree with statements like "I am not a worrier" or "Frightening thoughts sometimes come into my head." Neuroticism is roughly 50 percent heritable, meaning that 50 percent of individual differences in the trait (from weak to strong) come from genetic differences.

A varying genetic factor found on chromosome 17 involves a short or a long segment of DNA, reflecting a corresponding difference in how serotonin is regulated in the brain. Individuals with the shorter DNA segment tend to be more anxious and less happy-go-lucky than individuals with the longer segment. This gene–trait relation is relatively weak; the DNA variant explains less than 10 percent of the trait's 50 percent heritability. Clearly, additional genes must be involved.

Two research groups have each reported a connection between a gene called DRD4 located on chromosome 11 and yet another personality trait: novelty seeking, which includes being excited by novel stimuli, taking pleasure in exploring new things, and being extroverted more than conscientious or deliberate. The DRD4 gene, or gene that codes for the D4 variant of dopamine receptor, comes in a short and a long variant, depending on how much DNA it contains. These variants make a difference in how brain cells respond to the neurotransmitter dopamine.

Compared to people with the short variant, people with the long variant tended to be seekers of novel experience, and the difference was evident regardless of sex; racial, religious, socioeconomic, or ethnic group; or country of origin. Twin studies suggest a heritability of about 40 percent—that genetic variation explains 40 percent of the variation in novelty seeking. If variation in the DRD4 gene can explain only a small part of that genetic 40 percent, additional genes would have to be involved.

A similar story may be emerging with heroin addiction: Apparently, the long variant of DRD4 is observed more than twice as often in male heroin addicts than in male control subjects. Yet again, even if the DRD4 gene proves a true culprit, other genes are likely involved in the vulnerability. The long variant of the DRD4 gene seems also to make a modest contribution to attention-deficit/hyperactivity disorder (ADHD). Compared to control subjects children with ADHD appear far more likely to have the long rather than the short variant of the DRD4 gene. This DRD4-ADHD connection nicely fits with another observation: that male alcoholics are often impulsive and hyperactive during childhood.

A cautionary approach to all these genetic findings is advised, given the failures to replicate some of the connections, in particular between novelty seeking and the DRD4 gene or neuroticism and the serotonin regulator DNA sequence. On the other hand, failure to confirm need not mean that an original finding was illusory, for it might be real yet limited to certain families or populations. After all, a genetic influence found in one species may not be found in another; likewise, a genetic influence found in one strain of a species may not be found in another. Given that families are at least like strains within a species, we should not be surprised that genetic influence demonstrated in one cannot be found in another. Proof that the original finding was real is not so much in the replication of the finding, but in the ability of the experimenter to demonstrate the physiological mechanism.

Differences in personality emerging right from the beginning will be appreciated by the parents of more than one child. Not surprisingly, twin studies of infants and young children show that fraternal twins, like non-twin siblings, are much less alike than are identical twins for traits as sociability (or preference for being with and the tendency to respond positively to others) and for impulsivity (or lack of control), discipline, and reflectivity. Such findings suggest all the more why a child's environment is more than just something imposed arbitrarily from the outside, why it is, rather, something selected and created by virtue of the child's own temperament.

Consider the trait of well-being, or how happy one generally feels whatever one's abilities, personal achievement, or standing in the community, and regardless of mood shifts that naturally come with changes in life's circumstances. About 50 percent of variation in well-being comes from genetic influence. The rest comes from passing events, nonshared environmental influences that push people around emotionally. In addition, the genetic influence in well-being seems to express itself in patterns of electrical activity that can be recorded from the front part of the brain. Happy people show relatively greater activity on the left side, unhappy people relatively greater activity on the right.

What, then, is the heritability of the *stable component* of well-being, one's *typical level* of well-being, say, over a 10-year period? This question has been addressed by psychologists David Lykken and Auke Tellegen in a study of 127 pairs of twins (79 identical, 48 fraternal). For each twin, two well-being scores were obtained by self-report—one 10 years after the other. For all the twins, the correlation between well-being scores at the two points in time was 50, suggesting modest stability in the scores.

To answer the question about genetic influence, the researchers did the following: For each pair of twins, they compared the well-being score of twin A at the initial point in time with the well-being score of *twin B* 10 years later—also the well-being score of Twin B at that same initial point in time with the well-being score of *twin A* 10 years later. For identical twins, this cross-twin/cross-time correlation was about 40, or 80 percent of 50, that stable aspect of the well-being scores. Since the corresponding cross-twin/cross-time correlation for the fraternal twins was negligible, the implication is dramatic: The heritability of *stable* well-being is about 80.

As Lykken and Telligen say, "The reported well-being of one's identical twin, either now or 10 years earlier, is a far better predictor of one's self-rated happiness than one's own educational achievement, income, or status." Sex, race, and socioeconomic status contribute next to nothing. Surprisingly, despite comparatively low status, unfair discrimination, stereotyping, or obvious disadvantages, women, blacks, people with mental illness, people with handicaps, and the poor tend to rate themselves as happy and satisfied as do other groups.

The similar levels of well-being reported by identical twins whether raised together or apart suggests further that a particular rearing has little to do with the trait. In this, well-being is like other personality traits, or even physical traits, like the heritable disposition toward adult obesity that appears to have just about nothing to do with how one was fed or other aspects of the rearing environment.

What about attitudes, values, and interests, for example, in athletics, travel, or religious activities? People generally think of these as being socially engendered, but this is only partly true. For while only modest heritabilities of about 30 are found for certain interests, such as camping or making furniture, higher estimates of about 45 are found for athletics, travel, and religious activities. Even higher estimates (about 50) are found for adventurous occupations, such as the military, skilled activities, such as arts and crafts and industrial arts, and religious orientation.

So, too, with attitudes—for example, about the death penalty, sex crimes, the importance of religion, life after death, sex before marriage, patriotism, sterilizing people with incurable diseases, and euthanasia: It is usually assumed that these are merely the products of rearing; biology is hardly considered. Yet, the heritability of these attitudes ranges from 40 to 60, which is sufficiently high to have prompted psychologist David Lykken to raise an intriguing rhetorical question: Could William F. Buckley—could any strong conservative or liberal, for that matter—have resisted eventually arriving at his particular views on politics, religion, capital punishment, abortion, and the rest? The question may be rhetorical, but the implication, like the evidence, is increasingly clear. Each of us will come to resemble others with similar genes. Find someone with our exact genetic match, and we discover much of our self.

Chapter Eight

Vulnerability and Creativity

If you cannot get rid of the family skeleton, you may as well make it dance.

—*George Bernard Shaw*

A young graduate student of philosophy seems a bit too preoccupied with some rather idiosyncratic notions about the mind-body problem, the way mental life relates to the physiological activity of the brain. Weeks later, he appears increasingly odd and distracted, pacing back and forth while speaking in a rapid-fire manner. His appearance is agitated, not the usual look of the typical student come to a professor's office for a chat. Despite their logic, memos he slips surreptitiously under the door seem increasingly inappropriate and surreal—in a word, schizophrenic.

In an early memo, he talks about "the enlightenment, or 'awakening' of mystic alchemy [being] correlable with a relatively greater number of 'alpha waves' than the unenlightened states. . . ." Later, his ideas become more idiosyncratic, subjunctive. Everything is hyperabstract, with quote-enrapped words that invoke everything and mean nothing. He writes about things seen in dreams being a metaphor such that, "by any empiric criterion, 'It is not true that: "Things are things, such that 'Those things are members of the class of "things seen in dreams" ' " ' ", i.e., –p, if: p $\overset{\text{df}}{\equiv}$ $\exists$ (x) : x $\in$ A, A $\overset{\text{df}}{\equiv}$ "The class of 'things seen in dreams" '.

As if from some twilight zone, he thus continues with a mess of embedded quotation marks: "If one thinks that, ('heuristically' speaking) one was "dreaming", then, one thinks that, "One has thought (or, falsely assumed) that, 'There are (empirically speaking) members of the class of "things seen in dreams" ' '." A final message, sent anonymously before he disappeared, begins with "Dear Dr. Cohen: (p1 > p2 > p3) ^ – p4," and ends with a formula—$(2)^x o > o$—that is part of an egocentric argument about consciousness. To the casual observer, none of it will seem real, though it is intensely real to him. Here is a tortured soul, desperate and importunate, but without insight into his deteriorating condition.

With the slide into schizophrenic illness come preoccupations less anchored in reality and common sense, that subtle ability to understand the rules of social exchange, to know intuitively what is relevant, appropriate, and expected. In such a state, heady and grandiose abstractions may bring some satisfaction, but no real insight. With illness come apathy and social withdrawal, a disheveled or strange appearance, and inappropriate behavior—perhaps collecting garbage or talking to windows, pacing late at night, laughing or shouting spontaneously, speaking in a vague or distracted manner, or withdrawing in the middle of a conversation.

Is it mostly nature or nurture that determines why some people are at greater than normal risk for succumbing to such dreadful states of mind? Good answers reveal much about the mystery of normal, and even creative, behavior. At least one such good answer, a specifiable genetic abnormality, is evident from studies of twins, which brings up a story.

Paul's Astonishing Question

Years ago, while exploring the genetic argument with a classroom of undergraduate students, I mentioned that to find a psychologically normal person with the highest risk for schizophrenia, find a person who has a schizophrenic identical twin. That person will have a 40 percent chance of falling ill, which is 40 times the usual rate of 1 percent.

Finding such a person is not easy, because identical twinning occurs in just 1 out of 250 births, and schizophrenia affects just 1 in 100 persons. Multiplying these two fractions yields the rather slim chance of about 1 in 25,000 that a person is both an identical twin and a schizophrenic, regardless of the other twin's mental health. Clearly, there is only the smallest chance of finding a psychologically normal identical twin whose co-twin is schizophrenic.

After explaining this, a student, Paul, volunteered that indeed he was one of those identical twins, and would I comment on his obviously singular situation? Please understand, here was no incidental question posed out of idle curiosity. Paul understood the significance of what he was asking. If only for a moment, we were to explore his personal link to an insidious and unforgiving illness.

Most students wouldn't dream of thus exposing their personal lives to public scrutiny in a classroom full of strangers. We need to love, but also to *be* loved. We need to understand, but also to *be* understood. In some people, the press for love and understanding is magnified by painful circumstances. In others, it is pathologically transformed by a self-destructive or socially disruptive element. In them the need is great, the seeking urgent, and the interpersonal effects strong. Sometimes the balance shifts toward love, sometimes, as with Paul, toward understanding.

Most obvious now, after so many years, is how much Paul's singular question represented the need for understanding—in particular, a need to come to grips with the experience of loss. Paul could not indulge in the illusion that he was free from genetic influence. Compared to his wellness, his brother's schizophrenia was surely something different, but what about deep down? In his brother's illness, was Paul reading the handwriting on the wall, or were there nongenetic factors on which he could rest his hope—factors that would mean continued wellness rather than eventual illness?

Paul had asked his big question. What I offered in response were undeniable facts softened by a bit of evasiveness, probably because I wasn't really sure how to proceed—how to be truthful, without hurting Paul or scaring other students. Only after describing what he mostly already knew about the darker, genetic side of his dilemma could the elements of a more hopeful, partly nongenetic scenario be laid out.

One in 10 offspring of a schizophrenic parent will in like manner become ill. That 10 percent lifetime rate is at least 10 times greater than the approximate 1 in 100 rate for people randomly chosen from the population. Thus, schizophrenia runs in families, but why? One of the best reasons is that the closer the genetic link to an ill person, the greater the chance for illness. For example, people unrelated to a person with schizophrenia have a risk of less than 1 percent. But the risk can be as high as 10 percent for people who are 50-percent related to a person with schizophrenia, as are siblings, children, or parents. In the unlikely case of people who are 100-percent related, as are identical twins, the risk is about 40 percent. That's three times greater than for the fraternal twins of a person with schizophrenia, and 40 times greater than for people picked at random. The 40-percent rate for identicals therefore suggests a strong genetic contribution to the schizophrenia potential.

Two additional observations confirm the genetic influence while suggesting that the influence of rearing is weak. First, the 10-percent rate applies even if the schizophrenia sufferer's offspring are reared by adoptive parents. Second, it also applies to those rare offspring of a psychologically normal adult whose identical twin has schizophrenia, which means one's risk for schizophrenia is relatively high if one's mother has schizophrenia *or if she is perfectly normal but her identical twin has schizophrenia.* The evidence of genetic influence is impressive, for schizophrenia certainly, but also for other disorders, such as manic depression, or bipolar disorder.

If genetic influence is so important in schizophrenia, why are most identical twin siblings of those with schizophrenia not likewise ill? The answer: Schizophrenia is more than mental illness. Rather, it is a *potential* for illness, one that varies in people from a little to a lot—in some, so much that, for practical purposes, they can't help but get ill. But most important, even when strong, that potential need not be fulfilled in manifest illness, just as high intelligence, a quite different kind of potential, need not be manifest in some remarkable way, say, in brilliant achievement.

The point, so often missed by combatants in the nature–nurture debate, was clearly relevant to Paul. For even if he was somehow pro- tected by, say, a fortuitous fluke of prenatal development that altered his brain chemistry and personality, he still carried as many genes for schizo- phrenia as did his twin. Genetically, he therefore had the same potential as his brother, meaning that his offspring would likely have roughly the same risk as would his brother's offspring—as high as 1 in 10.

Genetic potential need not be expressed. A young woman asked in the middle of a lecture how her eyes could be brown while both her parents' eyes were blue, meaning that neither of them had genes for brown eyes. Some believe that perhaps 1 child in 10 isn't the offspring of the apparent father. However, parents with a gene for brown eyes may be blue-eyed if, unlike the offspring, they lack other biochemical factors for synthesizing brown eye pigment. In short, two blue-eyed parents—as many as 10 per- cent—will have a brown-eyed child. It is important to remember that a genetic potential passed to an offspring need not be fulfilled in the parent.

A genetic vulnerability not fulfilled in manifest behavior is like a genetic talent not fulfilled in manifest creativity or technical achievement. Imagine a piano tuner with a surprisingly rough and intimidating appearance: heavyset, muscular, with thick hands and a tough, no-nonsense attitude. Yet, can *he* play the piano—Chopin, Liszt, Beethoven—and with such power, subtlety, and feeling! He, in fact, is the younger brother of a famous concert pianist. The difference between them is not so much in talent but in achievement, whose absence in the tuner seems to reflect a lifetime of stubborn, almost cultivated indifference toward disciplined study.

Clearly, temperament can make all the difference in how a talent is exploited or squandered. The tuner's great talent was evident in his playing, and in this remarkable story. While tuning a piano for a concert by Claudio Arrau at Carnegie Hall, he was asked by the great pianist to evaluate a sample of his playing. *Excellent* was the verdict—except for the pedaling, which could be improved, as the tuner promptly demonstrated upon request. Arrau followed the suggestions, and the concert was a success, with positive reviews—including one that explicitly praised the pedaling!

Inborn potentials can manifest themselves in diverse ways or, for various reasons, remain largely unexpressed. With the piano tuner, temperament was important. In Paul's case, it may have been prenatal events mitigating genetic influence. In still other cases, it is at least partly a matter of overwhelming social circumstance. For reasons of temperament or circumstance, a person may be a brilliant success. Yet if that person and another are genetically related, that other person's ordinary behavior can nevertheless mask an extraordinary potential that may be passed on to a child. So, too, with the genetic potential for mental illness. For reasons of temperament or circumstance, one person may have schizophrenia, but not another. Yet if they are genetically related, that second person's wellness may mask an abnormal potential that could well be passed on to a child.

Inheriting the genes for a mental illness is like being dealt a lousy poker hand, while inheriting the genes for competence or courage is like being dealt a good poker hand. In the game are family players, parental dealers, and a deck stacked with many predisposing cards. As dealers, parents are therefore causal, though not responsible. They have dealt the genetic cards, but they had neither control over which cards, nor a working appreciation of just how much the deck is stacked. As players, offspring, too, are not responsible in one sense, though they are responsible in another. They never asked to participate. Yet once in the game, they must play out their hands, neither squandering a good one nor giving in to a bad one. Then just how heritable are such hands?

Genetic Influence in Mental Illness

With twins, the heritability of anything can be measured along a continuum. This is clear enough with IQ and personality traits, for these are measured from low to high or from weak to strong. But what about a mental illness potential, whether manifest, as in Paul's brother, or latent, as in Paul? That, too, but here is a problem: Typically, illness potential isn't measured in everybody. Rather, in all-or-nothing fashion, manifest illness is diagnosed in a few people while the rest are ignored. People with schizophrenia obviously have strong potential, but what about everyone else? After all, most people aren't—surely Paul wasn't—interested in just the genetics of a schizophrenic illness, but in the genetics, or heritability, of the vulnerability.

Even without a vulnerability scale—without something like an IQ test that is applied to everyone—the heritability of a vulnerability can still be estimated. It's the equivalent of using tall twins to estimate the heritability of height or brilliant twins to estimate the heritability of intelligence, all of which is like using the visible tip of an iceberg to theorize about the whole berg. The tip-of-the-iceberg method relies on people diagnosed as ill or not ill and ignores shades of gray. Thus, we seek out twins who are either concordant (both twins ill) or discordant (only one twin ill). Even if that difference seems straightforward enough, look a little closer, first at discordance.

Imagine that you take a test and miss by one point the next higher grade in a college course; say you got the highest B. But can it really be said that a high-B student really knows significantly less than a low-A student? So, too, with a twin diagnosed with schizophrenia whose co-twin is not so diagnosed. Such discordance can also be misleading because while some not-ill twins may be normal, like Paul, others may display noticeable schizophrenic abnormalities. They may even be schizophrenic, though not quite severely enough to be formally diagnosable. Some have a generally unkempt manner of dress, including ink-stained or ill-fitting clothes. Some have inappropriate emotional expressions, relatively poor eye contact, a tendency to talk to themselves, and other peculiar mannerisms. They may be deficient in common sense, as evident in their frequent asking about self-evident things, or they may have difficulty distinguishing between the likely and the unlikely. Some experience much social anxiety, especially around unfamiliar people. This tends to make them socially isolated or aloof.

Collectively, such peculiar traits are *schizotypal*, meaning typical of schizophrenia. They are called that for three good reasons. First, people with these traits seem to have a relatively mild version of schizophrenia. Second, they perform somewhat like schizophrenics on laboratory tasks that measure attention, thinking, memory, and even brain waves. Finally, recall that they and their biological relatives have an elevated risk for the illness, which means the so-called not-ill twin, someone like Paul, might be highly vulnerable, perhaps as much as his schizophrenic brother.

What can be said about these either-or categories that ignore shades of gray between normalcy and illness? Don't we miss important clues to vulnerability in those people who, like Paul, *aren't* manifestly ill? Yes, but we can get around this problem so that our tip-of-the-iceberg approach really can estimate the heritability of vulnerability.

We've considered discordance; now consider concordance. Imagine that we have each pulled a coin out of our pockets and discover that we each have a penny. No surprise in that. Most people carry pennies, so there's a good chance that any two will be concordant for a penny. But what if we had both pulled out a Susan B. Anthony dollar? Now *that* would be surprising! It could have happened by chance, but suppose we two were reared-apart identical twins with a similar penchant for carrying odd or unpopular coins! Something like that could explain the otherwise near-impossible coincidence of two people independently doing the same oddball things or inventing the same unlikely gizmo, as in the Charles Addams cartoon.

Separated at birth, the Mallifert twins meet accidentally.

As with the penny example, one naturally understands that the likelihood of two events occurring together (co-incidence) depends on the likelihood of each event occurring alone (incidence). That's why concordance for carrying a Susan B. Anthony dollar is more impressive than concordance for carrying a penny. Likewise, a mere 15 percent concordance for something rare, like suicide, is more impressive than even a 30 percent concordance for something relatively common, like depression.

A mere 15 percent concordance is nevertheless really impressive when compared with an expected rate of 1 to 2 percent. Another way of viewing the 15 percent concordance is to imagine that your child achieved only 15 percent on a test, then discovering that of all the other children in the class, only one besides yours achieved the same percentage, and none of the others achieved better than 2 percent.

Because it can be so misleading, concordance may not be used like a correlation to estimate heritability. Nevertheless, with a few assumptions and statistical methods—with a sort of modern alchemy—a leaden concordance rate can be turned into a golden correlation. That done, the genetic basis of this or that vulnerability can indeed be estimated.

For schizophrenia, heritability estimates have ranged from about 40 to 87, with a best estimate from recent research suggesting something between 80 and 86. For Alzheimer's disease in people over 65, identical twins are much more concordant for the illness than are fraternal twins, the numbers suggesting a roughly 60 percent heritability for the vulnerability to that disabling illness.

What about severe anxiety and depression, disorders that tend to go together—why are some people especially vulnerable? Consider an anxiety or depressive disorder not severe enough to require hospitalization, *each taken separately*. Compared to fraternal twins, identical twins are a little more concordant—if one identical twin has an anxiety or depressive disorder, the co-twin has a relatively larger but still modest chance of having the same disorder, which suggests that either the anxiety or depressive disorder is at best modestly heritable.

Now consider anxiety and depression, *taken together*. Compared to fraternal twins, identical twins are much more concordant—if an identical twin has either disorder, the co-twin is rather likely to have the same one, or the other one, or both—any disorder that expresses the general vulnerability. As different currencies (dollars and yen) represent the same purchasing power, different disorders (anxiety and depression) represent the same emotional vulnerability. It is in this sense that, like currencies, these disorders are exchangeable.

What does all this mean? While the heritability of the general disposition is high—one estimate being 80—the heritability of the individual disorder is rather modest (in adolescents, for example, maybe 10 to 30). And the likely reason? Environmental circumstances—personal threats or interpersonal losses—largely determine which disorder occurs or, if both occur, whether they occur together.

Alcoholism, too, is a heritable vulnerability, as evident in studies showing that animals can be bred for alcohol preference and that adoptively reared offspring of an alcoholic and identical co-twins of an alcoholic twin have a markedly elevated risk for alcoholism. One study even found comparably high rates of alcoholism in male adoptees and their nonadopted biological brothers—this despite the adoptees' obvious advantage growing up in a more stable and loving family environment and despite a higher socioeconomic status than that enjoyed by the nonadopted brothers.

Of seven studies of male twins, six have found identicals to be strikingly more concordant than fraternals; a seventh found identicals to be just slightly more concordant. In five studies, the heritability of the alcoholism vulnerability was found to be roughly 50 to 60 percent; in a sixth, it was 98 percent! For females, however, the somewhat less reliable evidence suggests much lower, even insignificant, genetic influence, compared to more powerful social causes.

A point to remember is that all such heritability estimates as we have addressed depend on how behavior is measured. For example, the more averaging that goes into measuring a personality trait—the more reliable the measure—the higher the heritability. Reliability is not the only factor. Tightness of definition can be important. In the case of mental illness, the strictness of the diagnostic criteria can make a big difference in the concordance rates for identical and fraternal twins, and therefore a big difference in the estimate of heritability.

With very narrow, strict criteria for diagnosing schizophrenia or manic-depression, the concordance rates are relatively low even for identicals. It's just that they are *much* lower for fraternals. As a result of that big difference—remember, we double that difference—the heritability is relatively high. Thus, while the illness so defined is relatively rare, the genetic contribution to the *vulnerability*—the heritability of that rare disorder—is relatively great. In one study of depression, for example, the concordance rate for identicals was 66 percent when the criteria were broad, but 46 percent when the criteria were narrow. The corresponding figures for fraternals were 42 and 20 percent. With the broad criteria, heritability was only 39 percent—with narrow criteria, a whopping 79 percent. The principle is clear: All heritability estimates depend on how a trait or illness is measured.

Suicidal Potential: How Heritable Is It?

Among identical twins who commit suicide, roughly 15 percent of their co-twins also eventually kill themselves, which is at least 800 percent higher than the 1 to 2 percent for fraternal twins. It is this *difference*, not the size of each percentage, that really matters. Apparently, then, a vulnerability to suicide requires a rare combination of genes that only identicals share.

Among adoptively reared people who eventually commit suicide, suicide rates are elevated in their biological relatives, but not in their adoptive relatives. This observation, like the difference in concordance rates for identical and fraternal twins, suggests a genetic vulnerability. Then what about the connection between suicide and mental illness, especially the depressive kind? Is the heritability of suicide merely in its link with depression, or does it reflect a distinct, genetically influenced vulnerability? What if indeed there are two separate vulnerabilities, with one peculiarly suited to unlocking the other?

Suicide and depressive illness run together in families, as is evident in the Old Order Amish community of Pennsylvania, where 73 percent of the suicides have come from just four pedigrees, or connected families. Over many generations, 24 out of 26 suicides have clearly been associated with depressive disorder. This familial connection between depression and suicide is evident in the diagram on the next page. In this family tree, squares represent males, circles females. A horizontal line connecting them represents a marriage, and each of the five rows of circles and squares represents a generation.

Depressive illness and suicide are generally as closely related as the diagram suggests. Therefore, it stands to reason that the genetic factor in suicide is nothing more than the genetic factor in depression. Yet, consider the implications of the following observations.

While depressive illness may often be experienced before a suicide, suicide is committed by relatively few patients with depressive illness—at most 20 percent, according to most studies, but maybe somewhat higher, if the Amish data suggesting 33 percent (7 suicides out of 22 cases of depression) are any clue. What's the missing factor that explains why most severely depressed people *don't* commit suicide?

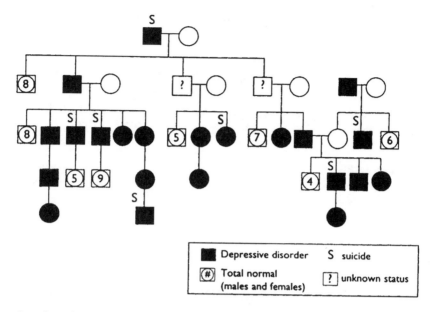

Suicide and affective disorder in an Old-Order Amish family (five generations).

It is not just the most seriously depressed people who kill themselves, for suicide is relatively frequent not just for people with depression, but for schizophrenics, sociopaths, and emotionally volatile people whose major psychiatric problem is confused thinking, frustration, and anger. For them, depression is no more powerful an element—and sometimes is relatively less powerful—than the depression of those with depressive illness. Apparently, there is more to suicide than just depression.

When *matched in mental health or illness* with the relatives of nonsuicides, the relatives of suicide victims still have an elevated rate of suicide. Again, it appears that there is something more to suicide than just severe depression or some other psychiatric disorder—that a suicidal disposition is genetically distinct from vulnerability to other psychiatric conditions. But how so?

One element of that disposition may be a variant of a gene that alters the availability of the neurotransmitter serotonin. A study of depressed people who had made numerous suicide attempts showed they were more likely (41 percent) to have the rare U form of the gene, compared to *equally depressed* people who displayed the same severity, same amount of suicidal thinking, and same number of past episodes of depression, but who had never tried to kill themselves (20 percent).

As for schizophrenic and sociopathic adoptees who commit suicide, it is their biological, not adoptive, relatives who also have elevated rates of suicide. This last observation suggests there may be something genetic about the suicide potential itself—that it need not be merely a matter of depression. Somerset Maugham once spoke about the pain and fear suffered silently by certain "people who seem in the best of health, prosperous, without any worry, and yet they are tortured by it." And he continued, "I've sometimes thought [this fear of life] was the most besetting humour of men, and I asked myself at one time if it was due to some deep animal instinct that man has inherited from that primeval something that first felt the thrill of life."

Depression, even more than other mental illness, may be an especially effective key to unlocking a distinct genetic vulnerability to suicide. Yet other keys include traits associated with nondepressive psychiatric disorders, the frustrations and impulsiveness of youth, or the hopelessness of old age. No surprise if such characteristics cause suicide more frequently when affected individuals feel put upon or are troubled by the consequences of drug abuse or soured relationships.

Vulnerability and Creativity: Is There a Genetic Connection?

We have looked at genetic influence on intelligence, personality, and vulnerability, but what about their connection, say, in certain forms of creative achievement? Aristotle noted a tendency toward madness in men of letters, politics, and the arts, but is there much truth to such observations, given the strong counterarguments? For example, the essayist Charles Lamb observed: "So far from the position holding true, that great wit (or genius, our modern way of speaking) has a necessary alliance with insanity, the greatest wits, on the contrary, will ever be found to be the sanest writers. It is impossible for the mind to conceive of a mad Shakespeare." And Lamb continues, "the ground of the mistake is that men, finding in the raptures of the higher poetry a condition of exaltation, to which they have no parallel in their own experience, besides the spurious resemblance of it in dreams and fevers, impute a state of dreaminess and fever to the poet. But the true poet dreams being awake. He is not possessed by his subject, but has dominion over it."

How can the connection between creativity and vulnerability be resolved, given our uncertainty about how to measure creativity? Should greatest emphasis be placed on original or beautiful works or on those ideas no one has thought of? Does creative thinking reflect, or at least sometimes get boosted by, a potential for mental illness? Schizophrenic tendencies, for example, can mean unconventional, even playful thinking. Manic tendencies can mean energetic, expansive, self-confident thinking. Both represent a loosening of mental inhibitions, with associations more plentiful and imagery more intense. With both come a chaotic richness, exuberant fertility, and playfulness of mind not otherwise possible. Is this what creativity is all about?

According to psychologists Philip Jackson and Samuel Messick, true creativity involves something more than being clever and inventive, novel and original. Creativity is also *apposite*, meaning so appropriate, so fitting, so truthful, that it has the handprint of necessity. It is also *transformative*, meaning that it forces a new, unconventional view eliciting not so much surprise and laughter as reflection and wonder. Finally, creativity is *poetic*, meaning that it expresses ideas in an especially concentrated, imaginative, and powerful way. In short, the highest forms of creativity have enduring truthfulness and engaging power that neither stems from nor depends on vulnerability but can surely be alloyed with it. As England's great literary critic Samuel Johnson put it: "The irregular combinations of fanciful invention may delight a-while, by that novelty of which the common satiety of life sends us all in quests; but the pleasures of sudden wonder are soon exhausted, and the mind can only repose on the stability of truth."

The enduring truthfulness and engaging power of true creativity require specialized talent, fine intellect, unerring instinct, good judgment, and a disciplined attitude—not often found with mental illness. Yet, combine these qualities with extreme sensitivity, strange originality, moody temperament, or ruthless egocentricity and perhaps an element of alcohol or other drugs, and what then? Possibly a creativity that goes beyond the classic type to something romantic with a special appeal and impact: the legacy of a poet like Lord Byron or Coleridge, a writer like Goethe or Hemingway, a composer like Tchaikovsky or Rachmaninoff, or a painter like Modigliani or Pollack. More vividly, philosopher-psychologist William James put it this way: "Borderline insanity, crankiness, insane temperament, loss of mental balance, psychopathic degeneration . . . when combined with superior quality of intellect in an individual make it more probable that he will make his mark and affect his age, than if his temperament were less neurotic."

Mood swings and inner conflict can mobilize talent through heightened consciousness, focused attention, poignant memories, and vivid imagery. All these enrich and enliven experience, causing a creative tension between a tortured soul and a gifted mind. Vulnerability can thus be both a blessing and a curse: a blessing when moderate doses energize and inform talent, but a curse when frank mental illness subverts it. Creative people with psychiatric problems often seem at once in touch and out of touch with social and physical reality. They are both insightful and irrational, right on and far out, realistic and dreamy, objective and egocentric. Compared to their less gifted and less troubled counterparts, they will be both in control and out of control, focused and diffuse, wise and immoral. On psychological tests, they display, on the one hand, industry, resiliency, and adaptability, but on the other, sensitivity, moodiness, or even craziness from an excess of associations and idiosyncratic ideas. A study of writers found that, compared to a representative group, the creative group showed high levels of ego strength and intellectual efficiency, but also symptoms of hysteria, anxiety, depression, and schizophrenia.

Ideally, great talent may transform the psychopathology that hobbles the spirit into a divine madness that liberates it. Much is in the balance, for it all depends on which part of the creative process dominates at any particular time, the talent or the vulnerability. The parts interact, each influencing the other, for better or for worse and often in unpredictable ways. In this admittedly speculative view, creativity influences vulnerability, palliating it with enhanced self-esteem from high achievement, but also intensifying it with the distress that comes from a compulsive commitment and the threat of failure. Creative people often work in self-imposed, self-centered isolation. Even when such single-minded, highly personal activity goes well, the work is intellectually taxing and emotionally frustrating.

Then how close are creativity and vulnerability? Given the observations just noted, the connection would seem clearest for gifted people in art, music, and literature. No surprise, then, that up to 70 percent of artists, writers, and poets surveyed have been found in several family studies to suffer major depressions, manic depressions, severe mood swings, and alcoholism, and to have an elevated risk for suicide.

In some fields of creative endeavor, the connection between nuttiness and genius is more likely. Yet most mentally ill people are not creative and most creative people are not mentally ill. If creative achievement occurs despite rather than because of emotional disorder, then we may agree with psychologist Robert Prentky, who suggests that without disorder, "more notables might have been paragons and paragons might have been demigods."

Whatever the creativity-vulnerability connection, could it have a genetic basis? The idea is as reasonable as the evidence is sparse and tentative, though we might note, with congressional librarian James Billington, that tentative answers to important questions are better than definitive answers to trivial ones. One study found excess depression, mood swings, alcohol problems, and personality disorders in the biological, but not adoptive, relatives of creative adoptees. Another found an excess of such disorders in creative adoptees and their biological parents, but not in noncreative adoptees and *their* biological parents. Also, there was no relation between the adoptees' creativity and their adoptive parents' mental health, meaning that creativity and mental illness seem to go together for genetic rather than social reasons.

Psychiatrist Leonard Heston's classic adoption study of schizophrenia also suggests a genetic connection between creativity and mental illness, but in a different way. In 1966, he reported that of 47 adopted offspring each born to a woman with schizophrenia, 5 eventually succumbed to the illness. In contrast, of 50 adopted offspring each born to a woman without schizophrenia, none ever succumbed. This difference strongly suggested a genetic cause in schizophrenia, yet there was something else. While some of the genetically vulnerable offspring were more often antisocial and neurotic as well as schizophrenic, some also seemed more spontaneous, colorful, and creative, with more interesting hobbies involving arts, crafts, and music. Apparently, the singular combination of intelligence, personality, and vulnerability evident in many creative people has a genetic basis, though its strength has yet to be estimated.

Chapter Nine

Conduct and Character

If it be not to come, it will be now; if it be not now, yet it will come; the readiness is all.

—*William Shakespeare*

Mary Shelley's gothic tale *Frankenstein, or the Modern Prometheus* shows how even the noblest individual can be damaged by unremittingly hostile and arbitrary conditions. The stunning eloquence of Shelley's tragic creature bears ironic testimony to a great soul's malignant transformation by cruel rejection, first by his creator and then by others whose emotional comfort and intellectual camaraderie he craved.

> *Once my fancy was soothed with dreams of virtue, of fame, and of enjoyment. Once I falsely hoped to meet with beings, who, pardoning my outward form, would love me for the excellent qualities which I was capable of bringing forth. I was nourished with high thoughts of honor and devotion. But now vice has degraded me beneath the meanest animal. . . . When I call over the frightful catalogue of my deeds, I cannot believe that I am he whose thoughts were once filled with sublime and transcendent visions of the beauty and the majesty of goodness. But it is even so; the fallen angel becomes a malignant devil. Yet even that enemy of God and man has friends and associates in his desolation; I am quite alone.*

The original tale gets perverted in the classic 1931 film version starring Boris Karloff. Shelley's creature received a normal brain with high intelligence and decent sentiments, making his monstrousness an artifact of a cruel society that cannot get past superficial appearance to the underlying goodness; he is a true victim whose malignant transformation is tragic. In contrast, Karloff's monster has received an abnormal brain with subnormal intelligence and antisocial sentiments, making *his* monstrousness inborn. He may be piteous, but he is no tragic figure, for he is as much a psychopath as a victim; his monstrousness is as inherent as it is acquired from a cruel society that recognizes in superficial appearances an underlying evil.

In Shelley's creature abuse and rejection—the crippling effects of rearing and social influence—create monstrousness where there was none before, while in Karloff's monster, they merely reinforce monstrousness that was already there. The difference is critical, for in only the former case can the social environment, including parents, be unequivocally blamed. In short, blaming the parents implies something more than evidence of what they have done. It implies a theory about the offspring who have been done to and done in—whether that offspring is more a Shelleyan creature or more a Karloffian monster.

Heart of Darkness: It *Is* a Jungle Out There

In 1992, a conference on genetic aspects of crime was scheduled, then canceled, by the National Institutes of Health. The immediate cause of the cancellation was a sociopolitical firestorm caused by remarks made by noted psychiatric researcher Frederick Goodwin, whose book (with Kay Jamison) on manic-depression has become a psychiatric classic and whose research suggested that among monkeys and chimpanzees, it is the relatively few genetically disposed males who cause much of the murder and mayhem in the wild. Does this idea apply to human society?

The elements of our antisocial potential—the impulsivity, egocentricity, selfishness, dishonesty, and ruthlessness—can run amok, as illuminated in *Lord of the Flies*. In William Golding's visionary story, English schoolboys stranded on an island revert to barbarism and predatory violence. When stripped of the civilizing forces of community and family, even nice little rich kids can become monsters. Peter Brook, director of the movie adaptation, was struck by the book's reality when his child actors, readily identifying with the story, were reverting to coalition and conflict. His impression was that the reversion described by Golding to have taken weeks or months would have actually taken days.

Something dark exists in the heart of human nature. Theologians speak of original sin, historians of constant warfare, philosophers of brutish willfulness, and naturalists of a nasty simian streak. Following St. Augustine, the sixth-century pope Gregory the Great argued that the tragedy of human experience is original sin from which come wicked inclinations in human nature. A more contemporary Will Durant wrote, "If one follows [human] nature and acts naturally he is much more likely to murder and eat his enemies than to practice philosophy; there is small chance of his being humble, and less of his being silent."

Political philosophers have offered similar observations. Seneca, stoic philosopher of ancient Rome, once offered this ironic comment: "I come home more greedy, more cruel and inhuman, because I have been among human beings." Renaissance philosopher Machiavelli wrote that "all men are bad and ever ready to display their vicious nature whenever they find occasion for it. If their evil disposition remains concealed for a time, it must be attributed to some unknown reason; and we must assume that it lacked occasion to show itself; but time . . . does not fail to bring it to light. . . ." More recently, James Burnham argued, "Men are driven chiefly by profound non-rational, often anti-rational, sentiments and impulses, whose character and very existence are not ordinarily understood by conscious reason. Many of these drives are aggressive, disruptive, and injurious to others and to society. Some . . . are destructive to the self: seeking pain and suffering, even death." Furthermore, he says, "only those who know very little about the history of mankind can suppose that cruelty, crime or weakness, mass slaughter or mass corruption, are exceptions from the normal human rule." Are such perennially gloomy visions scientifically justifiable? An answer starts with our nearest biological neighbors, the chimps.

Genetic overlap between the chimps and us is 98.4 percent, which is even more than the 98 percent overlap between chimps and gorillas. Such genetic overlap likely explains a lot: our curiosity, playfulness, and cleverness, but also our penchant for deception, aggressiveness, war—even genocide. Primate deception, for example, is well documented, as in pretended disinterest in some area discovered to contain food. In a creature with rudimentary language capability, it is a small evolutionary step from deception to lying, as is evident in this example from a chimpanzee named Lucy, who has learned to communicate with American Sign Language. Asked about a pile of chimp excrement on the living room floor, Lucy initially signs that she doesn't know what it is. Then, admitting that it is dirty, she blames one of her caretakers, Sue. When challenged, she blames Roger. Challenged again, she finally admits, "Lucy dirty, dirty. Sorry Lucy."

Innocent enough, yet chimps in the wild also delight in hunting down and killing hapless prey, for instance, a colobus monkey or an isolated chimp from another group. Anthropologist Craig Stanford describes how one skillful hunter devoured an infant monkey snatched from its frantic mother who was soon caught by other chimps and killed. The kill was just one detail of harrowing slaughter that occurred in Tanzania's Gombe National Park. A band of 30 chimps came across the troop of colobus monkeys Stanford was studying. During 4 hours of carnage, monkeys were torn apart and eaten. From the monkeys' perspective, it was devastating. It has been said men go to war because the women are watching. No doubt this oversimplifies a complex biological and social question. Nevertheless, Stanford says, the single best predictor of when chimps will hunt the colobus is the presence of at least one female with a swollen red rump signifying sexual receptivity.

Naturalist Jane Goodall has described cruel territorial wars in which one chimp community annihilates another. Bands of males will attack any hapless male or female of the other territory regardless of cries or struggle. Bitten and battered sometimes to insensibility, the maimed victims often die. Goodall points out that such murderous behavior is not the usual expression of territorial imperative, whereby animals clash but give way without inflicting or suffering mortal wounds. With chimps, territorial trespasser chimps are not just chased. They are caught and brutalized when not killed outright.

Chimps attack trespassers. They also raid neighboring territories, wreaking havoc when they can get away with it. One has the impression that were the chimps equipped with firearms they would readily kill off their enemies, and with relish. According to Goodall, "The chimp has clearly reached a stage where he stands at the very threshold of human achievement in destruction, cruelty, and planned intergroup conflict. If ever he develops the power of language—and . . . he stands close to that threshold, too—might he not push open the door and wage war with the best of us?"

Is there not something strangely familiar in the territorial, warlike, and genocidal behaviors of the chimps? "Let's face it," says psychologist Del Thiessen: "criminal-like behaviors could have been adaptive a million or so years ago, leaving us an ugly legacy. Male competition for social status and access to females was a particularly strong selective pressure for any behaviors of 'one-upmanship,' including aggression, oppression of others, murder, infanticide, and rape. Deception, cheating, nepotistic biases, paranoia, and conflicts with strangers added to our repertoire of offensive and defensive acts. Those behaviors were not called criminal among our hominid brothers and sisters; there were simply gene-survival devices. Today, when these behaviors disrupt our cultural system we call them antisocial or criminal behaviors. . . ."

Parenting, Poverty, and Antisocial Behavior

Many people believe that the root cause of crime is poverty. Poverty may be an excuse, but it is not a root cause. No, the root cause of crime is antisocial instinct and inadequate character nurtured by the moral deficiencies of families and society, all of which may, but need not, connect to poverty.

The poverty-crime connection, like any correlation, is fundamentally ambiguous. It has been argued that poverty frequently *causes* bad parenting, when often both poverty and bad parenting are the *common effects* of relatively strong antisocial instincts, poor judgment, and inadequate self-control. Poverty does not so much cause as facilitate and excuse antisocial ways. Arguing from a sociological perspective that poverty is the root cause of crime merely enables psychopaths and criminals to fulfill their antisocial potentials at others' expense, while allowing them to rationalize uncivilized conduct as the effect of circumstances imposed on innocent victims. It does not answer why, during periods of economic weakness and declining income, crime rates have often decreased while during periods of economic growth and increasing income they have often increased—and why, after declining for 30 years from 50 percent in 1940 to 15 percent in 1970, poverty has been relatively steady while crime has increased.

It would seem that the level of crime in a society has less to do with poverty than with character and decency reinforced by the civilizing influences of citizenship, marriage, and parenthood. The notion that poverty is the root cause of crime is a simplistic though appealing solution that confuses rather than illuminates a complex problem. The poverty-as-root-cause notion also does not explain why an inner-city boy from a single-parent home is twice as likely to commit crimes as an equally poor boy from a two-parent family. Rather it suggests that poverty can be the *consequence* of crime—the consequence of an early commitment to a life of crime and a neglect of education.

Poor people are mostly decent and law abiding; even during the Great Depression, most didn't revert to antisocial behavior. Many luminaries of science, literature, religion, politics—Copernicus, Gauss, Dickens, Luther, Lincoln, Hoover—grew up in impoverished conditions that were often abject and sometimes cruel. Pulitzer Prize winner James Michener described "how difficult and sometimes cruel life in America can be, for I was born a foundling, reared in genteel poverty, and was occasionally brought to the poorhouse when family funds diminished. My life till age 14 was a struggle with deprivation, and when I had worked my way out of poverty—I was constantly employed from age 11—I was faced by the Great Depression and World War II." The crime problem, according to Michener, is not so much about poverty of circumstances but poverty of character.

Professor Robert Hutchins tells about growing up poor. "In those far off days, ownership of an automobile showed you were rich, and not merely that you had a job. . . . In my home town there was only one boy whose father had one. He was a race apart. This was before radio, before television, almost before the movies, and not long after the phonograph and the telephone. (I never make a long-distance call now without looking over my shoulder to see whether somebody is watching, because I was brought up to believe it was a shameful extravagance. As the first John D. Rockefeller used to say to his children, 'A two-cent stamp is enough.') We had nowhere to go and no way to get there. . . . We had been granted the precious gift of poverty. Of course we didn't know we were poor because everybody was in the same situation, except the boy whose father owned the automobile. Because we were poor, we had to resort to 'fun' that didn't cost much," which, Hutchins tells us, meant reading everything he could possibly get his hands on. "Gradually I came to have some understanding of the difference between a good book and a poor one."

It was the same for the celebrated physicist Richard Feynman. In Feynman's Far Rockaway neighborhood, says author James Gleik, "was a consistency of belief and behavior. To be honest, to be principled, to study, to save money against hard times—the rules were not so much taught as assumed. Everyone worked hard. There was no sense of poverty—certainly in Feynman's family, though later he realized that two families had shared one house because neither could get by alone. 'But now I realize that everybody was struggling like mad. Everybody was struggling and it didn't seem like a struggle.' For children, life in such neighborhoods brought a rare childhood combination of freedom and moral rigor."

"The students who first made City College [CCNY] great during the early twentieth century," says City University of New York (CUNY) lecturer Robert Berman, "lived in crushing poverty in teeming, Lower East Side tenements, with parents who worked in sweat shops, or who during the Great Depression had no unemployment insurance, welfare Medicaid, WIC, or food stamp programs to soften the blows of long-term unemployment. And although before 1976 attendance at CUNY was free, students then received no financial aid." What was the result of all this economic poverty? Extraordinary academic and later social and intellectual achievement, including eight Nobel winners, more than for Harvard College or any other American undergraduate institution.

That poverty isn't the root cause of antisocial behavior is as empirical as anecdotal. A study of 397 males at risk for antisocial behavior was reported in 1966. In one group were people with a history of neurological problems and with parents who were psychologically disturbed but not poor. In a second group were people with a history of neurological problems only— no poverty or parental psychopathology. In a third group were people who grew up in impoverished conditions with social, economic, educational, and employment problems, but without neurological problems or disturbed parents. Those in the first group, those with a history of neurological problems and reared by disturbed parents, had over 2 times more criminal activity than the others. Those reared in poverty had the *lowest* crime rate of the three groups. As the researchers noted, their findings challenge the conventional notion that poverty is the root cause of a criminal lifestyle, and that the implied stigmatization of the poor, even if unintended, is unjustified.

Another reason to reject the poverty-as-root-cause argument, one that raises questions about parental influence more generally, is the dramatic sibling differences within the same family. Despite growing up with the same advantages or disadvantages, one sibling may turn out antisocial, as one—the least intelligent, the most hot-tempered—may lose ground socioeconomically. Psychologist Stanton Samenow tells of a young man who dealt drugs and whose father was an alcoholic tenant farmer. This man grew up poor, hungry, raggedy, and shamed by well-off peers. Yet only he of his eight siblings had turned to a life of crime and drug use. Of the others all had jobs and some were supporting families.

To submit that poverty is the root cause of crime evinces an inadequate appreciation of roots, of causality, and of crime. Biological variation can explain cruel indifference, antisocial behavior, and a criminal lifestyle— why even good families with decent parents can spawn a psychopath, a pervert, a mass murderer, for reasons out of a parent's control. In short, the crime problem cannot be *solely* a family matter, for biological variation within a family also matters.

Second, while bad parenting promotes antisocial behavior and uncivilized conduct, good parenting promotes—though it cannot guarantee—positive sentiments and civilized conduct. It is nothing more than simple-minded to assert that "people perform up—or down—to the expectations of those around them. We become what they think we are." Expectations may have some effect, but more on some kids and less on others; on some they will have just about no effect. Clearly, scientific answers are needed about how powerful is the effect of expectations, and on whom is the influence the greatest.

While some parents have strong expectations right from the beginning and regardless of a child's personality and behavior, expectations are as likely to reflect what the child's personality and behavior already have become. An irresponsible, antisocial, or unintelligent child is likely to create negative expectations in others. It is only natural, and blaming the parents for self-centered or otherwise inadequate ways merely fits in with an equally natural need to blame something external—anything, and why not parental expectations? A child's resentment of negative expectations always goes along with a lack of reflection on how much the self is responsible, but this resentment is a separate question from the one about how much those expectations influence not so much situational emotions but psychological development.

Just how much, then, do modifiable differences in parenting really matter? Only to that extent is there hope to improve children's social behavior by changing a parent's behavior. Social science findings, as one magazine article put it, are still a little fuzzy when it comes to answers. Well, they are more than a little fuzzy, for they can say nothing definitive about genetic or even environmental causality.

A Look at the Really Bad Guys

Why do families occasionally fail the awesome task of socializing and civilizing children? One answer is the parents or society; another is the child. Both are suspect, but the problem child is the more interesting, for despite having even the best of parents, some children seem to lack a psychological enzyme necessary for digesting the civilizing influences of family and society. That deficit, involving certain neurotransmitters, such as norepinephrine, and related enzymes, such as DBH, could explain the anxiety-free, predatory or the highly reactive, irritable child who is a candidate for aggressive and antisocial behavior. Does exceptional fearlessness stem from deficiencies of a norepinephrine mechanism?

Developmental psychologist Jerome Kagan found a strong connection between abnormal brain chemistry and conduct problems in boys. The difference implies that low norepinephrine levels means minimal apprehension about violating social standards. Since DBH is genetically controlled, it is likely that abnormal brain chemistry could explain the apparent fearlessness and manifest recklessness of extremely antisocial boys.

Failing to learn from the negative consequences of their acts, some individuals engage in antisocial behaviors that defy sociological explanation. But the problem is not just the antisocial behavior of criminals brutally reared and thriving in poor neighborhoods; it is also the antisocial behavior of sophisticated criminals lovingly reared with all the advantages of decent parents, good families, and safe neighborhoods. The worst are the mass murderers like Ted Bundy, and Kenneth Bianchi, the Hillside Strangler, of whom clinical psychologist Margaret Singer once opined: they are simply evil. In like manner, does Shakespeare's mystical character Prospero comment on the creature Caliban:

> *A devil, a born devil, on whose nature*
> *Nurture can never stick; on whom my pains,*
> *Humanely taken, all, all lost, quite lost. . . .*

The public is increasingly aware of the problem, for example, as illustrated by killer-kids. Forensic psychologist Helen Smith criticizes that society for looking not to the real root causes, but to everyone and everything else: the movies or the Internet for suggesting psychopathic scenarios, gun availability for making crimes more likely and heinous, immoral rock and roll music or rap. No, says Smith, "These are not normal, healthy teen-agers. They become killers because they are already deeply disturbed individuals who can be sent over the brink by all sorts of innocuous influences. (Charles Manson, after all, claimed to find inspiration for his crimes in a Beatles song.) It is not the ordinary kids who kill. It is usually those with subpar intelligence, mental disorders, and a history of cruelty to animals and siblings."

What then are the telltale behaviors and traits of those who are most disposed to criminal activity? Antisocial people are given to theft, vandalism, and pathological lying. They are deceitful, reckless, cruel to animals, irresponsible, and physically aggressive. Their hot-blooded traits include emotional volatility, impulsive behavior, and low frustration tolerance. Their cold-blooded (psychopathic) traits include a lack of anxiety, remorse, or guilt, and a lack of empathy. Though often superficially charming, antisocial people are egocentric and callously indifferent. For many reasons, they are unable or unwilling to follow rules, be controlled by others, or formulate realistic long-term plans. If such antisocial qualities are rooted in the variable genes of our species, they ought to be heritable.

Antisocial Personality: How Heritable Is It?

The best evidence of heritability in antisocial potential comes from studying twins and adoptees. Psychiatrist Raymond Crowe compared the arrest and incarceration records of two groups of adoptees. The high-risk adoptees were the offspring of female criminals with felony arrests for forgery, assault, breaking and entering, or prostitution. The low-risk adoptees were the offspring of noncriminal females. The two groups of offspring were comparable in age, sex, race, and age of adoption. Still, the high-risk adoptees were more likely to have been arrested (15 versus 2 percent), convicted (13 versus 1 percent), and incarcerated (10 versus 0 percent); they were also more likely to have a diagnosis of antisocial personality.

Here is the key to understanding two essential points: one, that the children of antisocial parents have a markedly elevated rate of conduct problems including troublesome antisocial behavior; and two, that the children of parents with other kinds of problems, for example depression or anxiety, have problems like their parents', yet a low rate of conduct problems and antisocial behavior. In short, parental antisocial personality and behavior correlate with offsprings' antisocial personality and behavior, not just maladjustment. Something specific is transmitted, but what?

Adoption studies offer a clear answer: a highly heritable vulnerability that *in some children* is so strong as to break through social constraints. Crowe's investigation surely says this, and other findings reinforce the idea. One study looked at 37 parents with 12-year-old adopted boys and girls diagnosed with an aggressive conduct disorder. Of the biological parents of these children, 30 percent had antisocial personality disorder; of the adoptive parents, none did. That 30-percent figure for the biological parents is virtually the same as what social science studies find for aggressive children and their parents. The 30-percent risk for the children of antisocials comes through regardless of whether they are reared by their antisocial parent or by normal adoptive parents. Apparently, the 30 percent represents those with the highest dose of a heritable vulnerability.

Psychologist Sarnoff Medick reported that in male adoptees the conviction rate for property crimes depends on convictions recorded for the biological parent. The more such convictions the parent has, the more likely the adopted-away son will have at least one conviction as well: 10 percent when the biological parent had no convictions, 12 percent when the biological parent had one conviction, 15 percent when biological parent had two convictions, and over 20 percent when the biological parent had three or more convictions. No such correlation was found for the adoptees and their adoptive parents. Apparently, what an uncivilized environment may produce despite normal genes, abnormal genes may create despite a normal environment.

Now, while some children are predisposed, others may be *counter-disposed*, or biologically insensitive, to the influence of antisocial rearing. Consider the biological sons of a criminal father who themselves may become criminal or remain law-abiding. Compared to the criminal sons, the law-abiding sons display a remarkable physiological pattern involving heart rate and the skin conductance of electrical signals. Apparently, the law-abiding sons are biologically resistant even to the influence of antisocial parenting, as if they had been inoculated against a communicable disease.

On average, however, adoptees born to antisocials do tend to have a higher rate of criminal activity (roughly 25 percent) than do adoptees born to normals (less than 15 percent). What then of adoptees with two strikes against them: those born to an adult with a criminal record and reared in troubled or otherwise disadvantaged conditions? These adoptees have even higher rates of antisocial or criminal behavior than would be expected from simply adding genetic and environmental influence.

This multiplicative rather than merely additive combination was found in a study of petty crime, such as nonviolent acts involving property. Of adoptees born to parents with no criminal record, just a small percentage had criminal records: 3 percent for those reared in normal adoptive homes and 7 percent for those reared in troubled homes. Of adoptees with a criminal birth parent, a larger percentage had a criminal record: 12 percent if reared in normal adoptive settings but 40 percent if reared in troubled settings. It would seem that bad genes and bad environments constitute a double whammy of interacting influences that can multiply risk.

These findings gain support from research on twins. According to 10

American and European studies, concordance in criminality—the percentage of adult twin pairs where both twins are criminals—is greater for identicals (51 percent) than for fraternals (21 percent). These findings are confirmed by an unusual study of eight adoptee-identicals, each with a criminal record. Four, or 50 percent, had a reared-apart co-twin who also had a criminal record. Taken together, twin studies suggest substantial genetic influence—a heritability of between 30 and 50 percent—that helps determine who is at greatest risk for achieving a criminal career, whatever the overall crime rate.

Compared to antisocial personality and career criminality, juvenile delinquency seems genetically less determined. In one study, the correlation for self-reported delinquent acts was 62 for identicals and 52 for fraternals, which is not much of a difference. So too with concordance rates: Pooled results for seven twin studies of juvenile delinquency yield 84 percent for identicals, 69 percent for fraternals—again, not a large difference. Apparently, many juvenile delinquents respond to sibling and peer pressure more than to parental authority. Delinquent behavior in adolescence may also express in unrestrained group activity the natural potential for conformity and aggregation that Golding so memorably dramatized in *Lord of the Flies*.

Juvenile delinquency aside, to assume that antisocial potential is heritable is not to deny environmental influence. Rather it is to recognize that environmental influence is only part of the reason for individual differences. Likewise, to assume that such differences are heritable does not deny that changing social conditions can influence the overall rate of criminal behavior. Finally, to assume that differences in antisocial potential are heritable does not deny that, *within families*, the quality of parenting can influence the overall rate of siblings' antisocial behavior.

How Does IQ Fit In?

Criminals generally have significantly lower IQs than their noncriminal siblings and peers. The evidence, summarized by psychologist Arthur Jensen, is as follows. First, delinquents who go on to become career criminals also average about 10 to 12 IQ points lower than law-abiding people in the same neighborhoods. Second, recidivists have lower IQs than one-time offenders, while those who manage not to become criminal have higher IQs, suggesting that relatively high IQ is a protective factor.

Finally, the most serious crimes against persons—rape, robbery, assault—are committed by males in the IQ range of 70 to 100, the peak rate occurring in the 80 to 90 range.

Whatever else promotes criminal behavior, IQ is clearly a risk factor. Furthermore, IQ is a greater risk factor than socioeconomic status, for when IQ is controlled—comparing people of the same IQ—there is little correlation between socioeconomic status and criminal behavior. Apparently, IQ is the more fundamental variable. Low IQ could reflect impulsivity, failure, and consequent low self-esteem. It could mean poor judgment and the greater ability to be led astray, or it could reflect a limited time horizon, which means poor foresight. Finally, it could imply an inability to reason morally, to recognize the adverse consequences of acts and how these harm innocent people.

Of course, an IQ estimate of intelligence doesn't measure all useful and desirable qualities, such as creativity and special talents. It doesn't tell us who is more conscientious, who shows more social adroitness or sheer energy and dogged persistence, and who is more dependable, charming, emotionally stable. Nevertheless, evidence from sociology to biology shows that IQ does estimate very well the capacities for analysis, reason, and good judgment. As two social scientists noted, "we know that many important tasks in life must be done by people with high intelligence. We know, for example, that we want the engineer who designs the plane we fly, or the pathologist who examines our biopsy tissue, to be a person with the analytic qualities that produce high IQ scores—and to hell with his interpersonal skills."

Relatively low intelligence, especially the verbal kind, goes with antisocial behavior regardless of rearing and socioeconomic status. Compared to their noncriminal siblings and peers, even middle-class adolescents with above-average IQs but who commit criminal acts have lower IQs than their siblings—about 10 to 12 IQ points less. Not surprisingly, they are worse at reading, spelling, listening, writing, remembering, planning, and controlling their impulses. All this is painfully evident in a letter written by a distressed school teacher regarding her psychopathic son. "He is inarticulate and quarrels quickly and finds fault. He writes like a child and misspells words." An antisocial sibling's *relatively* low verbal intelligence could indicate some neurological abnormality that compromises the functioning of an otherwise normal brain. This can explain even a bright antisocial's deficient reflection on the meaning and consequences of his actions.

Then how does relatively low intelligence elevate the risk for antisocial and criminal behavior? Social scientists have suggested four possibilities. One is failure and frustration in school and in the job market. Another is lack of foresight or ability to anticipate negative consequences when seeking immediate gratification. A third is an inability to recognize or be impressed by moral considerations that normally inhibit selfish instincts and appetites. A fourth is a callous disregard for others and an appetite for dangerous adventure. All of these plus low cunning—an ability to psyche out, exploit, and undermine a victim and all without guilt or remorse—will limit parental influence on such a person's social behavior.

The IQ-crime connection has an unusual aspect. In the 1960s and 1970s, the public's interest was stirred by a flurry of media stories about how inheriting an extra Y chromosome seems to make men even more prone to aggressiveness. One article described XYY men as supermales inclined toward aggression and mayhem. Yet this view was mostly anecdotal, based on isolated cases of violence in XYY males that proved the exception to a rule. Fueling speculation was the incorrect rumor that mass murderer Richard Speck was one of those XYY supermales.

One fact was correct—XYY men are indeed overrepresented in penal institutions—but their crimes are typically petty rather than violent. In one case, an XYY man committed two thefts for which the penalties were mild. In another, a career criminal spent many years in and out of prisons for burglary, embezzlement, and procuring for prostitution. One incidence of relatively mild aggression against someone else was noted. The cases show a surprising lack of violence for men so disposed to criminal behavior. In short, low intelligence and poor judgment appear to explain the elevated rate of criminal convictions found for men with an extra Y chromosome.

Given its rarity of 1 in 1,000 births, XYY obviously cannot contribute much to the crime problem. Yet the poor judgment it creates is the very model of an antisocial trait that *does* contribute mightily to the crime problem.

Hyperactivity, Psychosis, and Antisocial Behavior

The genetic potential for criminal behavior is marked by an antisocial temperament and by distractibility, impulsivity, and hyperactivity. Until recently, this triad was commonly called hyperactivity syndrome, but it is now known as attention-deficit/hyperactivity disorder (ADHD). In about 70 percent of clinic-referred cases, ADHD comes with conduct problems, including recklessness, explosive temper, incorrigibility, stealing, and pathological lying. Children with this kind of hyperactivity have a high risk of abusing drugs and committing crimes.

ADHD children are also at higher risk for becoming troubled adults. As one expert has observed, "The classic picture of the overactive and impulsive child often gives way to the disorganized and impulsive adult who suffers not only from academic and vocational underachievement, but also from troubled relationships. Those with ADHD bear the consternation of others for irresponsible behavior, angry outbursts, social faux pas, and missed appointments. As well, they often cause others to be impatient and irritable. These individuals are at markedly higher risk for serious antisocial behavior, depression, suicide, substance abuse, and for maltreatment of their own children and spouses."

ADHD can be viewed as a behavioral expression of antisocial tendencies, which would explain why many antisocials are diagnosed with ADHD. Or, as a distinctly separate abnormality, ADHD may be seen as reinforcing antisocial tendencies, which is why, without those tendencies, ADHD may not promote antisocial behavior.

ADHD has a strong genetic basis, so its connection to antisocial behavior further reinforces the latter's biological roots. First-degree relatives of people with ADHD are 5 times more likely than others to be similarly diagnosed. The offspring of adults diagnosed with ADHD are at special great risk, with an almost 60 percent rate found in one study. The biological (but not adoptive) fathers of hyperactive children are at least twice as likely to be hyperactive and alcoholic as the biological fathers of control children. The biological fathers are also more likely to have an antisocial personality—9 times more likely according to one study. It was also found that adoptively reared sons of a criminal parent have an elevated rate of ADHD as well as antisocial personality and aggressive behavior.

Twin studies confirm all this, suggesting a strong genetic influence in hyperactivity. Where one identical twin has the disorder, so does the other in most cases. In one study, the figure was 79 percent for identicals and 32 percent for fraternals. This difference in concordance implies high heritability, maybe 80 percent, meaning that genetic differences explain 80 percent of the differences in vulnerability to ADHD. In sum, like antisocial personality, hyperactivity with conduct problems figures in criminal behavior.

That biological view is reinforced by additional observations suggesting that antisocial behavior, especially the more violent kind, is associated with neurologically compromising factors that include head injury, birth complications, and minor physical anomalies such as a break in the crease running across the palm, flyaway hair, low-set ears, a small thumb, or an abnormally short distal phalanx (the last segment of a finger including the fingernail.) A large percentage of violent offenders show one or more of these brain-implicating factors, but also a double dose of these and other factors including hyperactivity and disorganized family life.

The biological view is further reinforced by yet another fact: An increased potential for criminal behavior reflects not only the highly heritable traits of antisocial personality and hyperactivity, but also alcoholism, which in males is highly heritable. Alcoholism also increases the risk of criminal behavior, especially the more violent kinds, and does so either by itself or by interacting with any coexisting mental illness. The result is an aggravation of antisocial tendencies, a subversion of judgment, and a sabotaging of competencies and social adjustment.

Damaged Brains, Altered Conscience: Where Lies the Soul of Saints and Sinners?

Social conditions can figure in the biology of antisocial potential. Poor prenatal care, including unrestrained abuse of drugs, abusive or neglectful parenting, and violence in the community can increase the chance of brain damage that sustains an antisocial disposition. Consider the apparent effect of a woman's cigarette smoking during pregnancy.

The children of women who smoked more than half a pack a day while pregnant have an elevated rate of conduct problems in school. However, compared to women who didn't smoke during pregnancy, smoker mothers are also more likely to have an antisocial disposition and a husband with an antisocial disposition, to be living in low socioeconomic circumstances, to be younger at the birth of the child, and to have an inadequate parenting style, including difficulty communicating clearly and a problem with supervising and disciplining the child. Why then are smoker mothers more likely to have a conduct-disorder child?

One possible answer is a genetic transmission of lower IQ and antisocial tendencies associated with smoking during pregnancy; smoking would thus be a marker of undesirable potentials. Another possible answer is that smoking is more than a marker, that it adds something extra to create or boost an antisocial potential. To find out, researchers compare the children of smoker and nonsmoker mothers who are comparable in personality, age, socioeconomic status, and the other relevant variables. The results were that smoker mothers' children are still more often diagnosable with conduct disorder. Apparently, nicotine intake during pregnancy adversely alters fetal brain development.

People can do damage to themselves if they have inherited a self-destructive vulnerability, for example, to alcoholism. A strong genetic disposition to abuse alcohol, through unmitigated pleasure seeking and an insensitivity to alcohol's adverse physiological effects, can lead to excessive drinking. After a time, drinking alters brain chemistry, directly as with any poison or indirectly through poor nutrition. Lowered levels of the neurotransmitter serotonin can cause paranoid feelings of being scrutinized, scorned, or cornered, and these can spur violent reactions to minor, even trivial, provocations. Aggressive behavior increases the risk of further brain damage through physical trauma. In this way, aggression breeds further aggression, the driving force being inborn defects and dispositions stimulated by social conditions. Assuming that drug addicts are both born and made, if made, then they are created by environmental conditions that are partly of their own making.

One neurological cause of violent antisocial behavior is a tumor that affects the hypothalamus, a primitive structure deep within the brain. As described by psychiatrist Harold Klawans, people with such tumors "can manifest increased emotional excitability, even building up to severe rage attacks, and aggressive behavior precipitated by paranoid ideation . . . [they] can react to insignificant events with excessive states of excitement, and they are capable of indiscriminate attacks against anyone who happens to be present."

Another neurological cause is an abnormality within the temporal lobes located just behind the ears. Damage in this area, especially in its deeper aspects, can cause irrationally violent behavior. Finally, antisocial behavior can stem from an abnormality within the frontal lobes, which are located right behind the eyes (the orbitofrontal area) and in the deep middle and lower parts of the brain (the ventromedial area). Researchers have been struck by a parallel between the behavior of people with damage to these areas and the behavior of psychopaths. Both have exaggerated sexual preoccupation and sexual behavior that is at once promiscuous and impersonal. Both lack good social judgment and a moral sense. Both seek immediate gratification while neglecting the long-term consequences of their actions. Both are irritable, apt to fly off the handle at the slightest provocation, yet display sluggish physiological reactivity.

The source of any brain damage underlying antisocial behavior is often unclear. It could be inherited or it could be acquired through physical traumas within an abusive family or in the wider community of violent peers and strangers. And, while many criminals are neither psychopathic nor neurologically abnormal, some are both. In some cases, damage to the temporal as well as frontal lobes can produce mood shifts and irritability that may be acted upon so violently, with so little self-control, and in such a grossly improper way that the behavior has a crazy quality.

Brain damage need not cause violent outbursts. Rather, it may simply diminish social judgment in matters of sex, money, or interpersonal behavior. It can also produce a singular apathy or indifference to others and a suspiciousness that may become paranoid. Neurologist Antonio Damasio describes an accountant who underwent an operation to remove a tumor located between his frontal lobes. The resulting damage transformed a normally well-adjusted and socially successful family man into an antisocial fellow. Despite preserved intelligence, he was now irresponsible, impulsive, shortsighted, and emotionally unresponsive to the pain and suffering of others. When tested with slides depicting violent or pornographic scenes, he showed no outward sign of emotion. It was as though, cut off from feelings that usually inform judgment, he had acquired a psychopathic indifference toward others.

The classic story of personality change with neurological damage goes back to September 1848, when a freak accident made Phineas Gage a legend in neurological circles. Gage was an intelligent, well-adjusted 25-year-old construction foreman who, working for the Rutland and Burlington Railroad, was responsible for laying track by using a blasting technique. Explosive powder and a fuse would be laid in a hole that was then covered with sand and tamped down with an inch-thick, 3-foot, 7-inch-long tamping bar. Inexplicably, Gage tamped down the blasting powder before the sand was poured in. The ensuing explosion blew the bar up into his cheek just below the left eye and out through the top of his forehead; the bar landed 100 feet away.

Weakened and bloodied, Gage nevertheless remained fully conscious. Eventually he recovered, though not normally. The now-classic report of attending physician John Harlow gives the following account: "The equilibrium or balance, so to speak, between his intellectual and animal propensities seems to have been destroyed. He is fitful, irreverent, indulging at times in the grossest profanity (which was not previously his custom), manifesting but little deference for his fellows, impatient of restraint or advice when it conflicts with his desires, at times pertinaciously obstinate, yet capricious and vacillating, devising many plans of future operations, which are no sooner arranged than they are abandoned in turn for others appearing more feasible. A child in his intellectual capacity and manifestations, he has the animal passions of a strong man. . . . In this regard his mind is radically changed, so decidedly that his friends and acquaintances said he was 'no longer Gage'."

Until his premature death at age 38, Gage had a recognizable frontal lobe syndrome. In this condition, intelligence may be largely intact, so that an affected person may still score over 130 (superior) on an IQ test, yet still manifest drastic changes in personality. Depending on the location and extent of the damage, a mature and responsible person becomes erratic, insensitive, impulsive, mischievous, remorseless, distractible, facetious, or sexually promiscuous. Modern neurology is replete with Gage-type studies of how environmental damage to different parts of the brain causes sometimes bizarre abnormalities in thinking, memory, language, emotion, personality, and social behavior.

Damasio's modern-day Phineas Gage case is surely interesting in itself, but also as a model for some forms of antisocial personality that involve lifelong brain abnormality caused by either genetic factors or traumatic circumstances affecting fetal or childhood development. How many people are impulsive, irresponsible, and indifferent to others—how many are given to criminal behavior—because something is wrong with their frontal lobes or other part of their brain?

Tentative answers to this question about the brain-behavior connection can be discovered in various clues: for example, a slightly abnormal heart rate or brain waves that have a "slow" or "spiky" aspect. Such anomalies, observable in early adolescence and even childhood, can predict criminal behavior. When tested in the laboratory at age 15, future male criminals display abnormally low heart rate and slow EEG. On the other hand, when tested at age 15, comparably antisocial adolescents who never became criminals display higher-than-normal heart rates. Such observations support what bears reiterating: *If brain damage can cause antisocial behavior, antisocial behavior must raise questions about brain abnormality, including a genetic reason for that abnormality.*

Some studies have also revealed an improvement in personality, which is just the opposite of what might be expected. In one, a man with intractable obsessive-compulsive disorder attempted suicide by shooting himself in the head. The ensuing damage to the frontal lobes appeared to have cured him of the disorder. In another, an antisocial teenager named Stephen, described as a "bad seed," got drunk and inadvertently put a .22-caliber bullet through his right temple. The ensuing damage to his frontal lobes cured his personality disorder—at least it seemed to. A year after the surgery, Stephen's neurosurgeon noted: "His speech had returned and his mind seemed intact. He had returned to school and was even doing reasonably well, at least when his record was compared with his dismal scholastic performance of the past. To his father's delight and to my surprise, Stephen's behavior had never been better. He no longer argued with his parents or teachers or had fits of rage."

Such studies, and in those with less happy outcomes, suggest how the distinct characteristics of neural machinery determine the unique capacities and traits that make us individuals. Given the evidence, one could argue that the quality of our very soul is a matter of brain physiology rather than parental influence. If this seems far-fetched, listen to Stephen's neurosurgeon: "[Phineas] Gage fell to damnation in an instant, while Stephen, like Saint Paul, was diverted from trouble's path by a single, blinding flash. Different as their outcomes were, Gage's tamping rod and Stephen's gun were both aimed at the anatomic substrate of our individuality, our humanity. [The philosopher] Descartes believed the soul resided in the pineal gland, a small, conical structure deep in the brain, below the frontal lobes. He was wrong by a mere six inches."

Genetic variation can explain why people differ in various psychological traits once ascribed to rearing and other social conditions. In fact, says David Rowe, "the best guess we could make about the psychological and physical traits of another person, without interviewing him or her directly, would be based upon the characteristics of the person's [identical] twin, assuming that one could be found. Nothing we might discover about conditions of rearing, schooling, neighborhood, religion, or school yard friends would come close to the usefulness of an [identical] twin in providing information about this person's height, weight, eye color, temperament, mental illness, habits, IQ, values, or nearly any other trait."

The best evidence of such genetic influence has usually come from twins and adoptees. With them, estimates can be made of *additive* influence—the cumulative effect of many genes whose small individual contribution adds up (that is, the more genes of one kind we inherit, the more intelligent or agreeable or conscientious or antisocial we are). In like manner, the more genes of another kind we inherit, the greater our risk for mental illnesses. Additive influence represents the blending of genetic inheritance from both parents, which is why parents can make reasonably good guesses about how their children will turn out—why, for example, the parental average IQ is a good predictor of a child's intelligence. It is also why adoption agencies sometimes try to place the offspring of parents with certain traits, say musical talent, with like-minded adoptive parents.

Additive influence, however, is only one part of the genetic story. The other is *nonadditive* influence, an all-or-nothing kind that doesn't add up, for example, because it involves a unique interaction of parental genes in a child or an effective double dose of a rare gene inherited from each parent. Such nonadditive influence can pop up unexpectedly in odd, awful, or wondrous ways that confound prediction based on knowing anything about either parent.

The next chapter considers some striking examples of nonadditive genetic influence that can dramatically and unexpectedly affect anything from mental life to sexual development. All of this confers a deeper appreciation than ever before, not just that parental influence may be less powerful, but that inborn influences may be more powerful, than we have yet imagined. The result is stunning unpredictability of behavioral outcomes.

Chapter Ten

Psyche and the Single Gene

It's quite an astonishing possibility that our genes may have a substantial influence on our behavior. Isn't it interesting to speculate that people behave as they do partly because of those little spheres of DNA that look like tapioca pudding in a glass dish? "So, that explains why Uncle Louie is such a son of a bitch!"

—*Steve Allen*

In 1903, a young Bavarian psychiatrist named Alois Alzheimer came to Munich to work with Emil Kraepelin, the celebrated psychiatrist famous for both his scientific investigations of psychopathology and his clinical work with the mentally ill. Like Kraepelin, Alzheimer was an expert diagnostician with a special interest in two brain diseases: One was a mental disease affecting young people, which is now called schizophrenia. The other was the senile dementia affecting the elderly, which is now called Alzheimer's. Alzheimer's discovery came from investigating a patient named Auguste D., a 51-year-old woman who, during the four years that Alzheimer followed her before she succumbed, had displayed memory loss and paranoid ideas.

Symptoms of Alzheimer's include severe memory loss, mental confusion, and personal disintegration. Brain scans reveal shriveled, prunelike structures with spaces where healthy tissue used to be. At the microscopic level are plaques, or clumps of dead neural tissue and a protein called beta amyloid. Higher magnification also reveals dying brain cells, or neurons, with their branchlike connections to other neurons that disintegrate as they break apart. While it disintegrates, a neuron may sprout new branches, which suggests either a pathological process that makes things worse or a compensatory process that makes things better, at least for a while. Still, it does look as if neurons, refusing to give in, are attempting to preserve life and limb.

Little neurons struggling against impossible odds: What a melancholy image. Apparently it was just that for a fiftysomething student of abnormal psychology who was as charming and literate as she was sensitive and who always sat in the front row and never missed a lecture. Throughout this one on Alzheimer's, she remained teary-eyed, occasionally weeping. Later, I learned she was losing her father to the disease. In her imaginative mind, an otherwise mechanical event in the microworld of the neurons had been transformed into something personal. For just one emotional moment, a dying neuron had become a dying father.

In a more reflective moment, another message could be appreciated: the power of a single gene or bit of DNA to alter the direction of a person's development and a new destiny quite out of keeping with hopes and expectations. This message comes from new research that, fulfilling the promise of the more traditional approach with twins and adoptees, offers us a future with more precise knowledge of genetic causation. Here are some of the newest findings and their stunning implications, beginning with some rather spectacular discoveries.

Sure Thing versus Increased Risk: Two Genetic Reasons for Alzheimer's

Alzheimer's disease wipes out billions of brain cells and their trillions of connections. The loss of about 15 percent per year, which is about 10 times that of normal aging, starts deep in the memory centers, eventually working outward to the thinking parts on the brain's surface. The result is memory loss, confusion, disorganized thinking, and striking changes in personality. Death is inevitable about 7 years from the time the symptoms are first identified.

Alzheimer's strikes up to 10 percent of people over 65 and 25 percent of people over 85: Currently about 4 million Americans are affected. One's risk depends on genetic relatedness to an ill person. First-degree relatives—offspring, for example—have a higher risk than do more distant relatives. Risk in relatives of a victim also depends on when the illness first became evident. It is higher when the illness began before age 65 than after age 85.

The rarer, more aggressive form is early-onset (presenile) Alzheimer's, which strikes people in their forties and fifties. The much more common, late-onset (senile) kind—maybe 95 percent of all cases—affects people over 65. Though the resulting dementia is indistinguishable both psychologically (with the same memory and thinking deficits) and neurologically (with the same buildup of amyloid plaques), the early- and late-onset kinds of Alzheimer's are nevertheless genetically different. The early one is genetically *determined;* having the rare genetic mutation—a pathologically altered dominant gene—means that we must succumb. The later one is genetically *disposed;* having the relatively common genetic variant means that we are merely at higher risk of succumbing.

Early-onset Alzheimer's is caused by any one of at least three mutations, the first one discovered in 1991. Normally, a certain gene located on chromosome 21 is the blueprint for producing a large precursor protein from which beta amyloid is derived. Apparently, because of a mutation of the *APP* gene (named for its product, Alzheimer precursor protein), too many big pieces of amyloid detach from the larger protein (APP) and accumulate in the brain.

These observations have implications for other genetic disorders, for example, Down's syndrome, which is associated with Alzheimer's. Young people with Down's have more than their fair share of amyloid deposits, an excess that increases even more as they reach their 40s. Alzheimer's disease seems to characterize *all* the autopsied brains of adults with Down's. Finally, Down's is caused by an extra chromosome 21, meaning three copies of the APP gene rather than the normal two. Could that one extra copy of APP in Down's act like the single APP mutation in normals?

In 1992, researchers discovered on chromosome 14 a mutation, called presenilin 1 (*PS1*), that may contribute to amyloid buildup. A similar mutation identified on chromosome 1, called PS2, may help researchers identify the fatal process that promotes the beta amyloid buildup common to all forms of Alzheimer's. And what if that knowledge could be exploited to figure out how the pathological effect of the mutation might be blocked? Inhibiting PS1 activity would be revolutionary therapy, demonstrating that *today's uncontrollable genetic determinism could be tomorrow's remediable genetic vulnerability.*

Late-onset Alzheimer's appears to be highly heritable, given that identical twins assessed in at least three studies are far more concordant (about 50 percent) than are fraternal twins (about 25 percent). This different genetic story for late-onset Alzheimer's seems also to involve the biology of longevity. A certain good genetic factor decreases the risk not only for this kind of Alzheimer's but also of dying prematurely from coronary disease and other infirmities. Conversely, a slightly different bad genetic factor increases these risks. For example, people suffering from brain hemorrhage are more likely to have a poor recovery or to die if they have the bad genetic factor than if they have the good one. Also, people who reach 100 are less likely to have a bad genetic factor and more likely to have the good one.

These good and bad factors, discovered in 1992, are not mutations. Rather, they are normal variants of a specific gene located on chromosome 19. This gene is called *apoE* because it serves as a blueprint for the E form of apolipoprotein, a kind of molecular ferry that shuttles cholesterol molecules around the bloodstream. Each of the three versions of the apoE protein—E2, E3, and E4—stems from a slightly different variant of the apoE gene.

Such variants are called *alleles* (pronounced ah-LEELS), as with the A, B, and O alleles of the ABO blood group gene. Every one inherits two of these alleles, one from each parent. With three alleles inherited two at a time, there are six possible pairs: AA, AB, AO, BB, BO, or OO. The A and B alleles are dominant, the O recessive. Therefore, people with two A alleles or an A and an O have blood type A. Those with two Bs or a B and an O have B-type blood. Those with an A and a B allele have AB blood. Only people with a double dose of the O allele have O-type blood.

Likewise with the three alleles of the apoE gene that each of us inherits, one from each parent. That means there are six possible combinations: E2E2, E2E3, E2E4, E3E3, E3E4, and E4E4. E4 is the bad allele because, especially in double doses, it increases the risk for both Alzheimer's and other diseases that reduce longevity. People with E4 who survive a head injury apparently have a poorer outcome 6 months later, and maybe a 10 times greater likelihood of developing Alzheimer's compared to people without E4. Furthermore, compared to boxers with the E3 variant, boxers with even one E4 variant are apparently far more likely to suffer from cognitive impairment, Parkinsonism (tremor, slowness of movements, expressionless face), poor coordination, and clumsy gait.

The rate of Alzheimer's appears to reflect the number of E4 alleles. In a study of families with at least one Alzheimer's sufferer, the Alzheimer's rate was 20 percent in those with no E4, 47 percent in those with one, and 91 percent in those with two. But the E4 allele is likely only a part of the Alzheimer's story, given that some late-onset cases involve no E4, while unaffected people can be found with an E4 double dose.

It seems the E2 is good because people with even one E2 seem to have a relatively low risk for Alzheimer's and other bad things. For example, people whose risk is elevated because of one E4 have less risk if their other variant is E2 rather than E3. Apparently, the greater the dose of E2 and the lower the dose of E4, the less the risk of dying prematurely.

The E2/E4 balance seems to influence brain integrity and mental ability. For one thing, E4 facilitates the buildup of amyloid plaques. Compared to other Alzheimer's patients, those with the E4 double dose are found upon autopsy to have more highly developed plaques throughout the brain. Also, on tests of mental ability, fraternal twins with an E4 allele but without Alzheimer's symptoms perform more poorly than their E4-free co-twins. Finally, in 50 percent of the cases of identical twins where one is suffering late-onset Alzheimer's and both share an E4 double dose, the other twin also has the illness. This 50 percent concordance rate, which is expected to increase with age, suggests a highly heritable vulnerability.

Additional risk factors for late-onset Alzheimer's are being discovered, for example a variant of the gene that codes for an enzyme called bleomycin hydrolase. Each person has one of three alleles of the bleomycin hydrolase gene: A/A, A/G, or G/G. Using tissue samples from 357 people with Alzheimer's disease and 320 control subjects, researchers found that, compared to individuals with the more common A/A allele, those with G/G have at least twice the risk. Moreover, that elevated risk is independent of whether an individual has an apoE4 allele.

It would be melodramatic to say that E4, G/G, or some other allele may do us in, that E2 may keep us alive, and the quality of life after 60 hangs in the balance. Still, we can imagine being genetically tested for a ticking time bomb of an E4 double dose, for some other "bad" genetic variant, or for those mutations that guarantee early-onset Alzheimer's. For just a moment, images of mental decline choreographed by the genes can threaten our complacency, our sense of free will, and our denial of mortality.

Rogue Genes for Mental Illness

Research on Alzheimer's raises a key question we began to explore in the last chapter: Could a single gene variant underlie an extroverted personality, a suicidal disposition, a scientific intellect, an evil nature, or a poetic soul? One answer to that question begins with an unusual example of antisocial behavior.

In the late 1970s, a woman approached the Dutch clinical geneticist H. G. Brunner. Apparently, none of her female relatives, but many of her male relatives, had been in serious trouble. One had raped his sister. Later, while in a mental institution, he used a pitchfork to attack a warden. Another forced his sister to undress at knifepoint. A third, feeling slighted, tried to run over his boss with a car. Two others were arsonists, committing their offense after a close relative had died. Fourteen such men were eventually known to the researchers. While all were given to aggressive or exhibitionistic behaviors or sexual outbursts, especially in frustrating situations, they were otherwise generally shy. In addition, their IQs averaged about 85, about where low-normal intelligence shades into borderline mental retardation.

One observation turned out to be especially important. No father of an affected man displayed antisocial behavior. Such behavior could therefore reflect a mutant gene located on the X chromosome that each son had inherited from his mother. If so, those mothers must somehow have been protected—and they are, for this reason: Only half of their X chromosomes have the mutation; the other half, lacking the mutation, affords a measure of protection. In contrast, all an affected male's X chromosomes have the mutation; given that the Y chromosome has no corresponding analog, there is no protection.

Using genetic techniques to probe the X chromosome, Brunner identified a mutation involving just one DNA letter: a C (cytosine) where a T (thymine) normally exists. This mutation appeared only in the violent men, not in any other male relative. With the mutation, a person lacks a key molecule that normally breaks down different neurotransmitters. The molecule is called *MAO-A*, short for the A form of monoamine oxidase. Without it, we get an imbalance in serotonin and other neurotransmitters that regulate mood, alertness, judgment, and self-control.

Brunner's study dealt with unpremeditated and relatively violent antisocial behavior, not the petty or opportunistic kinds that generally go with normal levels of serotonin. Yet his results comport with the conventional division of antisocial behavior into two kinds, of which only the emotionally unstable or violent one involves abnormal serotonin. His results comport also with what is known about serotonin. With too much or too little comes an increased propensity for antisocial behavior. For example, monkeys with an inherited excess of serotonin can be extremely aggressive, even if raised under normal conditions. Also, animals on diets that decrease brain serotonin become irritable and aggressive. Finally, lower serotonin levels can be found more often in naturally aggressive monkeys than in their less aggressive counterparts.

Serotonin has been linked to antisocial behavior in humans, too. Low levels are often found in people given to cruel disregard of others, hyper-activity, extreme impulsivity, recklessness, drug taking, and alcohol abuse. Low levels are also associated with unpremeditated violent aggression, impulsive fire setting, and violent suicide attempts. One observer has noted that, "Low serotonin level has been linked with impulsive violence and suicidality as tightly as love and marriage or horses and carriages."

Low serotonin can even predict future behavior. One study followed aggressive children over a 2-year period. Those with the lowest initial lev-els of serotonin activity were most likely to get into trouble. Another study found something similar in survivors of a suicide attempt. During a 5-year follow-up, those with the lowest serotonin activity were most likely to make another attempt. In a third study, released criminals convicted of manslaughter or arson were followed up for three years. Again, those with the lowest serotonin activity were most likely to commit a violent crime.

None of this is to deny that provocative situations can make genetically normal people antisocial, even violent. It merely reminds us that genetic influences, even a single rogue gene, can explain why typically some peo-ple are relatively immune, others are easily provoked, while still others are spontaneously antisocial even despite good families. Until now, however, most research has focused on the influence of additive genes. Take, for example, the case of depression, violent behavior, and disorganized think-ing. Often, these suggest a mental illness caused by many genes, each with a small influence that can add up to a big effect.

Yet, efforts to locate such additive genes have proven daunting. By the late 1980s, evidence of a gene for manic-depression located on the X chromosome had been discounted by later findings. A similar story was unfolding about a gene or genes located on chromosome 11. Working in the Old Order Amish community, researchers focused on families with at least one member diagnosable as manic-depressive. Initially it seemed a distinct region along chromosome 11 went with the illness. Though impressive, the findings were short-lived, undermined by additional cases and a closer examination of the statistics.

Another story about a schizophrenia gene located on chromosome 5 was likewise unraveling. Undaunted, psychiatric geneticists continue their search. Their method focuses on families with one or more people affected with a particular mental illness. From the blood cells of ill or nor-mal relatives, investigators extract chromosomes that are assessed with bits of special radioactive DNA that cleave to their different parts. Any pattern of markers that reliably differentiates ill people from their normal relatives can suggest a region along a chromosome where an illness-relevant gene might be located. Using such a method, four different groups in 1995 discovered a contributory gene for schizophrenia located on chromosome 6. Two other groups investigating other populations could not confirm this finding. Yet in the context of four confirmations, two failures may just mean the hunted gene contributes only to some cases of schizophrenia; the gene may be sufficient but not necessary.

Investigators are searching for genes that explain the heritability of alcoholism suggested by adoption and twin studies. One approach, like the one described for schizophrenia, is to look for DNA variations displayed by alcoholics but not by nonalcoholics. Such variations are most often found in so-called junk DNA—nonfunctional regions that separate the functional regions (genes). Identifying genetic markers, or hot spots, would suggest the presence of a nearby vulnerability gene.

Attention focuses on a region of chromosome 1 that might contain a vulnerability gene, and on a region of chromosome 4 that may indicate a genetic factor that protects against alcoholism. That region is already known to contain a gene that codes alcohol dehydrogenase, an enzyme that breaks down alcohol into harmless by-products. Those without benefit of this enzyme react to alcohol with flushed face and nausea, often strongly enough to dissuade them from abusing alcohol unless they are highly motivated by emotional distress or overwhelming social pressure.

Stunning new evidence suggests that additive genes may not be the culprit behind some forms of abnormal behavior or mental illness. In many cases, a single-dose recessive mutation in double dose may cause a medical disease. Consider the example of Wolfram syndrome, a rare diabetic condition associated with blindness, deafness, and other neurological abnormalities. About two-thirds of affected people also have psychiatric symptoms involving depression, anxiety, hostility, or violent behavior that may be quite severe.

The syndrome, affecting only one person out of about 100,000, comes from having two mutant genes located on chromosome 4, one inherited from the mother and one from the father. The gene is recessive, meaning that, having only one such gene, neither parent displays the medical symptoms of Wolfram syndrome. Yet each single-gene carrier has an increased risk—one study suggested a 4 to 5 times greater than expected risk—of psychiatric symptoms, in some cases severe enough to require hospitalization. Such symptoms as well as suicidal behavior are much more prevalent in the biological relatives of Wolfram patients than in genetically unrelated spouses or others in the population. What is the meaning of this connection between mental illness and the Wolfram mutation?

Blood relatives of Wolfram patients have a 25 to 100 percent chance of carrying a single mutation (100 percent for each parent). These are big percentages for a tiny group of people. Because a big percentage of a small number is still a small number, the troubled relatives of Wolfram patients cannot contribute much to the overall rates of mental illness. Yet people randomly picked from the population have a 1 percent chance of carrying a Wolfram mutation. Even 1 percent of a huge number, say, 300 million, is a large number—3 million. If just 5 percent of those people have psychiatric symptoms, that's 150,000.

The Wolfram story reminds us that some mental illness may arise sporadically, unpredictably, from single-gene quirks that cause devastating medical diseases. There are 300 such diseases with psychiatric symptoms. Some, like Wolfram, are unfamiliar to mental health professionals; others, like a common form of mental retardation called fragile X syndrome, are familiar. The evocative name *fragile X* comes from something curious that occurs when the chromosomes of affected people are stained for observation: The tip of the X chromosome seems to hang by a thread, as if it were ready to break off at the location where a gene has mutated—it doesn't, but it looks as if it would. The gene, which is given to mutating, is called *FRA*, meaning fragility at location A. In its mutated form, FRA cannot make a specific protein; the consequence is mental retardation.

The FRA mutation affects men differently from women. Because all of their X chromosomes have the FRA mutation, affected men show significant mental retardation. Because only half their X chromosomes have the FRA mutation, affected women often have relatively mild mental retardation: trouble perceiving spatial arrangements—say an object rotated in space—or trouble keeping things such as an unfamiliar telephone number they have just looked up in short-term memory. Even when not manifestly retarded, women with the FRA mutation have an elevated risk for peculiar mannerisms, gaze avoidance, and odd, eccentric, or disorganized thinking.

As with Wolfram, so with fragile X and many more such conditions: A single-gene mutation linked to medical disease can cause symptoms of psychopathology. All this suggests that, just as parental influence has been overestimated, genetic influence has been underestimated in our attempts to explain not just mental illness but other unusual and unexpected qualities that afford surprise and delight rather than sadness and despair.

Our Quirky Blueprint: Stuttering Genes and Other Strange Things

The fragile X story is important in another way, illustrating how, for genetic reasons, identical twins can be psychologically discordant for mental retardation—the fragile X kind, but Down's syndrome too. (There are five known cases of identical twins where one twin is normal and the other has Down's.) We have explored identical-twin discordance, but never its genetic basis. Yet increasing evidence shows that identical twins discordant for, say, mental retardation, are on certain chromosomal sites indeed genetically different.

Looking at the sentence *The dog bit the cat*, we see it includes five three-letter words. Over 800 such three-letter words can be fashioned from just the 26 letters making up the English alphabet. A gene is like a sentence that specifies not an idea but a sequence of amino acids, the building blocks of proteins. Each genetic "sentence" includes many three-letter "words," or triplets. Sixty-four triplets can be fashioned from the four DNA letters—A, C, G, and T—that make up the genetic alphabet. Though small, the alphabet is still big enough to generate the 20 amino acids necessary for life.

As a word can occur in many sentences, a DNA triplet can occur in many genes. In the FRA gene, the CGG triplet repeats many times: CGGCGGCGG, and so on. Normally, the repeat is about 30, and no greater than 52. In some people, however, it is greater than 200. Such an enormous repeat, or *stutter*, prevents the gene from working properly. The FRA mutation typically appears in a woman's unfertilized eggs. However, it can occur after fertilization, in the zygote, or even later in the embryo. It could even occur shortly after the embryo separates into twins, but in just one of them—which explains how one twin might be mentally retarded, the other not.

Another possibility is that each twin has a mutation, but of different size. This was evident in a set of identical twins, both of whom were mentally retarded because of the mutation. In one, however, the CGG repeat was 1,000 to 1,600, depending on cells sampled; in the other, it was 1,400 to 1,800. While such a difference might seem trivial, in identical twins there should be *no* difference; at least that's the conventional assumption. Could a genetic difference between identical twins explain some of the psychological differences that are typically given environmental explanations?

While a CGG repeat of 6 to 52 is normal and stable, a 54 to 200 repeat is a *premutation,* so called because it will likely expand to full mutation, say from 85 (premutation) in a mother to 150 (premutation) in a daughter to 215 (full mutation) in a granddaughter. The more repeats in a woman's premutation, the more likely they will increase into the full mutation range; beyond 90 repeats, such an expansion is a virtual certainty. That's bad news for female close relatives of someone with fragile X syndrome, since they average about 80 repeats, most between 60 to 110.

The premutation's expansion over the generations generally occurs only in females, typically in the ovarian cells that mature into a woman's eggs. In males—in the cells that give rise to their sperm—there is no such expansion. Nevertheless, a man can transmit his premutation to a daughter, in whom it can expand into a full mutation. That mutation can be passed to her offspring—his grandchildren. Thus, either sex can transmit the risk for fragile X, though males can transmit it only indirectly through a daughter (in whom the premutation expands) to a grandchild.

A genetic repetition is one thing, but a repetition that expands across generations, and differently in identical twins—that's *really* something. For in challenging the assumption of an immutable genetic blueprint, the idea of a genetic instability likewise challenges the assumption that any psychological difference between identical twins must be environmental, in particular social.

Excitement caused by the stunning discovery of genetic instability prompted this celebratory comment by molecular geneticist David Nelson. "The identification of a mutation that confers increased mutability onto itself is a rather astounding finding. . . . The idea that DNA is not necessarily inherited in the same form as the parents' or that it can be significantly altered from tissue to tissue within an individual is radical. . . . It is a rare delight when fundamentally new phenomena are uncovered in genetics, and unstable DNA that can be transmitted genetically from parents to offspring represents such a new principle. We can only hope that the continuing inquiry into the nature of our genes will yield more such insights."

Across the generations, the CGG expansion makes the fragile X syndrome more likely and more severe, and this raises the question, Does a similar genetic expansion explain why, over the generations, both panic disorder and schizophrenia seem to occur at an earlier age, in some cases attacking the victim with a greater severity? Does a genetic expansion, occurring after an embryo splits into twins, explain a panic disorder or schizophrenia in just one identical twin?

While this speculative possibility has only tentative support, it is another reason why psychological differences even between identical twins might not signify a difference in rearing, other social experience, or even prenatal life. See what happens once the door is opened even a little to difference at the genetic level? We face the possibility that it explains some of the psychological differences between identical twins, and if between them, then among everybody else.

A genetic repeat is not the only form of genetic instability. Sometimes genes can change location on a chromosome. So, even if the genes are identical, where they are located and how they interact with other genes might differ in each identical twin, possibly explaining psychological as well as physical differences.

Genetic differences can even explain how identical twins might differ in sex. Normally, a genetic male begins as a fertilized egg, an XY zygote with an X and Y chromosome, as compared to the XX female. A specific gene on the Y helps program the development of testes, whose secretion of male hormones, or androgens, cause an embryo to develop male characteristics. Without androgen, even an XY embryo will develop into what looks like a normal female.

The XY zygote has just divided, the two daughter cells separating into genetically identical XY twin cells. With one, cell division and fetal development will continue normally; the result is a male child. In the other, something odd happens: During its first division, when the chromosomes split up and rearrange themselves, the Y chromosome gets lost. All later divisions yield cells with an X but no Y, an abnormal arrangement called XO. With XO cells, the embryo undergoes female development, but with complications known as Turner's syndrome, which affects 1 of every 2,500 to 3,000 girls. A female with Turner's will be of short stature with an immature, little-girl appearance. She will also have serious deficits in spatial thinking, such as great difficulty reading maps.

Lacking ovaries, the female with Turner's is infertile, yet she will be feminine in her behavior and in the way she thinks about herself. In this, she'll resemble the stereotypically conventional girl who enjoys playing with dolls or caring for babies, and who looks forward to romance, marriage, pregnancy, and motherhood. So, despite sharing 99.9 percent of her genes with her sibling—all but the handful located on the missing Y chromosome—she and her brother will have lost the chance for that special relationship shared by identical twins.

An interesting twist to the Turner's story speaks to genetic influence on traits often assumed to be determined by rearing and other social conditions. One such trait is social cognition, or the ability to engage adroitly in social interactions. In this and in related cognitive abilities, girls with Turner's are often relatively impaired; for example, they can be socially disruptive.

Compared to girls with Turner's who received their single X chromosome from their father, those who received their single X chromosome from their mother are more impaired academically (40 versus 16 percent) and socially (72 versus 29 percent). They are more likely to lack awareness of others' feelings, to be excessively demanding of others' time, to be difficult to reason with when upset, to be insensitive to others' body language, and to be unaware of what is socially appropriate. They are also less able to concentrate: For example, when asked to alter a string of ones and twos, they have more trouble substituting a one for a two or a two for a one. The principal researcher noted that, based on social behavior, a good guess can be made regarding the origin of a Turner's syndrome girl's X chromosome, but what does this mean?

The answer may involve something called *genomic imprinting*, a genetic influence that depends on which parent transmits a gene. It is possible that genes for social cognition and self-control, if inherited from the mother, are actually switched off in the offspring. This might explain why boys, who get their sole X chromosome from their mother, are socially less adept than girls, who get switched-off genes on the X chromosome they inherit from their mother, but also active genes on the X chromosome they inherit from their father. The strong implication? Social behaviors— especially social behaviors that differentiate the sexes—are more than mere matters of rearing and other kinds of social conditioning.

Apparently, even slight genetic alterations during an embryo's development may cause unpredictable outcomes that make us different psychologically from what we would otherwise have been—different in ways having nothing to do with our upbringing. What then if a somewhat unstable genetic blueprint contributes to our unique ways of being? Genetic instability is good enough reason to question the usual social explanations for psychological differences, not just between identical twins but between any two people. It is also a reminder that, whatever their sometimes striking similarities, even identical twins are psychologically unique.

So, while the genes bias the way, they don't ensure how the trip will turn out, not for twins or for anybody. Even highly heritable dispositions can be magnified, blocked, or derailed by chancy and unpredictable gene–environment interactions, the result being inborn differences even between identical twins. In fact, there is now good reason to suspect at least 15 significant different reasons why identicals could differ genetically but also in other biological ways. As psychiatrist Robert Cole observes, "Our genes matter, of course, but they are not us. Fate, chance, luck, circumstance and nurture shape each of us decisively [and we] will still face the challenge of our humanity—the day-by-day emotional and moral experiences that so significantly make us who and what we are."

Sex Beyond our Sex Chromosomes

A lost Y chromosome is one way a male zygote can become a female. Another is through a mutation of the *SRY* gene, or sex-determining region of the Y chromosome. Normally, SRY sends a special signal to other genes for the development of testes, the major source of androgen. However, when mutated, SRY can't send the signal and the testes fail to develop. So, despite having a Y chromosome, the embryo develops female characteristics. Such rare anomalies remind us of how even a tiny DNA difference between people can sometimes make all the difference in the world.

Even with androgen, an XY embryo can still become female. This will happen if a genetic defect on the X chromosome creates an insensitivity to the hormone—a kind of biochemical blindness. The insensitivity doesn't apply to estrogen, a female hormone that in both sexes is produced in tiny amounts by the adrenal glands. Available estrogen means that upon reaching puberty, androgen-insensitive XY females will have a feminine appearance.

According to medical psychologists John Money and Anke Ehrhardt, an XY female typically has a lifelong feminine orientation, with dreams of being a wife, mother, and homemaker. She can be an attractive, statuesque woman with long legs, large breasts, radiant complexion, winning smile, and feminine ways. She may even look like a movie star or a fashion model. Her condition is usually not discovered until after puberty when a medical investigation of absent menstruation and an inability to bear children reveals two singular facts: the presence of undescended testes and a nonfunctional vagina, a short cavity or tube that dead-ends because no uterus exists.

While a genetic male (XY) fetus can become a female, a genetic female (XX) becoming a male almost never happens. Still, a female fetus can develop strikingly masculine characteristics. In the 1950s, some pregnant women took synthetic hormones to prevent miscarriage. Female offspring of these mothers were prenatally masculinized by such hormones. The girls developed a tomboy style complete with preference for cars and trucks over dolls, competition over cooperation, rough and tumble play over quiet talk, and blue jeans over frilly dresses. Whatever the social influence, fetal hormones had clearly made a big difference.

The influence of prenatal androgen on female development is evident in female fraternal twins with male co-twins. On tests of spatial ability that generally favor males, such women outperform female fraternals with female co-twins. They also show a greater preference for novel experiences, nonconformist or uninhibited behavior, and mind-altering drugs. Why would having a co-twin brother make a girl more masculine rather than more feminine? A biological answer—exposure to androgen during fetal development—fits what is known about animals. By chance a female mouse or gerbil fetus may develop between two male fetuses rather than between a male and a female or two females. A double dose of male neighbor means an extra dose of androgen, which in turn explains why such females tend to show more aggression and less sexual interest in males. It also explains why they are sexually less attractive to males.

The impact of prenatal androgen is illuminated by an unusual story of identical twin boys. At age 7 months, they underwent circumcision with a cauterizing needle rather than the usual scalpel. Unfortunately, one of the twins was the victim of a bizarre accident whereby his little penis was electrocuted, eventually drying up and falling off. After much anguish, the parents agreed to a sex reassignment, meaning that the victim's genitals would be surgically reconstructed to look female. She would be reared as a girl named Joan, and at puberty, estrogen therapy would be used to encourage mature female development.

This case has appeared in professional journals and psychiatry text-books, but mainly to illustrate alleged parental power to shape a child's sex-appropriate behavior and sexual identity. Yet a follow-up of this and other cases suggests that, quite the contrary, the genetically determined influence of androgens during fetal brain development is paramount. Far from being sexually neutral, newborns are strongly biased toward maleness or femaleness, some even more strongly than others. Social pressures merely reinforce this bias, they do not create it.

From the outset, even despite hormone replacement therapy and being reared as a female, Joan was unable to adopt a female sex role. In her mind, she was a boy, not a tomboy, with tendencies toward stubbornness and dominance. The masculine self-image was evident in her rejection of dresses, dolls, and any attempt to get her to imitate her mother's makeup ritual; if anything, she preferred to mimic her father shaving and to play with boys. These and other masculine qualities inspired her peers to call her "cave woman" and "gorilla."

Alas, encouraged by experts, Joan's parents continued to press for feminine behavior, all of which went against the grain of instinct and feeling. No wonder that by early adolescence, she was having serious psychological problems including conflict over her sexual identity, a sense of helplessness, and attempted suicide. Then, at age 14, Joan renounced her false female identity, deciding to live as a man named John and eventually to undergo extensive sex reassignment surgery including mastectomy with reconstruction of male genitals. It was at this point that John's father revealed the truth that John was a genetic (XY) male. "For the first time everything made sense," said John, "and I understood who and what I was." By age 25, he was happily married. Though still somewhat bitter, he was finally at reasonable peace with himself.

While John's case is exceptional, others make the same point. Regarding a group of six XY males born without penises castrated during infancy, and reared as girls, one researcher noted that all six were basically male in their mind and behavior. "They don't say, 'I wish I was a boy,' or 'I'd really rather be a boy,' or 'I think I am a boy.' They say, 'I *am* a boy.' " Additional evidence further suggests the paramount power of biological events to shape a person's psychological development despite unremitting social pressure from parents, peers, and professionals. The best known come from the testimony of homosexuals, but truly exotic phenomena make the point more convincing and memorable.

Consider genetically male (XY) children with a genetic deficiency of dihydrotestosterone, a male hormone that the body normally produces from testosterone. Because of the deficiency, such children have ambiguous, somewhat feminine external genitals with a clitoris-like penis, a labia-like scrotum, and a pouchlike vagina. However, because of their normal levels of testosterone, they have internal male genitals including seminal ducts and undescended testicles. With puberty comes a remarkable, Kafkaesque transformation. The usual surge of testosterone that normally causes masculine development has similar effects in these children, including enlarged penis, descended testicles, deepened voice, more muscle mass, and a new capacity for erection and ejaculation.

With these biological changes, and despite a lifetime of female upbringing, most such children living under reasonably tolerant social conditions develop a normal male-gender identity and adopt male roles, including husband and (adoptive) father. Apparently, much of what they have learned—much of the parental influence imposed during the so-called formative years—sloughs off, making clear just how superficial gender socialization can be in the face of powerful inborn dispositions from prenatal testosterone.

In a rare condition affecting about one person in 15,000, an overactive adrenal gland produces too much prenatal androgen. Congenital adrenal hyperplasia, or CAH, stems from a double dose of a recessive gene located on chromosome 6. Compared to normal females, CAH girls tend to be somewhat masculine in their preferences and behaviors. They are intensely energetic, enjoy rough and tumble play, and are seen as tomboys. When given a choice, they tend to display a preference for traditionally male toys: cars and blocks, for example, rather than dolls and crayons. While most CAH girls identify themselves as females, some show little enthusiasm for that role. While most become heterosexual, some become bisexual or homosexual. On personality tests, they tend to score more like males in attitudes toward aggression and in reactions to stress. So, too, on tests of spatial ability, for example recognizing an object rotated in space: CAH females tend to perform more like males.

These observations on sexual and gender development support our main theme: Parental and peer influence is limited, even blocked, by strong inborn potentials involving intelligence, personality, gender identity, vulnerability to mental illness, and special talents. We have seen this power of nature over nurture, not just in the findings of twins and adoption studies but in the striking effects of even slightly altered DNA and in marked differences that siblings show right from birth. Finally, despite the most unremitting pressure from families and communities, unconventional sexual and gender development could not be altered in the child.

With CAH, masculine behavior occurs despite social influences that encourage feminine behavior. With male homosexuality, feminine behavior occurs despite even stronger expectations and demands for masculine behavior. Looking forward, roughly 75 percent of strikingly effeminate boys become homosexual men; looking back, 85 percent of homosexual men responding to questionnaires endorse one or more questions about early effeminacy. Some of these are aversion to rough and tumble play, preference for the company of girls, interest in dolls, dressing in women's clothes, and being considered a sissy.

In males, the homosexual disposition is about 50 percent heritable, with estimates varying between 30 and 75 percent. That at least some of the disposition is transmitted by the mother is evident in a relatively high rate of male homosexuality on the maternal side of the family. This in turn implicates the X chromosome that a male inherits only from his mother. Genetics researcher Dean Hamer searched the X chromosome of 40 pairs of homosexual brothers. From each subject he isolated and identified the same set of 22 genetic markers—short, easily distinguished stretches of DNA that vary from person to person and that geneticists use to flag a particular spot on a chromosome. If two brothers shared a marker, chances were pretty good that they also shared genes in the neighborhood of that marker—genes presumably involved in their homosexual disposition. Thirty-three of the 40 pairs of brothers did indeed share the same set of five markers located in a region on the X chromosome called q28—far too many matches to be coincidental.

A follow-up study found essentially the same thing: 67 percent of homosexual brother pairs shared genetic markers in the same region of the X chromosome, compared to 22 percent of heterosexual brother pairs. Since 50 percent sharing is expected by chance, one or more genes in the q28 region of the X chromosome may very well contribute to male homosexuality. If homosexuality is indeed a heritable disposition, then those with its most obligate form have no more freedom to choose their sexual orientation than those whose heterosexual disposition is likewise obligate.

A similar point can be made of other dispositions—for example, cigarette smoking—that in some are powerfully addictive while in others, though pleasurable, are nevertheless dispensable when circumstances and good judgment prevail.

Heritability implies differences in brain, physiology, and psychology. Some structures in the male homosexual's brain look more female than male, for example the hypothalamus, a structure that regulates needs, drives, appetites, and circadian rhythms, and the anterior commissure, a structure that helps the left and right cerebral hemispheres communicate with each other. Physiological differences have also been found: For example, in response to an injection of the female hormone estrogen, women react with a big increase in another hormone called luteinizing hormone (LH); males have little or no increase. Male homosexuals show either the strong female pattern or an intermediate one involving a modest increase in LH. As for psychological differences, male homosexuals tend to perform more like heterosexual females on certain psychological tests that normally tend to differentiate males and females. Males tend to outperform females and male homosexuals on test of spatial rotation, for example the ability to recognize a target object that has been rotated left to right and front to back and placed among other similar objects.

Absent direct genetic evidence, a convincing argument that homosexuality is as inborn as heterosexuality would have to be founded on a definitive study of people adoptively reared by genetically unrelated homosexuals—a study showing that the rates of homosexuality in such adoptees are no different from the expected rate of roughly 2 to 5 percent. That finding would at once illuminate the biological basis of the homosexual disposition and demonstrate that it is no more contagious than, say, high intelligence or extroversion. At the same time, it would be one more example of just how really superficial if not illusory parental influence can be where the inborn dispositions of any one child are especially strong—just how, despite intense social pressure, some children can develop in such an alien way that they become like strangers to their parents.

A Brief Look Back at Genetic Influence

The heritability studies explored in Chapters 9 and 10 suggest that genetic influences on our lives are more powerful than heretofore considered—so too the studies of single-gene or chromosomal influences. Before proceeding in the next chapter to influences beyond the genetic, consider the newly discovered or strongly suspected single-gene influences noted earlier:

Single-Gene Influences on Heritable Conditions

CONDITION	GENETIC DETERMINANT	INFLUENCE
Pathological Conditions		
Schizophrenia	Gene on chromosome 6(?)	Vulnerability factor
Schizotypal behavior	One mutation (fragile X)	Vulnerability factor
Alzheimer dementia (early)	Three mutations (e.g., presenilin 1 and 2)	Determinant
Alzheimer dementia (late)	Genetic variants (e.g., apoE 4)	Vulnerability factor
Episodic violence (males)	One mutation (MAO-A)	Determinant
Depression	One mutation (Wolfram)	Vulnerability factor
Poor social conduct	Gene(s) on chromosome X	Vulnerability factor
Attention deficit	Gene on chromosome 7 (DRD4)	Vulnerability factor
Alcoholism	Gene on chromosome 7 (DRD4)	Vulnerability factor
Nonpathological Deviations		
Homosexuality (males)	Gene(s) on chromosome X	Vulnerability factor
Tomboy behavior (CAH females)	Gene(s) on chromosome 6	Determinant

These mostly preliminary findings need further assessment for their reliability—how well do they hold up across many studies?—and their generalizability—do they apply to the population or only to single families? Granted, whether additive or nonadditive, such genetic influence will prove responsible for a lot, even though it surely isn't everything.

Which is why someone like Paul, whose co-twin had schizophrenia, could truly be hopeful. Despite his brother's illness, his genetic vulnerability could be relatively weak. Good news for Paul, for if an identical twin has schizophrenia, the co-twin has at least a 60 percent chance of *not* becoming ill. Also, the chance of that co-twin also developing schizophrenia diminishes greatly after just a few years of wellness, and disappears almost entirely after 4 years. With each passing year, then, Paul's odds were rapidly improving, suggesting that he was carrying a relatively weak genetic vulnerability, and that would mean a relatively more favorable outlook for any children he might be contemplating.

Paul had to understand that there are natural influences beyond parental influence that could make all the difference, to him and to all of us—positive, compensatory qualities of intellect and temperament that we have already seen are themselves genetically inspired, but also prenatal influences that make the story of inborn potential and limited parental influence so interesting.

Chapter Eleven

A Prenatal World

Good wombs have born bad sons.

—Shakespeare

Psychologist Henry A. Murray once quoted a Vermont farmer who wisely noted, "People is mostly alike, but what difference they is can be powerful important." So, too, with identical twins: They are mostly alike, but what differences there are can be plenty important. Studying them reminds us that psychological explanations have more than scientific significance; they have personal significance.

What does someone with a twin who has schizophrenia want to hear, what does he or she need to hear, about the genesis of schizophrenia—that it is mostly in bad genes or mostly in lousy upbringing? Neither explanation can be of much comfort to anyone who plans to have children or anyone who loves his parents and believes they have raised the ill sibling equally well. Can there be a third explanation?

Beyond the Blueprint: Genes Aren't Everything

The genetic blueprint, or *genome*, is a set of instructions packed in 23 pairs of chromosomes that include up to 100,000 genes, the equivalent of thousands of books of information. Each gene serves as a little blueprint, or code, for fashioning a protein, and proteins enable cells to do everything from carrying oxygen to carrying ideas. Genetic information goes into forming our bodies and brains, which means our biological readiness to interact with environments and, therefore, to be biased in what we perceive, what we learn, and what we prefer to do.

Yet our genetic blueprints cannot be preserved over the generations. We can pass on only a part of them, for only a random half of a genetic blueprint's elements gets transmitted from a parent to each offspring. This key fact of life goes to the heart of an individual's biological uniqueness. So consider this fact: Each successive child gets a decreasing percentage of a parent's genes that have not already been received by the older children. Here's how it works, given the simplest scenario, which ignores a spouse for whom the same applies.

Your first child gets 50 percent of his genes from you. Likewise, your second child gets 50 percent of her genes from you, but of these only half (25 percent) differ from those already carried by the first sibling. So, while one child carries 50 percent of your genes into the next generation, two children carry 75 percent (50 + 25 percent). A third child gets 50 percent of his genes from you, but of these only 12.5 percent differ from those carried by the first two siblings. With three children, 87.5 percent of your genes get transmitted to the new generation (50 + 25 + 12.5 percent). And so it goes, each successive child getting a random 50 percent of your genes, but a smaller percentage of genes not already carried by older offspring.

With only two or three offspring, you can insure that most of your genes will survive. But even if you could pass them all on, your genetic blueprint—your unique pattern of genes—wouldn't survive. Thus, there can be immortality, but only for individual genes. For a generation or two, recognizable aspects of your heritable self survive in close relatives. Yet the continuities weaken with increasing genetic distance within and across generations, meaning that there's some of you in your siblings but less in your cousins, some in your parents or children but less in your grandparents or grandchildren. Across five links, just about all similarity disappears. For practical purposes, then, a person no more resembles a fifth-generation relative, or any fifth-degree relative, than does someone of the same sex and ethnic group chosen at random.

A unique genome inspires the development of a person about whom it can be said that there never has been nor ever will be another. Then what about identical twins—does a shared blueprint diminish their individual uniqueness? Not really, because there is more to uniqueness than a unique set of genes. With the same blueprint and builder, two houses built on adjacent lots may wind up so much alike that people call them identical, yet they won't be identical. Differences will get built in for many reasons. It could be availability of materials or the timing of events. It could be the effort and attitude of the workers on any particular day, or the gimmicks they use to compensate for deficiencies. It may even be just plain luck. One of the workers might be inebriated or preoccupied with the arrival of a new baby the day that the crew or the builder makes a crucial decision for assembling parts.

Identical twins may have identical genes, but their prenatal experience is different. This point is dramatically illuminated by psychologist Victor Denenberg and colleagues, who found that genetically identical mouse embryos implanted in different wombs grew into mice that differed in mental task performance. All the mouse embryos used in the study had an autoimmune disease similar to the human version of lupus. One third were transplanted into the wombs of mice without the disease, the rest into the wombs of mice with other autoimmune disorders. Despite having the genes for autoimmune disease, mice born of a mother with no autoimmune disease did relatively better on four of the five performance tests. Clearly, the prenatal environment made a difference. Generalizing to humans, it can be said that while identical twins may have the same genetic blueprint, they can never have the same prenatal environment—which is why they will always be different physiologically and psychologically.

Likewise with the genetically identical *cells* that make up a young embryo: Each contains the same genetic information; it is in this sense an identical twin of any other cell. Yet such genetically identical cells go their very different ways, one becoming a brain cell, another a muscle cell, a third a cell of the stomach lining, each physically different and carrying out completely different functions. The reason must involve the interaction of genes and environmental factors that differ, if only slightly, for cells throughout the embryo. The interaction can explain why cells experimentally moved to the back of a young embryo develop into parts of a leg or tail, or why cells moved to the front will develop into eyes or a brain. Behavioral embryologist Gilbert Gottlieb once suggested that we are sitting with bodily parts that could have been used for thinking.

Two points can be made. First, genetic influence depends on nongenetic events, in this case, the stage of cellular development. Second, evolutionary theory is supported by the fact that many genes are the same across species: The same genes are responsible for creating eyes in flies, squid, and humans. The same genes responsible for circadian rhythms can be found in flies, mice, and humans.

Genes and the prenatal environment interact in fairly reliable ways, which is why members of a species are similar and why close relatives show family resemblance. Nevertheless, gene–environment interactions are not entirely reliable, for they involve complex processes and chancy events. This is why members of a species—even identical twins—are different, and why predicting the psychological development of even highly heritable potentials is difficult. It would still be difficult even with perfect knowledge of the genes and full control of the environment.

A surviving twin's touching memorial posted on the Internet in 1997 implies as much:

> *I am an identical twin who has been shattered by the death of my very much loved sister at the age of 40. When I first saw the reports about cloning . . . I could think of nothing else all day. I must admit that, in my excitement, my first thought was "I can get her back, I'll find a way to get twinnie back." And this is an identical twin talking—supposedly, as one half of a monozygote, I am already a perfect genetic copy of my sister.*
>
> *But from birth we began growing into two very different people—we were a pair with complementary differences. We were physically alike, close, and empathic, in a way which I will be unable to repeat, and very comfortably different. And I realized that, of course, I knew her as her own vibrant person, whom I always regarded as separate and different from me. Beside this consideration, the genetic code hardly figured. It was simply a component of the whole. So, it would be impossible to recreate my sister in her totality as a person—the nurture context, the myriad minutiae of random environmental influences which modified her development, could not be repeated.*

Granted, certain psychological differences even between identical twins might involve strong parenting or other social influences; one can't dismiss the possibility out of hand. At the same time, however, other psychological differences, say in IQ, seem to have little or nothing to do with those parenting or other social influences. Then what *are* they due to? Well, most reflect genetic differences and just about all the rest—up to 20 percent of all individual differences in IQ—may reflect *prenatal* factors, such as fetal infection or maternal abuse of nicotine, alcohol, or other drugs. Yet prenatal factors include something else that could partly explain the individual differences: biological noise, events so complex, even random, that they can't be predicted—events that in a sense are surely genetic and environmental yet, in the usual sense of those terms, are neither clearly genetic nor clearly environmental.

The influence of prenatal life can be illustrated in the singular case of the notorious Genain quadruplets, four genetically identical sisters who displayed the social withdrawal, thought disorder, and hallucinations that mark schizophrenia, yet who differed in the severity of their symptoms and in other ways: in the number of their hospitalizations and their response to medications; in the amount of education achieved, from 4 years of high school to 2 years of business school; and on laboratory tests that measured, for instance, their ability to respond quickly and accurately to moving or changing stimuli.

Such differences in the genetically identical imply that genetic purpose is always subject to the influence of chance events having nothing to do with rearing or other social influences. For further insight into all this, consider twinning and then the sometimes stressful conditions of the womb. The details may be about twins, but the story, rooted deep in our evolutionary history, is about all of us.

Genes We Share and Genes We Don't

Unlike identical twins, fraternal twins, as with any two siblings, come from two eggs, each fertilized by a different sperm. The technical term for a fertilized egg is *zygote;* hence, fraternal twins are more accurately called *dizygotic.* Coming from two separately fertilized eggs means that, like any pair of siblings, fraternal twins share only 50 percent of their genes, on average. But fractional sharing involves only those genes that vary from one person to another.

To start with, most of our roughly 100,000 genes, about 70 to 85 percent, are *invariant,* meaning that they are identical for all humans. Some of the invariant genes are shared with all vertebrates—mammals, birds, reptiles, amphibians, and fish. Some are shared even with invertebrates whose evolution split off from ours at least 500 million years ago. Human invariant genes ensure that everybody has two eyes, one nose, and other invariant traits that mark our species. Psychological universals that express invariant genes are evident in the capacity to learn a language and much more. As evolutionary psychologist Del Thiessen suggests:

> *The character of our love, desires, and yearnings exalt us now as they have for thousands of generations. Jealousy, hate, and paranoia stalk us like the tigers of old; hunger, thirst, and tiredness consume us no less than ever; and the dread of death still fills our moments of contemplation. Nothing fundamental has changed by our experiences, languages, science, or technology—not one biological thread, not one genetic breath, not one trivial emotion. We are no less* H. sapiens *because of our cultural knowledge than a dog on a skateboard is other than a dog. Our psychological designs are those of our parents, their parents, and their parents, and so on to our "African Eve." It is our destiny to be what we were, what we are, and whatever we will be.*

Yet what we are is somewhat different from what the other person is, and part of that involves variation on phylogenetic themes—in other words, individual differences in sociability or intelligence that are caused by variable genes. Says geneticist Theodosius Dobzhansky:

> *Natural selection has always favored in mankind the development of educability, i.e., the capacity to learn what a given culture makes necessary in its members, to profit by experience, and to modify and adjust one's behavior in the light of circumstances. Educability is a fundamental trait of the species* Homo sapiens; *it's what makes human behavior so different from that of nonhuman animals; yet this trait is individually variable. Some individuals learn more easily and successfully certain things, and other individuals other things. Every individual is unique and unrepeatable; people are not interchangeable.*

Variable genes, then, ensure that people will always differ—in eye color and nose shape, but also in personality, intelligence, and a lot more. It is thus the variable genes that are always implied whenever we speak about genetic sharing, or *overlap:* roughly 0 percent for strangers, 50 percent for first-degree relatives, including fraternal twins, and 100 percent for identicals.

An overlap of 100 percent originates from the splitting of a single fertilized egg, which is why identical twins are more accurately called *monozygotic* (one-egg). Clearly, the colloquial term "identical" is misleading because even identical twins can sometimes be surprisingly different right from infancy. The individuality of identical twins can be illuminated by exploring two things having little or nothing to do with rearing: the process of twinning and the conditions of prenatal life.

Early versus Late Separation: Why Identical Twins Aren't Identical

Right after egg and sperm unite, the fertilized egg, or zygote, divides into two daughter cells that soon divide to make four granddaughter cells. Each of the four then divides to make eight, and so on, with each division doubling the total number. In this way, the clump of cells quickly develops as an embryo (from the Greek, meaning to swell within), then a fetus (from the Latin, meaning young one). Occasionally, something odd happens. Up to about the fifteenth day, the clump may split into two roughly equal clumplets that will become identical twins. Such twinning can occur early or late during this 15-day window of opportunity.

With early separation, occurring by day 4, the few cells of each twin are identical not only genetically, but in just about every other physical way.

Here are the beginnings of identical twins who should be much alike. Yet prenatal circumstances may change all that, for after some development each fetal twin gets its own placenta, the structure that connects it to the mother. So, while these early-separated identicals may be biologically alike, their separate placentas, and therefore separate blood supplies, create environmental differences that can make even identical twins in some ways so different.

With late separation, occurring after day 4, the original embryonic clump continues to grow past the time when different parts of the clump have responded to local conditions and are becoming ever more different. This increases the chance that the twins will be mirror images of each other, their hair whirling in opposite directions, their freckles or moles on opposite sides of their bodies. Some sort of mirror imaging occurs in about 25 percent of identicals, and it implies relatively late splitting. But mirror imaging also occurs in fraternal twins, meaning that late splitting is sufficient but not necessary for the condition.

In one case, a right-handed twin had a lifetime left facial weakness. She smiled somewhat asymmetrically and was unable to wink with her left eye. Her left-handed sister had a lifetime right facial weakness. She, too, smiled somewhat asymmetrically but was unable to wink with her right eye. Moreover, only the right-handed twin suffered a hormone disorder called adrenal insufficiency, probably caused by an autoimmune disease of unknown origin, which gave her face a thin and swarthy appearance.

About 25 percent of identical twins, almost certainly twins whose separation occurred after day 8, display some mirror imaging. In rare cases, mirror imaging even includes a reversal of the heart, the liver, and other internal organs. Given the high death rate of at least one fetal twin, the occasional singleton with such organ reversal could be the lone survivor of a twin pair. One researcher estimates that at least 15 percent of singletons are actually survivors of a twinship.

Perhaps over 70 percent of twin conceptions fail in one way or another. Twins who do survive also have a higher rate of congenital malformations, such as an extra finger. (The word *congenital*, from the Latin *congenitus*, means born together with.) Evident at birth, malformations suggest anomalous development caused, for instance, by prenatal stress from viral infection or compromised blood supply. Because malformations are more likely the later the embryo splits, conjoined twins have the highest risk. Finally, twins are generally born about 3 weeks prematurely. This may mean abnormally small birth weights, slightly lower IQ overall, and a

6-times-greater rate of mental retardation compared to singletons. With advances in both prenatal and postnatal care, such disadvantages are becoming less evident and less consequential.

A clue to the survivorship of a twin occasionally comes with coincidental evidence from sonograms taken on two separate occasions. Thus, a twin pregnancy revealed in a sonogram taken when the fetuses are 10 weeks old may no longer be evident in a later sonogram, suggesting the loss of a twin. Lost twins may also be identified in spontaneous abortions or in births of a singleton along with an amorphous twin, a remnant that never made it. A remnant can be anything from ambiguous tissue to an incomplete body—sometimes bits and pieces including teeth or hair.

Late splitters, including just about all mirror image twins, share the same placenta and, therefore, the same blood supply. Does such intimate sharing really explain why, for certain traits or conditions, twins are even more alike than twins who split before day 4 and therefore have their own placenta? Apparently so, for compared to early-splitting identicals, late-splitting identicals show comparatively greater resemblance on certain personality traits involving poor peer relations, shyness, irritability, and antisocial inclinations.

Sharing a placenta means sharing other qualities, such as a mental illness. Most identical twins are alike, or concordant, in handedness: Both are right- or left-handed. But there are exceptions. Apparently, identicals *discordant* for handedness—one right-handed, the other not—are mostly concordant for schizophrenia. In 60 percent of the cases where one twin had schizophrenia, the other also had schizophrenia. On the other hand, identicals concordant for handedness—both right- or left-handed—were mostly discordant for schizophrenia. Where one was ill, the other was also ill in only 32 percent of the cases.

Actually, these numbers make sense if different handedness indicates later splitting, which, in turn, means a higher chance that the twins will share a placenta. Sharing a placenta and concordance for schizophrenia raises the old idea of shared viral infection. Schizophrenics are more likely than others to have been exposed prenatally to maternal influenza, to have been in their second trimester of fetal life when their mothers got the flu. This means that they were at greatest risk of becoming infected during a time of incredibly complex brain development.

Thousands of new cells are laid down every day, each one migrating to its correct position, orienting itself, and sending out thousands of connections to thousands of its equally complex neighbors. Infection could disrupt this development, possibly helping to increase the risk for schizophrenia in someone already genetically disposed. If infection comes through the placenta, placental sharing should enhance both twins' risk of infection if either one becomes infected.

If sharing or not sharing a placenta really does affect identicals' risk for schizophrenia, then the implication is clear: Even highly heritable traits are subject to nongenetic influences from an embryo's own development and from events in the prenatal environment, none of which has to do with rearing.

Twins Lost, Hidden, or Conjoined: Why Identicals Can Be Quite Different

The influence of prenatal life is dramatically underscored by some of nature's strangest phenomena, arising when embryonic splitting is so late—after day 13—that twinning is incomplete. In rare cases, an x-ray reveals the anatomical parts of a hidden twin, or even a complete fetus, embedded within the body of an otherwise normal singleton. One such case involved an unborn sibling discovered in the abdomen of a 6-week-old child. Another case was described in a newspaper article beginning with the headline, "The Man Who Had a Baby." It told of a teenage Japanese man whose complaints of chest pain proved to have an unexpected cause: a female embryo about the size of a fist growing in his chest. Apparently, during early gestation the young man's twin sister had been incorporated into his fetal body, where it remained dormant until awakened by an upsurge of his adolescent hormones. Even more bizarre is the extraordinary case of an infant girl from whose brain were removed five fetuses.

Sometimes a lost twin appears in the form of extra body parts—for example, a trunk with legs and arms sticking out of the host's chest. In the rarest cases—called Janus, after the Roman god of beginnings, who appeared on temples and coins as a head with two faces looking in opposite directions—two complete and functional faces appear on either side of a head. One such person was Edward Mordake of England, a reclusive scholar, musician, and heir to a peerage. Along with his rather handsome face, Mordake sported a second face on the back of his head, a masklike feminine face supposedly given to smiling, sneering, and, according to Mordake, whispering all night long, though only the movement of the lips was verified. No longer able to tolerate his condition, Mordake committed suicide.

A more typical though still rare form of incomplete separation called *conjoined twinning* occurs in roughly 1 out of 50,000 births. Apparently, circus promoter P. T. Barnum first spoke of the condition as Siamese after hearing of the most famous case, a pair of twins connected by a thick cartilage running from their breastbone to their navel. Chang and Eng, Siamese names for left and right, were born in 1811 to Chinese parents. They lived in a village near Bangkok, the capital of what was then called Siam, now Thailand.

The twins were discovered by a British merchant who brought the teenagers first to America and then to England, where they were studied and enjoyed much notoriety. (Given current surgical techniques, the two could have been easily separated, for they shared no organs.) They traveled extensively throughout Europe, eventually changing their name to Bunker and settling in North Carolina. There they sired 22 children, 10 by Chang and his wife, 12 by Eng and *his* wife. Though two of Chang's children were deaf mutes, all the children were otherwise normal, intelligent, and even quite successful, one becoming the president of the Union Pacific Railroad. To minimize squabbling, each family was located in a different place, the twins shifting domiciles once a week or once every 3 days.

Chang was the smaller of the two, more feeble but also more temperamental and given to alcohol abuse. Eng was a teetotaler who, despairing of arguments and fights, often gave in to his dominating and temperamental brother. One cold, drizzly day Chang wanted to go out. Again he managed to prevail over his more docile and sensible brother, who wanted to remain indoors. Alas, Chang got sick and, after another characteristic quarrel followed by agreement to go to bed, he promptly died. In a panic over his untenable situation, the otherwise healthy Eng had a nervous breakdown and died a few hours later.

Chang and Eng fit a pattern suggested by mostly clinical and anecdotal evidence that conjoined twins are in many ways unalike. The differences, some as great as those seen with fraternal twins, are not just in physical characteristics of size, dexterity, or mirror imaging. There are also differences in thinking, opinions, and temperament, say, with one twin more dominant, confident, sensitive, extroverted, or creative than the other. Conjoined twins also may differ in states of mind and health, with one being ill, the other well. Even sleep-wake discordances have been observed, with one twin asleep, the other awake.

From where do such great nongenetic differences come? One answer is self-consciousness and other social effects of being conjoined, all of which create an urgent need to cultivate a separate identity. Another often over-looked possibility is that the biology of very late separation causes inborn differences that underlie lifelong psychological differences. Again, despite their sometimes stunning similarities, even identical twins must develop into unique persons—likewise, artificial clones, who would display even less psychological resemblance, given that they would have even greater differences in their prenatal and social environments.

That identical twins can be anything from highly similar to as different as a viable person and a clump of tissue again underscores a key point that applies to all people, whether singletons or twins. Despite the power of genetic influence on human behavior—despite even the power of social influences—there will be many surprises along the way. The genes may be an excellent guide, but they are no guarantee of exactly how a person will turn out, which is why, despite their identical genes and shared social environments, despite being treated alike, even identical twins reared together can differ in one or another trait.

Exotic Littles: Handy Clues to Prenatal Influence

The brain's development comes from two sources: external events involving the prenatal environment and internal events governing fetal growth. In conjoined twins, even more than in other identicals, brain development will always be somewhat different. Differences can be seen in brain scans revealing obvious differences in the size and shape of brain parts—even in the microstructure of the brain, which explains why both could have Tourette's syndrome, yet be markedly different in their tics, twitching, and gross movements. No surprise, then, that genetically identical people like Paul and his brother could differ, even strikingly, for biological reasons that have nothing to do with rearing. This idea is being addressed by new evidence from research on the hand.

Identical twins are usually alike in the length or shape of any part of their hands. A substantial difference would therefore suggest some prenatal event that has altered the genetically intended development of at least one of the twins. The events that cause hand differences occur from the third to fifth months of gestation. Could such events really make the difference between being ill with schizophrenia or being spared? The likely answer is yes, given what is known about identical twins who, like Paul and his twin brother, are discordant for the illness.

Ill twins tend to display certain odd characteristics on their hands: a break in the crease running across the palm, a smaller thumb, or an abnormally short distal phalanx, that last segment of the finger that includes the fingernail. Compared to well twins, ill twins have four times more such anomalies. Moreover, identical twins discordant for schizophrenia show certain telltale differences in their fingerprints, a sign that some adverse prenatal event during the second trimester has affected at least one of the twins.

All humans have fingerprints; it is a matter of those invariant genes. Each person has unique fingerprints; it is a matter of the variable genes that individuals share only with their biological relatives. The prints of genetically unrelated people are different, while the prints of identical twins are as alike as those of either twin's right and left hands. As with the fingers, so it is with other parts of the hand. The number and shape of the print ridges, the loops, whorls, and arches, are laid down at slightly different points in a fetus's development. Those at the tips of the fingers appear earlier (11 to 13 weeks after conception) than those at the base of the fingers, where the fingers connect to the hand (15 weeks after conception). The specific location of any print abnormality can, therefore, suggest when a prenatal insult most likely occurred.

A print is, for the most part, genetically determined, but a *difference* in prints between identical twins implies an environmental cause: It could be a defect of placental circulation that makes the fetus swell, thereby causing more fingerprint ridges to be laid down, or oxygen deprivation that causes retarded growth and, therefore, fewer fingerprint ridges. For identical twins, such differences are typically small. Nevertheless, a significant difference in prints has been found for identical twins who are discordant for schizophrenia. Furthermore, the location of that difference—at the base of the index and third fingers—points to a prenatal insult during the early part of the second trimester.

Clearly, what is important is not so much the prints themselves but what they might signify about psychological development. Ridges are laid down while the brain is undergoing unimaginably complex growth. This is reason enough to suspect that environmental insults that alter brain development could affect various psychological potentials, including vulnerability to mental illness.

Consistent with this are two other observations regarding relatively large left–right differences in finger or palm prints. First, any such difference, or *asymmetry*, is relatively frequent in very premature infants, in those with mental retardation, and in those with severe schizophrenia. Second, asymmetry also occurs in identical twins who show little of the spectacular resemblance normally displayed by identicals on certain personality traits.

From their fingerprints, pairs of identical twins can be separated into two groups: symmetrical pairs, in which both twins show little left–right difference, and asymmetrical pairs, in which one or both twins show a large difference. With many personality traits—extroversion, masculinity/femininity, and religious beliefs, for example—both the asymmetricals and the symmetricals show the expected strong resemblance. With other traits—anxiety, depression, phobias, concerns about health and morale, and schizophrenialike peculiarities of thinking—the asymmetricals show surprisingly little resemblance. On these traits, asymmetrical identicals seem to have gone their separate ways, but why?

One possibility is that some adverse prenatal event alters brain development and, therefore, inborn potentials, which raises an interesting question: Can such an event bring out a genetic vulnerability, as in Paul's brother, that might not otherwise be manifest, as in Paul? Alas, no one knows the answer, but people with certain medical and psychiatric conditions are more likely than others to show two kinds of evidence that they experienced an adverse prenatal event.

One kind, the *minor physical anomaly*, includes low-set ears, a severely curved pinkie, two or more hair whorls, abnormally fine wispy hair, an abnormally large or small head circumference, a large space between the big toe and the second toe, a third toe that is longer than second toe, and left–right asymmetries in the size and shape of the face or the ears, teeth, hands, or other body parts. Another kind is the *neurological soft sign:* a behavioral peculiarity that is evident on a neurological test (for example, an abnormal grasping movement made when the palm is stroked) and also in everyday behavior (for example, awkward gait, clumsiness, minor confusion regarding left and right, or an odd way of splaying the fingers with the wrist slightly bent forward).

Parents will note the occasional physical anomaly or behavioral soft sign, then ignore it—and rightly so, for it is probably of little consequence. Yet three or more such signs could very well be signs of genetic vulnerability. Then again, they could represent some fetal stress that magnifies, weakens, or derails a genetic potential. A child's psychological development can thus be altered, for better or worse, in sometimes novel and unpredictable ways—for *better* or worse because, conceivably, a fetal stress could occasionally cause a fortuitous outcome: an appealing quirkiness of the personality or a creative element of the intellect.

One candidate for such a prenatal influence is suggested by the fact that a male child's chance of becoming a homosexual depends on the number of older brothers, but not on the number of older sisters. This fraternal birth-order effect has prompted many social psychological explanations involving, for example, feelings of inadequacy in later-born boys relative to older brothers. Such hypotheses—we've seen them before—are not only unconvincing on logical and empirical grounds, they are demeaning. A more compelling hypothesis offered by behavioral scientist Ray Blanchard involves the minor histocompatibility, or H-Y, antigen, a Y-chromosome-coded protein that studs the surface of cells, especially brain cells. Presumably, with each subsequent pregnancy involving a male fetus, a maternal immunological reaction to H-Y antigen—increased production of maternal antibodies—becomes progressively strong, making more likely homosexual brain development and therefore homosexual motivation and behavior.

With this hypothesis, we find social psychological explanations yet again giving way to a biological explanation with no implication that a child, his siblings, or his parents are in some way personally responsible for his unconventional psychological development.

What about Clones?

Though we have no problem with the idea of twinning, we do have problems with the idea of cloning. For many, the idea is still confusing and morally troublesome, more like science fiction than medical science. It raises the strange specter of individuals with an odd pair of mothers: one a DNA donor, the clone's identical twin, the other a birth mother, the one who carried the embryonic clone to term. Stranger still, those two mothers could be the same person: A woman might give birth to her own identical twin sister, who would be her daughter.

Apprehension gets reinforced when scientists or theologians characterize cloning as a kind of human xerography. Who isn't intrigued by the notion that a copy of oneself could be made by the transfer of one's own genes? Trouble is, the notion is overblown and, strictly speaking, false. Like their natural counterparts, clones would surely look alike and be similar, if only because a genetic blueprint has a powerful influence over the direction of an individual's development. Yet they could never be replicas because each would have more than a common genetic endowment; each would have unique inborn potentials shaped by distinct personal experiences in different prenatal and social environments. In short, there can be no copying of a person because biology insures individuality. Yet how ironic that people who have never doubted the individuality of identical twins will fret about the individuality of human clones—that people, especially parents, who usually act as if the environment determined everything now react as if the genes determined everything!

No doubt, many of our concerns about cloning are both morally compelling and scientifically legitimate. Yet any argument must recognize what bears repeating: For biological as well as social reasons, even genetically identical people—twins or clones—will develop into unique individuals. Clones would no more be replicas of each other than are any two identical twins—in fact, less so, because differences in generations and, therefore, prenatal and social experience would make it so. Clones would not even be as identical genetically as are identical twins; unlike twins, they would not share the same DNA that is located outside the cell nucleus, the so-called mitochondrial DNA.

In short, it seems that our concern about cloning, like our insufficient attention to twinning, represents the twin dangers of overestimating and underestimating the power of genes over our destiny. We can avoid such dangers when we appreciate the vagaries of prenatal life. And yet, the cloning idea will not go away. Initial apprehensions are giving way to an acceptance of the scientifically inevitable as scientists and fertility experts begin considering or actually researching the possibility of cloning primates and humans, along with genetic engineering to enhance certain traits. Apparently, it's a brave new world.

Implications

These alternatives to genetic influence suggested by prenatal life make it that much clearer how much the uniqueness of the individual applies even to identical twins, whether natural or artificially created. In this message are hooks that Paul could hang his hopes on: reasons why, quite independent of rearing, only his brother had become—why he might be the only one *ever* to become—mentally ill. For Paul, then, the notion that genes aren't everything was more than a cliché; it was an inspiration.

Someone like Paul can take comfort in the idea that genetic vulnerability is modified by the flukes of prenatal development. Schizophrenia is highly heritable, meaning that a twin's illness signals a genetic potential in the co-twin, but is it strong enough to make the outcome inevitable? Suppose his brother's illness represented a strong genetic potential, with something nongenetic suppressing it in Paul. This would be bad news, for even if he never succumbed, his children would still have that relatively high 1 in 10 risk. Yet his brother's illness might represent a weak genetic potential strongly boosted by something nongenetic that the brothers didn't share. This would be good news because it would mean a considerably lower risk for both Paul and his offspring.

Hopefully, the illness of Paul's brother reflected something the brothers didn't share, something nongenetic that will be insufficient to defeat Paul. On the other hand, if the illness was mostly a matter of genes, well, that would put him in the same boat with his brother. How could Paul know which scenario was most likely? The question was surely more than a matter of his genes or of his characteristic behavior and appearance. Roughly 40 percent of schizophrenics will display no obvious signs of their potential, no schizotypal or other personality disturbance, before becoming ill. Paul's seeming normalcy could, therefore, have little bearing on his prospects over the next few years. But what about *our* prospects?

Pursuing the question of Paul's destiny, we pursue the question of our own. Unlike Paul, most of us don't have the luxury of an identical twin whose conventional or extraordinary behavior gives us strong clues to our own potential. Nevertheless, we may know something more abstract and, therefore, rather less motivating although quite interesting: The balance of vulnerability and resiliency is but one facet of human potential, whose mysterious and chancy nature may confound our efforts to predict behavior, our own as well as that of others.

In the next chapter, a key question is explored: namely, why does scientific knowledge about certain groups of people—those with schizophrenia, for example—still not help us predict precisely what will become of someone like Paul? Addressing this question makes us understand in yet another way the limits of parental influence, but also the limited applicability of social and psychological knowledge to our own behavior. And what can be done in the future to make knowledge more applicable to the individual case, to *our* case and the case of our loved ones? Seeing that means seeing how to get past much of the current uncertainties that tempt us to embrace illusory assumptions that may flatter and encourage, but are neither realistic nor truly helpful.

Often, it is not so much a matter of our ignorance about psychological mechanisms but our inability to figure out how what we know applies to the individual case where the potentials lie hidden. Well, some hidden potentials can now be revealed by new kinds of tests whose effectiveness means less uncertainty, greater predictability, and more control over our destiny.

Chapter Twelve

Unmasked Potentials

If you can look into the seeds of time, and say which grain will grow and which will not, speak then to me. . . .

—William Shakespeare

Dionysius the Elder was a brutal but skillful despot who had made a superpower out of the ancient Greek city-state Syracuse. Legend says that one of his courtiers, a fellow named Damocles, was given to extolling his sovereign's powers, resources, good fortune, and happy life. More than a little discomforted by extravagant flattery and immoderate praise, Dionysius decided to teach Damocles an important lesson about the value of moving past superficial appearances and seeing things the way they really are.

As chronicled by the ancient Roman statesman Cicero, Dionysius asked, "Would you then, Damocles, as this life of mine seems so delightful, like to have a taste of it yourself and make a trial of my good fortune?" Upon receiving an enthusiastic reply, the tyrant gave a sumptuous feast at which Dionysius had Damocles "seated on a couch of gold, covered with beautiful woven tapestries embroidered with magnificent designs, and had several sideboards set out with richly chased gold and silver plate. Next, a table was brought and chosen boys of rare beauty were ordered to take their places and wait upon him with eyes fixed attentively upon his motions. There were perfumes, garlands; incense was burnt; the tables were loaded with the choicest banquet: Damocles thought himself a lucky man."

While thus surrounded by opulence and luxury, he was required to remain in place while Dionysius had a downward-pointing sword suspended from the ceiling by a single horse hair, the point of the menacing sword just above the courtier's neck. In that moment of great pleasure mitigated by great danger, Damocles realized how perilous and fleeting are life's pleasures and achievements. Thus did an instrument of war

191

become a poignant symbol of two great truths: the precariousness of our good fortune and the precariousness of our cherished beliefs. The legend is of Damocles, yet its meaning is universal, its message timeless, for in the end, is not everybody a Damocles, living by a thread?

Risk of Nervous Breakdown: Searching for Telltale Signs

For clues to disease, physicians have always had to pay close attention to what their patients say. What, then, does a schizophrenic person like Paul's brother tell us? Says one former patient:

> *At first, it was as if parts of my brain "awoke" which had been dormant, and I became interested in a wide assortment of people, events, places and ideas which normally would make no impression on me. . . . The walk of a stranger on the street could be a "sign" to me which I must interpret. Every face in the windows of a passing streetcar would be engraved on my mind, all of them concentrating on me and trying to pass me some sort of message.*
>
> *Now, many years later, I can appreciate what had happened. Each of us is capable of coping with a large number of stimuli, invading our being through any one of the senses. . . . It's obvious that we would be incapable of carrying on any of our daily activities if even one hundredth of all these available stimuli invaded us at once. So the mind must have a filter which functions without our conscious thought, sorting stimuli and allowing only those which are relevant to the situation in hand to disturb consciousness. . . . What had happened to me in Toronto was a breakdown in the filter, and a hodgepodge of unrelated stimuli were distracting me from things which should have had my undivided attention.*

What could explain such odd associations, peculiar ideas, and lapses of attention that suggest a faulty filter? One likely answer involves brain structures: for instance, the frontal lobes, located behind the forehead; the temporal lobes, located roughly behind the ears; and the cerebellum, at the base of the brain where the head and neck meet. Another involves telltale activity of the schizophrenia patient's brain, as is evident, for example, in a jerky movement of the eyes as they follow a smoothly moving object, say, on a computer screen: The eyes slow down, then speed up, lose track of, then overshoot, the moving stimulus. Jerkiness in what is normally *smooth pursuit eye movement (SPEM)* is detectable in most people with schizophrenia, certainly more often than in people with other illnesses.

SPEM characteristics, whether normal or abnormal, tend to run in families for genetic reasons, as is evident, for example, in identical twins who, though discordant for schizophrenia, are nevertheless concordant for SPEM. But the key point is that telltale signs signifying a potential for the illness, like SPEM, should be found not only in those who have recovered from schizophrenia but often in their biological relatives, and more so than in other mental illness patients and their biological relatives.

This suggests that the schizophrenia vulnerability of someone like Paul ought to be evident in a SPEM anomaly. However, the anomaly is neither necessary nor sufficient: not necessary, given that some people with schizophrenia don't show it, and not sufficient, given that some normal people do show it. Such apparent exceptions to the rule must be explained. Even if it did pan out, a SPEM anomaly would likely prove just one element of a complex brain abnormality. With enough of these elements the illness would be inevitable, but with even a few, there would be only an elevated vulnerability, which presumably is the case with many people whose relatives have schizophrenia. All well and good, but what is the relevance of all this to us?

Pluses and Minuses: How We Line Up in Vulnerability

If we could never become mentally ill, why should we care about the search for signs of vulnerability? To see why, think of illness potential as being scaled along a line from lowest to highest, as shown in the figure. The filled part of the line to the extreme right represents a rare potential so high as to ensure mental illness sometime during a person's lifetime.

lowest ← Illness Potential → highest

Imagine the vulnerability to schizophrenia as coming from a deck of cards. Some cards are genetic, some environmental, and each is marked with a plus or minus to indicate favorable or unfavorable influence. At the beginning, the genetic cards are shuffled and dealt by parental dealers. Throughout life, additional environmental cards are dealt. Thus, at any moment, a person's vulnerability is the sum of all the inherited and acquired pluses and minuses.

A few lucky people acquire many more pluses than minuses, placing them at the far left of the vulnerability continuum. A few unlucky others get many more minuses than pluses, placing *them* at the far right, maybe in the dark region representing guaranteed illness. Most people get the usual mix of pluses and minuses, which puts them somewhere in the middle.

Vulnerability to schizophrenia is thus like height, intelligence, and other traits that vary in bell-curve fashion from lowest to highest, with most people in the middle and relatively few at either extreme. Just 1 percent of the population is located to the extreme right, the darkened part of the line where schizophrenia occurs—where it has already occurred or will eventually occur. In dramatic contrast, as we have seen, the figures are roughly 10 percent for first-degree relatives of someone who has schizophrenia, and 40 percent for identical twins—people like Paul—whose co-twin has schizophrenia.

But, what about *us?* Assuming that we will never become mentally ill, that we are located somewhere to the left of the filled part of the scale, does it matter exactly where? Before answering, imagine that the line represented achievement potential. The filled part at the extreme right would then represent extraordinary achievement, anything from becoming the chairman of a board to winning the Nobel prize. As before, let's pretend that *we* will never enjoy such extraordinary achievement, that we are located anywhere except the filled part of the line. Does it matter exactly where? Of course it does. Regarding achievement potential, we readily understand the importance of our own location, as estimated, say, by an IQ or SAT score. Ours might not be genius-level potential, yet it might be enough for high achievement and personal satisfaction.

In the case of illness potential, however, there is a problem. For without a measure like an IQ score, the continuum of illness potential is mostly hidden. It is true, schizotypal traits can be measured, and the higher the score on a scale of schizotypal traits, the greater the vulnerability to developing schizophrenia. And yes, the biological relatives of people with schizophrenia have stronger tendencies to peculiar thinking—thinking that is somewhat disorganized, eccentric, and idiosyncratic—than do the biological relatives of other people. Finally, the biological relatives of adoptively reared people with schizophrenia have stronger tendencies to peculiar thinking than do the biological relatives of adoptively reared people with no history of psychiatric problems.

A tendency toward thought disorder is likely an outward sign of a vulnerability that is genetically transmitted to biological offspring. Yet signs of that tendency, however measured, aren't very useful because, first, many highly vulnerable people don't display such signs, and second, many who do display them aren't highly vulnerable. Schizotypal behavior is thus a poor measure of the potential to develop schizophrenia. If it is obvious where those who have ever had mental illness are located on the vulnerability line, the location of everyone else must remain mostly a mystery. And *our* location? Even if we are located somewhere to the left of the filled part of the line, it *does* matter where we fall. The genetic part of vulnerability can be transmitted by people who are located safely outside the darkened part of the line and who appear to be entirely normal.

For the offspring of parents with normal intelligence, the risk of having mental retardation is roughly 1 in 100. However, it is roughly 5 in 100—that's a 500 percent greater risk—if just one of those normal parents has a sibling with mental retardation. Most parents of an offspring with mental retardation are themselves intellectually normal, yet they have transmitted a genetic vulnerability. Likewise, most parents of an offspring with schizophrenia are psychologically normal, yet they, too, have transmitted a genetic vulnerability.

Regardless of one's psychological adjustment or the quality of one's rearing, the more "bad" genes one carries—the more to the right one's location on the vulnerability continuum—the greater is the offspring's risk for mental illness.

Unmasking a Vulnerability through Provocative Tests

Most people with a vulnerability to genetically transmittable mental illness have no suspicion of their potential or the influence it can have on their children. Others, like Paul, are acutely aware, forced to live under the threat of a singular sword of Damocles. In *A Mind That Found Itself*, an autobiography published in 1908, mental health crusader Clifford Beers described an obsessive preoccupation, a vulnerability that he recognized first in his brother's illness and then in his own increasing apprehensiveness.

Now, if a brother who had enjoyed perfect health all his life could be stricken with epilepsy, what was to prevent my being similarly afflicted. This was the thought that soon possessed my mind. The more I considered it, the more nervous I became; and the more nervous, the more I was convinced that my own breakdown was only a matter of time. Doomed to what I then considered a living death, I thought of epilepsy, I dreamed epilepsy. . . .

Mental illness in a first-degree relative is at best an imprecise measure of one's own vulnerability. Even without such evidence, even when relatives seem mentally healthy, people cannot know whether they are nevertheless carrying some genetic or other inborn cause that puts them and their children at risk. One problem is a lack of good biological signs of vulnerability. One day we will have them, though, and not just for schizophrenia but for disorders involving depression, anxiety, alcohol abuse, antisocial behavior, and obsessive-compulsive symptoms.

Some of these signs will involve a psychological function, as with abnormal eye movement (SPEM). New research suggests others that will be more purely physiological, one example being an abnormal heart rate plus a slow EEG—billowy brain waves like those seen in sleep—that predict antisocial potential. Fifteen-year-old males who display these and other such signs are more likely than their peers to wind up engaging in criminal activity by age 26. Another example is the time it takes before the occurrence of the first rapid eye movement (REM) period of a night's sleep, which can indicate an elevated risk for major depression. Another example is an EEG anomaly suggesting lower brain-wave activity in the front part of the left hemisphere in at-risk children. These are the offspring of parents with depression, who also show the low-anterior left activity pattern while ill and even when in remission.

Another way to get at hidden vulnerability is to unmask it with a biological challenge, as is done in medicine. In the glucose tolerance test, for example, a challenging dose of glucose is given in the form of a thick, syrupy drink. The body's ability to eliminate the excess blood sugar is then monitored for 3 hours. Compared to people with normal parents, people with even one diabetic parent eliminate the excess glucose at a slower rate. These effects suggest how a hidden vulnerability to a medical disease can be brought out by altering chemical balances in the body and brain. Likewise, a hidden vulnerability to psychiatric disorders can be brought out by chemical challenge, as illustrated by the following study of depressive symptoms. Compared to normal people with normal relatives, normal people with relatives who suffer from depression have greater vulnerability to depressive symptoms. While the two groups may look and act alike, deep down they are different, and that hidden difference should be evident in mood changes brought about by a strictly physiological manipulation. To test this idea, researchers had subjects spend a day at home on a low-protein diet. The second day was spent in the laboratory.

At the beginning of a 5-hour observation period, each subject received a specially prepared drink that either included or lacked tryptophan, a protein building block that is normally turned into serotonin, a major neurotransmitter. Serotonin is strongly implicated in some kinds of depression. It therefore makes sense to see what happens when serotonin levels are reduced, which is just what happened with the drink that lacked tryptophan. More important, the dietary challenge significantly worsened mood in normal subjects with relatives with severe depression, rather than in normal subjects with no relatives with depression. A hidden vulnerability of otherwise normal people was thus brought out by a biological challenge, as might occur under stressful life conditions.

Another example of how a potential for psychiatric disorder can be unmasked by a biological challenge involves the vulnerability to panic attacks, episodes of anxiety so intense that it seems as if one is dying or going crazy. Panic disorder is modestly heritable, meaning that genetic differences partly explain why the relatives of panic patients have a greater than normal risk of having the disorder. This, in turn, suggests the possibility that even the psychologically normal relatives of a person with panic disorder have a genetic disposition that could be revealed by some biological challenge, but what kind?

People who suffer panic attacks are especially responsive to an inhaled mixture of 35 percent carbon dioxide and 65 percent oxygen; they experience anxiety and even panic attacks after exposure. If at least one cause of panic disorder is signaled by a heightened sensitivity to CO_2 inhalation, then even some of the healthy relatives of panic sufferers should experience significant anxiety after inhaling CO_2. This idea has been tested by comparing the reactions of three groups: panic patients, their normal first-degree relatives—parents, siblings, or children—and normal people with no family history of panic disorder.

It is not surprising that after inhaling CO_2, panic patients experienced the greatest increase in anxiety and the most episodes of panic: 51 percent. The really interesting observation is that more anxiety and more panic were experienced by relatives of panic patients—22 percent of them experienced panic—than by people with no family history of panic disorder—only 2 percent.

Apparently, a vulnerability to alcoholism is signaled by a relatively *weak* reaction to alcohol. One measure of such alcohol insensitivity is self-reported intoxication. Another is body sway while standing with feet placed together and arms at the side. After drinking alcohol, the sons of alcoholics, who presumably have an elevated risk, report *less* intoxication and display *less* body sway than do the sons of nonalcoholics. Ten years later, alcohol-insensitive young men of whatever parentage are 4 times more likely than their alcohol-sensitive peers to develop problems with alcohol.

Again, here is an example of hidden vulnerability revealed by a biological challenge. That hidden vulnerability may have something to do with abnormal brain waves that seem to be normalized by drinking alcohol. Self-medication may explain why some people seem to others to be abusing alcohol, when the motivation is to feel better.

Someday certain measures, such as eye-movement abnormality, or reactions to specific biological challenges, such as CO_2 inhalation, will go into what could be called a *vulnerability quotient (VQ)*. That test score, like IQ, would place each of us on a risk continuum for one or more illnesses. As with IQ, VQ would make individuals' behavior more predictable, whatever their personality traits and whatever their rearing, family life, or other social conditions.

Ideally, the diagnostic signs comprising a VQ would give someone like Paul a clearer picture of his own risk. The signs might indicate a weak genetic factor and, given an absence of symptoms, predict only a 15 percent chance of eventually succumbing. On the other hand, they might indicate a strong genetic factor and an 85 percent chance. With or without such signs a person must live with some uncertainty regarding the chance of succumbing to mental illness. At best, people are often forced to rely on indirect statistical evidence suggesting, for example, that they, like Paul, have a 40 percent risk.

Should there be better tests of vulnerability; for example, tests for carrying a gene that either increases risk or, worse, guarantees that illness is likely? Should that information be disclosed? What if that information got out, say, to an insurance company? With a good diagnostic test, a person would at least have a choice of knowing or not knowing. The problem is as difficult as it is personal.

Scientists are making extraordinary progress to reduce that uncertainty with tests that can reveal hidden potentials. For now, however, only so much can be explained, and even less can be predicted.

Unpredictable Behavior: The Case of a Suicide

A student once privately confessed that she had been struggling with the debilitating effects of a lifelong, drug-resistant depression. Compounding the lack of energy and hopelessness were irrepressible nightmares about being invaded by bugs, embarrassed by friends, or cruelly abused by her brother. Dreams about her brother were a replay of personal history.

Throughout childhood, Julie had been abused physically and psychologically by an envious, antisocial older brother. Her parents and other older siblings had either ignored or denied her fears, which, by age 9, had become increasingly desperate after her brother began threatening to kill her. Starved for attention, always insecure, unremittingly depressed, and totally disenchanted with a religious devotion that should have been her salvation, she threw herself into endless activities: ballet (dancing and choreographing), church choir, sports (swimming and diving), piano, and special academic projects for the gifted (reading great books and doing math and science projects). Still, the anxiety and depression were getting worse, as if the self-medication of activities was no longer working. By the end of the fourth grade Julie had a nervous breakdown, during which time she tried to kill herself with pills stolen from an older sister who was being treated for a kidney condition. Convinced of her culpability, Julie imagined that her death would be a blessing for her and an advantage to her brother, who would then get the help he needed.

During her high school career, Julie made other suicide attempts, but these were different, as she had long since abandoned the delusional idea that she was to blame for her brother's cruel behavior and her depressing situation. Rather than signs of a genuine wish to die, her suicide attempts were manipulative expressions of angry frustration and a call for attention and help. By college, still clinically depressed, she was again preoccupied with suicide. Who can doubt that she was at high risk, but how confidently can one predict a suicide? Most people like Julie survive, likely out of sheer good fortune or an inner strength reinforced with life-affirming experiences.

Each year suicide occurs in roughly 1 person out of every 10,000. Psychological postmortems tend to reveal older males who were relatively isolated. They probably felt depressed or hopeless, surely ruminated on suicide as an escape from demoralization, and may have made prior suicide attempts. Finally, they probably had relatives who suffered from depression or had committed suicide. These signs distinguish people who have killed themselves from people who haven't. These signs are therefore valid, but do they enable us to *predict* a suicide? No, because any valid predictor is relatively common compared to what is being predicted.

Imagine a suicide-prediction test that is valid because people who will commit suicide, compared to others, tend to endorse questions about isolation, prior suicide attempts, depressed and hopeless feelings, and depressed and suicidal relatives. Naturally, one would predict that many more high scorers than low scorers will wind up killing themselves during some specified time, say, within a year. Strange to say, that prediction will likely fail. In one study, none of 46 suicides eventually identified in a group of almost 2,000 people proved to have been the highest scorers on such a test. Here is a real-world example of *a valid test that characterizes suicides but can't predict correctly who will commit the act*—this, even though the potential for suicide is highly heritable.

Identifying a future suicide is one thing; falsely identifying a future suicide—making a so-called false positive—is quite another. To appreciate the problem, remember that no psychological test is 100 percent valid; there's *always* some error, and usually quite a lot. Some people who commit suicide will, prior to killing themselves, have scored low (nonsuicidal) on the test; likewise, some people who do not commit suicide will have achieved a high score (suicidal).

Now, imagine we have a suicide test whose validity is impossibly high, say, *99 percent*. It is so high that *all* potential suicides are accurately identified. Therefore, all the errors—the 1 percent we commit by using our 99 percent valid test—must involve labeling nonsuicidal people as suicidal. Remember, each year suicide occurs in roughly only 1 person out of every 10,000. Using our test, we will falsely label 100 as suicidal—that's 1 percent of 10,000. This error renders the test impractical, for what good is even a 99 percent valid test that falsely identifies 100 suicidal people for every truely suicidal person?

What, then, can be done to predict suicide correctly? One possibility is to consider biological alternatives, for example, that people vulnerable to suicide may have a brain abnormality, a low level of the neurotransmitter serotonin being one likely candidate.

Serotonin levels appear to be relatively low in those who have attempted suicide—even lower in those who have attempted suicide more than once—compared to those who have never attempted it. Moreover, attempters with the lowest serotonin levels are at greatest risk for repeating the attempt. Apparently, depression sufferers with a certain genetic variant affecting serotonin are much more likely to attempt suicide repeatedly than are equally disturbed depression sufferers who lack this genetic variant.

Knowing more about a person's brain serotonin chemistry and its genetic basis will likely advance our understanding beyond what is possible by knowing about the psychology of that person's rearing and family life.

The surprising element in human behavior—our difficulty in making valid predictions even with valid signs of a highly heritable trait—is not just of theoretical interest regarding the limits of parental influence. It also has practical and personal significance. How do we know if we are carriers of a genetic vulnerability? Indeed, how do we know when such vulnerability, say, to schizophrenia, alcoholism, or suicide, like the potential for great achievement, can be passed on to our children, however they may be reared?

People may be in the dark when it comes to their vulnerability—or to many other potentials, for that matter. Even when they have good reason to suspect something, they often can't be sure. They may know a lot about the human condition and its biological sources. Yet because of limited knowledge, as with suicide prediction, they must recognize that there will always be an unpredictable element in any one person's behavior.

"One thing that struck me after thinking about all this," says an observer, "was that no one should have children. If we can pass on genes for disorders we don't even know we carry—even if we *did* know—we certainly can't predict how things will turn out. We couldn't predict whether the genetic load is strong or weak, for example. I look at my own children and wonder if I have passed on genes for depression or alcoholism (they're in the families), and therefore if I have destined them to heartbreaking futures." Yes, but what of other genes that could be passed on, genes for courage, creativity, and good character that can override the harmful tendencies? Clearly, we are dealing with more than just a one-sided problem, which is no reason to rule out having children. We must all take risks in this life if we are to catch the brass ring. Having children is risky, but what's the alternative?

True, many things, both genetic and environmental, are so complex and subject to happenstance as to be unforeseeable and unmanageable. Accepting this can help all of us better appreciate the tragic as well as the comic aspects of life, its absurdity as well as its unpredictability. In what follows, this idea is explored in an unorthodox effort to answer a question about a curious phenomenon: Is unexpected creativity mostly a matter of genes, or social conditions, or maybe something entirely different, something still quite mysterious?

Chapter Thirteen

Out of the Blue

Men of talent as well as men of genius are born not made. Genius implies a much stronger force, less adaptable to environment, less tractable by education, and also far more exclusive and despotic. Its very intensity explains its frequent precocity. If the necessary opportunities do not arise, ordinary abilities may remain hidden indefinitely; but the stronger the ability the smaller need the inducement be to awaken them. In the extreme case, the case of genius, the ability is so strong that, if need be, it will force its own outlet.

—George Sarton

When he was little, Aaron's varied interests included piano, violin, karate, bike riding, magic, and writing stories. Later they included math, music composition, and debate. All these were if not ordinary at least understandable, given his parents' above-average mathematical, literary, and musical talents. But there was something else no one had predicted.

Exceptional Talent: Aaron's Story

Around age 5, one year after he began reading, Aaron got a little computer. Though primitive by today's standards, it unlocked an extraordinary talent. Over the next few years, and with virtually self-taught skills in a programming language called BASIC, he began creating fairly sophisticated programs for games of strategy and adventure. By age 10 he was also programming in the HyperCard language of the Macintosh computer. His programming became as diverse as his burgeoning ideas and interests. An interest in the stock market, for example, inspired him to create a game allowing two players to buy or sell up to eight stocks, set up accounts, buy on margin, and keep track of gains, losses, and margin interest. They could also try to outguess the trend of the overall market as well as the partly random movement of each stock.

At about the same time Aaron began composing music using both the piano and a computer keyboard. He was also experimenting with a rudimentary form of artificial intelligence. The idea was to get the computer to acquire bits of knowledge so it could eventually recognize an instance of a concept. By age 12, Aaron had created a novel program to simulate interactions among little creatures he called BITs. Each had the capacity to "see," "smell," and move either quickly or slowly, thus to behave as predator or prey. Aaron got the idea for BITs from reading a book on the geometry of curved surfaces, which is unsuitable to the plane geometry of the Macintosh. It meant Aaron had to teach himself a lot more math than he already knew.

Each new idea learned at school or during a piano lesson he would try to work out on the computer. So, for example, he experimented with it to compose original musical pieces or to solve quadratic equations and display the results graphically. The following year, just for fun, he worked out an algebraic proof that there can be no more than five platonic solids: cube, pyramid, octahedron, dodecahedron, and icosahedron. By age 14, he was teaching himself new programming languages, first Pascal and then C++. Just shy of his 16th birthday, he was exploring ways to get these languages to understand mathematical functions, for example to solve differential equations.

By the end of his 16th year, Aaron had created his own programming language constituting 150,000 lines of code. The language can, among many other things, simplify complex mathematical and logistical computations. A real-world problem requiring a month of programming in C++ took just 5 days using Aaron's language. The consensus was that this creation was PhD-level work. Just before the end of his senior year, Aaron had developed a second, more generally useful programming language. Both languages were acquired by publishers and made available on CD-ROM. That summer, he landed a full-time job with a local aerospace defense electronics company. His work so impressed his colleagues they offered him a part-time job during his senior year. Also, he was getting contract work from different companies needing help with programming for the Macintosh, all of which he would do in his spare time after school. During his freshman year at college, Aaron had teamed up with a top-flight software engineer with whom he was developing software products to be sold on the Internet.

Aaron's technical achievements were self-generated. There was in him something like what Will Durant once described as "the creative fury that soon throws off guidance and cuts a path almost violently for its own way." None of his high school friends, not even the most mathematically gifted of them—one was ranked fourth in the world—did anything like what he was doing. His sole high school course in programming was so elementary he wound up co-teaching it. While his parents always supported his work with encouragement and the necessary hardware and software, neither had more than rudimentary knowledge about computer programming, and neither was a math whiz. It was as if Aaron had an intuitive facility for the underlying logic of programming, a biologically prepared readiness for learning its underlying principles requiring no formal instruction.

No doubt his parents' enthusiasm for learning and high standards for intellectual accomplishment had some influence, yet not so much on Aaron's talent or creative capacity as on the opportunity for these to take shape. The operative rule was simple. Give him a decent computer, make sure he eats, then get out of his way. This rule was practical, for what else could they do? Yet it was more than practical, for it raised a philosophical question: Would it be wise to do more? How does one know that what comes with guidance and encouragement is always better than what comes naturally?

The question surely applies to special talent, as illustrated by the story of an extraordinary boy who grew up in a one-room adobe hut in southern India. Srinivasa Ramanujan had just a few basic textbooks and practically no mathematical instruction. Nevertheless, through a seemingly magical process of self-education, he became one of the modern world's most innovative mathematicians. The English mathematician G. H. Hardy, upon receiving notes sent by Ramanujan, commented that "a single look at them is enough to show that they could only be written down by a mathematician of the highest class. They must be true because, if they were not true, no one would have had the imagination to invent them."

Hardy noted that Ramanujan's work lacked "the simplicity and inevitableness of the very greatest work; it would be greater if it were less strange. One gift it has which no one can deny—profound and invincible originality. He would probably have been a greater mathematician if he had been caught and tamed a little in his youth. He would have discovered more that was new, and that, no doubt, of greater importance. On the other hand, *he would have been less of a Ramanujan, and more of a European professor and the loss might have been greater than the gain.*"

Hardy raises the question, How can one know when well-intentioned efforts are really in the best interest of another person? The question applies not just to those with special talents but to other children as well. When and how long must children be forced to learn the piano, to read certain books, to visit museums—all for their own good? Should they be forced to interact more with friends, again for their own good? How does one know what's really best for them as individual persons—apart from the obvious, that they must be at least minimally civilized and educated? And one other question: How does one know when to keep pushing and when to back off?

Think of how much the average parent invests in developmental toys for toddlers; flash cards for children; karate, dance, and piano lessons for grade school children; religious schooling for older children; Ivy League college education for young adults. Well-meaning parents make such educational investments, and no doubt these learning experiences represent parental care, personal involvement, and responsibility—all good for children. Children need affection and discipline just as they need opportunities and restrictions. Beyond that, they are probably best left to their own devices.

Some Genes Add Up, Some Don't: What Does It All Mean?

It might be argued that the source of Aaron's talent and much of his creativity was mostly genetic, but is that a sufficient explanation? As we have seen, there are two kinds of genetic influence: additive and nonadditive. With the additive kind, small influences accumulate in graded manner, such that the more genes, the more likely and intensely the trait will be expressed. For example, the more genes one has for tallness, intelligence, or anxiousness, the taller, smarter, or more anxious one tends to be. Additive genes are like players and instruments of an orchestra, in that the more there are, the bigger the effect.

Additive traits run in families, such that the greater the genetic overlap—the more genes shared by any two relatives—the greater the family resemblance. Thus, identical twins show roughly twice the resemblance on these traits that fraternal twins do; adoptees show little or no resemblance. Children will tend to resemble their parents on additive traits, which is why the best predictor of a child's IQ is the average of the parents'

IQ. This is no surprise, given that each parent supplies half the complement of additive genes. Clearly, there was much in Aaron's makeup that genetically added up: analytical intelligence, obsessive attention to detail, and a wry sense of humor.

What then about the creative achievement apparently so discontinuous with the rest of his personality and intellect? That, too, could be the effect of additive genes. Suppose 100 genes were involved, say, for special talents, a zest for working autonomously, and the ability to resist peer pressure, criticism, or distractions from the popular culture. Let's say that 30 of the relevant genes yield a little of that creativity, while 50 yield some, 70 a lot, and 90 or more real genius. Aaron might have inherited much more than average. This would be unusual because most children of bright or distinguished parents are themselves somewhat less endowed and much less accomplished. Yet regression toward the mean includes occasional exceptions to the rule. These can have genetic, but also social, reasons, for example special talents brought out by felicitous changes in social conditions affording children advantages their parents never enjoyed.

Inheriting more than one's fair share is not the only genetic explanation for extraordinary achievement, say twin researchers David Lykken and colleagues. Most differences among thoroughbred horses are due to modest variations in genes, training, nutrition, and other veterinary techniques. Each of these causes adding to the others contributes in somewhat different measure to the total effect that is reasonably predictable. "And then along came Secretariat, a great red stallion who lay down and took a nap on the day of the Kentucky Derby and then got up and broke the course record, not by just a whisker but by seconds. He did the same thing at Pimlico and then won the Belmont—and the Triple Crown—by more than 30 lengths. Put out at once to stud, where only the most promising mares could afford his fees, Secretariat sired more than 400 foals—most of them disappointments, none of them remotely in their sire's class. Secretariat had a distinguished lineage, of course, although none of his forebears could have run with him, but whatever he received at the great lottery of his conception could not be easily passed on in random halves."

To explain such out-of-the-blue achievement, Lykken's group is suggesting a nonadditive kind of inheritance in which each gene or set of genes is an essential aspect of a genetic pattern or configuration required for some trait, such as activity level—the pace and vigor of running, climbing, and talking. With that genetic configuration there is a good chance of standing out on the trait; without it, there's little chance, for if even one of the relevant genetic factors were missing, the genetic configuration and therefore the trait would be dramatically reduced or lost. The configuration is like a telephone number that doesn't work if its digits are rearranged or a radio that doesn't work if even one of its parts is removed.

With nonadditive traits, resemblance will be found for identical twins, even if reared apart, but not for close relatives including fraternal twins even though reared together. Such a trait would thus be heritable (strong resemblance of identicals), but it wouldn't run in families (negligible resemblance for all other relatives). For example, identical twins show substantial resemblance for the trait of activity level; they correlate at about 60. Fraternal twins show virtually zero resemblance, the difference suggesting a nonadditive genetic influence.

Likewise with the trait of happiness: A study by psychologists David Lykken and Auke Telligen found that for self-reported well-being, identical twins show a respectable correlation of about 45 whether they are reared together or apart. In contrast, fraternals show virtually no correlation even though they are reared together.

As with so many other traits, resemblance for well-being therefore seems to come from a shared genetic configuration rather than from shared environments. Given the mostly random roll of biased genetic and environmental dice, Lykken and Telligen conclude that "individual differences in human happiness—how one feels at the moment and also how happy one feels on average over time—are primarily a matter of chance," and that "trying to be happier is as futile as trying to be taller and therefore is counterproductive."

Is high-powered achievement likewise genetically nonadditive? Assuming so surely explains why, unlike intelligence and talent, it sometimes emerges even from relatively ordinary soil and why, as psychologist Arthur Jensen put it, most geniuses seem to arise out of the blue.

Neurocompensation: Bouncing Back, Perhaps to Something Better

Short of identifying the responsible genes, one can estimate but not specify how much of the genetic influence on a trait is additive, nonadditive, or both. Even less certain are those configurations of traits—intelligence, talent, imagination, persistence, curiosity, ambition—that figure in, say, creative achievement. No doubt genes are involved, but what about non-genetic influence?

When a developing brain is injured, while some neurons die, others sprout new connections and become more active. At the same time, undamaged parts of the brain can take over, as when the right hemisphere becomes more dominant after injury to the left. Such compensatory change can explain recovery of language skills that seemed forever lost. It is like becoming dexterous with one hand after losing the other.

What happens in the case of amputation? Normally, all parts of the body are mapped in the cerebral cortex. Each map can be identified from a pattern of electrical activity caused by stimulating the corresponding body part. After a finger is stimulated by forcing it to be active in learning a new task, the brain's electrical map of that finger actually gets bigger; many more neurons are recruited to serve its function. On the other hand, if the finger is surgically removed, the usual signals from the now-missing finger no longer flow to the cortical map. Without this inflow, the now sensory-deprived—literally, senseless—finger map gradually disappears. The change occurs as the sensory-deprived neurons that once mapped the missing finger now help map an adjacent finger. A new four-finger map now exists where a five-finger map used to be. This change enables the amputee to remain as handy as possible.

Exotic examples of neurocompensation include a type of hydrocephaly, or water on the brain, that occurs in infancy. In this condition, much of the developing brain is destroyed by internal pressure building from fluid that cannot properly drain. However, if a shunt is surgically implanted early enough, the worst scenario of profound retardation can be avoided. Even so, the brain develops abnormally. Brain scans give the impression that most of the tissue making up the cerebral mass is missing, though it isn't clear if neurons and connections are lost or highly compressed. In any case, an abnormally thin layer of highly active, seemingly disorganized tissue surrounds a hollow, fluid-filled cavity.

Occasionally, a hydrocephalic child with such brain abnormalities displays not only normal personality, but intelligence enough for success at college and work. It is mysterious how a brain so disorganized can carry out its functions. Intelligence must be more than just the number of neurons and neuronal connections or speed of neuronal information. There must be some quality of brain tissue that somehow knows what it is supposed to do, and manages to do it. What can all this mean?

Severe damage to the brain usually brings major dysfunctions: comprehension deficits, learning disabilities, distractibility, impulsivity, and mood swings. On the other hand, when the brain is stressed rather than damaged, recovery from any psychological problems can occur. In a minimally damaged brain, a permanent but minor reorganization of neural activity can occur. For example, after a right hemisphere stroke, control of certain aspects of left limb movement, say extension but not flexion, could shift to the undamaged left hemisphere, thus restoring limb function.

Would such neurological change, for example, in the thinking parts of the brain, occasionally be so advantageous, and in a bright brain so powerful, as to produce giftedness? Novel neural compensations, like novel genetic combinations, could explain certain surprising developments—a special talent, eccentric interests, a peculiar habit—that seem to arise spontaneously and unpredictably. How could special talent arise from neurocompensation?

The late neuropsychologist Norman Geschwind proposed a controversial answer that has stimulated thinking about how often-unforeseeable conditions can modify genetic endowment to produce novel, sometimes wonderful, effects. Simply stated, the theory holds that a fetal brain's left hemisphere develops more slowly than the right. Slower development means greater susceptibility to harm. This is relatively more likely in the male fetus because of either too much, or too great a sensitivity to, testosterone. To compensate for a weakened left hemisphere, the right hemisphere becomes abnormally dominant.

The left hemisphere has the major responsibility for language and other kinds of analytical thinking. A shift to greater right dominance can therefore cause problems, such as a learning disability. Occasionally, however, it may cause an especially effective interplay of verbal, spatial, intuitive, and mathematical abilities. At the highest levels of intelligence, this could explain surprising giftedness or creative achievement. It explains why more boys than girls are gifted in mathematics, but also why more of them are vulnerable to childhood autism, stuttering, and learning disabilities.

Geschwind's theory addresses other questions. Many people believe that highly intelligent children are sickly or psychologically abnormal, that they are awkward, peculiar, introverted. True, super-bright children may have psychological and interpersonal problems. They are too sophisticated for children their own age, but emotionally or socially too immature for people at their intellectual level. Yet, compared to children with average intelligence, super-brights typically grow up to be larger, healthier, happier, more accomplished, socially more responsible, and longer-lived.

How can one explain the belief that super-bright children have more than their fair share of psychological problems? One possibility is unconventional personality. The most creative super-brights are sometimes egocentric, even egotistical, and insensitive to peer pressure. All of this may give the impression of psychological abnormality, especially to envious people of an ordinary stamp. Yet consider the possibility that super-bright children are stunning examples of what Geschwind called *neuropathology of superior intellectual function*. They are bright and creative, yet they display some telltale deficiency or awkwardness. This need not imply outright brain damage, with its mostly negative consequences. Rather, it may imply some stress that altered brain development prenatally or during infancy that boosts or changes talent. It could even be that these kids won't have the larger brains expected for the normally high-IQ population.

There is no way to know if any of Aaron's talent reflected neurocompensation. A more likely explanation is the conventional one involving a unique combination of heritable traits. One thing that can surely be ruled out is that Aaron's talent came from systematic instruction and encouragement. Arthur Jensen points out the inevitable failure of even heroic efforts by parents to turn their energetic and talented children into little geniuses—or the opposite, to dissuade them along those lines. There is no evidence that even the best teaching could ever turn any of a random sample of children into something like a Shakespeare, a Beethoven, a Newton, a Michelangelo, a Gandhi, or a Babe Ruth. Even environmental influence designed to suppress talent is likely to fail, as is dramatically evident in the example of Leonard Bernstein's parents, who, fearing he might become a professional musician, tried to dissuade him by getting rid of the family piano.

Savant Tricks: What They Say about Learning and Family Influence

Some people excel despite severe cognitive handicaps. In the *savant syndrome*, special, even spectacular, talent may exist in the context of mental retardation or autism. One mentally retarded savant could give accurate answers within minutes or even seconds to questions like, How many inches are there in the diameter of the earth? or How many seconds are there in 1½ years? Another, a 38-year-old savant with a mental age of 12 and a vocabulary of less than 60 words, could accurately recall the 1910 population of all American towns over 2,000. He could also give the names, number of rooms, and locations of 2,000 major American hotels, the populations of 1,800 foreign cities, dates, and facts regarding 2,000 inventions and discoveries.

How can extraordinary skill in art, music, memory, or arithmetic calculation occur in people otherwise crippled by severe mental retardation, autism, or both? Such unusual islands of excellence irresistibly move even the skeptical, for without scientific explanations, even they may be reduced to metaphor.

Savantlike skills can be taught to normal people. Ordinary college students can learn to tell the day of the week given any date or to memorize large strings of numbers. One of them, S. F., was able, despite average memory, to learn a string of 84 numbers. He could even start in the middle and work backward or forward. Apparently he had discovered a well-known mnemonic device to help promote memorization: Bundle information into meaningful chunks. As a cross-country runner, S. F. might recognize the sequence 3492 as 3 minutes, 49.2 seconds, which is close to the record time for the mile. Such extraordinary performance with strings of numbers did not generalize, for without a mnemonic device, S. F.'s memory for strings of letters was ordinary.

Mentally retarded savants with limited memory outside their islands of expertise follow certain rules. A spoken narrative published in 1924 illustrates this ruleful sense in a savant who memorized the number 30,249,385,274, just as a college student might. The trick was to make otherwise meaningless information meaningful by connecting it to personal facts. Thus, "30 is the number of days in the month. . . . 385—I once paid $3.85 railroad fare going from Cheyenne, Wyoming to Wheatland, Wyoming. 274—I can remember that by putting a 6 in front of it for the time being. 6274 is the seating capacity of the Hippodrome."

Psychologists K. Anders Ericcson and Irene Faivre give many more examples of how the mechanical application of rules can make a seemingly impossible problem solvable. Savants have somehow learned rules for normally difficult things including memorization, multiplication, and calendar calculation. But what is the source of this learning—how can an otherwise intellectually deficient person learn such impressive tricks of memory? It doesn't seem possible that the answer is specific instruction by parents, like that given to college students by experimenters, for how many parents know the rules? Does the social environment really make a contribution, if only in the form of mere encouragement? Is this credible, given that oftentimes the savant's skill is discovered only after having developed over years of physical and mental isolation?

Social causes surely can't explain the phenomenon, says psychiatrist Donald Treffert. "For if they did, why wouldn't every developmentally disabled, or autistic, or brain-damaged individual be a savant or have savant skills? Why would savant skills be seen more frequently in males than in females, with such a constant regularity? Why would some patients who live in the same unit, in the same institution . . . develop savant skills when others do not?" Says Treffert, "the savant syndrome is extremely rare, and the picture is very uniform, despite all sorts of different environments, families, and surroundings." In short, the savant's skill represents self-education through single-minded concentration and practice needing no instruction by others. If explicit instruction has little to do with the savant's talent, then it may also have little to do with the unique intellectual and temperamental traits of more conventional people.

Biographer George Sarton helps clarify the difference between talent and genius:

> *When genius evolves slowly it may be hard to distinguish from talent—but when it explodes suddenly, at the beginning and not at the end of life, or when we are at a loss to explain its intellectual genesis, we can but feel that we are in the sacred presence of something vastly superior to talent. When confronted with facts we can't explain in the ordinary way, is it not more scientific to admit our ignorance than to hide it behind faked explanations? Of course it is not necessary to introduce any mystical idea, but it is one's duty to acknowledge the mystery. When a work is really the fruit of genius, we cannot conceive that a man of talent might have done it "just as well" by taking the necessary pains. Pains alone will never do; neither is it simply a matter of jumping a little further, for it involves a synthetic process of a higher kind. I do not say that talent and genius are essentially different, but that they are of different orders of magnitude.*

Seven Rules of Parenting

It would seem, says journalist Lawrence Wright of identical twins reared apart, that life experiences we think have shaped us are little more than "ornaments or curiosities we have picked up along the way; and that the injunctions of our parents and the traumas of our youth which we believed to be the lodestones of our character may have had little more effect on us than a book we have read or a show we have seen on television—that in effect we could have lived another person's life and still be who we are."

Nevertheless, many parents still believe in a strong deterministic connection between early childhood events and psychological development. Parents must know that they are essential to a child's psychological development. The intent has never been to question the obvious. Rather, it has been to question certain assumptions about the necessarily enduring impact and paramount importance of a particular kind of parenting on a child's development. And this means recognizing the limits of parents' influence—recognizing that a child's development is often unpredictable, uncontrollable, and in some ways quite alien, yet understanding how, by stimulating a child's potential, parenting can bear surprising and even wondrous fruit.

Children can be pushed around, their behavior modified at least for a time. In the end, though, they are their own people, and as adults they are responsible for themselves, for their biology makes it so. As one observer noted, "I think the biological view *is* comforting, more so than the view that we are produced by our environment! I can rest easy knowing that my personality is really mine, not a product of external influences. It gives a person individuality, not outside determination."

All the illustrations, research evidence, and arguments about nature, nurture and personal responsibility can be brought to bear on the theme of parental influence and responsibility.

Rule 1. Good Parents Respect—They Don't Just Love— Their Children.

Love and respect are both needed by a child, for respect without love is merely cold comfort, while love without respect is merely warm illusion. Parental love is best when it resonates to a child's talents and personality, when it celebrates and encourages what is best in a child. This means not only deferring to a child who is precociously talented or sensitive in some desirable way—intellectually, artistically, or interpersonally—but also celebrating when that child out-achieves a parent.

Parental love is worst when it strives in endless futility to induce what is really best for parents—for example, when parents try to impose their unique psychological agendas on their children, try to live vicariously through them, or try to keep their children in a state of emotional dependency—even though the parents resented it when their own parents tried to do the same thing. While they can try to impress their way of life on their children, parents cannot—and in most cases, should not—impose their unique ways of being, for unless severely neglected or abused, children are bound to follow their own psychological paths, despite what parents try to do.

Parents need to back off when something isn't there. Trying to make children much more intelligent, considerate, sociable, assertive, graceful, or accomplished than they naturally are prone to be will likely fail if not backfire, at least in the long run. And parents must let go even when their emotions tell them to hang on. As they grow up, children naturally tend to move away from their parents, psychologically and physically. Everything parents do, if truly in the child's interest, functions to train and nurture whatever natural competencies a child has for independent and autonomous development. Despite love, loyalty, and family resemblance, children naturally go their separate ways, and parents must learn to accept this biological reality.

Rule 2. Good Parents Help a Child Become Civilized and Self-actualized.

Good parents try to promote happiness, civilized conduct, and academic achievement. They understand that it is their obligation to create opportunities that help their children fulfill inborn potentials in art, music, science, or sport. They know it may take a variety of educational experiences before a child's hidden ability or talent is finally triggered. And they understand that for many reasons some children have little capability or interest, let alone talent, but that even such children should likewise be encouraged. Wise parents are smart enough not to push children beyond their abilities, and are also intuitive enough to recognize the signs of futility and ease off.

Good parenting is essential to civilized society. Without good parenting, children can easily be spoiled and more selfish, immature, antisocial. However, even good children left to their own devices will get into mischief, or worse. That is why good parenting instills in children a sense of responsibility for their behavior, so, for example, lying and cheating are unacceptable. The absence of moral education can stunt a child's psychological development.

Rule 3. Good Parents Recognize that Each Child Is Unique Psychologically.

Children are not motivated to confirm anything or validate anyone, including a parent. Children are not miniature replicas of their parents; they can feel pressure to conform to parental hopes and expectations; they may even identify with these, at least for a while. Eventually, though, hollow accommodations tend to fade as inner potentials ripen. Children must follow their own sometimes surprising and divergent psychological paths, despite what their parents try to make them do.

Children can be taught to control themselves, but they cannot be taught to be themselves. Under normal (nonabusive) conditions, much of the learning that sticks, like language learning, comes from self-education through self-satisfying experience that needs little or no formal instruction.

Children must learn what is expected while they learn to be themselves. Parents need to be attentive, caring, controlling, authoritative, and resourceful—as much as possible in ways that accommodate a child's unique intellect and temperament, yet in ways that promote a parent's and a society's reasonable expectations.

Rule 4. Parents Have Limited Ability to Predict Their Children's Development.

Predicting a child's eventual development is hazardous at best. Because of the roll of genetic and other inborn "dice," extraordinary offspring—great leaders, creative geniuses, psychotics—can come from ordinary people, while surprisingly ordinary offspring can come from extraordinary people. After a relatively stormy childhood, positive and desirable traits may ripen as the problem child becomes a happy and productive adult. Contrariwise, after a relatively normal childhood, a vulnerability may ripen during adolescence or young adulthood, the risk period for schizophrenia, manic depression, and other disorders. In short, though some predictions are relatively straightforward, parents are continually surprised.

Parents can never know what incident or experience will trigger something wonderful (or terrible). Therefore good parents should provide as many opportunities as possible for self-discovery and insist that the schools provide such opportunities. Parents can never know whether a child's apparent talent is special or ordinary, or whether the apparent absence of talent is mistaken.

Rule 5. Parents Have Limited Ability to Control Their Child's Development.

Normally, we cannot bend others—our children, parents, spouses, colleagues, citizens—to our will except in the superficial sense of getting them to do things. Absent totalitarian, traumatic, or other abusive influences, we cannot transform personality, improve intelligence, or create character where the instincts of ability, disposition, or humanity are lacking. Parents should recognize that given the strength or weakness of inborn talents and dispositions, much of what children learn—especially the deepest, most personal and enduring kind of learning that figures in their personality development—doesn't necessarily follow from what they are exposed to or what they are taught.

Love doesn't conquer all. It may make the world go 'round, but it can't make the schizophrenic whole, the manic-depressive happy, the psychopath humane, the introvert sociable, the ordinary person talented. Even with the best parenting, children may still be insecure, uninspired, unfulfilled, uncivilized. They may be freighted with so much cognitive disability or emotional vulnerability that a parent can do relatively little, even with special education or psychotherapy.

Most children have the inner resiliency to bounce back from adversity. The supposed mistakes most parents make will likely have no more long-term consequence than a bruise that leaves no scar. Good parents must accept that they can't be perfect and realize they will make mistakes with their children.

Parental influence is often transitory, as is most evident in the dissolution of any resemblance between adoptees and their adoptive relatives—in particular, their parents and siblings—as adoptees reach maturity and go their own ways. Children slough off what lacks personal relevance, in the home but also in school: Ask anyone without mathematical talent who did well in high school math what he remembers about logarithms, cosines, or polynomials. Ask anyone without literary inclinations who did well in high school English what she remembers about *Julius Caesar* or *Silas Marner*. There's a good reason why all those courses, music lessons, museum trips, and ethical instruction often have so little predictable long-term effect on a child's competence and personality.

Much parental influence is nonspecific and inadvertent. Even when ineffective for shaping behavior in specific directions desired by a parent, rewards and punishments usually still signify an emotional engagement that normally encourages security, well-being, self-confidence, and identity, also serving to bind family members in affection and loyalty. But alienation of affection is more likely when a child's need for autonomy, privacy, respect, and personal responsibility is frustrated by overcontrolling, oversolicitous, excessively intrusive parenting, which fundamentally is self-centered more than child-centered.

Much parental influence is reactive, orchestrated by the child rather than simply imposed by a parent. By influencing their parents' behaviors, children, however unwittingly, help engineer just those social forces that figure in their becoming adults and fulfilling their potential; if children are clay, they are also their own potters.

Some parental influence is simply illusory. Rewards need not reinforce behavior, nor punishments inhibit it, since what parents do with their children need not have effects—at least not intended or lasting effects. Apparent parental influence may not reflect so much what parents have done to their children as what genes they share with them.

Rule 6. Parents Have Limited Moral Responsibility for How a Child Turns Out.

Some parents and their children are just victims of bad luck that, with limited current educational or biomedical technology, cannot be cured and maybe not even well remedied. The chancy nature of genetic combinations, the vagaries of prenatal life, and the flukes of fetal development and social life mean that there simply may be no causal relation between parenting and dysfunctional behavior. Therefore:

Parents need to lighten up! They must take less blame for their "failures" and less credit for their "triumphs." Much of what happens, the good as well as the bad, will happen regardless because no one—neither the parent nor the child—has ultimate control of psychological development. Nevertheless, parents should continue to encourage desirable behavior and discourage undesirable behavior.

Taking too much credit or blame for a child's successes or failures denies a child's special genius for self-determination and it denies the personal responsibility, the accountability, and therefore the dignity of the person. Finally, it strengthens the false illusion that one has more influence over another and worse, that one ought to have such influence.

Parents need to be "good" not because they will get what they want, but because good parenting is their job. In the end, parents simply must go on doing what most of them do reasonably well: providing love, comfort, and understanding, but also the discipline and consistent ethical examples that educate the social instincts while dissuading the uncivilized instincts.

These six rules reflect the power of a child's inborn potentials that can limit both a parent's influence and a parent's moral responsibility. How often as a parent or even spouse or friend do we try to make others over according to some image or idea, and how often does such effort bear fruit? We need to back off more and let others be themselves, to recognize how much inborn potential, no less than social influence, can be unpredictable and uncontrollable, its consequences unforeseeable and unmanageable, all of which makes our life both tragic and comic when it isn't absurd. Only when we understand all this are we likely to grasp the last rule of parenting:

Rule 7. That We Can Be Anything We Want, and Therefore that Our Children Can Be Anything We Want, Is Dangerous Myth and Delusion.

We are most likely to abuse our power to control others when we treat them as so much moldable clay, yet at the same time consider ourselves to be free agents. Thus does the unstable illusion of free will become a delusion of power that makes people assume things that are false, say things that are futile, and do things that alienate and harm spouses, children, friends, and themselves.

Enchanted by an illusory sense of free will, parents lack the proper insight and respect for the natural limits on what they and their children can be. If adults think they can be anything they want, parents are likely to think children can be anything the parents want, which would mean that the parents too would have to be anything that their own parents wanted them to be.

Perhaps the rules are familiar. Some will even seem self-evident, given our personal experience and common sense. Yet sometimes even what is considered common knowledge can get derailed or displaced when other things, like parent-child conflicts, spousal arguments, and media stories, loom large. The fact that something well understood in one situation can become inaccessible in another is charmingly illustrated by what happens when 6-year-olds are asked how they would retrieve a bead floating on water inside a stationary tube.

Some children do come up with a float-up solution—pour more water into the tube to make the bead rise to the top. Yet half of these successful children failed to retrieve the bead when later shown a real bead floating in a real test tube affixed to a table. Distracted by bottles, tweezers, and other irrelevant things, they could not remember what they had articulated earlier.

Likewise adults who know the rules often act as though they don't know them. Ultimately, how many otherwise sophisticated parents still blame themselves for what they could not have predicted or controlled? The trick is to remember what the seven rules collectively say: that although parenting is essential to a child's development, a specific kind of parenting will normally have rather limited effects on the specific directions of that development. This must be so, for each person(ality), largely autonomous and self-creating, naturally resists all countervailing influences.

In the end then, despite what parents may try to make happen, children will strive instinctively to be themselves, which means that in some ways they will be strangers in the nest. This is not necessarily a bad thing. After all, more than caretakers and teachers, parents are witnesses to a miracle of nature that with reasonably normal rearing will manifest itself in the ineluctable unfolding of unique potentials. More than a scientific message, the seven rules offer a moral message: respect for others; responsibility for oneself; the dignity of the individual.

Chapter Fourteen

Beyond the Nest

I have been very near the gates of death, and have returned very weak and an old man, feeble and tottering, but not in spirits and life, not in the real man, the imagination, which liveth forever.

—*William Blake*

As I come to the end of a journey that for personal as well as intellectual reasons has proven more challenging and rewarding than I could have ever anticipated, I see myself again on the "Sunday side" of Ocean Parkway, across from where I used to play. In a somewhat distracted mood, I visualize scenes of my childhood, lovely evanescent things all too soon crowded out by thoughts of another kind: This Sunday side, what does it mean?

Scientific and intellectual ideas come to mind, then fade as I muse on something that touches me more deeply, something that Thoreau once wrote in his essay on walking: "When I go out of the house for a walk uncertain yet whither I will bend my steps, and submit myself to my instinct to decide for me, I find, strange and whimsical as it may seem, that I finally and inevitably settle south-west. . . . My needle is slow to settle—varies a few degrees, and does not always point due south-west, it is true, and it has good authority for this variation, but it always settles between west and south-south-west. The future lies that way to me, and the earth seems more unexhausted and richer on that side."

How curious, for in walking with my dad to see the Sunday-side trains I, too, went in a southwesterly direction—likewise moving from New York and Michigan to Texas, which for me was the moral equivalent of moving to the Sunday side, where insights have seemed, as Thoreau put it, more unexhausted and richer. How curious that my book likewise celebrates human nature and self-determination, even as the specter of genetic determinism seems to mock our sense of free will.

What then is revealed by the exploration offered by *Stranger in the Nest?* Most basically, when it comes to individual development, the influence of heredity and prenatal life (nature) is surprisingly strong, the influence of rearing and family life (nurture) is surprisingly weak, and the somewhat chancy interactive effects of nature and nurture are often surprisingly perverse. The three guiding hypotheses that served as our major theme are indeed amply sustained by evidence that is as compelling as it is consistent.

At the end of the last chapter, the major themes of the book were represented in the seven rules of parenting. Here, those themes are addressed by answering seven essential, albeit provocative, questions about social science and biological determinism, and their personal as well as social implications for us as individuals and as parents.

Can Social Science Answer Deep Questions about Individual Development?

No social science can credibly answer the deepest questions about psychological development if it fails to come to grips with a basic fact of life: that, *for biological reasons*, individuals determine their fates, creating as well as reacting to environments, exploiting opportunities, avoiding dangers, resisting social pressure, and recovering from adversity. And nowhere is the limitation of social science more evident than in its inability to offer convincing answers to such key questions as the following.

- *Assuming the power of the family's influence over a child's psychological development*, how come adoptively related siblings resemble one another in so many psychological traits no more than they resemble strangers from their neighborhood, yet show the usual modest (family) resemblance to their biological parents and siblings, whom they've never met and may not even know exist? And how come identical twins reared apart often show striking coincidences in some emotional expression, personal preference, or behavioral style, coincidences rarely or never shown by fraternal twins reared together? Finally, how come identical twins misidentified by their parents as fraternal (and presumably treated less alike) nevertheless turn out as similar psychologically as identicals correctly identified (treated more alike); likewise, how come fraternal twins misidentified by their parents as identical (treated more alike) are nevertheless no more similar psychologically than fraternals correctly identified (treated less alike)?

- *Assuming the great influence of parenting and family life in shaping the development of a child's intelligence,* how come adult adoptively related siblings resemble one another in IQ no more than strangers from their neighborhood, yet show the usual modest family resemblance in IQ to their biological parents and siblings, whom they've never met and may not even know exist? And how come, unlike fraternal twins reared together, adult identical twins reared apart have almost the same IQs as identical twins raised together? How come IQ is better predicted by the size of a person's brain than the size of his parents' bank account or the length of their education? And how come bright parents have children with IQs typically lower then theirs, while dull parents have children with typically higher IQs?

- *Assuming the great influence of parenting and family life in shaping a child's development of vulnerability to major mental illness and behavior disorder,* how come the elevated rate of schizophrenia or manic-depression is about the same for the offspring of a normal parent if that normal parent has a schizophrenic or manic-depressive identical twin? And how come the adoptively reared offspring of criminal or hyperactive parents nevertheless have the same rate of criminal activity or hyperactivity as do children actually reared by their own antisocial or hyperactive parents—a rate significantly higher than that of children (adopted or not) born of normal parents?

- *Assuming the family's power to influence language learning and other specific behaviors,* how come children use creole expressions ("Nobody don't like me") that they've never heard, while they resist using irregular expressions (past-tense verbs, such as "went" or "came") that they frequently hear and even have used when they were younger, preferring, for example, "comed" and "goed"? And how come the parent-child correlation for smoking is substantial for blood relatives but roughly zero for parents and children adoptively related? Finally, how come the newborns of all cultures studied spend more time staring at—how come they apparently prefer—attractive faces over plain faces?

This book has offered answers to such questions, every one suggesting the same thing—namely that rearing influences heretofore widely believed to shape a child's psychological development in general and in particular actually are, for biological reasons, quite limited, inconsequential, or even illusory. We may understand and approve of the implications of the evidence, but truly appreciating the big picture and the moral of the story represented by this book means recognizing the personal and social as well as scientific implications of the evidence. And that means addressing six additional questions.

How Should We Appreciate Evidence of Genetic Influence in Our Lives?

It is one thing to acknowledge an idea; it is quite another to embrace it as one's own—not because it is fashionable, self-evident, comforting, or even delightfully counterintuitive but because it comports with the relevant evidence. Understanding the meaning and accepting the implications of any idea must therefore benefit from a familiarity with diverse, sometimes surprising observations that are often compelling, sometimes provoking, yet in the end wholly convincing; and so it is with the power of biology— in particular, genetic factors—to limit or even trump parental influence.

Nevertheless, like the theory of evolution, the specter of genetic determinism unsettles all kinds of people: optimists, because it seems to deny our ability to change for the better; conservatives, because it seems to threaten free will and personal accountability; liberals, because it implies big differences between groups in intelligence or criminal behavior that can't be remedied, however heroic the effort; and religious people, because it seems to deny the spiritual element in human nature.

Despite any such apprehension, we are best served by the free debate of objective evidence. Yet influences allied against open debate can become uncomfortable if not outright nasty. A couple of researchers complain that "It has been difficult to entertain the genetic hypothesis about individual differences in IQ and still remain on speaking terms with many of one's colleagues." Another states: "This pressure is so stressful that faculty soon begin to censor themselves in the interest of avoiding future problems. When this process works itself to its final conclusion the professor or student becomes careful to avoid even a thought that may lead to unwanted questions. At this point, he is deemed fit to join the herd where conspicuous benevolence . . . controls both teaching and research." It seems like a modern replay of the tragedy of Galileo—an ambitious scientific spirit quashed by misguided ideology.

A philosopher of biology has suggested in all seriousness that the public would be better off being kept in the dark about any gene discovered to predispose a person to certain patterns of behavior, such as dyslexia or homosexuality. But how can such a statement serve the public's interest? Do we really want to live in a society where some people keep others in the dark about certain things, where some knowledge is forbidden and a few people are in charge of what can come to light?

The difference between the science-minded and the ideological isn't merely political or even intellectual, but moral, for it turns on the high principle that ideas should be *falsifiable*—not necessarily false, but if false, capable of being disproved. Embracing the falsifiability concept means accepting that because most hypotheses are probably false or at least misleading, most will eventually fall by the wayside. Accepting this implies a special kind of conscience, a willingness to transcend naive credulity, irrationality, and self-serving prejudice—even common sense.

There is no shame in a passionate defense of preferred ideas, sometimes to the point of irrationality. We can all relate to the alcoholic who, hung over on scotch and water, swears off water. The question isn't whether people can ever be free of bias, prejudice, and defensiveness. No, the question is whether they are free to engage in scientific investigation as a public process in a marketplace of ideas, which usually means applying the principle of falsifiability to the *other* guy's ideas. Since those other guys have the same intention, there is plenty of scrutiny, skepticism, and correction of errors to make the enterprise work. The result is progress, and this means progress in the biological sciences, which is increasingly forcing profound changes in the way we view individual differences, especially those involving inequalities.

Yet in 1993, a survey of American sociologists revealed an overwhelming preference for denying that biology has anything to do with personal achievement or psychological traits. "We may well admit," said one, "that certain forms of so-called mental and moral deficiency are inborn and ineradicable. . . . But to apply this to the normal or the allegedly supernormal is to fly in the face of all democratic principles. Those who appear to be intellectually superior—those [with high IQs]—generally owe their apparent superiority, not to some innate gift, but to the economic and cultural privileges they enjoy in middle class homes."

To deny profound differences in inborn potentials is to confuse democracy with egalitarianism, equity with equality. Is middle-class status an unearned privilege rather than a natural—an honest—achievement? Then one must also ignore many observations, for example, the large variation in IQ among siblings who share the same family environment, and the fact that the relatively brighter children do better than their siblings, the duller worse, no matter what the efforts made by parents and teachers to equalize the outcomes.

All children may be special, for that is largely a matter of value, but not all are gifted or driven to succeed, for that is largely a matter of biology. Like parents, teachers must take pains with all their charges, for "it is obvious," says Mark Van Doren, "that not all can be philosopher-kings, but it is just as obvious that all must not be less than they are; and a democracy must be prepared to give the entire quantity of itself that can be taken."

Given that children are naturally talented or motivated in different ways and to different degrees, then it is false philanthropy to pretend either that all children are gifted and talented or that they are inherently equal in ability or decency—and worse, to pretend that undesirable differences among children, being socially engendered, say by faulty parenting, are therefore remediable by schooling. Any curriculum based on such egalitarian visions will poorly serve children (and their parents) if it is dumbed down even more to ensure what the Dodo observed in *Alice in Wonderland*: that if everybody is a winner all must have prizes.

Social critic Allan Bloom warned that language is corrupted and concepts are trivialized in the effort to promote some social agenda. "Words that were meant to describe and encourage Beethoven and Goethe are now applied to every schoolchild. It is in the nature of democracy to deny no one access to good things. If those things are not really accessible to all, then the tendency is to deny the fact—simply to proclaim, for example, that what is not art is art." Yet even good intentions will be confounded by a tyranny of mediocrity that must arise when educators, politicians, and judges legislate equal outcomes rather than create equal opportunity—yet never for themselves or their kids. By embracing the egalitarian view, we deny creativity and thus life. The hereditarian position celebrates the environmental as well as the genetic, the cultural as well as biological, all of which gives us creativity and life.

Efforts to enforce equality of outcome in the name of fairness yield neither fairness nor equality. Rather, they yield increasing indifference to education, dislike of schooling, and resentment of authority. In contrast, a curriculum good in the moral as well as the educational sense recognizes individual differences while challenging each child to maximize inner potential. It strives to prepare each child to become an educated and productive citizen, for this is the goal of society; yet it expects different outcomes for each child, for this is the way of biology.

Is a Balanced View of Nature and Nurture Necessarily a Good Thing?

The arguments and evidence for a biological perspective are quite compelling, and many people are newly convinced. Some psychologists who once embraced a purely social view now recognize biological influence, but in this many of them are like the cock in Aesop's fable of the cock and the horses. "The cock was gotten to roost in the stable among the horses; and there being no racks or other conveniences for him, it seems, he was forced to roost upon the ground. The horses jostling about for room, and putting the cock in danger of his life, he gives them this grave advice: 'Pray, gentlefolks! let us stand still! for I fear we should tread upon one another!' "

Commenting on this fable, novelist Daniel Defoe noted that some people, after having been reduced to an equality with others—unperched, as it were—now crow about a brand of fair play for which, not so long ago, they showed rather little enthusiasm. Likewise, some social scientists, increasingly forced by compelling evidence of nature's power over nurture—thus likewise unperched—now crow about the need for a more balanced view.

The call for a more balanced view often seems more lip service than genuine conviction, a matter of the head more than the heart; no sooner is it articulated in theory than it is forgotten in practice. After hearing about a new finding that suggests genetic influence, we almost always get something like: Of course, environmental influences are important too. Yet, after hearing about a new finding that suggests social influence, we *never* get something like: Of course, genetic influences are important too—*not even when genetic influences are demonstrably more powerful!*

The new fashion of embracing a balanced view, albeit reassuring, can be misleading, for example, when the problem of obesity is chalked up to environmental as well as genetic influences. But just how do the words *as well as* really clarify anything? That the children of obese parents have twice the normal risk of obesity suggests a genetic factor; so, too, does research on twins. Yet, as one researcher notes, Americans are getting fatter year by year, which must mean that environmental influence is more important than genetic influence. After all, our genes aren't changing that fast. Rather, children are imitating their parents' eating and exercise habits. (See how parent blaming can sneak into even what may seem like the nicest of explanations?) Nevermind that environmental influence may have nothing to do with children imitating their parents. In short, proclaiming that a problem is both genetic and environmental may stir good feelings, but cannot serve the truth. At best it is empty, at worst diverting, suggesting an illusory solution to an important and interesting problem.

Clearly, it will no longer do to say that because we've now made peace with nature, the nature-nurture debate is no longer interesting. Neither will it do to underscore an egalitarian sincerity by announcing that we now credit nature more than we did a couple of decades ago, that we were bad but now we are good. For this insight misses the deeper question: Why, many decades even before *that*, did we give lots of credit to nature, and why the endless shifting? Perhaps we never really understood the nature argument or never really believed it.

People may be steeped in magazine articles about genetic influence and, if asked, are willing to admit that genetic influence is real enough. Fine in the abstract, yet what if ambivalence is so deep that knowledge of genetic influence is piecemeal and its usefulness unreliable? Can anyone then truly claim to have confronted the biological basis of human behavior, its personal and social implications, but also its deeper truths and subtle beauty?

Is a Genetic Perspective Really Hostile to Social Influence?

"When the question is posed as Nature vs. Nurture," says psychologist Earl Hunt, "the debate looks like a stomping match between Godzilla and Bambi. For those who did not see the movie, Godzilla wins." However, Godzilla and Bambi can both win. We can accept nature's surprising powers over our destiny while understanding that, depending on a child's receptivity, parenting and family life can foster security, learning, civility, and self-confidence. In short, the nature-nurture argument should not be viewed as a zero-sum game in which one side loses while the other wins. Embracing the scientific evidence of heredity and prenatal life need not mean rejecting—just reevaluating—social scientific notions about the *relative* power of parenting and family life (nurture).

A major misconception promoted by standard social science is that, because genetic researchers don't really care about environmental influence, their genetic perspective threatens to make social factors irrelevant. But of course genetic researchers *do* care about environmental influence; they merely refuse to favor that influence in their theories of behavior. An enthusiastic view of genetic influence on individual differences does not mean indifference to the importance of social conditions or family life. We can agree with psychologists Tom Bouchard, David Lykken, and their colleagues that "the genes sing a prehistoric song that today . . . would be foolish to ignore." We can also agree with psychologist Urie Bronfenbrenner that "the family is the most powerful and by far the most economical system known for making and keeping human beings human." Both statements address what is universal and enduring, the one influence that makes us uniquely human—the main focus of this book—and the other that makes us optimally human.

A critic of the genetic viewpoint complains that individuals cannot be desegregated into separate components of genetic and environmental influence—as if any informed person would ever argue such a thing. Without either genes or environments, no one could exist. It is therefore imperative that we distinguish among three ideas: *a false psychological distinction* when applied to any individual, in whom both nature and nurture are 100 percent influential; *a valid statistical fact* about the relative importance of nature and nurture to individual differences; and *a misleading theoretical notion* that suggests an opposition of two influences that are not necessarily opposed.

To appreciate better the interrelation of nature and nurture, imagine a great pool filled with people who must spend their entire lifetimes mostly swimming, with occasional rests at the shallow end. Their risk of drowning will depend on many things, such as swimming ability, shrewdness about getting to the shallow end, securing aid, or inventing flotation devices. Assuming the vulnerability to drowning involves just two factors, the depth of the pool and the height of the swimmers, we can create an example of how nature constrains nurture.

Pool depth is analogous to environmental stress, so, the greater the overall depth—the more stressful the environment—the higher the overall rate of drowning. A swimmer's height is analogous to vulnerability: the shorter the swimmers—the less able they are to stand at greater depths or to push to the shallow end—the greater their risk of drowning. Because height is highly heritable, with differences mostly genetic, the potential for drowning must likewise be heritable. This is true even if, at any given time, no one drowns. If there were little water in the pool, differences in height would account for nothing. It is only when water levels are high that individual differences, in this case genetic differences, can be significant.

Just as swimmers' height is analogous to vulnerability, pool depth is analogous to stress from parents and siblings (family life), peers and politics (community life). Thus, by illuminating the role of environmental influence, the pool metaphor helps disentangle two things, the rate of some behavior and individual differences in the potential for that behavior. Why, for example, did the suicide rate of young American men increase 300 percent from 1960 to 1990? Since no significant genetic changes can occur in so short a time, something environmental must be at work, a cultural sea change reflecting a quality of parenting making it more difficult for children. Perhaps an increase in family instability, divorce rates, and levels of violence or a decrease in influence of traditional standards factor in the changing environment. In the pool, this change in parenting and peer influence is like raising the water level, which makes things more difficult for all children.

Too often, though, a crucial distinction is missed between enduring individual differences in vulnerability, reflecting mostly nature, and a changing rate of a certain behavior, reflecting nurture and other social influences. No wonder people have erroneously interpreted a zero shared-environment effect on sibling *resemblance* to mean that parents have no influence on children, when in fact parents likely have significant influences on at least the general quality of a child's behavior. Parents may not be able to make their little "row boats" into "yachts," but to some extent—the research is still unclear on just where and how much—parents may affect the water levels that make "boats" rise of fall, thus maximizing or squandering potentialities.

People argue past each other, some focusing on the vulnerability (nature), others on the change in rates (nurture). To address that problem, we can visualize the pool metaphor in three different scenarios, each with something new added: extra weight that swimmers must carry. Extra weight represents suboptimal parenting and peer influence (nurture), and again the swimmers' height represents the unchanging genetic vulnerability (nature).

In the *life-is-arbitrary* scenario, bad luck determines which swimmers must carry extra weight and which are spared. Some taller swimmers loaded with extra weight will be at greater risk of drowning than some shorter swimmers with little or no extra weight. Still, unless the arbitrary environmental influence is so powerful as to reduce heritability dramatically, the shortest swimmers will continue to be at greatest risk; they will be most likely to contribute to the increased rate of drowning. In short, the more arbitrary the environmental influence—the less it correlates with genetic risk—the lower the heritability, in this case, of drowning.

In the *life-is-fair* scenario, every swimmer must carry the same extra weight. Additional weight increases everyone's risk, as evident in a higher overall drowning rate, yet the short swimmers still have the greatest risk while the tall ones have the least. Nothing has altered the rank order of height, and because height remains highly heritable, so too does vulnerability in the pool. Thus, the heritability of the swimmers' vulnerability doesn't change with the increase in the rate of drowning.

We see then that a new environmental influence may lower heritability, as in the life-is-arbitrary scenario, or it may have no effect on heritability, as in the life-is-fair scenario. Environmental influence might even increase heritability. To see how, consider a third *life-is-cruel* scenario in which the shorter the swimmer, the more extra weight he must carry. The short swimmers could be exploited victims who are loaded up for no fault of their own, or they might be perpetrators who, through their own irrational behavior or poor judgment, seek out or create social situations that weigh them down. Either way, because the amount of added weight correlates with height, it magnifies the genetic influence, meaning it increases the heritability of risk.

All these pool scenarios make clear how much environmental influence is part of any genetic theory of behavior. With the genetic approach explored in the book, the question has never been genetic *or* environmental influence but *how much* each explains individual differences and the implications of the evidence for a theory about parental influence and responsibility. Individual differences in many psychological traits have proven to be affected more strongly by differences in biology than by differences in rearing. Accepting evidence that, after all, might have gone the other way cannot properly be called hostility to environmental influence.

In sum, we now know well that genetic influence is a powerful factor in explaining family resemblance as well as sibling and parent-child differences. We don't know as well the power of parents and peers to determine the behavioral expression of an individual's potential, especially over the long term. Those who promote the self-evident idea that parents or peers powerfully influence language learning and social behavior may not justifiably argue that parents or peers likewise powerfully influence an individual's personality and other potentials, for the scientific evidence on such an assumption is limited or nonexistent.

Does Genetic Influence Rule Out Therapeutic Change?

A major misconception promoted by social science is that genetic researchers push a strong form of genetic determinism that denies the possibility of therapeutic change. The idea is that if some undesirable behavior is environmentally engendered we can do something about it with education or therapy, but if it is genetically determined, the behavior is beyond the power of self-control and social influence.

"One keeps reading," says journalist Daniel Seligman, "that the evidence points to homosexuality being 'immutable, not a personal choice' (*Los Angeles Times*), or that 'sexual orientation is innate' (*New York Times*), or that it is 'biologically determined' (*Boston Globe*). Or when the subject is data pointing to genetic and biochemical markers for violent behavior, that 'biology is destiny' (*Time*)." The problem with all these "facts," says Seligman, "is that *none* of the data now emerging postulates any such determined outcomes. The news is about probabilities, not about destiny. In every case the data concern genetic effects that 'predispose' one in this or that direction and thereby change the odds of particular outcomes."

Seligman's observation is only partly true because in some people a predisposition may indeed be so powerful that behavior has an obligatory quality, as if it were driven by some genetic mutation. Such obligatory behavior gives the false impression that all genetically determined behavior is likewise obligatory. Yet genetic influence is often a matter of graded probability rather than an all-or-nothing fate—of potential as much as manifest behavior, possibility as much as inevitability. But what does all this say about therapeutic change?

A generation ago, psychologist Bernard Rimland said that educators, social workers, politicians, and the like often seem "oblivious to history, which shows that centuries of lawmaking, teaching, preaching, threatening, punishing, explaining, persuading, and cajoling have not resulted in a notably more exemplary Man. Preventive and remedial medicine, on the other hand, have made remarkable strides, even in many disorders that were called [socially caused]." Rimland was putting his money on therapeutic advances in genetically determined psychopathology, the classic example being PKU, a strictly inherited form of mental retardation.

A double dose of a recessive allele causes this rare condition which affects roughly one in 10,000 newborns. The single dose (one recessive allele) is rather common at about 1 in 50, and is associated with a slightly lower IQ than would have been the case without the allele. The double dose of PKU alleles, located on chromosome 12, causes a metabolic error that leads to brain damage. A major culprit in all this is a bit of protein called phenylalanine, phenyl being the P of PKU. Knowing all this, we can readily understand why, without a diet free of phenylalanine, PKU infants become profoundly retarded children, many with unpleasant personalities marked by restlessness, fearfulness, hyperactivity, or even psychosis.

Successful treatment of PKU shows how even strong genetic determinism can be thwarted by a strictly nongenetic intervention. A contemporary example involves drugs like Prozac that can induce brighter mood, greater achievement, increased affection, and higher self-esteem. Thus a little pill taken for a few short weeks can accomplish what neither rearing, self-help, nor psychotherapy could accomplish over the years, which is altering personal qualities normally not regarded as mechanical. A psychiatrist observes: "It is all very well for drugs to do small things: to induce sleep, to allay anxiety, to ameliorate a well-recognized syndrome. But for the drug's effect to be so global—to extend to social popularity, business acumen, self-image, energy, flexibility, sexual appeal—touches too closely on fantasies about medication for the mind."

It's not just diet or drugs. A powerful psychological therapy that teaches a person how to control anxiety can thwart the genetic tendency toward panic attacks. Better educational mechanisms for rearing, schooling, or therapy might be developed to enhance or suppress genetic determination. Thus with new educational as well as physiological technology, yesterday's genetic determinism becomes today's genetic potential—and perhaps tomorrow's cure. Then where is the inevitability in genetic determinism?

Does Genetic Influence Rule Out Personal Responsibility?

We are witnessing a dizzying acceleration of new genetic discoveries for diseases like Alzheimer's, mental illnesses like manic-depression, behavior disorders like obesity and alcoholism, personality traits like extroversion, and sexual traits involving homosexuality. At this rate, we wonder, what *won't* turn out to be genetically determined, and what effect will all this have on the way we think about what it means to be responsible for one's behavior? Notes one observer: "It's as though we are witnessing the bio-molecular deconstruction of humanity, the abdication of all responsibility and will to our evolutionarily preprogrammed computer chips. The scales of the ongoing nature-nurture debate are so tipped that it is perhaps more pertinent to ask, Where do genes finally leave off and people begin?"

If we mostly can't help being more (or less) intelligent, extroverted, manic-depressive, or psychopathic than others, are we not up the creek without a paddle? Yes and no. Yes, our psychodynamics and personality traits are probably a lot more heritable than we have thought—and no, this doesn't foreclose on self-control or improved behavior through education and psychotherapy. After all, genetic determinism, like the environmental kind, is often about dispositions and potentials, some of which are strong and resistant to change but some of which are weak and malleable.

Even the strongest genetic potentials are subject to at least some influence, and not just the parental, educational, and therapeutic kind that derives from the social environment. As a social species, we have evolved traits that push for socially acceptable behavior, inner potentials for good as well as for bad. The self-control we bring to bear on impulses, emotions, habits, and the willingness to take medications to inhibit pathology or enhance personality—all these heritable traits are matters of nature. So too ingenuity or courage, individual responsibility or the possibility of self-control and personal growth—even redemption: All such human qualities are biologically inspired. We are biased toward being responsible, even more so when social conditions press for responsible behavior.

In this view, the moral dimension of human experience, the conflict between good and bad, is as much a matter of nature as of nurture. Yet the point will be missed if we assume that only what is cruel and selfish necessarily derives from our biology, while what is kind and good necessarily derives from our culture—if we assume that our mindless urges for selfish gratification (id impulses) are necessarily more heritable than our capacity for socially responsible behavior (superego). In short, a genetic influence does not rule out personal responsibility, given that our personal responsibility is partly a matter of genetic influence.

The moral drama is universal, it is historical, and in the modern world, it is increasingly tied to high technology, which gives us greater power to master as well as fulfill inborn potentials. Using abnormal brain chemistry as an excuse for bad behavior is simply not acceptable. The epileptic is not responsible for her disease; but she *is* responsible for any decision to drive, given the danger of having a seizure. Likewise the alcoholic is not responsible for his disease. Despite a tougher row to hoe, he is still responsible for avoiding drink, as a diabetic is responsible for taking insulin. The militant teetotaler, if still fundamentally an alcoholic, is nevertheless a morally superior one.

Is a Genetic Perspective Incompatible with the Traditional View of Parenting?

The potential for personally responsible behavior is at least partly genetic, but genetic potential is affected by parenting and social pressure from peers and other factors outside the family. When any of these potentials— the genetic, the parental, the cultural—is inoperative or defective, behavior naturally reverts to antisocial forms. Considering the power of biology and culture to trump parental influence, how can parents hope to maximize their influence? The best answer may be the most obvious one: old-fashioned disciplined rearing.

Requiring work (chores); insisting on restrictions (say, for TV-watching); employing discipline with the occasional and judicious use of mild physical punishment; having strong expectations for good conduct, which means deprivation of privileges after strikingly offensive or repeated instances of unacceptable behavior: old-school conditions may be emotionally demanding to a child—frustrating too. They will surely seem noxious, even abusive, to someone who prefers new-school permissiveness justified by assumptions about unconditional positive regard.

Yet looking back, such rigorous parenting often brings a powerful nostalgia and respectful gratitude like what one feels when reminiscing about those toughest of teachers who had uncompromisingly high standards.

Comedian Chris Rock's success can be chalked up to the right combination of wit, perspicacity, ambition, insecurity, charm, and something else: parents with the highest standards for good conduct.

60 MINUTES' ED BRADLEY: You were a strict parent?

CHRIS ROCK'S MOM: Very strict. I spanked; I grounded; I timed out.

BRADLEY: So you didn't tolerate things in the house?

MOM: Oh no. They always say, "Momma don't let you get away with nothing." Chris says something on some show that my mother was the president and my father was the troops. You know, if there was any trouble, they call in the troops.

Except for obvious instances of neglect and abuse, a demanding rearing environment need not harm personality—on the contrary, it may facilitate emotional maturity, good character, and self-confidence. Yet a seemingly benevolent rearing environment need not benefit personality—on the contrary, it may discourage it. A student of mine from Sierra Leone once described a local custom whereby middle- or upper-class families take in children of poorer relatives, exploiting them as servants, and using physical punishment to boot. Yet, according to my student, these Cinderella children, these victims of discipline and deprivation, seem to grow up happier, more confident, better educated, and better adjusted than one may have expected, while the spoiled biological children living under the same roof grow up less happy, less confident, less educated, and less well adjusted.

Well, it's just an observation and certainly no reason for arguing that children should be treated harshly. Yet during his high school years, my son agreed that, while no fun, imposed requirements to do chores and to be responsible for conduct are best, for they engender a sense of boundaries and therefore a sense of self. He was impressed that such requirements and strict guidelines were virtually absent in the lives of his rather well-off peers, most of whom used illicit drugs, including the kind one smokes and sniffs and the kind one injects. He was observing something that, alas, is all too frequent in our culture: wayward children reared by self-indulgent—that is, neglectful—parents for whom high standards for academic achievement and social conduct are abstract, if not alien, concepts.

What if the old school is closer to what common sense suggests and what many parents still assume, even in this day and age: that if not too extreme, even the strictest parenting done out of love and respect maximizes healthy child development? Granted, common sense isn't scientific evidence and the scientific evidence is based mostly on animal behavior, whose relevance to humans is uncertain. Yet we are impressed that animals emotionally stressed during infancy by rough handling nevertheless develop into emotionally hardy, more relaxed, longer-lived individuals.

Along with the animal research, social criticism supports the view that something insidious is occurring in our society that, like inborn potentials, can limit parental influence to the detriment of child development. Philosophy professor Christina Hoff Sommers observes that "Too many young people are morally confused, ill-informed, and adrift. This confusion gets worse rather than better once they go to college. If they are attending an elite school, they can actually lose their common sense and become clever and adroit intellectuals in the worst sense. George Orwell reputedly said, 'Some ideas are so absurd that only an intellectual could believe them.' Well, the students of such intellectuals are in the same boat."

Hoff Sommers observes further: "I often meet students incapable of making even one single confident moral judgment. And it's getting worse. The things students now say are more and more unhinged. Recently, several of my students objected to philosopher Immanuel Kant's 'principle of humanity'—the doctrine that asserts the unique dignity and worth of every human life. They told me that if they were faced with the choice between saving their pet or a human being, they would choose the former." And the result of all this? Students "taught that 'all knowledge is a social construct' were doubtful that the Holocaust ever occurred," though some averred that it was "a perfectly reasonable conceptual hallucination."

Looking at the problem of society today from a different angle, attorney and author Andrew Peyton Thomas has written most eloquently that "In all humans, there is a constant struggle between the selfishness designed to preserve the individual and the social instincts that preserve the species. Of the two, selfishness naturally predominates. As any parent can attest, only years of training and habit can curb this tendency. Thus, when society—through its values, social pressure, and legislation—actually enters into this internal contest on the side of self-centeredness, then chaos must prevail."

In the end says Thomas, "life is a series of obligations to be fulfilled as honorably as possible, with occasional interludes for moderate self-indulgence." Yet we are pursuing the reverse course of moderate self-indulgence rationalized as much as possible, with occasional interludes for fulfilling obligations. Is it any surprise then when a society that increasingly tolerates bad behavior—indeed, redefines as normal what a generation ago was considered immoral or psychopathic—winds up with high rates of crime?

In this regard, remember that episodes of seemly harsh treatment may have a salutary effect, as lawyer and psychologist Barbara Lerner points out in the strongest moral terms. "Consider spanking," she says. "The experts' conclusion and the research it is based on treat all spankings alike, assuming that the reasons why a child is struck are irrelevant—the message is always the same: violence is OK. Whenever I hear this nonsense, I think of my friend Donald's grandfather." Lerner goes on to describe Donald's friendship with a black boy he palled around with on a farm in West Virginia. The two boys got along fine most of the time, but they did quarrel, and on those occasions, Donald's grandfather would separate them and send them home to think about their conflict, and come to be friends another day—except one day when Donald's grandfather overheard him calling his friend a nigger.

"The old man didn't say a word. He hauled off and struck Donald with his fist, hitting him square on the jaw, hard enough to knock him down, then turned sharply on his heel and walked away, leaving his grandson sprawled in the dirt, more shocked than hurt. The message was violent, and it came with no verbal explanation at all. It was everything today's experts deplore. But Donald got the message his grandfather was trying to send, and it wasn't about the acceptability of violence. It was a message about the utter unacceptability of bigotry, and it had a powerful effect. Donald never used the N-word again, and his grandfather never struck him again.

"Contrast that with a parent who whacks his kid every time the youngster does something mildly irritating or inconvenient, and the idiocy of pretending that all spankings are the same becomes clear." Our kids need to understand "the difference between right and wrong—and between true evils like being a bigot or a bully and minor infractions like forgetting to pick up your socks or take out the garbage. And if, on rare occasions, it take a whipping to make that distinction really sink in, forget the chorus of experts, and remember Donald's grandfather."

Seemingly good-hearted, tolerant rearing can be a form of neglect, in some ways as irresponsible and harmful to a child's development as is abusive parenting. Following this thought, author Diana West remarks that a big problem of parents who were steeped in 1960s culture is not so much a failure to know their children but to judge them, to make the all-important distinction between right and wrong. "Such parents . . . mirror our cracked culture of relativism—one of the most insidious innovations of the '60s—which prizes toleration above all else. Lacking the moral fortitude to take a stand—any stand—these parents fail to offer their children even a fortune cookie's worth of wisdom. No wonder their kids are chronically troubled, perplexed by the array of behavior 'choices' before them. The fact is, nobody—not parents, schools or society—is passing onto these youngsters the fundamentals of right and wrong."

In this culture, a powerful combination of biological disposition and peer pressure can trump even the most responsible parental influence; the result is often irresponsible, self-indulgent behavior. Few children have the good judgment, emotional autonomy, and presence of mind to choose friendships intelligently and to conduct themselves wisely.

Social scientist Charles Murray neatly summarized what he calls the three core premises of popular wisdom regarding citizens and their government. First, people respond to incentives and disincentives; sticks and carrots work. Second, people are not inherently hardworking or moral; without countervailing influences, they will avoid work and be amoral. Finally, people must be held responsible for their actions, that is, whether they are responsible in some ultimate philosophical or biochemical sense cannot be the issue if society is to work. And children too: Generally, they respond to incentives and disincentives; in the absence of countervailing influences, they will avoid work and be amoral; and whether they are responsible in some ultimate philosophical or biochemical sense cannot be the issue if a family is to work.

The principle of self-control is vital to any society. It is a major component in the story of civilization, one that reflects our biology no less than our rearing. It is what good parenting and family life try to engender even when a good outcome cannot be guaranteed. It is what gives us hope for our future and the future of our children.

Chapter Notes

Introduction

3   Source is Kiester, E., & Kiester, S. V. (1996, October). You can raise your child's IQ. *Reader's Digest*, 137–141. Media stories often lead readers to just the opposite of the truth, as is well illustrated by this example. Consider the headline: "*Playing Dungeons and Dragons Makes Teens Suicidal.*" The implication is that teens caught up in the game become obsessed and emotionally disturbed because the game has an insidious effect on vulnerable minds. An alternate explanation is that teens who choose to play—roughly 3 million of them—are *less* likely to commit suicide than other teens. But consider this: Roughly 360 is the expected number of yearly suicides for 3 million teens, given that the rate of teen suicide is about 12 per 100,000 per year. Yet only 28 teens who often played the game committed suicide in 1 year. Now the implication is different: Because playing Dungeons and Dragons reflects self-selection, forcing more kids to play the game won't appreciably reduce the teen suicide rate. See Paulos, J. A. (1988). *Innumeracy: Mathematical illiteracy and its consequences*. New York: Hill & Wang (Farrar, Strauss & Giroux).

5   Quote from Harris, J. R. (1995). Where is the child's environment? *Psychological Review, 102,* 458–489.

7   Quote from Watson, J. B. (1924). *Psychology from the standpoint of a behaviorist*. Philadelphia: J. B. Lippincott.

Chapter 1

9   Landers, A. (1976, July 27). Parents can't absorb total blame. *Austin American-Statesman*, p. C2. For those whose personality contains the elements of character and courage, a desperate situation can bring about a kind of personal redemption, an uplifting and strengthening of the self. In his novel *Far from the Madding Crowd*, Thomas Hardy described the effect of a disastrous investment on his main character, Gabriel Oak.

"He had passed through an ordeal of wretchedness which had given him more than it had taken away. He had sunk from his modest elevation as pastoral king into the very slime-pits of Siddim; but there was left to him a dignified calm he had never before known, and that indifference to fate which, though it often makes a villain of a man, is the basis of his sublimity when it does not. And thus the abasement had been exaltation, and the loss gain."

10   Bouchard, T. J., Jr., Lykken, D. T., McGue, M., Segal, N. L., & Tellegen, A. (1990). Sources of human psychological differences: The Minnesota study of twins reared apart. *Science, 250,* 223–228.

10   Bouchard, T. J., Jr., & McGue, M. (1990). Genetic and rearing environmental influences on adult personality: An analysis of adopted twins reared apart. *Journal of Personality, 58,* 263–292; Wright, L. (1995, August 7). Double mystery. *The New Yorker,* 45–62.

13   Quote from Gordon, M. (1996, May 12). Hot dog. *New York Times Magazine,* 38–41. In like vein, it seems safe to say that if ego and intellect are as biologically determined as are id qualities, then in the biological as well as the personal sense, we are determined to be ourselves—*however unpredictable the outcome, and whatever inferences about free will we derive from our experiences making choices.* Yes, we can paint our wagons, but we are probably stuck with them. Our choice of colors and mode of application? These, too, are more than mere matters of chance or free will; surely they, too, arise from sources outside our personal volition: dispositions that push us inexorably from within, and external influences that coerce and seduce. Dispositions remain, while external pressures and their manifest effects change or dissolve. In time, fashionable paint jobs wear thin, crack, and flake off, revealing inner grain. Thus does the telling comment, "I open my mouth and out comes the voice of my father/mother," strike middle-aged people with a mixture of surprise and rueful amusement. (Source is Cohen, D. [1994]. *Out of the blue: Depression and human nature.* New York: Norton.)

14   Case of Beth and Amy from Abrams, S. (1986). Disposition and environment. *The Psychoanalytic Study of the Child, 41,* 41–60.

15   Quote from Sulloway, F. J. (1996). *Born to rebel: Birth order, family dynamics, and creative lives.* New York: Pantheon.

16   Quote from Samenow, S. (1989). *Before it's too late: Why some kids get into trouble—and what parents can do about it.* New York: Times Books (Random House).

16   Quote from Montini, E. J. (1998, February 13). The mother of all scandals. *Austin American-Statesman,* p. A15.

16   Rowe, D. C. (1977). A place at the policy table? Behavior genetics and estimates of family environmental effects on IQ. *Intelligence, 24* (1), 1133–1158.

17   Eysenck, H. (1995). *Genius: The natural history of creativity.* New York: Cambridge University Press.

17   Quote from Stone, M. H. (1993). *Abnormalities of personality: Within and beyond the realm of treatment.* New York: Norton.

18   Source is Brandon, K. (1998, May 24). An Oregon tale: Good parents who failed. *Austin American-Statesman,* pp. A1, A11. Such stories have far-reaching implications, for example, for legions of parents with a wayward child, who wonder if they are to blame yet long for some sort of reconciliation. One such parent put it in this bittersweet way: "My teenage daughters went hormonally berserk, and the loving children they had been mutated into raging monsters who treated my wife and me with hatred, contempt, and indifference . . . my children have grown, gone, and become quite decent people again." (Source is Elfeinbein, D. [Ed.]. *Living with Prozac and other selective serotonin reuptake inhibitors [SSRIs].* New York: Harper San Francisco, 1995.)

Sometimes, as with this example, there is no good news, not even the suggestion of a happy ending. According to government researchers, Daniel Fletcher ripped off 200,000 individuals and dozens of telephone companies of millions of dollars in long-distance scams by phony advertisement that capitalized on religious themes. Mr. Fletcher, a seminary student and the son of a minister, "took advantage of the phone companies' huge appetite for customers by dealing with them honestly for a time, and then gradually feeding them thousands of apparently counterfeit callers." By the time his scams were fully uncovered, Fletcher was on the run.

He had been "a good kid," said Fletcher senior, who simply could not explain how his son had become such a criminal. After being away from home, "he came back totally foreign"; the father then offered up some of the usual suspects, including stress from too many courses and too much study—but what kind of explanation is that, and is it any better than blaming the parents? Just how much are parents responsible for a child's psychological destiny? (Quotes from Keller, J. J. [1998, April 23]. How a minister's son discovered "slamming" and then disappeared. *The Wall Street Journal,* pp. A1, A6.)

Adoptive parents fret over a wayward child's hyperactive and antisocial behavior or a failing child's unremitting dullness and poor scholastic achievement—any of this despite years of unconditional devotion or remedial tutoring. Yet what relief it is to discover that the problem isn't something in the quality of rearing, but something in the genetics transmitted by the biological parents. Relief, yes, but at the cost of heightened consciousness of limited influence and a sobering question that many parents secretly harbor: Whose child is this, anyway—have we been rearing a stranger?

19   Quote from Frankl, V. E. (1984). *Man's search for meaning*. New York: Washington Square Press (Pocket Books).

21   Quote from Frankl, V. E. (1984). *Man's search for meaning*. New York: Washington Square Press (Pocket Books).

21   Source for opening paragraph, "Getting Perspective" section, is Baumrind, D. (1993). The average expected environment is not enough: A response to Scarr. *Child Development, 64*, 1299–1317.

21   Pressing or traumatic situations can derail even instinctively preferred ways of behaving. People driven by hunger, fear, pain or other exigencies of the moment will do all sorts of things that don't fit their personality: Extroverts will study for exams, introverts will socialize, and children will clean up their rooms. Laboratory rats can be made to do what, from a rat's perspective, are rather dumb things. For instance, normally they won't just run through a maze; blind alleys are leisurely explored, not just to discover potential escape routes, but to satisfy their curiosity. Yet when sufficiently hungry and with few options, those very rats will scurry through the maze if, during an earlier excursion, they had found food at the end.

   College students can be induced by researchers to do even bizarre things they wouldn't imagine doing under ordinary situations. Asked to role-play a person accused of murdering three women, they can, while under hypnosis, act like someone with multiple personality disorder. Without coaching, some of them display different personalities, each with its own name. They even claim amnesia for the interviews done under hypnosis during which they had mostly denied, but eventually admitted, having carried out murders. (See Spanos, N. P., Weekes, J. R., Menary, E., & Bertrand, L. D. [1986]. Hypnotic interview and age regression procedures in the elicitation of multiple personality symptoms: A simulation study. *Psychiatry, 49*, 298–311.)

   No doubt, these are realistic performances, and why not? There is in human nature a deep capacity for dramatic and theatrical self-expression and suggestibility. (See Ey, H. [1982]. History and analysis of the concept. In A. Roy [Ed.], *Hysteria*. Chichester, England: Wiley.) The point, though, is that making something happen under controlled conditions in the laboratory supposedly means we know something about how it happens in the real world, but is this necessarily so? Getting people to quack like ducks, even to believe under hypnosis that they are ducks, doesn't make them ducks, for there is more decoy than duck in their behavior. With hypnotic instructions, one can get college students to simulate multiple personality; so, too, with teaching gimmicks, one can get them to solve quadratic equations. Yet, does any of this explain real-world individual differences, why some people are so disposed to multiple personality or why others are so mathematically gifted?

Chapter 2

25   Louis, A. M. (1981, January 26). Schlitz's crafty taste test. *Fortune*, 32–34.

26   Quote from Irving, J. (1989). *A prayer for Owen Meany*. New York: William Morrow.

27   Does the specter of being an adoptee affect psychological development? One study found that there were no differences in mental health or in quality of the relationship with the adoptive parents between adoptees who knew and those who didn't know about their adoptive status. See Eldred, C. A., Rosenthal, D., Wender, P. H., Kety, S. S., Schulsinger, F., Welner, J., & Jacobsen, B. (1976). Some aspects of adoption in selected samples of adult adoptees. *American Journal of Orthopsychiatry, 46*, 279–290.

29   Scarr, S. (1996). How people make their own environments: Implications for parents and policy makers. *Psychology, Public Policy, and Law, 2*, 204–228. A classic example of a cause that proves least salient is the work of physician Joseph Goldberger, who worked for the U.S. Public Health Service at the turn of the twentieth century. Goldberger had a theory about pellagra, a disease marked by diarrhea, dermatitis, running sores, vomiting, dizziness, impaired reasoning, agitation, and depression. People with poor diets are especially vulnerable, as are people with poor sanitation facilities. So then, which one was crucial: the salient factor that most physicians assumed to be critical—poor sanitation—or some dietary factor, as Goldberger believed?

To convince his colleagues, Goldberger did two things. He manipulated diet by shifting subjects to a high-carbohydrate and low-protein diet lacking B vitamins. The result was pellagra, just as he predicted. (The missing factor, niacin, one of the B vitamins, wouldn't be discovered until 1937, 8 years after Goldberger's death.) He also tested the supposed sanitary cause, incredibly, by injecting himself with the blood of pellagra victims. The result: no pellagra, not even after he ate their nose secretions and consumed little pellagra balls made of their urine and feces, scrapings from their sores, and flour! (Source is Stanovich, K. [1989]. *How to think straight about psychology*. Glenview, IL: Scott, Foresman.)

People with one watch always know the time; just ask them and they will tell you without the slightest hesitation or doubt. People wearing two watches can never be sure. Inevitable discrepancies will keep them wondering, which is good because it keeps them open to alternative explanations and therefore new possibilities.

Two-watch people take to heart that, as the wit Artemis Ward said, "It ain't so much the things we don't know that gets us into trouble. It's the things we know that ain't so." They are thus less likely to be taken in or upset by razzle-dazzle findings that spark the imagination and galvanize public policy, but that so often fail to bear up under the weight of close inspection and the passing of sufficient time. But let's make no mistake; it's not just a matter of looking at two sides of an argument or a finding. It means doing the hard work of figuring out which, if either, side is the better answer.

30   Even if poor parents were somehow induced to talk three times more, and if talking more really made a difference, their children still wouldn't have enough hours in a day to catch up. According to the researchers, professional-class achievement would take working-class children 43 hours of language study per week, low-income children much more. But if talking *expresses* rather than causes cognitive ability, the lasting value of such programmed instruction would be questionable. See Hart, B., & Risley, T. R. (1995). *Meaningful differences in the everyday experience of young American children.* Baltimore: Paul H. Brooks.

30   In response to so-called new findings celebrated in 1998 by both the press and the politicians, professor emeritus Gordon M. Harrington wrote:

> *What strikes me is the feeling I am in a time warp. I taught early stimulation and brain connection research in my introductory psychology course 40 years ago. The White House conference press reports have not identified any ideas that were unknown 40 years back. (I have just scanned Hebb's 1958* Textbook of Psychology *and the notes I gave him for the 2nd edition to verify the accuracy of my memory.) The press reports do indeed ignore the genetic. By the mid 60's we had manipulated brain growth and synaptic proliferation in rats both genetically and environmentally finding differences between longitudinal and lateral brain development according to the manipulation. Has it indeed taken 40 years for the impact of the basic research to reach the level of application or is America being rediscovered?*

One other point worth noting is that findings with animals need not generalize to the human condition. Forty years ago, researchers discovered that animal crowding causes increased rates of hypertension, arteriosclerosis, infection, and infant mortality (Calhoun, J. B. [1962]. Population density and social pathology. *Scientific American, 206,* 139–146). Yet a subsequent look at human crowding yielded no consistent and convincing evidence of similar effects. Thus, animal research on brain and behavior need not always reveal important truths about human needs and individual development.

32   Quote from St. Augustine (413–426). *City of God: Book V,* chap. 4, sec. 4. "Why, then," asks mathematician John Paulos, "do so many people

believe in astrology? One obvious reason is that people read into the generally vague astrological pronouncements almost anything they want to, and thus invest them with a truth which is not inherent in the pronouncements themselves. They are also more likely to remember true 'predictions,' overvalue coincidences, and ignore everything else. . . ." Paulos adds two other likely reasons. One is the "flattering insistence on the connection between the starry vastness of the heavens and whether or not we'll fall in love this month." The other is that "during individual sessions astrologers pick up on clues about a client's personalities from their facial expressions, mannerisms, body language, etc." (Quotes from Paulos, J. A. [1988]. *Innumeracy: Mathematical illiteracy and its consequences.* New York: Hill & Wang [Farrar, Strauss & Giroux].)

People who don't accept astrology might yet believe in the efficacy of talking to their plants, never stopping to ask if the words or just the hot air—the CO_2 of breath—could be the beneficial factor. Admittedly, talking is the more romantic—dare one say, inspiring?—notion, but might breathing alone do as well, assuming that there is anything to the belief? And it's a testable question. Get a bunch of plants and randomly assign them to one of four conditions: talked to, sung to, quietly breathed on, and, mercifully, left alone.

32   Correlations from Plomin, R., Loehlin, J. C., & DeFries, J. C. (1985). Genetic and environmental components of "environmental" influences. *Developmental Psychology, 21,* 391–402.

33   Methods reported in Baumrind, D. (1967). Child care practices anteceding three patterns of preschool behavior. *Genetic Psychology Monographs, 75,* 43–88; Sears, R. R., Maccoby, E. E., & Levin, H. (1957). *Patterns of child rearing.* Evanston, IL: Row, Peterson.

33   That current methods to test parent–child correlations are more sophisticated than this doesn't really change the basic results or critical comments about such results. Also, see Jensen, A. R. (1998). *The g factor: The science of mental ability.* Westport, CT: Praeger.

33   Thomas, A., Chess, S., & Birch, H. G. (1968). *Temperament and behavior disorders in children.* New York: New York University Press.

33   Liem, J. H. (1974). Effects of verbal communication of parents and children: A comparison of normal and schizophrenic families. *Journal of Consulting and Clinical Psychology, 42,* 438–450.

33   Bell, R. Q. (1968). A reinterpretation of the direction of effects in studies of socialization. *Psychological Review, 75,* 81–95.

34   Quote from Thomas, A., Chess, S., & Birch, H. G. (1968). *Temperament and behavior disorders in children.* New York: New York University Press.

36   Chira, S. (1995, March 19). Multiple divorces multiple scars. *Austin American-Statesman,* pp. A1, A15.

36   Cherlin, A. J., Furstenberg, J. F. F., Chase-Lansdale, P. L., Kiernan, K. E.,

Robins, P. K., Morrison, D. R., & Teitler, J. O. (1991). Longitudinal studies of effects of divorce on children in Great Britain and the United States. *Science, 252,* 1386–1389; McGue, M., & Lykken, D. T. (1991). Genetic influence on risk of divorce. *Psychological Science, 3,* 368–373.

37   Dodge, K. A., Bates, J. E., & Pettit, G. S. (1990, December 21). Mechanisms in the cycle of violence. *Science, 250,* 1678–1683; Kendall-Tackett, K. A., Williams, L. M., & Finkelhor, D. (1993). Impact of sexual abuse on children: A review and synthesis of recent empirical studies. *Psychological Bulletin, 113,* 164–180; McCord, J. (1983). A forty-year perspective on effects of child abuse and neglect. *Child Abuse and Neglect, 7,* 265–270.

37   Estimates from Widom, C. S. (1989, April 14). The cycle of violence. *Science, 244,* 160–166.

37   Simons, R. L., Wu, C., Johnson, C., & Conger, R. D. (1995). A test of various perspectives on the intergenerational transmission of domestic violence. *Criminology, 33,* 141–171.

37   Dodge, K. A., Bates, J. E., & Pettit, G. S. (1990, December 21). Mechanisms in the cycle of violence. *Science, 250,* 1678–1683; Kendall-Tackett, K. A., Williams, L. M., & Finkelhor, D. (1993). Impact of sexual abuse on children: A review and synthesis of recent empirical studies. *Psychological Bulletin, 113,* 164–180; McCord, J. (1983). A forty year perspective on effects of child abuse and neglect. *Child Abuse and Neglect, 7,* 265–270.

38   Quote from Hobson, J. A. (1994). *The chemistry of conscious states.* Boston: Little, Brown (Back Bay Books).

38   Our imaginary study includes two groups of adoptees, each differing in genetic background but not in rearing. Ideally, the study would include four groups, each differing in genetic background but also in quality of rearing. We'd have the same two groups of adoptees born of abusive or nonabusive biological parents. Half of each group would be reared by normal parents, the other half by abusive parents. In this way, we would be testing the effect of environments usually not sampled in even the best of studies. True, abusive adoptive parents would be difficult to find, given the generally high standards used by agencies to select adoptive parents; yet with these four groups, we could go a long way toward disentangling the relative influence of heredity and rearing under the widest range of environmental conditions.

We would start with the rate of abusiveness found for adoptees whose biological and adoptive parents are both normal. Compared to that, other rates of abuse would be telling. A relatively high rate in the abusively reared offspring of normal biological parents would clearly support an environmental explanation, namely that abusive rearing in itself increases the risk of becoming an abuser. On the other hand, a relatively high rate of abuse in the normally reared offspring of abusive biological parents would support a genetic explanation, namely that an abusive genetic background in itself increases the risk of becoming an abuser. The genetic and social risk factors might add up to elevate the risk by their combined effects; more interesting, however, would be if the two factors yielded a *much higher* risk, suggesting that genetic and environmental influences don't just add up, but multiply the potential for deviant behavior.

39   Smoking correlation from Rowe, D. C. (1994). *The limits of family influence: Genes, experience, and behavior.* New York: Guilford.

39   Body weight correlation from Grilo, C. M., & Pogue-Geile, M. F. (1991). The nature of environmental differences. *Psychological Bulletin, 110,* 520–537.

39   Frick, P. J., & Jackson, Y. K. (1993). Family functioning and childhood antisocial behavior: Yet another reinterpretation. *Journal of Clinical Child Psychology, 22,* 410–419.

Chapter 3

41   Quote from Rader, D. (1997, May 18). Be open to whatever happens. (An interview of Lauen Bacall). *Parade Magazine,* 4–5.

42   Walker, S., III. (1996). *A dose of sanity: Mind, medicine, and misdiagnosis.* New York: John Wiley & Sons.

42   Quote from Pollak, R. (1997). *The creation of Dr. B.: A biography of Bruno Bettelheim.* New York: Simon & Schuster.

43   Sources and quotes from Kimball, R. (1997, August 8). The death of decency. *The Wall Street Journal,* p. A12; and from Beck, J. (1990, October 7). Bettelheim image deserves to suffer. *Austin American-Statesman,* p. D3.

44   See Akiskal, H. S., Djenderdejian, A. H., Rosenthal, R. H., & Khani, M. K. (1977). Cyclothymic disorder: Validating criteria for inclusion in the bipolar affective group. *American Journal of Psychiatry, 134,* 1227–1233.

44   Bennett, M. I., & Bennett, M. B. (1984). The uses of hopelessness. *American Journal of Psychiatry, 141,* 559–562.

45   Quote from Cameron, M. (1965, Winter). Why psychosis. *Michigan Quarterly Review, 4,* 14–18.

45   Hobson, J. A. (1994). *The chemistry of conscious states.* Boston: Little, Brown (Back Bay Books).

47   Rutter, M., Bailey, A., Bolton, P., & Le Couteur, A. (1993). Autism: Syndrome definition and possible genetic mechanisms. In R. Plomin & G. McClearn (Eds.), *Nature, nurture, and psychology* (pp. 269–284). Washington, DC: American Psychological Association.

47   Gottesman, I. I. (1991). *Schizophrenia genesis: The origins of madness*. New York: Freeman.

48   Source on obsessive-compulsive behavior is Davison, G. C., & Neale, J. M. (1998). *Abnormal psychology* (7th ed.). New York: John Wiley & Sons.

49   Source on Freud is the classic textbook of psychoanalytic theory by Fenichel, O. (1945). *The psychoanalytic theory of neurosis*. New York: Norton.

49   Source on evidence regarding fraternals and identicals is Livesley, W. J., Jang, K. L., Jackson, D. N., & Vernon, P. A. (1993). Genetic and environmental contributions to dimensions of personality disorder. *American Journal of Psychiatry, 150,* 1826–1831.

50   Quote from Cameron, N. (1963). *Personality development and psychopathology*. New York: Houghton Mifflin.

50   Rauch, S. L., Jenike, A., Alpert, N. M., Baer, L., Breiter, H. C. R., Savage, C. R., & Fischman, A. J. (1994). Regional cerebral blood flow measured during symptom provocation in obsessive-compulsive disorder using oxygen 15-labeled carbon dioxide and positron emission tomography. *Archives of General Psychiatry, 51,* 62–70.

50   Schwartz, J. M., Stoessel, P. W., Baxter, L. R., Martin, K. M., & Phelps, M. E. (1996). Systematic changes in cerebral glucose metabolic rate after successful behavior modification treatment of obsessive-compulsive disorder. *Archives of General Psychiatry, 53,* 109–113.

50   Pauls, D. L., Towbin, K. E., Leckman, J. F., Zahner, G. E. P., & Cohen, D. J. (1986). Giles de la Tourette's syndrome and obsessive-compulsive disorder: Evidence supporting a genetic relationship. *Archives of General Psychiatry, 43,* 1180–1182.

51   Murphy, T. K., Goodman, W. K., Fudge, M. W., Williams, J. R. C., Ayoub, E. M., Dalal, M., Lewis, M. H., & Zabriskie, J. B. (1997). B lymphocyte antigen D8/17: A peripheral marker for childhood-onset obsessive-compulsive disorder and Tourette's syndrome. *American Journal of Psychiatry, 154,* 402–407.

51   Swedo, S. E., Leonard, H. L., Mittleman, B. B., Allen, A. J., Rapoport, J. L., Dow, S. P., Kanter, M. E., Chapman, F., & Zabriskie, J. (1997). Identification of children with pediatric autoimmune neuropsychiatric disorders associated with streptococcal infections by a marker associated with rheumatic fever. *American Journal of Psychiatry, 154,* 110–112.

51   See Neubauer, P. B., & Neubauer, A. (1990). *Nature's thumbprint: The new genetics of personality*. New York: Addison-Wesley. A similar anecdote makes the same point. Ellen is being treated for a mental illness that her therapist attributes to being raised by emotionally distant parents. Across town, Alice is being treated for the same mental illness—which *her* therapist attributes to being raised by emotionally high strung and intrusive parents. Here, then, are two different social explanations

for the same problem. However, Ellen and Alice are identical twins separated early in life and reared apart. This suggests that their illness has nothing to do with a particular rearing, good or bad, but everything to do with a shared genetic abnormality.

52 Hobson, J. A. (1994). *The chemistry of conscious states*. Boston: Little, Brown (Back Bay Books).

52 Walker, S., III. (1996). *A dose of sanity: Mind, medicine, and misdiagnosis*. New York: John Wiley & Sons. When speaking of illness potential, we speak of *vulnerability*, but this term is somewhat misleading. Vulnerability refers to a psychological defect, deficiency, or other weakness of mental life, and to the brain activity sustaining it. It can involve, for example, the insecurity that elevates the risk for anxiety attacks, or the inferiority feelings that elevate the risk for paranoia, or the hopelessness that elevates the risk of depression and suicide. It can also involve an abnormality of the brain's left hemisphere. Vulnerability is therefore not only about *why*, but about *how* a psychological breakdown occurs.

When speaking of illness potential, we can also mean *liability*, or risk, whatever the psychological mechanism (vulnerability). Liability is commonly estimated from the relatives of ill people. For example, compared to people randomly chosen from the population, the first-degree relatives of bipolar sufferers are 10 times more likely to succumb to that illness. We can say that their liability is 10 times higher—that there is something familial about bipolar disorders—even if we have no theory of what it is. When we speak of the heritability of some disorder, we really mean the heritability (genetic factor) of liability to that disorder.

If our goal is precision, then two terms—*vulnerability* and *liability*—are probably better than one. On the other hand, given that either meaning should be clear from the discussion, the goal of simplicity suggests that the more familiar term *vulnerability* should suffice.

53 Goggans, F. C., Allen, R. M., & Gold, M. S. (1986). Primary hypothyroidism and its relationship to affective disorders. In I. Extein & M. S. Gold (Eds.), *Medical mimics of psychiatric disorder*. (pp. 95–109). Washington, DC: American Psychiatric Press.

53 Hall, R. C. W. (Ed.). (1980). *Psychiatric presentations of medical illnesses: Somatopsychic disorders*. New York: SP Medical Scientific Books.

53 Koranyi, E. K. (1979). Morbidity and rate of undiagnosed physical illness in a psychiatric clinical population. *Archives of General Psychiatry, 36*, 414–419.

53 Roy, A. (Ed.). (1982). *Hysteria*. Chichester, England: Wiley.

53 Associated Press (1990, January 17). Women's "false" pains tied to artery ailment. *Austin American-Statesman*, p. A4.

54 Hall, R. C. W. (Ed.). (1980). *Psychiatric presentations of medical illnesses: Somatopsychic disorders*. New York: SP Medical Scientific Books; Walker,

S., III. (1996). *A dose of sanity: Mind, medicine, and misdiagnosis.* New York: John Wiley & Sons.

54   Source is an exposé on memory in children entitled "Truth on Trial." It was created by John Stoessel for the television show *20/20* and aired on September 8, 1995.

55   Quote from Ofshe, R., & Watters, E. (1993, March–April). Making monsters. *Society,* 4–16.

56   Quote from Rabinowitz, D. (1995, January 30). A darkness in Massachusetts. *The Wall Street Journal,* p. A12.

57   Quote from editorial (1997, September 11). A citizen of Massachusetts. *The Wall Street Journal,* p. A14.

57   Quote from Hill, J. J. (1997, September 23). Where is the sense of shame? [Letter to the editor]. *The Wall Street Journal,* p. A23.

57   Quote from Isaac, R. J. (1997, June 30). Abusive justice. *National Review,* pp. 31–35.

57   Quote from Loftus, E. (1997, September). Creating false memories. *Scientific American,* 70–75.

58   Comment by Isaac, R. J. (1997, June 30). Abusive justice. *National Review,* pp. 31–35.

58   Quote from Kundera, M. (1985, June 13). Man thinks, God laughs. *New York Review of Books,* 11–12.

58   Quote from Durant, W. (1935). *The story of civilization: Part I. Our oriental heritage.* New York: Simon & Schuster.

59   Durant, W. (1953). *The story of civilization: Part V. The Renaissance.* New York: Simon & Schuster.

59   Quotes from Li, C. C. (1971). A tale of two thermos bottles: Properties of a genetic model for human intelligence. In R. Cancro (Ed.), *Intelligence, genetic and environmental influences.* New York: Grune & Stratton; and from Russell, B. (1957). *Understanding History.* New York: New York Philosophical Library.

60   Quote from Russell, B. (1957). *Understanding History.* New York: New York Philosophical Library.

60   Especially when emotionally stirred, the preference for good stories over critical thinking becomes all too evident. People feel a special need to make up stories, even for behavior that isn't all that embarrassing. (See Nisbett, R. E., & Wilson, T. D. [1977]. Telling more than we can know: Verbal reports on mental processes. *Psychological Review, 84,* 231–259.) After memorizing word pairs, such as ocean-moon, individuals are twice as likely as others to answer "Tide" when asked later to name a detergent. Yet when asked to explain their answers, they almost never refer to the word pair that really mattered, and which they recall but seem to discount; rather, they make up something like, "Tide is the most popular detergent."

How often, it seems, there's no impediment to facile, self-serving storytelling whose truth is more important than its accuracy. A wonderful illustration of this comes from research on so-called split-brain subjects, in a 1978 study of a neurology patient described by neuropsychologists Michael Gazzaniga and Joseph LeDoux. (See Gazzaniga, M., & LeDoux, J. [1978]. *The integrated mind.* New York: Plenum.) Life-threatening epileptic seizures can be treated by severing the neural bridge that connects the left and right hemispheres of the brain. After this so-called split-brain procedure, the verbally inarticulate right hemisphere can no longer communicate directly with the self-conscious, verbal left hemisphere. Nevertheless, the mute right hemisphere can still express what it knows through emotion or by pointing to relevant things with the *left* hand. You need remember only that each hemisphere receives information from the opposite half of the body and external world, and each controls the opposite half of the body. Thus the left hemisphere, responding to information on the right, controls the right hand while at the same time the right hemisphere, responding to information from the left, controls the left hand.

Now, consider a split-brain subject sitting in front of a screen and staring at a fixation point at its center. For an instant, two pictures are flashed on either side of the fixation point: a chicken claw to the right, a snow scene to the left. Immediately after the screen goes blank, each picture has become a memory locked in one of the two hemispheres, the chicken-claw memory held in the left hemisphere, the snow-scene memory held in the right hemisphere. Thus, the subject—actually, his verbally proficient left hemisphere—reports having seen a chicken claw in the right visual field but nothing in the left. At the same time, though he cannot report it, his right hemisphere has mutely perceived a snow scene in the left visual field but nothing in the right. How strange, but there is more.

The subject must next look at eight pictures lined up in a row on the table and point to one that best relates to what he has just seen. The subject—actually, his right hand—voluntarily points to a chicken head, which makes sense, given that his left hemisphere remembers the chicken claw. At the same time, his left hand involuntarily points to a shovel, which also makes sense, given that his right hemisphere remembers the snow scene. Here's the dilemma: The subject—actually, his left hemisphere—has only one thing in his conscious mind, namely the memory of a chicken claw. Yet he perceives himself pointing to two seemingly incompatible things: a chicken and a shovel. Now what? Only one solution to this embarrassing inconsistency seems evident: Make up a good story. Thus, "I saw a claw and I picked the chicken, *and you have to clean out the chicken shed with a shovel.*" I've added emphasis to make the point about how readily and without reflection we make up stories that may be true for us, may be passionately believed and even promoted, but that prove to be flat-out false.

Chapter 4

62   Koluchová, J. (1976). Severe deprivation in twins: A case study. In A. M. Clarke & A. D. B. Clarke (Eds.), *Early experience: Myth and evidence* (pp. 45–55). New York: The Free Press (Macmillan); Koluchová, J. (1976). A report on the further development of twins after severe and prolonged deprivation. In A. M. Clarke & A. D. B. Clarke (Eds.), *Early experience: Myth and evidence* (pp. 56–66). New York: The Free Press (Macmillan).

In rare cases involving obscenely abusive or neglectful conditions, alas, no part of personality or even intelligence seems deep enough to remain unscathed. (Different aspects of the story are given in Curtiss, S. [1977]. *Genie: A psycholinguistic study of a modern-day "wild child."* New York: Academic Press; and in Rymer, R. [1993]. *Genie: An abused child's flight from silence.* New York: HarperCollins.) In 1970, a 13-year-old girl, code-named Genie, was discovered to have been living all her life confined to a bedroom. There, year after year, she was harnessed to a potty seat while awake, and was restrained in a sleeping bag while asleep. She remained hungry, isolated, and unable to move much or even to hear much language. Deprived of linguistic stimulation, Genie developed only primitive speech that lacked the intuitive grammatical sense for word arrangement. She might utter, "Genie have Momma have baby grow up."

All of her thinking seemed to be done with her brain's right hemisphere, and this raises a question: Could lack of language stimulation have prevented proper development of the brain's left hemisphere, which in most people is the one specialized for language? To test for such brain imbalance, investigators use laboratory tasks that make one hemisphere compete against the other. For instance, verbal or nonverbal information can be directed by earphones to the left and right ear, simultaneously. The details are complicated but the main fact is relatively simple: Left-hemisphere dominance for language is signaled by faster and more accurate response to verbal information presented to the opposite, or right, ear. In contrast, right-hemisphere dominance, say for musical sounds, is signaled by faster and more accurate response to music presented to the opposite, or left, ear.

On such tests, Genie's left hemisphere seemed completely nonfunctional, an investigator noting that her performance was like that of children who have no left hemisphere. Mostly right-hemisphere thinking was also evident in her adult-level performance on many nonverbal tests—for example, on tests of spatial ability, where one must quickly recognize an object that has been rotated, altered in perspective, or hidden amongst other objects. Genie was object-oriented rather than people-oriented; that is, she attended more to color, shape, and number than to stories, and more to the physical relations among objects than to social relationships among people. Similarly intact or even superior were her other mostly nonverbal abilities, such as the ability to categorize or memorize things.

Most remarkable is not so much what Genie lacked, but how much of her intellectual and even social ability remained despite the worst rearing imaginable. One biographer observed that she "was the most disturbed person I'd ever met. But the lights were on. There was somebody home." After much intellectual catch-up over the years, her achievements, if selective, were truly remarkable. As psychologist Irwin Sameroff noted, "The human organism appears to have been programmed by the course of evolution to produce normal developmental outcomes under all but the most adverse circumstances. Any understanding of deviancies in outcome must be seen in the light of this self-righting and self-organizing tendency which appears to move children towards normality in the face of pressure towards deviation" Clarke, A. M. & Clarke, A. D. B. (1976). *Early experience: Myth and evidence* (p. 270). New York: The Free Press.

62   Psychic wounds: see Vachss, A. (1994, August 28). You can carry the cure in your heart. *Parade Magazine*, 4–6.

62   Kluft, R. P. (1996, July). Treating the traumatic memories of patients with dissociative identity disorder. *American Journal of Psychiatry, 153* [Festschrift Supplement], 103–110.

63   Information on children separated during World War II from Garmezy, N. (1981). Children under stress: Perspectives on antecedents and correlates of vulnerability and resistance to psychopathology. In A. I. Rabin, J. Aronoff, A. Barclay, M., & R. A. Zucker (Eds.), *Further explorations in personality* (pp. 196–269). New York: John Wiley & Sons.

63   Quote from Kagan, J. (1996). Three pleasing ideas. *American Psychologist, 51,* 901–908.

63   Information on infant stress from Levine, S. (1971). Stress and behavior. In Readings from Scientific American (Eds.), *Progress in psychobiology* (pp. 143–148). San Francisco: W. H. Freeman; Meaney, M. J., Aitken, D. H., van Berkel, C., Bhatnagar, S., & Sapolsy, R. M. (1988, February 12). Effect of neonatal handling on age-related impairments associated with the hippocampus. *Science, 239,* 766–768.

63   Quote from Torrey, E. F., Bowler, A. E., Taylor, E. H., & Gottesman, I. I. (1994). *Schizophrenia and manic-depressive disorder: The biological roots of mental illness as revealed by the landmark study of identical twins.* New York: Basic Books.

66   Soumi, S. J. (1991). Uptight and laid-back monkeys: Individual differences in the response to social changes. In S. E. Brauth, W. S. Hall, & R. J. Dooling (Eds.), *Plasticity of development* (pp. 28–56). Cambridge, MA: MIT Press (Bradford Book).

66   Kagan, J. (1989). Temperamental contributions to social behavior. *American Psychologist, 44,* 668–674; Kagan, J. (1994). Distinctions among emotions, moods, and temperamental qualities. In P. Ekman & R. J. Davidson (Eds.), *The nature of emotion: Fundamental questions* (pp. 74–78.). New York: Oxford University Press.

66   Timid versus normal children from Biederman, J., Rosenbaum, J. F., Hirschfield, D. R., Faraone, S., Bolduc, E., Gersten, M., Meminger, S., Kagan, J., Snidman, N., & Reznick, J. S. (1990). Psychiatric correlates of behavioral inhibition in young children of parents with and without psychiatric disorders. *Archives of General Psychiatry, 47,* 21–26.

67   Cairns, R. B. (1979). *Social development: The origins and plasticity of interchanges.* San Francisco: W. H. Freeman; Cairns, R. B., Gariépy, J.-L., & Hood, K. E. (1990). Development, microevolution, and social behavior. *Psychological Review, 97,* 49–65.

67   Loehlin, J. C., Willerman, L., & Horn, J. M. (1982). Personality resemblances between unwed mothers and their adopted-away offspring. *Journal of Personality and Social Psychology, 42,* 1089–1099; and Loehlin, J. C., Willerman, L., & Horn, J. M. (1987). Personality resemblance in adoptive families: A 10-year follow-up. *Journal of Personality and Social Psychology, 53,* 961–969.

68   Breland, K., & Breland, M. (1961). The misbehavior of organisms. *American Psychologist, 16,* 661–664.

68   Lorenz, K. (1963). *On aggression.* New York: Harcourt, Brace & World/ Bantam (1966). Lorenz' observations reconfirm what has always been known, if not always sufficiently appreciated, about reversion to type. While imprisoned and awaiting execution by orders of Theodoric, Ostrogothic king and master of sixth-century Italy, the philosopher-statesman Boethius wrote in his *Consolation of Philosophy:* "If the bird who sings so lustily upon the high tree-top, be caught and caged, men may minister to him with dainty care, may give him cups of liquid honey and feed him with all gentleness on plenteous food. Yet if he fly to the roof of his cage and see the shady trees he loves, he spurns with his foot the food they have put before him. The woods are all his sorrow calls for; for the woods he sings with his sweet tones."

68   McCartney, K., Harris, M. J., & Bernieri, F. (1990). Growing up and apart: A developmental meta-analysis of twin studies. *Psychological Bulletin, 107,* 226–237.

69   Quote from Hutchins, R. M. (1972). The great anti-school campaign. In R. M. Hutchins & M. J. Adler (Eds.), *The Great Ideas Today* (pp. 155–227). New York: Encyclopaedia Britannica.

70 See Frank, G. H. (1965). The role of the family in the development of psychopathology. *Psychological Bulletin, 64,* 191–205.

70 Buss, D. (1987). Selection, evocation, and manipulation. *Journal of Personality and Social Psychology, 53,* 1214–1221.

71 Rushton, J. P. (1995). *Race, evolution, and behavior.* New Brunswick, NJ: Transaction; Thiessen, D., & Gregg, B. (1980). Human assortative mating and genetic equilibrium: An evolutionary perspective. *Ethology and Sociobiology, 1,* 111–140. Assortative mating sustains human diversity by promoting psychological extremes that would get washed out by random mating. (See Herrnstein, R. J., & Murray, C. [1994]). *The bell curve: Intelligence and class structure in American life.* New York: The Free Press.) It accounts for over 70 percent of very superior intelligence (IQ over 130) and probably over 90 percent of extremely superior intelligence (IQ over 145). Because of assortative mating, we have at least 30 times more people with genius intelligence (IQ over 160) than we otherwise would have. Simply said, without assortative mating, the dullest of our population would be less dull, but the brightest would be less bright.

Assortative mating thus confers benefits to society, albeit at some cost, ensuring a steady supply of those gifted individuals who contribute most to intellectual life and technological achievement. Apparently, it also pays off interpersonally, in that the marriages of couples who mate assortatively are more stable than the marriages of couples who don't mate assortatively. (See Thiessen, D., & Gregg, B. [1980]. Human assortative mating and genetic equilibrium: An evolutionary perspective. *Ethology and Sociobiology, 1,* 111–140.) Incidentally, the more assortative an unmarried couple seems to be, the more positively it is viewed; such a couple is also more likely to be seen as eventually settling down and having children. Finally, assortative mating also pays off for the individual. Compared to opposites, birds of a feather have more children together, and the more similar the birds, the more offspring they have. Assortative mating thus promotes Darwinian fitness, or the number of offspring who carry one's genes into the next generation.

71 Thiessen, D., & Gregg, B. (1980). Human assortative mating and genetic equilibrium: An evolutionary perspective. *Ethology and Sociobiology, 1,* 111–140.

72 Twins study from Plomin, R., Lichtenstein, P., Pedersen, N. L., McClern, G. E., & Nesselroade, J. R. (1990). Genetic influence on life events during the last half of the life span. *Psychology and Aging, 5,* 25–30.

73 See Rowe, D. C. (1994). *The limits of family influence: Genes, experience, and behavior.* New York: Guilford.

73 Kendler, K. S. (1997). Social support: A genetic-epidemiological analysis. *American Journal of Psychiatry, 154,* 1398–1404.

73 Saudino, K. J. (1997). Moving beyond the heritability question: New directions in behavioral genetic studies of personality. *Current Directions*

in Psychological Science, 6, 86–90. Note that the environment is heritable also to the extent that the behavior of people with whom a person interacts is heritable.

73   Plomin, R., DeFries, J. C., McClearn, G. E., & Rutter, M. (1977). *Behavioral genetics* (3rd ed.). New York: W. H. Freeman.

Chapter 5

74   Meltzoff, A. N., & Moore, M. K. (1977). Imitation of facial and manual gestures by human neonates. *Science, 198,* 75–78.

76   Hecht, H., & Proffitt, D. R. (1995). The price of expertise: Effects of experience on the water-level task. *Psychological Science, 6* (2), 90–95.

76   Weimer, W. B. (1973). Psycholinguistics and Plato's paradoxes in the *Meno. American Psychologist, 28,* 15–33.

77   Gordon, P. (1986). Level-ordering in lexical development. *Cognition, 21,* 73–93.

77   Slobin, D. I. (1971). *Psycholinguistics.* Glenview, Illinois, (ch. 3).

77   Alexander, R. (1995, July 12). Metropolitan diary. *The New York Times,* p. C2.

78   McNeill, D. (1966). Developmental psycholinguistics. In F. Smith & G. A. Miller (Eds.), *The genesis of language: A psycholinguistic Approach.* Cambridge, MA: MIT Press.

79   Radetsky, P. (1994, August). Silence, sounds, wonder. *Discover,* 62–68.

79   Quote from Diamond, J. (1991, May). Reinventions of human language. *Natural History,* 22–28.

80   Quote from Twain, M. (1889). *A Connecticut Yankee in King Arthur's court.* New York: Aerie Publisher.

80   Source and quotes from Pinker, S. (1994). *The language instinct: How the mind creates language.* New York: William Morrow.

80   Marler, P., & Peters, S. (1981). Sparrows learn adult song and more from memory. *Science, 213,* 780–782. Even a cursory look at a child's dreams suggests the autonomous, instinctive quality of so much experience. We all dream maybe for 10 years—certainly for the roughly 5 years we spend in the rapid eye movement (REM) phase of sleep, that state which consumes roughly 20 to 25 years of our 75-year lifespan. As children, we have more REM sleep/dreaming than we do as adults, and as newborns we have even more. What then is the purpose of all the self-generated experience? No one can be certain because, given the limits of our current technology, hard evidence is all but impossible to get; worse, our uncertainty is not likely to change in the foreseeable future.

Nevertheless, this intriguing—even haunting—notion remains: that all of us develop, not just through externally influenced waking experiences, but through self-generated dream experiences, and why not?

Dream experiences are emotionally compelling, so why not developmentally so—why couldn't they be a fundamental way in which our very self explores and creates experiences whose connection to external reality is tenuous at best, but whose connection to *our* reality is intimate, and therefore whose personal effects on our psyche help shape what we are to become?

We can think of waking experience as food for thought, as something digested and transformed quite unconsciously into the very structure of the self. How else can we explain why a loved and protected 3-year-old can have nightmares about being abandoned by his parents—like Selma Fraiberg's little David who worried that his parents would fly off to Yurp without him? It may make no sense to guilty parents fretting over their child's fearful imagery and overwhelming anxiety, but it actually makes all the sense in the world, for it is a what-if dream that asks, as it were, suppose the world were not so comfortable, caring, and safe—what then?

81 Source and quotes from Pinker, S. (1994). *The language instinct: How the mind creates language*. New York: William Morrow.

81 Jacobs, W. J., & Nadel, L. (1985). Stress-induced recovery of fears and phobias. *Psychological Review, 92*, 512–531.

82 Quote from Hutchins, R. M. (1972). The great anti-school campaign. In R. M. Hutchins & M. J. Adler (Eds.), *The great ideas today* (pp. 155–227). New York: Encyclopaedia Britannica.

82 Garcia, J., & Koelling, R. A. (1966). Relation of cue to consequence in avoidance learning. *Psychonomic Science, 4*, 123–124; Garcia, J., & Rusiniak, K. W. (1980). What the nose learns from the mouth. In Muller-Schwarze & R. M. Silverstein (Eds.), *Chemical signals* (pp. 141–146). New York: Plenum.

82 Of course, when universal needs for nourishment, security, and information are especially intense, behavior can be shaped in ways that may be inconsistent with biologically preferred ways. (See Jacobs, W. J., & Nadel, L. [1985]. Stress-induced recovery of fears and phobias. *Psychological Review, 92*, 512–531.) Most interesting is not so much that we can be taught to do all sorts of things, but that certain things are difficult or impossible to learn no matter how hard the effort, or they are difficult or impossible to retain once conditions return to normal.

83 Source and quotes from Pinker, S. (1994). *The language instinct: How the mind creates language*. New York: William Morrow.

83 Bouchard, T. J., Jr., Lykken, D. T., McGue, M., Segal, N. L., & Tellegen, A. (1990). Sources of human psychological differences: The Minnesota study of twins reared apart. *Science, 250*, 223–228.

83 Source and quotes from Fraiberg, S. H. (1959). *The magic years*. New York: Charles Scribner's Sons.

84   There is another way to appreciate the great chasm between the educational environment at home or school and what a child has perceived and learned: delightful confabulations, for example, of Bible stories earnestly taught and raptly attended, but to what end? "The Jews were a proud people and throughout history they had trouble with the unsympathetic Genitals." "Moses led the Hebrews to the Red Sea, where they made unleavened bread, which is bread made without any ingredients." "Moses died before he ever reached Canada. Then Joshua led the Hebrews in the battle of Geritol. The greatest miracle in the Bible is when Joshua told his son to stand still and he obeyed him." "When Mary heard that she was the mother of Jesus, she sang the Magna Carta. When the three wise guys from the East Side arrived, they found Jesus in the manger. Jesus was born because Mary had an immaculate contraption." "The people who followed the Lord were called the twelve decibels. The epistles were the wives of the apostles." "St. Paul cavorted to Christianity. He preached holy acrimony, which is another name for marriage. A Christian should have only one wife. This is called monotony." (Source is Lederer, R. [1995, December 31]. Question and answer. *National Review*, 38.)

Chapter 6

85   See Paulos, J. A. (1988). *Innumeracy: Mathematical illiteracy and its consequences.* New York: Hill & Wang (Farrar, Strauss & Giroux).

88   For the classic paper on regression to the mean and other factors that make intuitive thinking error prone, see Tversky, A., & Kahneman, D. (1974). Judgment under uncertainty: Heuristics and biases. *Science, 185,* 1124–1131.

88   Quote from Durant, W. (1935). *The story of civilization: Part I. Our oriental heritage.* New York: Simon & Schuster.

88   Waller, J. H. (1971). Achievement and social mobility: Relationships among IQ score, education and cooperation in two generations. *Social Biology, 18,* 252–259.

91   Ellwein, M. C. (1984, January 20). Early education [Review of the book *As the twig is bent . . . Lasting effects of preschool programs.* Consortium for Longitudinal Studies (1983). Hillsdale, NJ: Erlbaum]. *Science,* 273–274. Horn, J. M. (1981). Duration of preschool effects on later school competence. *Science, 213,* 1145.

92   Johnson, J. L., McAndrew, F. T., & Harris, P. B. (1991). Sociobiology and the naming of adopted and natural children. *Ethology and Sociobiology, 12,* 365–375.

93   Massie, R. K. (1980). *Peter the Great: His life and world.* New York: Knopf.

93   Quote from Branden, B. (1986). *The passion of Ayn Rand*. New York: Anchor Books (Doubleday).

95   Losing sight of statistical reality, even professionals can get so caught up in their imagery, feelings, or personal experiences, as in this story told by historian and financial advisor Peter Bernstein. "One winter night during one of the many German air raids on Moscow in World War II, a distinguished Soviet professor of statistics showed up in his local air-raid shelter. He had never appeared there before. 'There are seven million people in Moscow,' he used to say. 'Why should I expect them to hit me?' His friends were astonished to see him and asked what happened to change his mind. 'Look,' he explained, 'there are seven million people in Moscow and one elephant. Last night they got the elephant'." (Source is Bernstein, P. [1996]. *Against the gods: The remarkable story of risk*. New York: John Wiley & Sons.)

Chapter 7

101   Source is Rushton, J. P. (1995). *Race, evolution, and behavior*. New Brunswick, NJ: Transaction.

101   Quotes from Bernstein, P. (1996). *Against the gods: The remarkable story of risk*. New York: John Wiley & Sons.

102   Langlois, J. H., & Roggman, L. A. (1990). Attractive faces are only average. *Psychological Science, 1* (2), 115–121; Langlois, J. H., Roggman, L. A., & Musselman, L. (1994). What is average and what is not average about attractive faces. *Psychological Science, 5*, 214–220.

102   Langlois, J. H., Ritter, J. M., Roggman, L. A., & Vaughan, L. S. (1991). Facial diversity and infant preferences for attractive faces. *Developmental Psychology, 27*, 79–84. No one knows for certain the nature of this preference in infants for attractive faces, though it does seem to be instinctive. One possibility is that, like adults, infants prefer the gist over specific experiences. Other things being equal, an attractive face representing a kind of statistical average—a gist—will therefore tend to be preferred over a specific face and certainly over an unattractive face.

That we are naturally disposed toward the gist of our experiences is suggested by laboratory studies that use artificial prototypes. (See Franks, J. J., & Bransford, J. D. [1971]. Abstraction of visual patterns. *Journal of Experimental Psychology, 90*, 65–74; also Langlois, J. H., Roggman, L. A., & Musselman, L. [1994]. What is average and what is not average about attractive faces. *Psychological Science, 5*, 214–220.) An instinctive tendency to favor the gist of things experienced would explain why 6-month-old babies seem to prefer attractive faces, whether real or computer-averaged. But, asks Judy Langlois, what if *newborns* who lack personal experience also prefer attractive faces? Could certain prototypes—averaged faces, for instance—have a special appeal for us because they resonate with instinctive knowledge, or *archetypes*, about what is likely to be normal or healthy? No one knows.

Psychologist C. G. Jung popularized the concept of archetypes, by which he meant genetically based potentialities for experiencing and responding to specific aspects of the world as our ancestors did. Psychologists Hall and Nordby explain that, in Jung's view, "There are as many archetypes as there are typical situations in life. [For example], every infant throughout the world inherits a mother archetype. This preformed image of the mother is then developed into a definite image by the actual mother's appearance and behavior, and by the relationships and experiences the baby has with her."

What Jung called a preformed image is analogous to language ability that, because of human evolution, is common to individuals in all cultures. What he called *actual image* is analogous to language competence individuals gain from the speech patterns of a particular culture. The distinction is important. Jung was not saying to skeptics that we inherit ideas, at least not ideas we can think or imagine at will. Rather, we inherit mental templates or molds that are the *potentials* for ideas. (See Hall, C. S., & Nordby, V. J. [1973]. *A primer of Jungian psychology*. New York: New American Library.)

104 Information reconstruction concept based on Flavell, J. H. (1963). *The developmental psychology of Jean Piaget*. Princeton, NJ: D. Van Nostrand.

104 Kendler, K. S. (1993). Twin studies of psychiatric illness: Current status and future directions. *Archives of General Psychiatry, 50*, 905–915; Kendler, K. S., Neale, M. C., Kessler, R. C., Heath, A. C., & Eaves, L. J. (1993). A test of the equal-environment assumption in twin studies of psychiatric illness. *Behavior Genetics, 23*, 21–27; Rowe, D. C. (1993). Genetic perspectives on personality. In R. Plomin & G. E. McClearn (Eds.), *Nature, nurture, and psychology* (pp. 179–195). Washington, DC: American Psychological Association.

104 Rowe, D. C. (1993). Genetic perspectives on personality. In R. Plomin & G. E. McClearn (Eds.), *Nature, nurture, and psychology* (pp. 179–195). Washington, DC: American Psychological Association; Scarr, S., & Carter-Saltzman, L. (1979). Twin method: Defense of a critical assumption. *Behavior Genetics, 9*, 527–542.

104 Loehlin, J. C., & Nichols, R. C. (1976). *Heredity, environment, & personality: A study of 850 sets of twins*. Austin, TX: University of Texas Press; Rowe, D. C. (1994). *The limits of family influence: Genes, experience, and behavior*. New York: Guilford. I noted two ways to estimate the effect of the shared environment. One is to look for resemblance in unrelated people (adoptees) reared together; the other is to compare the resemblance of identical twins reared together versus apart. There is yet another method.

In identical twins, a correlation measures the resemblance coming from two influences: 100 percent genetic overlap g plus shared environment e—in short, $g + e$. In fraternals, however, a correlation represents the influence of only *50 percent* genetic overlap plus shared environment—in short, $\frac{1}{2} g + e$. Question: How can we get rid of the g term so we are left with e?

The answer: First we double the fraternals' correlation, which is the same as doubling the genetic and environmental influences represented by that correlation. Thus, 2 times $\frac{1}{2} g + e$ becomes $g + 2e$. Next, we subtract the identicals' correlation, which represents $g + e$. In this way, the g term drops out (g minus g leaves 0), and $2e$ minus e leaves e.

We can illustrate this with figures from a study on juvenile delinquency, specifically self-reported delinquent acts. The correlations were 62 for identicals and 52 for fraternals, which means the identicals tend to be more alike than the fraternals, but not by much. The influence of the common environment e is estimated by doubling the fraternal twin's correlation of 52, which yields 104, then subtracting the identical twins' correlation of 62. The result, 42, is our estimate of the shared environment's influence. So, of all the influences that determine how juveniles will line up in delinquency potential, about 42 percent come from the environmental influences from parents and peers that siblings share. The rest comes from genetic and nonshared environmental influences.

Juvenile delinquency, unlike adult criminality, is weakly heritable; identicals and fraternals show similar resemblance for various measures of juvenile delinquency found in many other studies. Pooled results for seven twin studies yield concordance rates of 84 percent for identicals, 69 percent for fraternals. The interesting observation, however, is the relatively large shared environment effect of parenting and peer influences that we usually don't see with IQ, personality traits, and some vulnerabilities, though we do see it with alcoholism.

105 Doubling the difference would not be necessary if the comparison was between not identicals and fraternals but identicals and *genetically unrelated* twins; such a difference would reflect the entire range of possible genetic variation from 100 percent (in identical twins) to 0 percent (in genetically unrelated twins). Genetically unrelated twinning is possible by implanting in a woman's uterus two fertilized eggs from two sets of parents. In 1997, an Italian woman, acting as a surrogate mother, was reported to be expecting two boys in a pregnancy involving five people: herself and two sets of genetically unrelated parents.

105 McClearn, G. E., Johansson, B., Berg, S., Pedersen, N. L., Ahern, F., Petrill, S. A., & Plomin, R. (1997, June 6). Substantial genetic influence on cognitive abilities in twins 80 or more years old. *Science, 276,* 1560–1563.

105   Comparative studies from McGue, M., Bouchard, T. J., Jr., Iacono, W. G., & Lykken, D. T. (1993). Behavior genetics of cognitive ability: A life-span perspective. In R. Plomin & G. E. McClearn (Eds.), *Nature, nurture, and psychology* (pp. 59–76). Washington, DC: American Psychological Association.

106   Miller, E. M. (May, 1997). Could nonshared environmental variance have evolved to assure diversification through randomness? *Evolution and Human Behavior, 18,* 195–221.

107   Rowe, D. C. (1994). *The limits of family influence: Genes, experience, and behavior.* New York: Guilford.

108   Vernon, P. A. (1993). Intelligence and neural efficiency. In D. K. Detterman (Eds.), *Current topics in human intelligence* (pp. 171–187). Norwood, NJ: Ablex.

108   Willerman, L., Schultz, R., Rutledge, J. N., & Bigler, E. D. (1991). *In vivo* brain size and intelligence. *Intelligence, 15,* 223–228.

109   Waller, J. H. (1971). Achievement and social mobility: Relationships among IQ score, education and cooperation in two generations. *Social Biology, 18,* 252–259.

109   Willerman, L., Schultz, R., Rutledge, J. N., & Bigler, E. D. (1991). *In vivo* brain size and intelligence. *Intelligence, 15,* 223–228.

110   McCrae, R. R., & Costa, P. T. (1997, May). Personality trait structure as a human universal. *American Psychologist, 52,* 509–516. Loehlin, J. C., McCrae, R. R., & Costa, P. T., Jr. (1998). Heritabilities of common and measure-specific components of the Big Five personality factors. *Journal of Research in Personality, 32,* 431–453.

110   Buss, D. M. (1995). Evolutionary psychology. *Psychological Inquiry, 6,* 1–30.

110   See Loehlin, J. C., & Nichols, R. C. (1976). *Heredity, environment, & personality: A study of 850 sets of twins.* Austin, TX: University of Texas Press; Livesley, W. J., Jang, K. L., Jackson, D. N., & Vernon, P. A. (1993). Genetic and environmental contributions to dimensions of personality disorder. *American Journal of Psychiatry, 150,* 1826–1831.

111   The argument is developed by Judy R. Harris in her 1998 book *The nurture assumption: Why children turn out the way they do,* published by The Free Press in New York. Her "zilch" comment appears on p. 265.

112   Loehlin's paper, entitled "A test of J. R. Harris's theory of peer influences on personality," appeared in the *Journal of Personality and Social Psychology, 72,* 1197–1201.

112   Raine, A. (1993). *The psychopathology of crime: Criminal behavior as a clinical disorder* (pp. 191–316). San Diego: Academic Press.

112   Given that identicals are genetically identical, any correlation between their personality resemblance and either peer sharing or parental treatment can reflect only environmental influence—the social environmental aspect of that influence being about 15 percent for peers and

10 percent for parents, if we accept Loehlin's correlations. On the other hand, given that fraternals are genetically as well as environmentally different, any correlation between *their* personality resemblance and either peer sharing or parental treatment can reflect genetic as well as environmental influence. Thus, *a larger correlation for fraternals than for identicals* suggests a genetic disposition to select and identify with peers and parents, to influence, as well as to be influenced by, the environment.

113   Lesch, K.-P., Bengel, D., Heils, A., Sabol, S. Z., Greenberg, B. D., Petri, S., Benjamin, J., Müller, C. R., Hamer, D. H., & Murphy, D. L. (1996, November 29). Association of anxiety-related traits with a polymorphism in the serotonin transporter gene regulatory region. *Science, 274*, 1527–1531.

113   Ebstein, R. P., Novick, O., Umansky, R., Priel, B., Osher, Y., Darren, B., Bennett, E. R., Nemanov, L., Katz, M., & Belmaker, R. H. (1996). Dopamine D4 receptor (D4DR) exon III polymorphism associated with the human personality trait of novelty seeking. *Nature Genetics, 12*, 78–80; Obler, L. K., & Fein, D. (Eds.). (1988). *The exceptional brain: Neuropsychology of talent and special abilities.* New York: Guilford.

114   Gelernter, J., Krazler, H., Coccaro, E., Siever, L., New, A., & Mulgrew, C. L. (1997). D4 dopamine-receptor (DRD4) alleles and novelty seeking in substance dependent, personality disorder, and control subjects. *American Journal of Human Genetics, 61*, 1144–1152; Jönsson, E. G., Nöthen, M. M., Gustavsson, J. P., Neidt, H., Brené, S., Tylec, A., Propping, P., & Sedvall, G. C. (1997). Lack of evidence for allelic association between personality traits and the dopamine D4 receptor gene polymorphism. *American Journal of Psychiatry, 154*, 697–699.

114   Buss, D. M. (1995). Evolutionary psychology. *Psychological Inquiry, 6*, 1–30.

114   Goleman, D. (1996, July 21). The secret of happiness: It's in the genes. *Austin American-Statesman*, pp. D1, D4.

114   Lykken, D., & Telligen, A. (1996). Happiness is a stochastic phenomenon. *Psychological Science, 7*, 186–189.

115   Diener, E., & Diener, C. (1996). Most people are happy. *Psychological Science, 7*, 181–185.

115   Gibbs, W. W. (1996). Gaining on fat. *Scientific American*, Volume 275 88–94.

116   Lykken, D. T. (1982). Research with twins: The concept of emergenesis. *Psychophysiology, 19*, 361–373.

Chapter 8

119   Heston, L. L. (1966). Psychiatric disorders in foster home reared children of schizophrenic mothers. *British Journal of Psychiatry, 112*, 819–825.

120   Fischer, M. (1971). Psychoses in the offspring of schizophrenic monozygotic twins and their normal co-twins. *British Journal of Psychiatry, 118*, 43–52.

120   Kendler, K. S. (1993). Twin studies of psychiatric illness: Current status and future directions. *Archives of General Psychiatry, 50*, 905–915; Crowe, R. R. (1974). An adoption study of antisocial personality. *Archives of General Psychiatry, 31*, 785–791; Reiss, D., Plomin, R., & Hetherington, E. M. (1991). Genetics and psychiatry. *American Journal of Psychiatry, 148*, 283–291.

The actual rate of schizophrenia in the population is somewhere between 0.5 and 1 percent; rounding up to the larger figure merely simplifies discussion. What counts, however, is not so much an absolute number but the size of one statistic relative to another; 10 percent for the offspring of schizophrenics versus 1 percent for the population has more or less the same meaning as 5 versus 0.5 percent.

122   DiLalla, D. L., & Gottesman, I. I. (1995). Normal personality characteristics of identical twins discordant for schizophrenia. *Journal of Abnormal Psychology, 104*, 490–499; Torrey, E. F., Bowler, A. E., Taylor, E. H., & Gottesman, I. I. (1994). *Schizophrenia and manic-depressive disorder: The biological roots of mental illness as revealed by the landmark study of identical twins.* New York: Basic Books.

124   Concordance to correlation from Reiss, D., Plomin, R., & Hetherington, E. M. (1991). Genetics and psychiatry. *American Journal of Psychiatry, 148*, 283–291.

124   Schizophrenia heritability estimates from McGuffin, P., & Katz, R. (1993). Genes, adversity, and depression. In R. Plomin & G. McClearn (Eds.), *Nature, nurture, and psychology* (pp. 217–230). Washington, DC: American Psychological Association.

125   Heritable disorder occurrence from Eley, T. C. (1997). General genes: A new theme in developmental psychopathology. *Current Directions in Psychological Science, 6*, 90–95.

125   Kendler, K. S., Prescott, C. A., Neale, M. C., & Pedersen, N. L. (1997). Temperance board registration for alcohol abuse in a national sample of Swedish male twins, born 1902 to 1949. *Archives of General Psychiatry, 54*, 178–184; McGue, M. (1993). From proteins to cognitions: The behavioral genetics of alcoholism. In R. Plomin & G. E. McClearn (Eds.), *Nature, nurture, and psychology* (pp. 245–268). Washington, DC: American Psychological Association.

125   Goodwin, D. W., Schulsinger, F., Hermansen, L., Guze, S. B., & Winokur, G. (1973). Alcohol problems in adoptees raised apart from alcoholic biological parents. *Archives of General Psychiatry, 34*, 238–243.

125   But see Kaij, L. (1960). *Alcoholism in twins.* Stockholm: Almqvist and Wiksell.

125 Concordance figures from McGuffin, P., & Katz, R. (1993). Genes, adversity, and depression. In R. Plomin & G. McClearn (Eds.), *Nature, nurture, and psychology* (pp. 217–230). Washington, DC: American Psychological Association.

126 Wender, P. H., Kety, S. S., Rosenthal, D., Schulsinger, F., Ortmann, J., & Lunde, I. (1986). Psychiatric disorders in the biological and adoptive families of adopted individuals with affective disorders. *Archives of General Psychiatry, 43,* 923–929.

127 Miles, C. P. (1977). Conditions predisposing to suicide: A review. *Journal of Nervous and Mental Disease, 164,* 231–246.

127 Brent, D. A., Bridge, J., Johnson, B. A., & Connolly, J. (1996). Suicidal behavior runs in families: A controlled family study of adolescent suicide victims. *Archives of General Psychiatry, 53,* 1145–1152.

128 Mann, J. J., Malone, K. M., Nielsen, D. A., Goldman, D., Erdos, J., & Galerntner, J. (1997). Possible association of a polymorphism of the tryptophan hydroxylase gene with suicidal behavior in depressed patients. *American Journal of Psychiatry, 154,* 1451–1453.

128 Quote from Maugham, S. (1946). *The razor's edge.* New York: Pocket Books.

128 Quote from Lamb, C. (1963). Sanity of true genius. In R. M. Hutchins & M. J. Adler (Eds.), *Gateway to the great books* (Vol. 5). Chicago: Encyclopaedia Britannica.

129 Johnson Quote from Bloom, H. (1994). *The western canon: The books and school of the ages.* New York: Harcourt Brace.

129 Jackson, P. W., & Messick, S. (1968). Creativity. In P. London & D. Rosenhan (Eds.), *Foundations of abnormal psychology* (pp. 226–250). New York: Holt, Rinehart & Winston.

130 Writers study from Barron, F. (1969). *Creative person and creative process.* New York: Holt, Rinehart & Winston.

130 Jamison, K. R. (1995, February). Manic depressive illness and creativity. *Scientific American,* 62–67; Post, F. (1994). Creativity and psychopathology: A study of 291 world famous men. *British Journal of Psychiatry, 165,* 22–34.

131 Prentky, R. A. (1980). *Creativity and psychopathology.* New York: Praeger.

131 Creativity-vulnerability connection based on Post, F. (1994). Creativity and psychopathology: A study of 291 world famous men. *British Journal of Psychiatry, 165,* 22–34; Prentky, R. A. (1980). *Creativity and psychopathology.* New York: Praeger.

131 McNeil, T. (1971). Prebirth and postbirth influence on the relationship between creative ability and recorded mental illness. *Journal of Personality, 39,* 391–406.

131 Heston, L. L., & Denny, D. (1968). Interactions between early life experience and biological factors in schizophrenia. In D. Rosenthal &

S. S. Kety (Eds.), *The transmission of schizophrenia* (pp. 363–376). Oxford, England: Pergamon. Aside from the artistic and creative element, is there a silver lining—a value to the self or to the culture—of vulnerability to mental illness or other abnormal behavior? Anthropologist Peter Farb described a cross-cultural example of the neurotic person's value as shaman, or medicine man, in Inuit (Eskimo) culture. Some Inuit think they can spot the peculiar and malevolent symptoms of a future shaman. The child "is meditative and introverted; he may have fits or fainting spells; he is disturbed by dreams and suffers from hallucinations and hysteria. The shaman is a psychological type known as the neurotic, borderline schizoid—which is perfectly all right with the Eskimo, since he believes the shaman needs extraordinary abilities in his traffic with the supernatural." (See Farb, P. [1968]. *Man's rise to civilization as shown by the Indians of North America from primeval times to the coming of the industrial state.* New York: Dutton.)

In an essay entitled "Is Mental Illness Necessary?" psychiatrist Max Hamilton also addresses the indirect value of mental illness, for example, the association of depression with the gift of creative writing; likewise, people with hysterical personalities who excel in the performing arts and the uncanny capacity of people with neuroses for detecting hidden motives and feelings. Hamilton also describes two kinds of English aviators. One is the obsessional bomber pilot who has a job to do a certain way no matter what else is happening, the other is the cold-blooded fighter pilot who intends to hunt and kill someone. In his view, many people owed their very lives to those psychopathic fighter pilots who flew during the summer of 1940. (See Hamilton, M. [1981]. Paul Hoch address: Is mental illness necessary? In D. F. Klein & J. Rabkin (Eds.), *Anxiety: New research and changing concept.* New York: Raven Press.) Likewise suggesting that amoral, even antisocial, people have a potentially useful role, Del Thiessen argues that "many deviant behaviors of today are only distortions of adaptive responses of yesterday. They are exaggerated, ill-timed, misused, and socially damaging, but not abnormal in their origin." (See Thiessen, D. [1996]. *Bittersweet destiny: The stormy evolution of human behavior.* New Brunswick, NJ: Transaction.)

If some mental illness is the price societies must pay for certain kinds of creativity, then a magic bullet to knock out genetic factors, say, in schizophrenia or manic depression might reduce a culture's creative potential. The argument, once articulated by psychiatrist Henry Maudsley, is this: "To forbid the marriage of a person sprung from an insanely disposed family might be to deprive the world of a singular genius or talent, and so be an irreparable injury to the race of men. . . . If, then, one man of genius were produced at the cost of one thousand or fifty thousand insane persons, the result might be a compensation for the terrible cost." It's an interesting problem, but the solution is not all that obvious.

Chapter 9

134 Quote from Durant, W. (1935). *The story of civilization: Part I. Our oriental heritage.* New York: Simon & Schuster.

134 Quotes from Durant, W. (1953). *The story of civilization: Part V. The Renaissance.* New York: Simon & Schuster.

134 Quote from Burnham, J. (1985/1964). *Suicide of the west: An essay on the meaning and destiny of liberalism.* Washington, DC: Regnery Gateway.

134 Attributing these and other similarities of chimp and human behavior to extraordinary overlap in DNA can be misleading. Cognitive scientist Steven Pinker clarifies the possible meaning of a little difference in DNA, for example, between humans and chimps. "Indeed, a 1% difference in total DNA does not even mean that only 1% of human and chimpanzee genes are different. It could, in theory, mean that 100% of human and chimpanzee genes are different, each by 1%. DNA is a discrete combinatorial code, so a 1% difference in the DNA for a gene can be as significant as a 100% difference, just as changing one bit in every byte [in computer code], or one letter in every word, can result in a new text that is 100% different." Pinker, S. (1994). *The language instinct: How the mind creates language* (p. 351). New York: William Morrow.

   That even a tiny difference in DNA can be a big deal is illustrated by evolutionary physiologist Jared Diamond, referring to Lake Victoria's 200 species of cichlid fishes, all of which evolved over 200,000 years from a common ancestor. "Some graze on algae, others catch other fish, and still others variously crush snails, feed on plankton, catch insects, nibble the scales off other fish, or specialize in grabbing fish embryos from brooding mother fish. Yet all those Lake Victoria cichlids differed from each other on the average by only about 0.4 percent of their DNA studied. Thus it took even fewer genetic mutations to change a snail crusher into a specialized baby killer than it took to produce us from an ape."

134 Quote from Goodall, J. (1986). *The chimpanzees of Gombe: Patterns of behavior.* Cambridge, MA: Belknap (Harvard University Press).

135 Stanford, C. B. (1995, January). To catch a colobus. *Natural History,* 48–54.

135 This and the next quote from Goodall, J. (1986). *The chimpanzees of Gombe: Patterns of behavior.* Cambridge, MA: Belknap (Harvard University Press).

136 Quote from Thiessen, D. (1996). *Bittersweet destiny: The stormy evolution of human behavior.* New Brunswick, NJ: Transaction.

136 Colson, C. W. (1996, January 24). The new criminal class. *The Wall Street Journal,* p. A14.

136   Langley, M. (1996, April 2). My son, the teen-age predator. *The Wall Street Journal*, p. A14.

137   Quote from Michener, J. (1998, October 27). Will the U.S. prevail? *Parade Magazine*, 6–7.

137   Quote from Hutchins, R. M. (1963). A letter to the reader. In R. M. Hutchins & M. J. Adler (Eds.), *Gateway to the great books* (pp. 1–14). Chicago: Encyclopaedia Britannica.

137   Quote from Gleick, J. (1992). *Genius: The life and science of Richard Feynman.* New York: Pantheon.

138   Source and quote from Berman, R. (1998, Spring). Making up the grade: Notes from the Antiversity. *Academic Questions,* 39–40.

138   Raine, A., Brennan, P., Mednick, B., & Mednick, S. A. (1996). High rates of violence, crime, academic problems, and behavioral problems in males with both early neuromotor deficits and unstable family environments. *Archives of General Psychiatry, 53,* 544–549.

139   Quote from Pitts, L. (1998, April 13). Kids' success still depends on parents. *Austin American-Statesman*, p. A9.

140   Kagan, J. (1994). *Galen's prophecy: Temperament in human nature.* New York: Westview (HarperCollins).

140   Quote from Smith, H. (1997, December 19). It's not the Internet, movies, guns but we want something to blame when kids kill. *Austin American-Statesman*, p. A15.

140   American Psychiatric Association (1994). *Diagnostic and statistical manual of mental disorders* (4th ed.). Washington, DC: Author.

141   Crowe, R. R. (1974). An adoption study of antisocial personality. *Archives of General Psychiatry, 31,* 785–791.

141   See Frick, P. J., & Jackson, Y. K. (1993). Family functioning and childhood antisocial behavior: Yet another reinterpretation. *Journal of Clinical Child Psychology, 22,* 410–419.

141   See Jarey, M. L., & Stewart, M. A. (1985). Psychiatric disorder in the parents of adoptive children with aggressive conduct disorder. *Neuropsychobiology, 13,* 7–10.

142   Mednick, S. A., Gabrielli, W. F. J., & Hutchings, B. (1984). Genetic influences in criminal convictions: evidence from an adoption cohort. *Science, 224,* 891–894.

142   Brennan, P. A., Raine, A., Schulsinger, F., Kirkegaard-Sorensen, L., Knop, J., Hutchings, B., Rosenberg, R., & Mednick, S. A. (1997). Psychophysiological protective factors for male subjects at high risk for criminal behavior. *Archives of General Psychiatry, 154,* 853–855.

142   Cloninger, C. R., & Gottesman, I. I. (1987). Genetic and environmental factors in antisocial behavior disorders. In S. A. Mednick, T. E. Moffitt, & S. A. Stack (Eds.), *The causes of crime* (pp. 92–109). Cambridge, England: Cambridge University Press.

142 Raine, A. (1993). *The psychopathology of crime: Criminal behavior as a clinical disorder.* San Diego, CA: Academic Press.

143 Raine, A. (1993). *The psychopathology of crime: Criminal behavior as a clinical disorder.* San Diego, CA: Academic Press; Lyons, M. J., True, W. R., Eisen, S. A., Goldberg, J., Meyer, J. M., Faraone, S. V., Eaves, L. J., & Tsuang, M. T. (1995). Differential heritability of adult and juvenile antisocial traits. *Archives of General Psychiatry, 52,* 906–915; Rowe, D. C., & Waldman, I. D. (1993). The question "How?" reconsidered. In R. Plomin & G. McClearn (Eds.), *Nature, nurture, and psychology* (pp. 355–373). Washington, DC: American Psychological Association.

143 Harris, J. R. (1995). Where is the child's environment? *Psychological Review, 102,* 458–489. The good news is that many delinquents outgrow their antisocial ways, despite all the conditioning and bad habits acquired in crime-ridden environments that are supposed to explain why others continue their criminal ways. Delinquency out of expedient conformity more than inner conviction would explain why they are likely to improve once they get into college, get a job, or get married.

An informal dissenting view is offered by psychologist Stanton Samenow. "I question that 'most delinquents outgrow their antisocial ways.' My experience tells me that they decide to abandon certain types of behaviors, perhaps to take fewer risks. But the errors in thought patterns, the attempts to control others, the dishonesty, etc. tend to persist. In other words they remain irresponsible but become more cautious."

There is a continuum from the worst of the delinquents who just miss becoming career criminals and the good kid who for a short while gets caught up in the gang atmosphere until opportunity calls him away. Samenow may be speaking of delinquents at the psychopathic end of this spectrum. Researchers may be speaking to the rest of the continuum that includes relatively normal individuals who, for a time, have indulged the antisocial tendencies at the heart of our species.

144 Jensen, A. R. (1998). *The g factor: The science of mental ability.* Westport, CT: Praeger.

144 Herrnstein, R. J., & Murray, C. (1994). *The bell curve: Intelligence and class structure in American life.* New York: The Free Press.

144 Raine, A. (1993). *The psychopathology of crime: Criminal behavior as a clinical disorder.* San Diego, CA: Academic Press. The negative relation between IQ and antisocial behavior does not appear to stem from higher-IQ antisocials escaping detection because low IQ also reflects *self-reported* acts of antisocial behavior regardless of whether the acts have been detected or not (see Moffitt, T. & Silva, P. A. [1988]. IQ and delinquency: A direct test of the differential detection hypothesis. *Journal of Abnormal Psychology, 97,* 330–333).

145 Witkin, H. A., Mednick, S. A., Shulsinger, F., Bakkestrom, E., Chris-

tiansen, K. O., Goodenough, D. R., Hirschorn, K., Lundsteen, C., Owen, D. R., et al. (1977). Criminality, aggression, and intelligence among XYY and XXY men. In S. A. Mednick & K. O. Christiansen (Eds.), *Biosocial bases of criminal behavior.* New York: Gardner Press. In the definitive study headed up by psychologist Hy Witkin, blood samples to assess chromosomal anomalies were taken from over 4,000 Danish men at least 6 feet ½ inches tall. XYYs are on the tall side and therefore more likely to be found in a group of tall men. From this sample, the investigators identified 12 XYYs, 16 XXYs (Kleinfelter's syndrome), and 4,096 XYs. The rate of criminality—convictions for violating the Danish penal code—was 9 percent for the XYs, 19 percent for the XXYs, and 42 percent for the XYYs. That's a very high rate, yet the crimes committed by the XYYs tended to be petty rather than violent, directed toward property rather than against persons. According to the investigators, "Among all the offenses committed by XYYs there was only a single instance of an aggressive act against another person; and in that case the aggression was not severe."

146   Weiss, G., & Hechtman, L. T. (1986). *Hyperactive children grown up.* New York: Guilford Press.

146   Quote from Kopplewicz, H. S. (1997, October 6). ADD, chemistry, and self-control. Letter to the editor. *The Wall Street Journal,* p. A23.

146   Biederman, J., Faraone, S. V., Mick, E., Spencer, T., Wilens, T., Kieley, K., Guite, J., Ablon, J. S., Reed, E., & Warburton, R. (1995). High risk for attention deficit hyperactivity disorder among children of parents with childhood onset of the disorder: A pilot study. *American Journal of Psychiatry, 152,* 431–435.

146   Cadoret, R. J., & Stewart, M. A. (1991). An adoption study of attention deficit/hyperactivity/aggression and their relationship to adult antisocial personality. *Comprehensive Psychiatry, 32,* 73–82.

147   Raine, A. (1993). *The psychopathology of crime: Criminal behavior as a clinical disorder.* San Diego, CA: Academic Press.

147   Cadoret, R. J., Yates, W. R., Troughton, E., Woodworth, G., & Stewart, M. A. (1995). Adoption study demonstrating two genetic pathways to drug abuse. *Archives of General Psychiatry, 52,* 42–52; Tiihonen, J., Isohanni, M., Räsänen, P., Koiranen, M., & Moring, J. (1997). Specific major mental disorders and criminality: A 26-year prospective study of the 1966 Northern Finland birth cohort. *American Journal of Psychiatry, 154,* 840–845.

148   Wakschlag, L. S., Lahey, B. B., Loeber, R., Green, S. M., Gordon, R. A., & Leventhal, B. L. (1997). Maternal smoking during pregnancy and risk of conduct disorder. *Archives of General Psychiatry, 54,* 670–676.

148   McGue, M. (1993). From proteins to cognitions: The behavioral genetics of alcoholism. In R. Plomin & G. E. McClearn (Eds.), *Nature, nurture,*

and psychology (pp. 245–268). Washington, DC: American Psychological Association.

148   Quote from Klawans, H. L. (1988). *Toscanini's fumble and other tales of clinical neurology.* Chicago: Contemporary Books.

148   Mark, V. H., & Ervin, F. R. (1970). *Violence and the brain.* New York: Harper & Row.

149   Willerman, L., & Cohen, D. B. (1990). *Psychopathology.* New York: McGraw-Hill; LaPierre, D., Braun, C. M. J., & Hodgins, S. (1995). Ventral frontal deficits in psychopathy: Neuropsychological test findings. *Neuropsychologia, 33,* 139–151.

149   Raine, A. (1993). *The psychopathology of crime: Criminal behavior as a clinical disorder.* San Diego, CA: Academic Press.

149   Damasio, A. R. (1994). *Descartes' error: Emotion, reason, and the human brain.* New York: G. P. Putnam's Sons (Grosset/Putnam).

150   Quote from Blumer, D. (1975). Temporal lobe epilepsy and its psychiatric significance. In D. F. Benson & D. Blumer (Eds.), *Psychiatric aspects of neurological disease* (pp. 171–197). New York: Grune & Stratton.

150   Raine, A., Venables, P. H., & Williams, M. (1990). Relationships between central and autonomic measures of arousal at age 15 and criminality at age 24 years. *Archives of General Psychiatry, 47,* 1003–1007; Raine, A., Venables, P. H., & Williams, M. (1995). High autonomic arousal and electrodermal orienting. *American Journal of Psychiatry, 152,* 1595–1600.

151   This and the next quote from Vertosick, J. F. (1996, October). A bullet to the mind. *Discover,* 38–40.

151   Quote from Rowe, D. C. (1994). *The limits of family influence: Genes, experience, and behavior.* New York: Guilford.

Chapter 10

154   Heilman, J. R. (1995, August 13). The good news about Alzheimer's. *Parade Magazine,* 12–15.

154   Swerdlow, J. L. (1995). The quiet miracles of the brain. *National Geographic,* Vol. 187, 2–41.

154   Heston, L. H., Mastri, A. R., Anderson, V. E., & White, J. (1981). Dementia of the Alzheimer type: Clinical genetics, natural history, and associated conditions. *Archives of General Psychiatry, 38,* 1085–1090.

156   Maher, J. (1997, July 12). Boxer's genetic fate. *Austin American-Statesman,* pp. E1, E9.

156   Corder, E. H., Saunders, A. M., Strittmatter, W. J., Schmechel, D. E., Gaskell, P. C., Small, P. C., Roses, A. D., Haines, J. L., & Pericak-Vance, M. A. (1993, August 13). Gene dose of apolipoprotein E type allele and the risk of Alzheimer's disease in late onset families. *Science,*

261, 921–923; Tsai, M. S., Tangalos, E. G., Petersen, R. C., Smith, G. E., Schaid, D. J., Kokmen, E., Ivnik, R. J., & Thibodeau, S. N. (1994). Apolipoprotein E: Risk factor for Alzheimer disease. *American Journal of Human Genetics, 54,* 643–649.

157   Most dramatically, compared to normal controls, Alzheimer patients *without* apoE4 have a fourfold greater chance of having the G/G variant. See Montoya, S., Aston, C. E., DeKosky, S. T., Kamboh, M. I., Lazo, J. S., & Ferrell, R. E. (1988). Bleomycin hydrolase is associated with risk of sporadic Alzheimer's disease. *Nature Genetics, 18,* 211–212. As *Stranger in the Nest* went to press, a preliminary announcement was being made of yet another genetic risk factor, this one—apparently as potent as apoE—a mutation of the gene that codes for a protein called α_2-macroglobulin, or α_2-M. One theory is that the protein produced by the normal gene helps eliminate proteins, such as beta amyloid, that tend to have a toxic effect on the brain. According to theory, risk for Alzheimer's increases either because the abnormal protein created by the mutated α_2-M gene doesn't work or because the normal protein produced by the normal α_2-M gene can't work when another risk factor, such as apoE4, blocks its function. For a more complete explanation, see Marx, J. (1998, July 24). New gene tied to common form of Alzheimer's. *Science, 281,* 507–509.

157   Brunner, H. G., Nelen, M., Breakefield, X. O., Ropers, H. H., & van Oost, B. A. (1993). Abnormal behavior associated with a point mutation in the structural gene for monoamine oxidase A. *Science, 262,* 578–580.

158   Arato, M., Tothfalusi, L., & Banki, C. M. (1989). Serotonin and suicide. *Biological Psychiatry, 25,* 196A–197A; Coccaro, E., & Murphy, D. (Eds.). (1991). *Serotonin in major psychiatric disorders.* Washington, DC: American Psychiatric Association.

158   Cases, O., Seif, I., Grimsby, J., Gaspar, P., Chen, K., Pournin, S., Müller, U., et al. (1995, June 23). Aggressive behavior and altered amounts of brain serotonin and norepinephrine in mice lacking MAOA. *Science, 268,* 1763–1766; Doudet, D., Hommer, D., Higley, J. D., Andreasen, P. J., Moneman, R., Soumi, S. J., & Linnoila, M. (1995). Cerebral glucose metabolism, CSF 5-HIAA levels, and aggressive behavior in rhesus monkeys. *American Journal of Psychiatry, 152,* 1782–1787.

158   Coccaro, E., & Murphy, D. (Eds.). (1991). *Serotonin in major psychiatric disorders.* Washington, DC: American Psychiatric Association; Virkkunen, M., Rawlings, R., Tokola, R., Poland, R. E., Guidotti, A., Nemeroff, C., Bissette, G., Kalogeras, K., Karonen, S. L., & Linnoila, M. (1994). CSF biochemistries, glucose metabolism, and diurnal activity rhythms in alcoholic, violent offenders, fire setters, and healthy volunteers. *Archives of General Psychiatry, 51,* 20–27; Virkkunen, M., Kallio, E., Rawlings, R., Tokola, R., Poland, R. E., Guidotti, A., Nemeroff, C.,

Bissette, G., Kalogeras, K., Karonen, S. L., & Linnoila, M. (1994). Personality profiles and state aggressiveness in Finnish alcoholic, violent offenders, fire setters, and healthy volunteers. *Archives of General Psychiatry, 51,* 28–33.

159 Quote from Marzuk, P. M. (1996). Violence, crime, and mental illness: How strong a link? *Archives of General Psychiatry, 53,* 481–486.

159 Kelsoe, J. R., Ginns, E. I., Egeland, J. A., Gerhard, D. S., Goldstein, A. M., Bale, S. J., Pauls, D. L., Long, R. T., Kidd, K. K., Coute, G., Houseman, D. E., & Paul, S. M. (1989). Re-evaluation of the linkage relationship between chromosome 11p loci and the gene for bipolar affective disorder in the Old Order Amish. *Nature, 342,* 238–243.

159 Watt, D. C., & Edwards, J. H. (1991). Doubt about evidence for a schizophrenic gene. *Psychological Medicine, 21,* 279–285.

161 Swift, R. G., Perkins, D. O., Chase, C. L., Sadler, D. B., & Swift, M. (1991). Psychiatric disorders in 36 families with Wolfram syndrome. *American Journal of Psychiatry, 148,* 775–779; Swift, R. G., Polymeropoulos, M. H., Torres, R., & Swift, M. (1998). Predisposition of Wolfram syndrome heterozygotes to psychiatric illness. *Molecular Psychiatry, 3,* 86–91.

161 Willerman, L., & Cohen, D. B. (1990). *Psychopathology.* New York: McGraw-Hill.

161 Sobesky, W. E., Hull, C. E., & Hagerman, R. J. (1994). Symptoms of schizotypal personality disorder in Fragile X women. *Journal of the American Academy of Child and Adolescent Psychiatry, 33,* 247–255; Freund, L. S., Reiss, A. L., Hagerman, R., & Vinogradov, S. (1992). Chromosome fragility and psychopathology in obligate female carriers of the fragile X chromosome. *Archives of General Psychiatry, 49,* 54–60.

Why is it that only half of women's X chromosomes have the FRA mutation, and therefore a relatively mild fragile X-type mental retardation? The answer lies in a sex difference that, psychologically speaking, can make all the difference in the world.

Unlike affected men, who would have the mutation on all their X chromosomes, carrier mothers would have that mutation on only *half* their active X chromosomes, which is not enough to affect their behavior. I say half their *active* X chromosomes because half of a woman's X chromosomes are inactive, which means that men and women have only one active X chromosome per cell.

Consider a female embryo grown to 32 cells. At about this point in normal female development, one of the X chromosomes in each cell gets chemically inactivated. But which one—the A or the B member of the XX pair? There's no way to predict, because X inactivation is random. Simply by chance, the A chromosome is inactivated in about half the 32 cells, the B chromosome in the other half.

Now imagine a mutation such as the one that causes fragile X syndrome exists on the A member of the X chromosome pair. By chance, 50 percent of those A chromosomes will be inactivated, and 50 percent of the B chromosomes will be inactivated. In effect, half of a woman's active X chromosomes will have the mutation. The other half will be free of the mutation; it is this 50 percent that affords the protection. Further protection comes to some women for whom, also by chance, even more than 50 percent of the X chromosomes are the B kind without the mutation. (For less fortunate others, more than 50 percent are the A kind with the mutation.)

Now we have an explanation of why, even with the CGG mutation, females are less likely than males to have the fragile X syndrome—why fragile X syndrome occurs in at least 80 percent of the males but only 30 percent of the females, and why, typically, those males are more severely affected, the females less affected, sometimes so little as to escape being diagnosed by relatives and friends. In short, the reason for the sex difference is largely in the fact that males have only one X chromosome per cell, each with the mutation; females, on average, have only half their X chromosomes with the mutation, the other half affording the affected female a measure of protection.

162 Tsujita, T., Niikawa, N., Yamashita, H., Imamura, A., Hamada, A., Nakane, Y., & Okazaki, Y. (1998). Genomic discordance between monozygotic twins discordant for schizophrenia. *American Journal of Psychiatry, 155*, 422–424.

163 Kruyer, H. (1994). Fragile X syndrome and the (CGG)n mutation: Two families with discordant MZ twins. *American Journal of Human Genetics, 54*, 437–442.

164 Battaglia, M., Bertella, S., Bajo, S., Binaghi, F., & Bellodi, L. (1998). Anticipation of age at onset in panic disorder. *American Journal of Psychiatry, 155*, 590–595.

164 Gorwood, P., Leboyer, M., Falissard, B., Jay, M., Rouillon, F., & Feingold, J. (1996). Anticipation in schizophrenia: A new light on a controversial problem. *American Journal of Psychiatry, 153*, 1173–1177.

164 Petronis, A., & Kennedy, J. L. (1995). Unstable genes—unstable mind? *American Journal of Psychiatry, 152*, 164–172.

164 Côté, G. B., & Gyftodimou, J. (1991). Twinning and mitotic crossing-over: Some possibilities and their implications. *American Journal of Human Genetics, 49*, 120–130.

164 Money, J., & Ehrhardt, A. A. (1972). *Man & woman/boy & girl.* Baltimore: Johns Hopkins University Press; Vogel, F., & Moltulsky, A. G. (1986). *Human genetics: Problems and approaches.* New York: Springer-Verlag.

165 Skuse, D. H., James, R. S., Bishop, D. V. M., Coppin, B., Dalton, P., Aamodt-Leeper, G., Bacarese-Hamilton, M., Creswell, C., McGurk, R.,

& Jacobs, P. A. (1997). Evidence from Turner's syndrome of an imprinted X-linked locus affecting cognitive function. *Nature, 387*, 705–708.

166 Martin, N., Boomsma, D., & Machin, G. (1997). A twin-pronged attack on complex traits. *Nature Genetics, 17*, 387–392.

166 Quote from Cole, R. (1997, May 2). Will cloning beget disaster? *The Wall Street Journal*, p. A14.

166 Roberts, L. (1988, January). Zeroing in on the sex switch. *Science, 239*, 21–23.

166 Money, J., & Ehrhardt, A. A. (1972). *Man & woman/boy & girl.* Baltimore: Johns Hopkins University Press.

167 Resnick, S. M., Gottesman, I. I., & McGue, M. (1993). Sensation seeking in opposite-sex twins: An effect of prenatal hormones? *Behavior Genetics, 23*, 323–329. Also see Miller, E. M. (1998). Evidence from opposite-sex twins for the effects of prenatal sex hormones. In L. Ellis & L. Ebertz (Eds.), *Males, females, and behavior: Towards biological understanding* (pp. 27–58). Westport, CT: Praeger.

167 New, M. I., & Levine, L. S. (Eds.). (1984). *Adrenal diseases in childhood.* London: S. Karger.

168 Diamond, M., & Sigmundson, H. K. (1997). Sex reassignment at birth: Long-term review and clinical implications. *Archives of Pediatric and Adolescent Medicine, 151*, 298–304.

169 Imperato-McGinley, J., Guerrero, L., Gautier, T., & Peterson, R. E. (1974). Steroid 5-alpha reductase deficiency in man: An inherited form of male pseudohermaphroditism. *Science, 186*, 1213–1215; Imperato-McGinley, J., Peterson, R. E., Gautier, T., & Sturla, E. (1979). Androgens and the evolution of male-gender identity among male pseudohermaphrodites with 5-alpha reductase deficiency. *The New England Journal of Medicine, 300*, 1233–1237.

169 Berenbaum, S. A., & Hines, M. (1992). Early androgens are related to childhood sex-typed toy preferences. *Psychological Science, 3* (3), 203–206; Collaer, M. L., & Hines, M. (1995). Human behavioral sex differences: A role for gonadal hormones during early development? *Psychological Bulletin, 118*, 55–107.

170 Willerman, L., & Cohen, D. B. (1990). *Psychopathology.* New York: McGraw-Hill.

170 Bailey, J. M., & Pillard, R. C. (1991). A genetic study of male sexual orientation. *Archives of General Psychiatry, 48*, 1089–1096; Bailey, J. M., Pillard, R. C., Neale, M. C., & Agyei, Y. (1993). Heritable factors influence sexual orientation in women. *Archives of General Psychiatry, 50*, 217–223.

170 LeVay, S. (1993). *The sexual brain.* Cambridge, MA: The MIT Press (A Bradford Book).

171 Gladue, B. A. (1994, October). The biopsychology of sexual orientation. *Current Directions in Psychological Science, 3*, 150–154.

173 Belmaker, R., Pollin, W., Wyatt, R. J., & Cohen, S. (1974). A follow-up

of monozygotic twins discordant for schizophrenia. *Archives of General Psychiatry, 30,* 219–222.

Chapter 11

176 Steinmetz, H., Herzog, A., Huang, Y., & Hackländer, T. (1994). Discordant brain-surface anatomy in monozygotic twins [Letter to the editor]. *The New England Journal of Medicine, 331,* 952–953.

177 Horgan, J. (1990, December). Double trouble: When identical twins are not identical. *Scientific American,* 25–26. The point about predicting behavior even with knowledge of genes and environment is nicely illustrated in a lyrical, century-old observation on the wasp *Ammophila urnaria:* "While one . . . was beguiled from her hunting by every sorrel blossom she passed, another stuck to her work with indefatigable perseverance. While one stung her caterpillar so carelessly and made her nest in so shiftless a way that her young could survive only through some lucky chance, another devoted herself to these duties not only with conscientious thoroughness, but with an apparent craving after artistic perfection." If such relatively simple, highly instinctive, genetically alike mechanical creatures can be so different in personality, why not people—why not even identical twins—*and for reasons having little to do with parenting or other social conditions?*

177 Miller, E. M. (1997). Could nonshared environmental variance have evolved to assure diversification through randomness? *Evolution and Human Behavior, 18,* 195–221.

177 Mirsky, A., & Quinn, O. W. (1988). The Genain quadruplets. *Schizophrenia Bulletin, 14* (4), 595–612; Rosenthal, D. (1963). *The Genain quadruplets.* New York: Basic Books.

178 Gaddis, V., & Gaddis, M. (1972). *The curious world of twins.* New York: Hawthorn Books; Gedda, L. (1961). *Twins in history and science.* Springfield, IL: Charles C. Thomas; Moody, P. A. (1975). *The genetics of man* (2nd ed.). New York: Norton.

178 Many human genes have their counterparts in worms, such that replacing a worm's gene with a human counterpart has no deleterious effect; the human gene works well in the worm. Even human genes that cause Alzheimer's, colon cancer, and other diseases have their counterparts in the worm. Their strikingly similar chemical structure means that many genes of worm and human must have evolved from the DNA of some distant common ancestor. See Wade, N. (1997, June 24). Worm tells secrets of human genetic code. *The New York Times,* p. C1.

178 Quote from Thiessen, D. (1996). *Bittersweet destiny: The stormy evolution of human behavior.* New Brunswick, NJ: Transaction.

179 Quote from Dobzhansky, T. (1974). Advancement and obsolescence in science. In R. M. Hutchins & M. J. Adler (Eds.), *The great ideas today* (pp. 51–61). New York: Encyclopaedia Britannica.

180 Davis, J. O., & Phelps, J. A. (1995). Twins with schizophrenia: Genes or germs. *Schizophrenia Bulletin, 21* (1), 13–18. Sharing a placenta may be a problem. Within a single placenta, the tiny arteries of one twin may become connected to the tiny veins of the other, making one twin something of a blood donor. Both twins are disadvantaged, though typically one more than the other. The difference can be seen in retarded physical growth, occasionally to the point of damage or even death. Where just one of two identical twins has schizophrenia, as with Paul and his brother, the mentally ill twin is the one most likely to show such a disadvantage. See Torrey, E. F., Bowler, A. E., Taylor, E. H., & Gottesman, I. I. (1994). *Schizophrenia and manic-depressive disorder: The biological roots of mental illness as revealed by the landmark study of identical twins.* New York: Basic Books.

180 Côté, G. B., & Gyftodimou, J. (1991). Twinning and mitotic crossing-over: Some possibilities and their implications. *American Journal of Human Genetics, 49,* 120–130.

181 Sokol, D. K., Moore, C. A., Rose, R. J., Williams, C. J., Reed, T., & Christian, J. C. (1995). Intrapair differences in personality and cognitive ability among young monozygotic twins distinguished by chorion type. *Behavior Genetics, 25,* 457–466.

181 Kirch, D. G. (1993). Infection and autoimmunity as etiologic factors in schizophrenia: A review and reappraisal. *Schizophrenia Bulletin, 19* (2), 355–370; Mednick, S. A., Machon, R. A., Huttenen, M. O., & Bonett, D. (1988). Adult schizophrenia following prenatal exposure to an influenza epidemic. *Archives of General Psychiatry, 45,* 189–192.

182 Schinzel, A. A. G. L., Smith, D. W., & Miller, J. R. (1979). Monozygotic twinning and structural defects. *Journal of Pediatrics, 95,* 921–930.

182 Source on hidden twins is Wright, L. (1997). *Twins.* New York: John Wiley & Sons.

183 Conjoined twinning figure from O'Connell, J. E. A. (1976). Craniopagus twins: Surgical anatomy and embryology and their implications. *Journal of Neurology, Neurosurgery, and Psychiatry, 39,* 1–22.

183 Details on Chang and Eng from Blumer, M. G. (1970). *The biology of twinning in man.* Oxford, England: Clarendon.

184 Source on brain differences is research by Dr. David E. Comings and associates (1996) at the City of Hope Medical Center in Duarte, CA. *American Journal of Medical Genetics, 67,* 741–748.

185 Bracha, H. S., Torrey, E. F., Bigelow, L. B., Lohr, J. B., & Linington, B. B. (1991). Subtle signs of prenatal maldevelopment of the hand ectoderm in schizophrenia: A preliminary monozygotic twin study. *Biological Psychiatry, 30,* 719–725; Bracha, H. S., Torrey, E. F., Gottesmann, I. I., Bigelow, L. B., & Cunniff, C. (1992). Second-trimester markers of fetal size in schizophrenia: A study of monozygotic twins. *American Journal of Psychiatry, 149,* 1355–1361.

185   Davis, J. O., & Bracha, H. S. (1996). Prenatal growth markers in schizophrenia: A monozygotic co-twin control study. *American Journal of Psychiatry*, *153*, 1166–1172.

186   Livshits, G., & Kobyliansky (1991). Fluctuating asymmetry as a possible measure of developmental homeostasis in humans: A review. *Human Biology*, *63* (4), 441–466.

186   Tupper, D. E. (Ed.). (1987). *Soft neurological signs*. New York: Grune & Stratton; Waldrup, M. F., Pedersen, F. A., & Bell, R. Q. (1968). Minor physical anomalies and behavior in preschool children. *Child Development*, *39*, 391–400.

188   Many scientists believe that cloning research would mean more effective and cheaper medicines and treatments, perhaps cures, for diseases, including cancer and AIDS. One doctor asserted that if one of her relatives got cancer, she would want to clone that person and use the bone marrow for a transplant. Geneticist Eldon Sutton notes that it might even help us understand how many lizards can grow a new limb, and who knows what potential medical benefits might come of this? Nevertheless, moral objections are numerous, for example, that cloning violates the human dignity and the right to be conceived and born within the context of marriage. Some say that clones would be the children of science rather than of nature, of manufacture rather than procreation, and that such cloning is playing God.

The image of replicate Hitlers distresses us as we imagine how cloning research might get out of control. Almost all attempts to create clones from adult cells have failed. The notorious cloned sheep, Dolly, was the only one of 277 attempts that survived; the others failed either to develop, to come to term, or to live long after birth. So, we can imagine all sorts of cloning errors that might produce sometimes monstrous defects. To which psychiatrist Robert Coles replies, "I wonder whether such cloning, if realized, challenges us biologically or psychologically any more than nature does, when it presents us with identical twins— who, however, are usually quite able to become two distinctive individuals. Yes, cloning might go awry, but so not rarely does nature when it offers parents deformed fetuses." And we might add, all kinds of medical procedures likewise go awry, sometimes horribly, as with the inadvertent death of patients. Yet we accept the risk, refusing to ban those procedures. More Americans die every year on the highways than were killed in the Vietnam war; yet we don't insist on banning cars, or limiting speed to 20 or 30 mph.

Those who worry about exploitation imagine brain-dead clones— even headless clones—created for spare body parts. If, as evidence now suggests, headless cloning can be done with laboratory animals, can the commercial exploitation of such work with humans be far away? A person frets, "Many people will argue that the clone will provide the perfect donor organs. This may involve the murder of the clone for the benefit of the original. This idea is completely unethical. I would rather die than bring someone into the world just to end up killing them." Another fears that cloning would be misused to produce one or another kind of person, in particular, males or geniuses.

Another argues: "The one drawback to widespread cloning I can think of is that it could lead to an imbalance of the sexes in the world. This could have a negative impact on society. I don't think cloning will ever become widespread enough for this to happen." Other people have a more sociological apprehension of rich people having an unfair advantage, with greater access to a technology that would enable them to design siblings or replace children rather than take their chances like everyone else. Does this mean, others reply, that if not everyone can afford a big car, a trip to Europe, a college education, or a heart transplant, no one should have one?

More compelling, it seems to me, are two other arguments. One is that because the DNA of a person cloned from an adult would be relatively old, the clone might have a dramatically shortened life expectancy. We don't know if the age of a person's DNA determines life expectancy, but shouldn't we at least consider the possibility? The other objection can be posed as a question: Would it be ethically proper that young clones would have to witness their considerably older identical twins going through the processes of aging, disease, and death—in a very real sense, to have to witness their own physical destiny? Wouldn't that take some of the mystery out of life? Worse, wouldn't it make it harder for clones to deny vulnerability and mortality, something everyone else gets to do despite seeing a parent in decline?

There is yet another implication that has hardly been explored: With cloning, we would lose our advantage over bacteria, viruses, and fungi, whose rapid evolution into more lethal forms would do us in as a species were it not for the genetic mixing that comes with sexual reproduction. Science writer Jim Holt describes it in this droll fashion: "It has been observed of sex that the pleasure is fleeting, the contortions ridiculous, and the expense damnable. If and when we start making humans by other means, though, we might be surprised to discover that sex has been preserving us from some very nasty things. That there is, to put it another way, a very good reason why we go to all the trouble." (Quote from Holt, J. [1998, February 13]. Why courtship beats cloning. *The Wall Street Journal*, p. A14.)

The ethical considerations of cloning are clearly daunting. At least, as one observer noted, they force us to consider "a set of questions about what it means to be human; questions that go to the heart of the way we think families and relationships between generations, our concept of individuality, and the potential for treating children as objects, as well as issues of constitutional law that might be involved in the area of procreation." (Quote from Shapiro, H. T. [1997, July]. Ethical and policy issues of human cloning. *Science, 277,* 195–196.)

188   Kolata, G. (1997, December 2). Cloning debate turns sharply. *Austin American-Statesman,* p. A1, A7.

Chapter 12

192   Quote from Willerman, L., & Cohen, D. B. (1990). *Psychopathology.* New York: McGraw-Hill.

192   The frontal lobes are implicated in motivation, emotions, personality, and a sense of self, all of which are markedly disturbed in schizophrenia. They are also important to working memory, the ability to hold information, anything from an unfamiliar telephone number to an interesting idea.

The temporal lobes are responsible for language, memory, and thinking, so it is no surprise that temporal lobe abnormalities are found in schizophrenia. One involves the fluid-filled spaces, or *ventricles,* in the very center of the temporal lobes. In many people with schizophrenia, these spaces are either unusually large, indicating a loss of brain tissue, or asymmetrical, with one being noticeably larger than the other. The greater the asymmetry—such asymmetry is found along the surface of certain parts of the temporal lobe, especially those areas that serve language—the more severe the symptoms. (See Aso, M., Kurachi, M., Suzuki, M., Satoru, Y., Mié, M., & Saitoh, O. [1995]. Asymmetry of the ventricle and age of the onset of schizophrenia. *European Archives of Psychiatry and Clinical Neuroscience, 245,* 142–144; also Barta, P. E., Pearlson, G. D., Brill, L. B., II, Royall, R., McGilchrist, I. A., Pulver, A. E., Powers, R. E., Casanova, M. F., Tien, A. Y., Frangou, S., & Petty, R. J. [1997]. Planum temporale asymmetry reversal in schizophrenia: Replication and relationship to gray matter abnormalities. *American Journal of Psychiatry, 154,* 661–667.) Located along the inner surface of the temporal lobe is the *hippocampus.* In schizophrenia, the hippocampus tends to be abnormally small, and the smaller its size, the more severe the symptoms.

Another structure likely involved in the faulty filter is the *thalamus,* located deep in the brain, which manages information flow: the inflow of sensory information from the body and the outside world; the outflow of motor information in gait, balance, and coordination; and the flow of information from long-term memory relevant to learning, thinking and consciousness. An abnormal thalamus could mean disrupted filtering of sensory information. Overwhelmed by stimuli, a person would experience poor attention, disorganized or eccentric thinking, and misperceptions of the delusional and hallucinatory kind; such a person could become apathetic and lose motivation to do anything. (See Andreasen, N. C., Arndt, S., Swayze, V., II, Cizadlo, T., Flaum, M., O'Leary, D. O., Ehrhardt, J. C., & Yuh, W. T. C. [1994]. Thalamic abnormalities in schizophrenia visualized through magnetic resonance image averaging. *Science, 266,* 294–298.)

"An abnormality in this [midbrain] structure," says psychiatric researcher Nancy Andreasen, can cause "abnormalities in filtering stimuli, focusing attention, or sensory gating. A person with a defective thalamus is likely to be flooded with stimuli. That person may consequently experience the striking misperceptions that we refer to as delusions or hallucinations or may withdraw and retreat and display [apathy and a loss of motivation to do anything]." See also Martin, P., & Albers, M. (1995). Cerebellum and schizophrenia: A selective review. *Schizophrenia Bulletin, 21* (2), 241–248.

192 Levy, D. L., Holzman, P., Matthysse, S., & Mendell, N. R. (1993). Eye tracking dysfunction and schizophrenia: A critical perspective. *Schizophrenia Bulletin, 19* (3), 461–536. Another sign of abnormal brain activity in schizophrenia can be recognized in electroencephalographic waves, or EEGs. An EEG represents both spontaneous brain activity and activity excited by distinct stimuli that cause a momentary disturbance of spontaneous activity. Any brain wave evoked by a stimulus will, therefore, be messy and difficult to identify in the restless and ever-changing EEG. Yet messy evoked waves can be smoothed out by computer averaging. With computer-assisted averaging, the unsystematic ups and downs of evoked waves cancel each other out. The result is a smoother averaged wave.

Now, imagine a volunteer subject, perhaps someone like Paul, sitting comfortably in the EEG lab, hooked up with electrodes and wearing a headphone. Once he's relaxed, the headphones begin to deliver pairs of clicks, a half-second apart: click click . . . click click . . . click click. . . . Thirty pairs might be presented, each separated by a 10-second interval. Under such conditions, we get two distinct brain waves. Each wave is called a *P50* because it occurs 50 milliseconds—a twentieth of a second—after a click.

Normally, the second P50 is much smaller than the first. For many patients with schizophrenia, the second P50 seems to be too big, even to be as big as the first one. Perhaps this anomaly is an objective indicator of the faulty filter—but is it a marker of the schizophrenia vulnerability? For that to be true, the P50 anomaly should occur in patients with schizophrenia, but not in patients with other psychiatric illnesses; and it should occur in many of the patient's relatives, even normal ones like

Paul. Finally, it should go together with abnormal SPEM in patients with schizophrenia, yet appear individually in some of their relatives. These hypotheses have been mostly, but not always, sustained by research evidence.

Two additional observations bear on schizophrenia and the P50 wave. The first involves cigarette smoking. According to one survey, almost 90 percent of people with schizophrenia smoke, many heavily. These rates are high compared to the 70 percent rate for people with manias, the 50 percent rate for people with other mental illnesses, and the roughly 30 percent rate for the general population. Why such high rates for schizophrenics?

Consider this intriguing observation: After abstaining for 1 night followed by unrestricted smoking in the morning, the second P50 of smokers with schizophrenia is smaller—more normal, less characteristic of schizophrenia. Incidentally, normal smokers tend to show the opposite pattern. Smoking makes their second P50 bigger, or slightly more characteristic of schizophrenia. These opposite effects of nicotine are like the effects of amphetamines, which normalize the behavior of children with hyperactivity disorders but disrupt the behavior of normal people.

Though extremely short-lived, the nicotine effects seem to be real enough, especially when you consider another observation. Nicotine gum seems to normalize the characteristic P50 of the relatives of people with schizophrenia. Could this evident normalization of brain activity mean that smoking is a kind of self-medication against the faulty filter? Could such self-medication serve a similar purpose even for normal people with some vulnerability to schizophrenia? Smoking might buy immediate, albeit subtle, relief at the cost of future harm.

All these observations and a highly technical theoretical model are offered by Lawrence Adler and colleagues. See Adler, L., et al. (1998). Schizophrenia, sensory gaiting, and nicotinic receptors. *Schizophrenia Bulletin, 24* (2), 189–202.

194   Kinney, D. K., Holzman, P. S., Jacobsen, B., Lennart, J., Faber, B., Hildebrand, W., Kasell, E., & Zimbalist, M. E. (1997). Thought disorder in schizophrenic and control adoptees and their relatives. *Archives of General Psychiatry, 54,* 475–479.

195   Beers, C. W. (1981/1907). *A mind that found itself.* Pittsburgh, PA: University of Pittsburgh.

196   Raine, A., Venables, P. H., & Williams, M. (1990). Relationships between central and autonomic measures of arousal at age 15 years and criminality at age 24 years. *Archives of General Psychiatry, 47,* 1003–1007.

196   Giles, D. E., Kupfer, D. J., Rush, A. J., & Roffwarg, H. P. (1998). Controlled comparison of electrophysiological sleep in families of probands with major depression. *Archives of General Psychiatry, 155,* 192–199.

196 Tomarken, A. J., Simien, C., & Garber, J. (1994). Resting frontal brain asymmetry discriminates adolescent children of depressed mothers from low-risk controls. *Psychophysiology, 31*, 97–98. See also Henriques, J. B. & Davidson, R. J. (1990). Regional brain electrical asymmetries discriminate between previously depressed and healthy control subjects. *Journal of Abnormal Psychology, 99*, 22–31.

196 Benkelfat, C., Ellenbogen, M. A., Dean, P., Palmour, R. M., & Young, S. N. (1994). Mood-lowering effect of tryptophan depletion: Enhanced susceptibility in young men at genetic risk for major affective disorders. *Archives of General Psychiatry, 51*, 687–697.

197 Hidden vulnerability to depression has been revealed by using another building block of brain serotonin in three groups of children. One group included only those suffering from manifest depression. Another included only high-risk children, those not manifestly depressed but with at least two depressed biological relatives. A third included those with neither depression nor elevated risk of depression. In comparison to the normal control-group children, both the depressed and high risk-nondepressed children showed the same characteristic hormonal reactions to the serotonin challenge: weak for the stress hormone cortisol, strong, in girls only, for the female hormone prolactin. See Birmaher, B., Kaufman, J., Brent, D. A., Dahl, R. E., Perel, J. M., Al-Shabbout, M., Nelson, B., Stull, S., Rao, U., Waterman, G. S., Williamson, D. E., & Ryan, N. D. (1997). Neuroendocrine response to 5-hydroxy-l-tryptophan in prepubertal children at high risk for major depressive disorder. *Archives of General Psychology, 54*, 1113–1119.

197 Perna, G., Cocchi, S., Bertani, A., Arancio, C., & Bellodi, L. (1995). Sensitivity to 35% CO_2 in healthy first-degree relatives of patients with panic disorder. *American Journal of Psychiatry, 152*, 623–625.

197 Schuckit, M. A. (1984). Subjective response to alcohol in sons of alcoholics and controls. *Archives of General Psychiatry, 41*, 879–884; Schuckit, M. A. (1994). Low level of response to alcohol as a predictor of future alcoholism. *American Journal of Psychiatry, 151*, 184–189.

198 Self-medication with alcohol from Willerman, L., & Cohen, D. B. (1990). *Psychopathology.* New York: McGraw-Hill.

199 Murphy, G. E. (1984). The prediction of suicide: Why is it so difficult? *American Journal of Psychotherapy, 38*, 341–349. The story of suicide prediction makes us appreciate that *some information, though emotionally powerful and seemingly useful, is of little or no consequence to making a good decision, while other information, though subtle and remote, makes all the difference.* And sometimes, ignoring what we know can get us into big trouble, as illustrated by a bizarre story that begins like this: "On Oct. 30, 1985, Sylvia Seegrist walked into the Springfield Mall in suburban Philadelphia and started to shoot at random with a .22 caliber semi-

automatic rifle. Her bullets hit 10 people, killing three of them. She was later ruled criminally insane."

An article by the criminologist Lawrence Sherman describes a Delaware County jury that determined that the mall was at fault and therefore liable for damages. The key question is this: What is the likelihood that a Seegrist event would *ever* take place? This question of likelihood—the so-called *prior probability* that an event will actually take place—must be asked. After all, when employing a valid theory about the proper responsibility of malls without considering the "priors," we are as likely to go wrong as when we employ a valid test for suicide without thought to its rarity. So again, what was the likelihood that a Seegrist event would ever take place?

Seegrist had apparently made threats, yet a study of 110 cases involving threats found that none had led to serious injury, let alone murder. As Sherman says, threats are almost always just talk. But there is more to consider, because "from 1976 to 1984, there was only about one crime a year similar to this one in the entire U.S.: simultaneous murder of three or more people by a stranger, not for monetary gain, using a gun. Only seven people a year, on average, die from such an offense. Fifteen people, on average, die from planes falling out of the sky on them. Lightning strikes some 80 people dead each year, and auto accidents kill 50,000. The odds of a plaintiff dying in a mass murder were about 1 in 30 million." But what about in the Seegrist crime?

"The annual odds (the priors) of Ms. Seegrist committing the crime were," Sherman says, "only 1 in 156 million, without considering her sex. The prior rate of such crimes by women nationwide was zero. There also had been no prior documented mass murder in a shopping center." The Seegrist crime was thus essentially unpredictable, much less so even than correctly predicting who would win the next year's lottery. Even a correct prediction wouldn't have meant preventing it, short of closing the mall or leaving it open but turning it into an armed camp! Apparently unimpressed by such statistics, a jury of presumably reasonable people nevertheless found the mall to be negligent. (Source is Sherman, L. W. [1990, April 4]. Was a mall to blame for a mass murder? *Wall Street Journal*, A24.)

200 Goldstein, R. B., Black, D. W., Nasrallah, A., & Winokur, G. (1991). The prediction of suicide: Sensitivity, specificity, and predictive value of a multivariate model applied to suicide among 1906 patients with affective disorder. *Archives of General Psychiatry, 48*, 418–422.

200 Heritability of potential for suicide from Murphy, G. E. (1984). The prediction of suicide: Why is it so difficult? *American Journal of Psychotherapy, 38*, 341–349.

200 Arato, M., Tothfalusi, L., & Banki, C. M. (1989). Serotonin and suicide. *Biological Psychiatry, 25*, 196A–197A.

200 Mann, J. J., Malone, K. M., Nielsen, D. A., Goldman, D., Erdos, J., & Galerntner, J. (1997). Possible association of a polymorphism of the tryptophan hydroxylase gene with suicidal behavior in depressed patients. *American Journal of Psychiatry, 154,* 1451–1453.

201 Predicting behavior from knowledge about the environment is often difficult or impossible, simply because of the sheer number of possible causes. Suppose that 10 factors combine in some unique way to create a vulnerability to some mental illness. If each of these 10 can be scored "present" or "absent," then there are 2^{10}, or 1,024, possible combinations, though the number is much larger if those factors must occur in a certain order. In a more complicated but realistic scenario, there might be 20 such causal factors, each with 3 possible classifications (severe, mild, absent), which would generate over 3 billion combinations! No wonder that psychologists, like historians, often must start from effects and work back to presumed causes. Unfortunately, such after-the-fact reconstructions can misidentify presumed causes or overestimate their importance. (See Cohen, D. B. [1994] *Out of the blue: Depression and human nature* [chap. 13]. New York: Norton.

Thus, the difficulty with theorizing about causality is that events insignificant in themselves may collectively cause a big effect, and no convincing causal sequence can be reconstructed. While theories may identify the big causal factors that occur with sufficient frequency or potency, we may never be able to devise any theory that can handle individual human beings in all their uniqueness, and this may be true for abnormal and normal variations in human behavior. (Source is Willerman, L., & Cohen, D. B. [1990]. *Psychopathology.* New York: McGraw-Hill.)

Chapter 13

204 Quote from Durant, W. (1953). *The story of civilization: Part V. The Renaissance.* New York: Simon & Schuster.

206 Lykken, D. T., McGue, M., Tellegen, A., & Bouchard, T. J. (1993). Emergenesis: Genetic traits that may not run in families. *American Psychologist, 47,* 1565–1577.

207 Lykken, D., & Telligen, A. (1996). Happiness is a stochastic phenomenon. *Psychological Science, 7,* 186–189.

207 Eysenck, H. (1995). *Genius: The natural history of creativity.* New York: Cambridge University Press.

208 Stein, D. (Ed.), (1974). *Plasticity and recovery of function in the central nervous system.* New York: Academic Press.

208 Lewin, R. (1980, December 12). Is your brain really necessary? *Science,* 1232–1234.

209 McManus, I. C., & Bryden, M. P. (1991). Geschwind's theory of cerebral lateralization: Developing a formal, causal model. *Psychological Bulletin, 110,* 237–253.

209   Obler, L. K., & Fein, D. (Eds.). (1988). *The exceptional brain: Neuropsychology of talent and special abilities.* New York: Guilford.

209   Hollingworth, L. (1942). *Children above 180 IQ (Stanford Binet): Origin and development.* New York: World Book.

209   Terman, L. M., & Oden, M. H. (1959). *The gifted child at mid-life.* Stanford, CA: Stanford University Press.

211   Quote from Treffert, D. A. (1989). *Extraordinary people: Understanding "idiot savants".* New York: Harper & Row.

211   Quote from Ericcson, K. A., & Faivre, I. A. (1988). What's exceptional about exceptional abilities? In L. K. Obler & D. Fein (Eds.), *The exceptional brain: Neuropsychology of talent and special abilities* (pp. 436–473). New York: Guilford.

212   Quote from Treffert, D. A. (1989). *Extraordinary people: Understanding "idiot savants".* New York: Harper & Row.

212   Quote from Sarton, G. (1963). Evarist Galois. In S. Rapport & H. Wright (Eds.), *Mathematics* (pp. 46–63). New York: New York University Press.

213   Quote from Wright, L. (1995, August 7). Double mystery. *The New Yorker,* 45–62.

218   Bortner, M., & Birch, H. G. (1970). Cognitive capacity and cognitive competence. *American Journal of Mental Deficiency, 74,* 735–744. Another example comes from a study of $2\frac{1}{2}$-year-olds. It seems they can use a photo of a room containing a toy to retrieve the real toy from the real room. Clearly, the children understand a photo can represent or map out something like room with toy. Nevertheless, they can't use a physical model of the room to solve the same problem. Distracted by the manipulative, playful aspects of a material object (model) needed to solve the problem, they lose sight of what they know. (Source is DeLoache, J. S. [1987, December 11]. Rapid change in the symbolic functioning of very young children. *Science, 237,* 1556–1557.)

Analogous failings can be observed in our nearest genetic neighbors. When distracted or excited, chimps too can lose sight of what they know. They can learn that plastic numbers printed on plastic cards represent actual amounts. For example, they will point to a plastic 4, thus showing they understand a plate contains four candies. After having learned the symbols, say from 0 to 9, they can learn to add using just the plastic numbers. They will point to the 7 after finding two plates, one with a 3 and the other with a 4. They can also learn a numerical rule. Pointing to the smaller of two numbers means another chimp gets a plate with that smaller number of candy. By following this rule, they specify what the other guy gets, meaning they wind up with more. But when faced with plates of candies rather than numbers, they can't keep the rule in mind. Distracted by feelings and wishful thinking, they repeatedly point to the plate with more candies that is promptly given to the other chimp. See Fischman, J. (1993, December 3). New clues surface about the making of the mind. *Science, 262,* 1517. Are these chimps really so different from humans who forget what they know: that the power of parenting over a child's psychological destiny is rather limited?

Chapter 14

223 Quote from Scarr, S., & Weinberg, R. A. (1979). Nature and nurture strike (out) again. *Intelligence, 3,* 31–39.

223 Quote from Horn, J. (1997). On the ineffectiveness and irrelevancy of tenure. *Academic Questions, 23.*

224 Source is Dennett, D. C. (1995). *Darwin's dangerous idea: Evolution and the meaning of life.* New York: Simon & Schuster.

225 Quote from Barzun (1959). *Liberal Education.* Boston: Beacon Press.

225 Quote from Bloom, A. (1987). *The closing of the American mind.* New York: Simon & Schuster.

226 Source is Eliot, C. (Ed.). (1910). *The Harvard Classics.* New York: P. F. Collier & Son.

227 See Fumento, M. (1997, September 29). Land of the fat. *The Wall Street Journal,* p. A2.

227 Quote from Hunt, E. (1997). Nature vs. nurture: The feeling of vujà dé. In R. J. Sternberg & E. L. Grigorenko (Eds.), *Intelligence, heredity, and environment.* Cambridge, England: Cambridge University Press.

228 Quote from Paulk, J. (1998, June 17). The real purpose of marriage [Letter to the editor]. *The Wall Street Journal,* p. A17.

231 Quotes from Seligman, D. (1994, October 10). A substantial inheritance. *National Review,* 56–60.

232 Quote from Rimland, B. (1969). Psychogenesis versus biogenesis: The issues and the evidence. In S. C. S. C. Plog & R. B. Edgerton (Eds.), *Changing perspectives in mental illness* (pp. 702–735). New York: Holt, Rinehart & Winston.

232 Quote from Kramer, P. D. (1993). *Listening to Prozac: A psychiatrist explores antidepressant drugs and the remaking of the self.* New York: Penguin. Such fantasies include the imagined power of "medications." Strong physiological responsiveness can occur to a pharmacologically inert substance, or placebo, presented as real treatment, all of which shows the high degree of suggestibility and imagination regarding bodily function. See Brown, W. A. (1998, January). The placebo effect. *Scientific American,* 90–95; Frank, J. D. (1982) *Persuasion and healing.* Baltimore: Johns Hopkins University Press; Tiger, L. (1979), *Optimism: The biology of hope.* New York: Touchstone Books (Simon & Schuster).

Warts may disappear when painted with a brightly colored but inert dye that the person believes is real medicine, and this may occur even for a wart that hasn't responded to surgical or other standard treatments. In one study, 70 percent of patients with bleeding ulcers showed improvement after injection with a salt solution they believed to be effective medicine. Only 25 percent of such patients showed improvement if they were told that the injection was experimental and therefore of uncertain effectiveness. Strong placebo responses can be found for depression, with as many patients (about a third) responding to placebo as to real antidepressants. See Fisher, S. and Greenberg, R. P. (1995, September/October), Prescription for happiness? *Psychology Today*, 32–37.

One of the most fantastic anecdotes about the placebo effect involves a man with advanced cancer whose tumors seemed to vanish after taking the "drug" krebiozen. After newspaper articles appeared exposing krebiozen as bogus, the patient experienced a resurgence of the cancer. It again faded, however, after the desperate physician pooh-poohed the stories and administered what he said was a larger and purer dose—but that was just distilled water. Eventually, with the truth of the placebo treatment no longer deniable, the cancer recurred and the man died. See Rosch, P. J. (1979). Stress and cancer: A disease of adaptation? In Taché, J., Selye, H., & Day, S. B. (Eds.) *Cancer, stress, and death*. New York: Plenum. Clearly, even a false but compelling idea can predominate over a true but less compelling one. But the question for us is the relevance of experimental research to help us understand individual differences, in particular, the nature-nurture question of where they come from.

Incidentally, the interesting derivation of the term *placebo* is given by psychiatric researcher Walter Brown. (See Brown, W. A. [1998, January], The placebo effect. *Scientific American*, 90–95.) "Latin for 'I shall please,' placebo is the first word of the vespers for the dead, and in the 12th century these vespers were commonly referred to as *placebos*. By the 1300s, the term had become secular and pejorative, suggesting a flatterer or sycophant, a meaning probably derived from the depreciation of professional mourners, those paid to sing placebos. When the word entered the medical terminology, the negative connotation stuck. It was defined as a medicine given to please patients rather than to benefit them," though, as we have seen, it often does benefit them.

233   Quote from Siebert, C. (1996, January 5). At the mercy of our genes. *The New York Times*.

234   Ratey, J., & Johnson, C. (1997). *Shadow syndromes*. New York: Pantheon.

234   Levine, S. (1971). Stress and behavior. In Readings from Scientific American (Eds.), *Progress in psychobiology* (pp. 143–148). San Francisco: W. H. Freeman; Meaney, M. J. Aitken, D. H., van Berkel, C., Bhatnagar, S., & Sapolsy, R. M. (1988). Effect of neonatal handling on age-related impairments associated with the hippocampus. *Science*, *239* (February 12, 1988), 766–768.

236 Common sense can be quite distracting, suggesting as it does that the sun revolves around the earth, which apparently over 25 percent of adult Americans believe. Source is Vos Savant, M. (1998, April 19). Ask Marilyn. *Parade Magazine*, p. 16.

236 Quote from Hoff Sommers, C. (1998, March). Are we living in a moral stone age? *Imprimis*, 8, 14.

237 Quote from Thomas, A. P. (1995, August 9). Can we ever go back? *The Wall Street Journal*, p. A8.

238 Quote from Lerner, B. (1998, April 21). Sometimes spanking can't be beat. *The Wall Street Journal*, p. A22.

238 Quote from West, D. (1998, April 22). Treat your children well. *The Wall Street Journal*, p. A20.

238 Source is Murray, C. (1984). *Losing ground: American social policy 1950–1980*. New York: Basic Books.

Bibliography

Abrams, S. (1986). Disposition and environment. *The Psychoanalytic Study of the Child, 41*, 41–60.

Alexander, R. (1995, July 12). Metropolitan diary. *The New York Times*, p. C2.

American Psychiatric Association (1994). *Diagnostic and statistical manual of mental disorders* (4th ed.). Washington, DC: Author.

Andreasen, N. C., Arndt, S., Swayze V., II, Cizadlo, T., Flaum, M., O'Leary, D. O., Ehrhardt, J. C., & Yuh, W. T. C. (1994). Thalamic abnormalities in schizophrenia visualized through magnetic resonance image averaging. *Science, 266*, 294–298.

Arato, M., Tothfalusi, L., & Banki, C. M. (1989). Serotonin and suicide. *Biological Psychiatry, 25*, 196A–197A.

Aso, M., Kurachi, M., Suzuki, M., Satoru, Y., Mié, M., & Saitoh, O. (1995). Asymmetry of the ventricle and age of the onset of schizophrenia. *European Archives of Psychiatry and Clinical Neuroscience, 245*, 142–144.

Associated Press (1990, January 17). Women's "false" pains tied to artery ailment. *Austin American-Statesman*, p. A4.

Bailey, J. M., & Pillard, R. C. (1991). A genetic study of male sexual orientation. *Archives of General Psychiatry, 48*, 1089–1096.

Bailey, J. M., Pillard, R. C., Neale, M. C., & Agyei, Y. (1993). Heritable factors influence sexual orientation in women. *Archives of General Psychiatry, 50*, 217–223.

Barron, F. (1969). *Creative person and creative process*. New York: Holt Rinehart & Winston.

Barta, P. E., Pearlson, G. D., Brill, L. B., II, Royall, R., McGilchrist, I. A., Pulver, A. E., Powers, R. E., Casanova, M. F., Tien, A. Y., Frangou, S., & Petty, R. J. (1997). Planum temporale asymmetry reversal in schizophrenia: Replication and relationship to gray matter abnormalities. *American Journal of Psychiatry, 154*, 661–667.

Battaglia, M., Bertella, S., Bajo, S., Binaghi, F., & Bellodi, L. (1998). Anticipation of age at onset in panic disorder. *American Journal of Psychiatry, 155*, 590–595.

Baumrind, D. (1967). Child care practices anteceding three patterns of preschool behavior. *Genetic Psychology Monographs, 75,* 43–88.

Baumrind, D. (1993). The average expected environment is not enough: A response to Scarr. *Child Development, 64,* 1299–1317.

Beers, C. W. (1981/1907). *A mind that found itself.* Pittsburgh, PA: University of Pittsburgh.

Bell, R. Q. (1968). A reinterpretation of the direction of effects in studies of socialization. *Psychological Review, 75,* 81–95.

Belmaker, R., Pollin, W., Wyatt, R. J., & Cohen, S. (1974). A follow-up of monozygotic twins discordant for schizophrenia. *Archives of General Psychiatry, 30,* 219–222.

Benkelfat, C., Ellenbogen, M. A., Dean, P., Palmour, R. M., & Young, S. N. (1994). Mood-lowering effect of tryptophan depletion: Enhanced susceptibility in young men at genetic risk for major affective disorders. *Archives of General Psychiatry, 51,* 687–697.

Bennett, M. I., & Bennett, M. B. (1984). The uses of hopelessness. *American Journal of Psychiatry, 141,* 559–562.

Berenbaum, S. A., & Hines, M. (1992). Early androgens are related to childhood sex-typed toy preferences. *Psychological Science, 3* (3), 203–206.

Biederman, J., Faraone, S. V., Mick, E., Spencer, T., Wilens, T., Kieley, K., Guite, J., Ablon, J. S., Reed, E., & Warburton, R. (1995). High risk for attention deficit hyperactivity disorder among children of parents with childhood onset of the disorder: A pilot study. *American Journal of Psychiatry, 152,* 431–435.

Biederman, J., Rosenbaum, J. F., Hirschfield, D. R., Faraone, S., Bolduc, E., Gersten, M., Meminger, S., Kagan, J., Snidman, N., & Reznick, J. S. (1990). Psychiatric correlates of behavioral inhibition in young children of parents with and without psychiatric disorders. *Archives of General Psychiatry, 47,* 21–26.

Birmaher, B., Kaufman, J., Brent, D. A., Dahl, R. E., Perel, J. M., Al-Shabbout, M., Nelson, B., Stull, S., Rao, U., Waterman, G. S., Williamson, D. E., & Ryan, N. D. (1997). Neuroendocrine response to 5-hydroxy-l-tryptophan in prepubertal children at high risk for major depressive disorder. *Archives of General Psychology, 54,* 1113–1119.

Blanchard, R. (1997). Birth order and sibling sex ratio in homosexual versus heterosexual males and females. *Annual Review of Sex Research, 8,* 27–67.

Blumer, M. G. (1970). *The biology of twinning in man.* Oxford, England: Clarendon.

Bortner, M., & Birch, H. G. (1970). Cognitive capacity and cognitive competence. *American Journal of Mental Deficiency, 74,* 735–744.

Bouchard, T. J., Jr., Lykken, D. T., McGue, M., Segal, N. L., & Tellegen, A. (1990). Sources of human psychological differences: The Minnesota study of twins reared apart. *Science, 250,* 223–228.

Bouchard, T. J., Jr., & McGue, M. (1990). Genetic and rearing environmental influences on adult personality: An analysis of adopted twins reared apart. *Journal of Personality, 58,* 263–292.

Bracha, H. S., Torrey, E. F., Bigelow, L. B., Lohr, J. B., & Linington, B. B. (1991). Subtle signs of prenatal maldevelopment of the hand ectoderm in schizophrenia: A preliminary monozygotic twin study. *Biological Psychiatry, 30,* 719–725.

Bracha, H. S., Torrey, E. F., Gottesmann, I. I., Bigelow, L. B., & Cunniff, C. (1992). Second-trimester markers of fetal size in schizophrenia: A study of monozygotic twins. *American Journal of Psychiatry, 149,* 1355–1361.

Breland, K., & Breland, M. (1961). The misbehavior of organisms. *American Psychologist, 16,* 661–664.

Brennan, P. A., Raine, A., Schulsinger, F., Kirkegaard-Sorensen, L., Knop, J., Hutchings, B., Rosenberg, R., & Mednick, S. A. (1997). Psychophysiological protective factors for male subjects at high risk for criminal behavior. *Archives of General Psychiatry, 154,* 853–855.

Brent, D. A., Bridge, J., Johnson, B. A., & Connolly, J. (1996). Suicidal behavior runs in families: A controlled family study of adolescent suicide victims. *Archives of General Psychiatry, 53,* 1145–1152.

Brunner, H. G., Nelen, M., Breakefield, X. O., Ropers, H. H., & van Oost, B. A. (1993). Abnormal behavior associated with a point mutation in the structural gene for monoamine oxidase A. *Science, 262,* 578–580.

Buss, D. (1987). Selection, evocation, and manipulation. *Journal of Personality and Social Psychology, 53,* 1214–1221.

Buss, D. M. (1995). Evolutionary psychology. *Psychological Inquiry, 6,* 1–30.

Cadoret, R. J., & Stewart, M. A. (1991). An adoption study of attention deficit/hyperactivity/aggression and their relationship to adult antisocial personality. *Comprehensive Psychiatry, 32,* 73–82.

Cadoret, R. J., Yates, W. R., Troughton, E., Woodworth, G., & Stewart, M. A. (1995). Adoption study demonstrating two genetic pathways to drug abuse. *Archives of General Psychiatry, 52,* 42–52.

Cairns, R. B. (1979). *Social development: The origins and plasticity of interchanges.* San Francisco: W. H. Freeman.

Cairns, R. B., Gariépy, J.-L., & Hood, K. E. (1990). Development, microevolution, and social behavior. *Psychological Review, 97,* 49–65.

Cases, O., Seif, I., Grimsby, J., Gaspar, P., Chen, K., Pournin, S., Müller, U., et al. (1995, June 23). Aggressive behavior and altered amounts of brain serotonin and norepinephrine in mice lacking MAOA. *Science, 268,* 1763–1766.

Cherlin, A. J., Furstenberg, J. F. F., Chase-Lansdale, P. L., Kiernan, K. E., Robins, P. K., Morrison, D. R., & Teitler, J. O. (1991). Longitudinal studies of effects of divorce on children in Great Britain and the United States. *Science, 252,* 1386–1389.

Chira, S. (1995, March 19). Multiple divorces multiple scars. *Austin American-Statesman,* p. A1, A15.

Cloninger, C. R., & Gottesman, I. I. (1987). Genetic and environmental factors in antisocial behavior disorders. In S. A. Mednick, T. E. Moffitt, & S. A. Stack (Eds.), *The causes of crime* (pp. 92–109). Cambridge, England: Cambridge University Press.

Coccaro, E., & Murphy, D. (Ed.). (1991). *Serotonin in major psychiatric disorders*. Washington, DC: American Psychiatric Association.

Collaer, M. L., & Hines, M. (1995). Human behavioral sex differences: A role for gonadal hormones during early development? *Psychological Bulletin, 118*, 55–107.

Colson, C. W. (1995, January 24). The new criminal class. *The Wall Street Journal*, p. A14.

Corder, E. H., Saunders, A. M., Strittmatter, W. J., Schmechel, D. E., Gaskell, P. C., Small, P. C., Roses, A. D., Haines, J. L., & Pericak-Vance, M. A. (1993, August 13). Gene dose of apolipoprotein E type allele and the risk of Alzheimer's disease in late onset families. *Science, 261*, 921–923.

Côté, G. B., & Gyftodimou, J. (1991). Twinning and mitotic crossing-over: Some possibilities and their implications. *American Journal of Human Genetics, 49*, 120–130.

Crowe, R. R. (1974). An adoption study of antisocial personality. *Archives of General Psychiatry, 31*, 785–791.

Damasio, A. R. (1994). *Descartes' error: Emotion, reason, and the human brain*. New York: G. P. Putnam's Sons (Grosset/Putnam).

Davis, J. O., & Bracha, H. S. (1996). Prenatal growth markers in schizophrenia: A monozygotic co-twin control study. *American Journal of Psychiatry, 153*, 1166–1172.

Davis, J. O., & Phelps, J. A. (1995). Twins with schizophrenia: Genes or germs. *Schizophrenia Bulletin, 21*, (1), 13–18.

Diamond, M., & Sigmundson, H. K. (1997). Sex reassignment at birth: Long-term review and clinical implications. *Archives of Pediatric and Adolescent Medicine, 151*, 298–304.

Diener, E., & Diener, C. (1996). Most people are happy. *Psychological Science, 7*, 181–185.

DiLalla, D. L., & Gottesman, I. I. (1995). Normal personality characteristics of identical twins discordant for schizophrenia. *Journal of Abnormal Psychology, 104*, 490–499.

Dodge, K. A., Bates, J. E., & Pettit, G. S. (1990, December 21). Mechanisms in the cycle of violence. *Science, 250*, 1678–1683.

Doudet, D., Hommer, D., Higley, J. D., Andreasen, P. J., Moneman, R., Soumi, S. J., & Linnoila, M. (1995). Cerebral glucose metabolism, CSF 5-HIAA levels, and aggressive behavior in rhesus monkeys. *American Journal of Psychiatry, 152*, 1782–1787.

Ebstein, R. P., Novick, O., Umansky, R., Priel, B., Osher, Y., Darren, B., Bennett, E. R., Nemanov, L., Katz, M., & Belmaker, R. H. (1996). Dopamine

D4 receptor (D4DR) exon III polymorphism associated with the human personality trait of novelty seeking. *Nature Genetics, 12,* 78–80.

Eley, T. C. (1997). General genes: A new theme in developmental psychopathology. *Current Directions in Psychological Science, 6,* 90–95.

Ellwein, M. C. (1984, January 20). Early education [Review of the book *As the twig is bent . . . Lasting effects of preschool programs.* Consortium for Longitudinal Studies (1983). Hillsdale, NJ: Erlbaum]. *Science,* 273–274.

Ericcson, K. A., & Faivre, I. A. (1988). What's exceptional about exceptional abilities? In L. K. Obler & D. Fein (Eds.), *The exceptional brain: Neuropsychology of talent and special abilities.* (pp. 436–473). New York: Guilford.

Eysenck, H. (1995). *Genius: The natural history of creativity.* New York: Cambridge University Press.

Farb, P. (1968). *Man's rise to civilization as shown by the Indians of North America from primeval times to the coming of the industrial state.* New York: E. P. Dutton.

Fischer, M. (1971). Psychoses in the offspring of schizophrenic monozygotic twins and their normal co-twins. *British Journal of Psychiatry, 118,* 43–52.

Flavell, J. H. (1963). *The developmental psychology of Jean Piaget.* Princeton, NJ: D. Van Nostrand.

Fraiberg, S. H. (1959). *The magic years.* New York: Charles Scribner's Sons.

Freund, L. S., Reiss, A. L., Hagerman, R., & Vinogradov, S. (1992). Chromosome fragility and psychopathology in obligate female carriers of the fragile X chromosome. *Archives of General Psychiatry, 49,* 54–60.

Frick, P. J., & Jackson, Y. K. (1993). Family functioning and childhood antisocial behavior: Yet another reinterpretation. *Journal of Clinical Child Psychology, 22,* 410–419.

Gaddis, V., & Gaddis, M. (1972). *The curious world of twins.* New York: Hawthorn Books.

Garcia, J., & Koelling, R. A. (1966). Relation of cue to consequence in avoidance learning. *Psychonomic Science, 4,* 123–124.

Garcia, J., & Rusiniak, K. W. (1980). What the nose learns from the mouth. In Muller-Schwarze & R. M. Silverstein (Eds.), *Chemical signals.* (pp. 141–146). New York: Plenum.

Garmezy, N. (1981). Children under stress: Perspectives on antecedents and correlates of vulnerability and resistance to psychopathology. In A. I. Rabin, J. Aronoff, A. Barclay, M., & R. A. Zucker (Eds.), *Further explorations in personality.* (pp. 196–269). New York: John Wiley & Sons.

Gedda, L. (1961). *Twins in history and science.* Springfield, IL: Charles C. Thomas.

Gelernter, J., Krazler, H., Coccaro, E., Siever, L., New, A., & Mulgrew, C. L. (1997). D4 dopamine-receptor (DRD4) alleles and novelty seeking in substance dependent, personality disorder, and control subjects. *American Journal of Human Genetics, 61,* 1144–1152.

Gibbs, W. W. (1996). Gaining on fat. *Scientific American,* Vol. 275, 88–94.

Giles, D. E., Kupfer, D. J., Rush, A. J., & Roffwarg, H. P. (1998). Controlled comparison of electrophysiological sleep in families of probands with major depression. *Archives of General Psychiatry, 155,* 192–199.

Gladue, B. A. (1994, October). The biopsychology of sexual orientation. *Current Directions in Psychological Science, 3,* 150–154.

Goggans, F. C., Allen, R. M., & Gold, M. S. (1986). Primary hypothyroidism and its relationship to affective disorders. In I. Extein & M. S. Gold (Eds.), *Medical mimics of psychiatric disorder* (pp. 95–109). Washington, DC: American Psychiatric Press.

Goldstein, R. B., Black, D. W., Nasrallah, A., & Winokur, G. (1991). The prediction of suicide: Sensitivity, specificity, and predictive value of a multivariate model applied to suicide among 1906 patients with affective disorder. *Archives of General Psychiatry, 48,* 418–422.

Goleman, D. (1996, July 21). The secret of happiness: It's in the genes. *Austin American-Statesman,* pp. D1, D4.

Goodall, J. (1986). *The chimpanzees of Gombe: Patterns of behavior.* Cambridge, MA: Belknap (Harvard University Press).

Goodwin, D. W., Schulsinger, F., Hermansen, L., Guze, S. B., & Winokur, G. (1973). Alcohol problems in adoptees raised apart from alcoholic biological parents. *Archives of General Psychiatry, 34,* 238–243.

Gorwood, P., Leboyer, M., Falissard, B., Jay, M., Rouillon, F., & Feingold, J. (1996). Anticipation in schizophrenia: A new light on a controversial problem. *American Journal of Psychiatry, 153,* 1173–1177.

Gottesman, I. I. (1991). *Schizophrenia genesis: The origins of madness.* New York: Freeman.

Grilo, C. M., & Pogue-Geile, M. F. (1991). The nature of environmental differences. *Psychological Bulletin, 110,* 520–537.

Hall, R. C. W. (Ed.). (1980). *Psychiatric presentations of medical illnesses: Somatopsychic disorders.* New York: SP Medical Scientific Books.

Hamilton, M. (1981). Paul Hoch address: Is mental illness necessary? In D. F. Klein & J. Rabkin (Eds.), *Anxiety: New research and changing concepts* (pp. 95–101). New York: Raven Press.

Harris, J. R. (1995). Where is the child's environment? *Psychological Review, 102,* 458–489.

Hecht, H., & Proffitt, D. R. (1995). The price of expertise: Effects of experience on the water-level task. *Psychological Science, 6* (2), 90–95.

Heilman, J. R. (1995, August 13). The good news about Alzheimer's. *Parade Magazine,* pp. 12–15.

Herrnstein, R. J., & Murray, C. (1994). *The bell curve: Intelligence and class structure in American life.* New York: The Free Press.

Heston, L. L. (1966). Psychiatric disorders in foster home reared children of schizophrenic mothers. *British Journal of Psychiatry, 112,* 819–825.

Heston, L. L., & Denny, D. (1968). Interactions between early life experience and biological factors in schizophrenia. In D. Rosenthal & S. S. Kety

(Eds.), *The transmission of schizophrenia* (pp. 363–376). Oxford, England: Pergamon.

Heston, L. H., Mastri, A. R., Anderson, V. E., & White, J. (1981). Dementia of the Alzheimer type: Clinical genetics, natural history, and associated conditions. *Archives of General Psychiatry, 38,* 1085–1090.

Hobson, J. A. (1994). *The chemistry of conscious states.* Boston: Little, Brown (Back Bay Books).

Hollingworth, L. (1942). *Children above 180 IQ (Stanford Binet): Origin and development.* New York: World Book.

Horgan, J. (1990, December). Double trouble: When identical twins are not identical. *Scientific American,* 25–26.

Horn, J. M. (1981). Duration of preschool effects on later school competence. *Science, 213,* 1145.

Imperato-McGinley, J., Guerrero, L., Gautier, T., & Peterson, R. E. (1974). Steroid 5-alpha reductase deficiency in man: An inherited form of male pseudohermaphroditism. *Science, 186,* 1213–1215.

Imperato-McGinley, J., Peterson, R. E., Gautier, T., & Sturla, E. (1979). Androgens and the evolution of male-gender identity among male pseudohermaphrodites with 5-alpha reductase deficiency. *The New England Journal of Medicine, 300,* 1233–1237.

Jackson, P. W., & Messick, S. (1968). Creativity. In P. London & D. Rosenhan (Eds.), *Foundations of abnormal psychology* (pp. 226–250). New York: Holt, Rinehart & Winston.

Jacobs, W. J., & Nadel, L. (1985). Stress-induced recovery of fears and phobias. *Psychological Review, 92,* 512–531.

Jamison, K. R. (1995, February). Manic depressive illness and creativity. *Scientific American,* 62–67.

Jensen, A. R. (1998). *The g factor: The science of mental ability.* Westport, CT: Praeger.

Johnson, J. L., McAndrew, F. T., & Harris, P. B. (1991). Sociobiology and the naming of adopted and natural children. *Ethology and Sociobiology, 12,* 365–375.

Jönsson, E. G., Nöthen, M. M., Gustavsson, J. P., Neidt, H., Brené, S., Tylec, A., Propping, P., & Sedvall, G. C. (1997). Lack of evidence for allelic association between personality traits and the dopamine D4 receptor gene polymorphism. *American Journal of Psychiatry, 154,* 697–699.

Kagan, J. (1989). Temperamental contributions to social behavior. *American Psychologist, 44,* 668–674.

Kagan, J. (1994). Distinctions among emotions, moods, and temperamental qualities. In P. Ekman & R. J. Davidson (Eds.), *The nature of emotion: Fundamental questions* (pp. 74–78). New York: Oxford University Press.

Kelsoe, J. R., Ginns, E. I., Egeland, J. A., Gerhard, D. S., Goldstein, A. M., Bale, S. J., Pauls, D. L., Long, R. T., Kidd, K. K., Coute, G., Houseman,

D. E., & Paul, S. M. (1989). Re-evaluation of the linkage relationship between chromosome 11p loci and the gene for bipolar affective disorder in the Old Order Amish. *Nature, 342,* 238–243.

Kendall-Tackett, K. A., Williams, L. M., & Finkelhor, D. (1993). Impact of sexual abuse on children: A review and synthesis of recent empirical studies. *Psychological Bulletin, 113,* 164–180.

Kendler, K. S. (1993). Twin studies of psychiatric illness: Current status and future directions. *Archives of General Psychiatry, 50,* 905–915.

Kendler, K. S. (1997). Social support: A genetic-epidemiological analysis. *American Journal of Psychiatry, 154,* 1398–1404.

Kendler, K. S., Neale, M. C., Kessler, R. C., Heath, A. C., & Eaves, L. J. (1993). A test of the equal-environment assumption in twin studies of psychiatric illness. *Behavior Genetics, 23,* 21–27.

Kendler, K. S., Prescott, C. A., Neale, M. C., & Pedersen, N. L. (1997). Temperance board registration for alcohol abuse in a national sample of Swedish male twins, born 1902 to 1949. *Archives of General Psychiatry, 54,* 178–184.

Kiester, E., & Kiester, S. V. (1996, October). You can raise your child's IQ. *Reader's Digest,* 137–141.

Kinney, D. K., Holzman, P. S., Jacobsen, B., Lennart, J., Faber, B., Hildebrand, W., Kasell, E., & Zimbalist, M. E. (1997). Thought disorder in schizophrenic and control adoptees and their relatives. *Archives of General Psychiatry, 54,* 475–479.

Kirch, D. G. (1993). Infection and autoimmunity as etiologic factors in schizophrenia: A review and reappraisal. *Schizophrenia Bulletin, 19* (2), 355–370.

Kluft, R. P. (1996, July). Treating the traumatic memories of patients with dissociative identity disorder. *American Journal of Psychiatry, 153* [Festschrift Supplement], 103–110.

Koluchová, J. (1976). A report on the further development of twins after severe and prolonged deprivation. In A. M. Clarke & A. D. B. Clarke (Eds.), *Early experience: Myth and evidence* (pp. 56–66). New York: The Free Press (Macmillan).

Koluchová, J. (1976). Severe deprivation in twins: A case study. In A. M. Clarke & A. D. B. Clarke (Eds.), *Early experience: Myth and evidence.* (pp. 45–55). New York: The Free Press (Macmillan).

Koranyi, E. K. (1979). Morbidity and rate of undiagnosed physical illness in a psychiatric clinical population. *Archives of General Psychiatry, 36,* 414–419.

Kruyer, H. (1994). Fragile X syndrome and the (CGG)n mutation: Two families with discordant MZ twins. *American Journal of Human Genetics, 54,* 437–442.

Landers, A. (1976, July 27). Parent's can't absorb total blame. *Austin American-Statesman,* p. C2.

Langley, M. (1996, April 2). My son, the teen-age predator. *The Wall Street Journal*, p. A14.

Langlois, J. H., Ritter, J. M., Roggman, L. A., & Vaughn, L. S. (1991). Facial diversity and infant preferences for attractive faces. *Developmental Psychology*, *27*, 79–84.

Langlois, J. H., & Roggman, L. A. (1990). Attractive faces are only average. *Psychological Science*, *1* (2), 115–121.

Langlois, J. H., Roggman, L. A., & Musselman, L. (1994). What is average and what is not average about attractive faces. *Psychological Science*, *5*, 214–220.

LaPierre, D., Braun, C. M. J., & Hodgins, S. (1995). Ventral frontal deficits in psychopathy: Neuropsychological test findings. *Neuropsychologia*, *33*, 139–151.

Lesch, K.-P., Bengel, D., Heils, A., Sabol, S. Z., Greenberg, B. D., Petri, S., Benjamin, J., Müller, C. R., Hamer, D. H., & Murphy, D. L. (1996, November 29). Association of anxiety-related traits with a polymorphism in the serotonin transporter gene regulatory region. *Science*, *274*, 1527–1531.

LeVay, S. (1993). *The sexual brain*. Cambridge, MA: The MIT Press (A Bradford Book).

Levine, S. (1971). Stress and behavior. In Readings from Scientific American (Eds.), *Progress in psychobiology* (pp. 143–148). San Francisco: W. H. Freeman.

Levy, D. L., Holzman, P., Matthysse, S., & Mendell, N. R. (1993). Eye tracking dysfunction and schizophrenia: A critical perspective. *Schizophrenia Bulletin*, *19* (3), 461–536.

Lewin, R. (1980, December 12). Is your brain really necessary? *Science*, 1232–1234.

Liem, J. H. (1974). Effects of verbal communication of parents and children: A comparison of normal and schizophrenic families. *Journal of Consulting and Clinical Psychology*, *42*, 438–450.

Livesley, W. J., Jang, K. L., Jackson, D. N., & Vernon, P. A. (1993). Genetic and environmental contributions to dimensions of personality disorder. *American Journal of Psychiatry*, *150*, 1826–1831.

Livshits, G., & Kobyliansky, E. (1991). Fluctuating asymmetry as a possible measure of developmental homeostasis in humans: A review. *Human Biology*, *63* (4), 441–466.

Loehlin, J. C., & Nichols, R. C. (1976). *Heredity, environment, & personality: A study of 850 sets of twins*. Austin, TX: University of Texas Press.

Lorenz, K. (1963/1966). *On aggression*. New York: Harcourt, Brace & World/ Bantam.

Louis, A. M. (1981, January 26). Schlitz's crafty taste test. *Fortune*, 32–34.

Lykken, D., & Telligen, A. (1996). Happiness is a stochastic phenomenon. *Psychological Science*, *7*, 186–189.

Lykken, D. T. (1982). Research with twins: The concept of emergenesis. *Psychophysiology, 19,* 361–373.

Lykken, D. T., McGue, M., Tellegen, A., & Bouchard, T. J. (1993). Emergenesis: Genetic traits that may not run in families. *American Psychologist, 47,* 1565–1577.

Lyons, M. J., True, W. R., Eisen, S. A., Goldberg, J., Meyer, J. M., Faraone, S. V., Eaves, L. J., & Tsuang, M. T. (1995). Differential heritability of adult and juvenile antisocial traits. *Archives of General Psychiatry, 52,* 906–915.

Maher, J. (1997, July 12). Boxer's genetic fate. *Austin American-Statesman,* pp. E1, 9.

Mann, J. J., Malone, K. M., Nielsen, D. A., Goldman, D., Erdos, J., & Galerntner, J. (1997). Possible association of a polymorphism of the tryptophan hydroxylase gene with suicidal behavior in depressed patients. *American Journal of Psychiatry, 154,* 1451–1453.

Marler, P., & Peters, S. (1981). Sparrows learn adult song and more from memory. *Science, 213,* 780–782.

Martin, N., Boomsma, D., & Machin, G. (1997). A twin-pronged attack on complex traits. *Nature Genetics, 17,* 387–392.

Martin, P., & Albers, M. (1995). Cerebellum and schizophrenia: A selective review. *Schizophrenia Bulletin, 21* (2), 241–248.

McCartney, K., Harris, M. J., & Bernieri, F. (1990). Growing up and apart: A developmental meta-analysis of twin studies. *Psychological Bulletin, 107,* 226–237.

McClearn, G. E., Johansson, B., Berg, S., Pedersen, N. L., Ahern, F., Petrill, S. A., & Plomin, R. (1997, June 6). Substantial genetic influence on cognitive abilities in twins 80 or more years old. *Science, 276,* 1560–1563.

McCord, J. (1983). A forty year perspective on effects of child abuse and neglect. *Child Abuse and Neglect, 7,* 265–270.

McCrae, R. R., & Costa, P. T. (1997, May). Personality trait structure as a human universal. *American Psychologist, 52,* 509–516.

McGue, M. (1993). From proteins to cognitions: The behavioral genetics of alcoholism. In R. Plomin & G. E. McClearn (Eds.), *Nature, nurture, and psychology* (pp. 245–268). Washington, DC: American Psychological Association.

McGue, M., Bouchard, J. Jr., T. J., Iacono, W. G., & Lykken, D. T. (1993). Behavior genetics of cognitive ability: A life-span perspective. In R. Plomin & G. E. McClearn (Eds.), *Nature, nurture, and psychology* (pp. 59–76). Washington, DC: American Psychological Association.

McGue, M., & Lykken, D. T. (1991). Genetic influence on risk of divorce. *Psychological Science, 3,* 368–373.

McGuffin, P., & Katz, R. (1993). Genes, adversity, and depression. In R. Plomin & G. McClearn (Eds.), *Nature, nurture, and psychology* (pp. 217–230). Washington, DC: American Psychological Association.

McGuffin, P., Katz, R., Watkins, S., & Rutherford, J. (1996). A hospital-based twin register of the heritability of DSM-IV unipolar depression. *Archives of General Psychiatry, 53,* 129–136.

McManus, I. C., & Bryden, M. P. (1991). Geschwind's theory of cerebral lateralization: Developing a formal, causal model. *Psychological Bulletin, 110,* 237–253.

McNeil, T. (1971). Prebirth and postbirth influence on the relationship between creative ability and recorded mental illness. *Journal of Personality, 39,* 391–406.

McNeill, D. (1966). Developmental psycholinguistics. In F. Smith & G. A. Miller (Eds.), *The genesis of language: A psycholinguistic approach.* Cambridge, MA: MIT Press.

Meaney, M. J., Aitken, D. H., van Berkel, C., Bhatnagar, S., & Sapolsy, R. M. (1988, February 12). Effect of neonatal handling on age-related impairments associated with the hippocampus. *Science, 239,* 766–768.

Mednick, S. A., Gabrielli, W. F. J., & Hutchings, B. (1984). Genetic influences in criminal convictions: Evidence from an adoption cohort. *Science, 224,* 891–894.

Mednick, S. A., Machon, R. A., Huttenen, M. O., & Bonett, D. (1988). Adult schizophrenia following prenatal exposure to an influenza epidemic. *Archives of General Psychiatry, 45,* 189–192.

Meltzoff, A. N., & Moore, M. K. (1977). Imitation of facial and manual gestures by human neonates. *Science, 198,* 75–78.

Miles, C. P. (1977). Conditions predisposing to suicide: A review. *Journal of Nervous and Mental Disease, 164,* 231–246.

Mirsky, A., & Quinn, O. W. (1988). The Genain quadruplets. *Schizophrenia Bulletin, 14* (4), 595–612.

Money, J., & Ehrhardt, A. A. (1972). *Man & woman/boy & girl.* Baltimore: Johns Hopkins University Press.

Montoya, S., Aston, C. E., DeKosky, S. T., Kamboh, M. I., Lazo, J. S., & Ferrell, R. E. (1988). Bleomycin hydrolase is associated with risk of sporadic Alzheimer's disease. *Nature Genetics, 18,* 211–212.

Moody, P. A. (1975). *The genetics of man* (2nd ed.). New York: Norton.

Murphy, G. E. (1984). The prediction of suicide: Why is it so difficult? *American Journal of Psychotherapy, 38,* 341–349.

Murphy, T. K., Goodman, W. K., Fudge, M. W., Williams, J. R. C., Ayoub, E. M., Dalal, M., Lewis, M. H., & Zabriskie, J. B. (1997). B lymphocyte antigen D8/17: A peripheral marker for childhood-onset obsessive-compulsive disorder and Tourette's syndrome. *American Journal of Psychiatry, 154,* 402–407.

New, M. I., & Levine, L. S. (Ed.). (1984). *Adrenal diseases in childhood.* London: S. Karger.

O'Connell, J. E. A. (1976). Craniopagus twins: Surgical anatomy and embryology and their implications. *Journal of Neurology, Neurosurgery, and Psychiatry, 39,* 1–22.

Obler, L. K., & Fein, D. (Ed.). (1988). *The exceptional brain: Neurospychology of talent and special abilities*. New York: Guilford.

Pauls, D. L., Towbin, K. E., Leckman, J. F., Zahner, G. E. P., & Cohen, D. J. (1986). Giles de la Tourette's syndrome and obsessive-compulsive disorder: Evidence supporting a genetic relationship. *Archives of General Psychiatry, 43*, 1180–1182.

Perna, G., Cocchi, S., Bertani, A., Arancio, C., & Bellodi, L. (1995). Sensitivity to 35% CO_2 in healthy first-degree relatives of patients with panic disorder. *American Journal of Psychiatry, 152*, 623–625.

Petronis, A., & Kennedy, J. L. (1995). Unstable genes—unstable mind? *American Journal of Psychiatry, 152*, 164–172.

Plomin, R., DeFries, J. C., McClearn, G. E., & Rutter, M. (1977). *Behavioral genetics* (3rd ed.). New York: W. H. Freeman.

Plomin, R., Lichtenstein, P., Pedersen, N. L., McClern, G. E., & Nesselroade, J. R. (1990). Genetic influence on life events during the last half of the life span. *Psychology and Aging, 5*, 25–30.

Plomin, R., Loehlin, J. C., & DeFries, J. C. (1985). Genetic and environmental components of "environmental" influences. *Developmental Psychology, 21*, 391–402.

Post, F. (1994). Creativity and psychopathology: A study of 291 world famous men. *British Journal of Psychiatry, 165*, 22–34.

Prentky, R. A. (1980). *Creativity and psychopathology*. New York: Praeger.

Rabinowitz, D. (1995, January 30). A darkness in Massachusetts. *The Wall Street Journal*, p. A12.

Radetsky, P. (1994, August). Silence, sounds, wonder. *Discover*, 62–68.

Raine, A. (1993). *The psychopathology of crime: Criminal behavior as a clinical disorder*. San Diego, CA: Academic Press.

Raine, A., Brennan, P., Mednick, B., & Mednick, S. A. (1996). High rates of violence, crime, academic problems, and behavioral problems in males with both early neuromotor deficits and unstable family environments. *Archives of General Psychiatry, 53*, 544–549.

Raine, A., Venables, P. H., & Williams, M. (1990). Relationships between central and autonomic measures of arousal at age 15 and criminality at age 24 years. *Archives of General Psychiatry, 47*, 1003–1007.

Raine, A., Venables, P. H., & Williams, M. (1995). High autonomic arousal and electrodermal orienting. *American Journal of Psychiatry, 152*, 1595–1600.

Rauch, S. L., Jenike, A., Alpert, N. M., Baer, L., Breiter, H. C. R., Savage, C. R., & Fischman, A. J. (1994). Regional cerebral blood flow measured during symptom provocation in obsessive-compulsive disorder using oxygen 15-labeled carbon dioxide and positron emission tomography. *Archives of General Psychiatry, 51*, 62–70.

Reiss, D., Plomin, R., & Hetherington, E. M. (1991). Genetics and psychiatry. *American Journal of Psychiatry, 148*, 283–291.

Resnick, S. M., Gottesman, I. I., & McGue, M. (1993). Sensation seeking in opposite-sex twins: An effect of prenatal hormones? *Behavior Genetics, 23,* 323–329.

Roberts, L. (1988, January). Zeroing in on the sex switch. *Science, 239,* 21–23.

Rosenthal, D. (1963). *The Genain quadruplets.* New York: Basic Books.

Rowe, D. C. (1977). A place at the policy table? Behavior genetics and estimates of family environmental effects on IQ. *Intelligence, 24* (1), 1133–1158.

Rowe, D. C. (1993). Genetic perspectives on personality. In R. Plomin & G. E. McClearn (Eds.), *Nature, nurture, and psychology* (pp. 179–195). Washington, DC: American Psychological Association.

Rowe, D. C. (1994). *The limits of family influence: Genes, experience, and behavior.* New York: Guilford.

Rowe, D. C., & Waldman, I. D. (1993). The question "How?" reconsidered. In R. Plomin & G. McClearn (Eds.), *Nature, nurture, and psychology* (pp. 355–373). Washington, DC: American Psychological Association.

Roy, A. (Ed.). (1982). *Hysteria.* Chichester, England: Wiley.

Rushton, J. P. (1995). *Race, evolution, and behavior.* New Brunswick, NJ: Transaction.

Rutter, M., Bailey, A., Bolton, P., & Le Couteur, A. (1993). Autism: Syndrome definition and possible genetic mechanisms. In R. Plomin & G. McClearn (Eds.), *Nature, nurture, and psychology* (pp. 269–284). Washington, DC: American Psychological Association.

Saudino, K. J. (1997). Moving beyond the heritability question: New directions in behavioral genetic studies of personality. *Current Directions in Psychological Science, 6,* 86–90.

Scarr, S. (1996). How people make their own environments: Implications for parents and policy makers. *Psychology, Public Policy, and Law, 2,* 204–228.

Scarr, S., & Carter-Saltzman, L. (1979). Twin method: Defense of a critical assumption. *Behavior Genetics, 9,* 527–542.

Schinzel, A. A. G. L., Smith, D. W., & Miller, J. R. (1979). Monozygotic twinning and structural defects. *Journal of Pediatrics, 95,* 921–930.

Schuckit, M. A. (1984). Subjective response to alcohol in sons of alcoholics and controls. *Archives of General Psychiatry, 41,* 879–884.

Schuckit, M. A. (1994). Low level of response to alcohol as a predictor of future of alcoholism. *American Journal of Psychiatry, 151,* 184–189.

Schwartz, J. M., Stoessel, P. W., Baxter, L. R., Martin, K. M., & Phelps, M. E. (1996). Systematic changes in cerebral glucose metabolic rate after successful behavior modification treatment of obsessive-compulsive disorder. *Archives of General Psychiatry, 53,* 109–113.

Sears, R. R., Maccoby, E. E., & Levin, H. (1957). *Patterns of child rearing.* Evanston, IL: Row, Peterson.

Simons, R. L., Wu, C., Johnson, C., & Conger, R. D. (1995). A test of various perspectives on the intergenerational transmission of domestic violence. *Criminology, 33,* 141–171.

Skuse, D. H., James, R. S., Bishop, D. V. M., Coppin, B., Dalton, P., Aamodt-Leeper, G., Bacarese-Hamilton, M., Creswell, C., McGurk, R., & Jacobs, P. A. (1997). Evidence from Turner's syndrome of an imprinted X-linked locus affecting cognitive function. *Nature, 387,* 705–708.

Sobesky, W. E., Hull, C. E., & Hagerman, R. J. (1994). Symptoms of schizotypal personality disorder in Fragile X women. *Journal of the American Academy of Child and Adolescent Psychiatry, 33,* 247–255.

Sokol, D. K., Moore, C. A., Rose, R. J., Williams, C. J., Reed, T., & Christian, J. C. (1995). Intrapair differences in personality and cognitive ability among young monozygotic twins distinguished by chorion type. *Behavior Genetics, 25,* 457–466.

Soumi, S. J. (1991). Uptight and laid-back monkeys: Individual differences in the response to social changes. In S. E. Brauth, W. S. Hall, & R. J. Dooling (Eds.), *Plasticity of development* (pp. 28–56). Cambridge, MA: The MIT Press (Bradford Book).

Stanford, C. B. (1995, January). To catch a colobus. *Natural History,* 48–54.

Stein, D. (Ed.). (1974). *Plasticity and recovery of function in the central nervous system.* New York: Academic Press.

Steinmetz, H., Herzog, A., Huang, Y., & Hackländer, T. (1994). Discordant brain-surface anatomy in monozygotic twins [Letter to the editor]. *The New England Journal of Medicine, 331,* 952–953.

Swedo, S. E., Leonard, H. L., Mittleman, B. B., Allen, A. J., Rapoport, J. L., Dow, S. P., Kanter, M. E., Chapman, F., & Zabriskie, J. (1997). Identification of children with pediatric autoimmune neuropsychiatric disorders associated with streptococcal infections by a marker associated with rheumatic fever. *American Journal of Psychiatry, 154,* 110–112.

Swerdlow, J. L. (1995, vol. 187). The quiet miracles of the brain. *National Geographic,* 2–41.

Swift, R. G., Perkins, D. O., Chase, C. L., Sadler, D. B., & Swift, M. (1991). Psychiatric disorders in 36 families with Wolfram syndrome. *American Journal of Psychiatry, 148,* 775–779.

Swift, R. G., Polymeropoulos, M. H., Torres, R., & Swift, M. (1998). Predisposition of Wolfram syndrome heterozygotes to psychiatric illness. *Molecular Psychiatry, 3,* 86–91.

Terman, L. M., & Oden, M. H. (1959). *The gifted child at mid-life.* Stanford, CA: Stanford University Press.

Thiessen, D., & Gregg, B. (1980). Human assortative mating and genetic equilibrium: An evolutionary perspective. *Ethology and Sociobiology, 1,* 111–140.

Thomas, A., Chess, S., & Birch, H. G. (1968). *Temperament and behavior disorders in children.* New York: New York University Press.

Tiihonen, J., Isohanni, M., Räsänen, P., Koiranen, M., & Moring, J. (1997). Specific major mental disorders and criminality: A 26-year prospective study of the 1966 Northern Finland birth cohort. *American Journal of Psychiatry, 154,* 840–845.

Torrey, E. F., Bowler, A. E., Taylor, E. H., & Gottesman, I. I. (1994). *Schizophrenia and manic-depressive disorder: The biological roots of mental illness as revealed by the landmark study of identical twins.* New York: Basic Books.

Treffert, D. A. (1989). *Extraordinary people: Understanding "idiot savants".* New York: Harper & Row.

Tsai, M. S., Tangalos, E. G., Petersen, R. C., Smith, G. E., Schaid, D. J., Kokmen, E., Ivnik, R. J., & Thibodeau, S. N. (1994). Apolipoprotein E: Risk factor for Alzheimer disease. *American Journal of Human Genetics, 54,* 643–649.

Tsujita, T., Niikawa, N., Yamashita, H., Imamura, A., Hamada, A., Nakane, Y., & Okazaki, Y. (1998). Genomic discordance between monozygotic twins discordant for schizophrenia. *American Journal of Psychiatry, 155,* 422–424.

Tupper, D. E. (Ed.). (1987). *Soft neurological signs.* New York: Grune & Stratton.

Vernon, P. A. (1993). Intelligence and neural efficiency. In D. K. Detterman (Eds.), *Current topics in human intelligence* (pp. 171–187). Norwood, NJ: Ablex.

Vertosick, J. F. (1996, October). A bullet to the mind. *Discover,* 38–40.

Virkkunen, M., Kallio, E., Rawlings, R., Tokola, R., Poland, R. E., Guidotti, A., Nemeroff, C., Bissette, G., Kalogeras, K., Karonen, S. L., & Linnoila, M. (1994). Personality profiles and state aggressiveness in Finnish alcoholic, violent offenders, fire setters, and healthy volunteers. *Archives of General Psychiatry, 51,* 28–33.

Virkkunen, M., Rawlings, R., Tokola, R., Poland, R. E., Guidotti, A., Nemeroff, C., Bissette, G., Kalogeras, K., Karonen, S. L., & Linnoila, M. (1994). CSF biochemistries, glucose metabolism, and diurnal activity rhythms in alcoholic, violent offenders, fire setters, and healthy volunteers. *Archives of General Psychiatry, 51,* 20–27.

Vogel, F., & Moltulsky, A. G. (1986). *Human genetics: Problems and approaches.* New York: Springer-Verlag.

Wakschlag, L. S., Lahey, B. B., Loeber, R., Green, S. M., Gordon, R. A., & Leventhal, B. L. (1997). Maternal smoking during pregnancy and risk of conduct disorder. *Archives of General Psychiatry, 54,* 670–676.

Waldrup, M. F., Pedersen, F. A., & Bell, R. Q. (1968). Minor physical anomalies and behavior in preschool children. *Child Development, 39,* 391–400.

Walker, S., III. (1996). *A dose of sanity: Mind, medicine, and misdiagnosis.* New York: John Wiley & Sons.

Waller, J. H. (1971). Achievement and social mobility: Relationships among IQ score, education and cooperation in two generations. *Social Biology, 18,* 252–259.

Watt, D. C., & Edwards, J. H. (1991). Doubt about evidence for a schizophrenic gene. *Psychological Medicine, 21,* 279–285.

Weimer, W. B. (1973). Psycholinguistics and Plato's paradoxes in the *Meno. American Psychologist, 28,* 15–33.

Weiss, G., & Hechtman, L. T. (1986). *Hyperactive children grown up.* New York: Guilford.

Wender, P. H., Kety, S. S., Rosenthal, D., Schulsinger, F., Ortmann, J., & Lunde, I. (1986). Psychiatric disorders in the biological and adoptive families of adopted individuals with affective disorders. *Archives of General Psychiatry, 43,* 923–929.

Widom, C. S. (1989, April 14). The cycle of violence. *Science, 244,* 160–166.

Willerman, L., & Cohen, D. B. (1990). *Psychopathology.* New York: McGraw-Hill.

Willerman, L., Schultz, R., Rutledge, J. N., & Bigler, E. D. (1991). *In vivo* brain size and intelligence. *Intelligence, 15,* 223–228.

Witkin, H. A., Mednick, S. A., Shulsinger, F., Bakkestrom, E., Christiansen, K. O., Goodenough, D. R., Hirschorn, K., Lundsteen, C., Owen, D. R., et al. (1977). Criminality, aggression, and intelligence among XYY and XXY men. In S. A. Mednick & K. O. Christiansen (Eds.), *Biosocial bases of criminal behavior.* New York: Gardner Press.

Wright, L. (1995, August 7). Double mystery. *The New Yorker, 45–62.*

Index